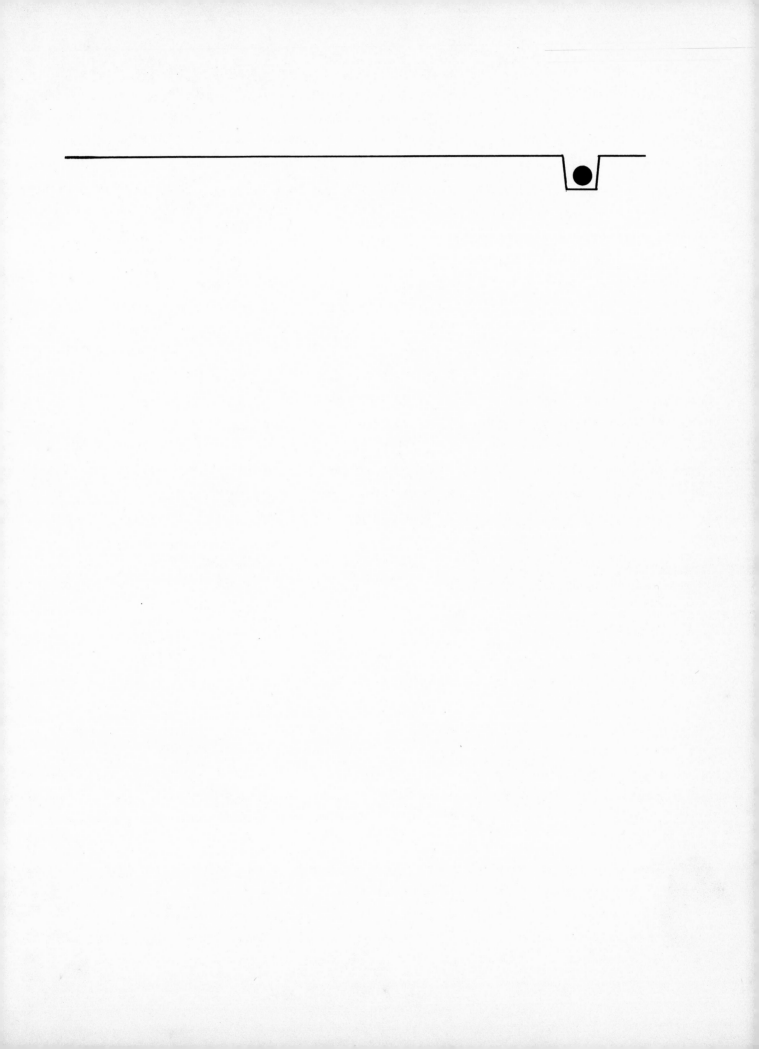

GOLF

ITS HISTORY, PEOPLE & EVENTS

By Will Grimsley

With Special Section by
Robert Trent Jones

Prentice-Hall, Inc., Englewood Cliffs, New Jersey

Golf: Its History, People & Events
by Will Grimsley with special section by Robert Trent Jones

Library of Congress Catalog Card Number: 66–12565

Printed in the United States of America

T 35800

Prentice-Hall International, Inc., London
Prentice-Hall of Australia, Pty. Ltd., Sydney
Prentice-Hall of Canada, Ltd., Toronto
Prentice-Hall of India (Private) Ltd., New Delhi
Prentice-Hall of Japan, Inc., Tokyo

Foreword

This present volume must represent the most ambitious attempt yet made to record between two covers the history and traditions of the game of golf, to illuminate the accomplishments of the great players of the past and present, and to provide the means of learning where the game has come from and where it stands today.

I have known the author for a number of years as one who has written competently and with integrity on a number of sports. No further testimony to his industry is needed than the knowledge that he has undertaken a work of this scope. Even though the book must have required an enormous amount of research, I should be very confident that Grimsley would have pursued it with thoroughness and intelligence.

I should think the result would be a welcome addition to any golfer's library.

ROBERT TYRE JONES, JR.

Preface

Golf is a game with a shady past. Its actual birth is shrouded in mystery. No one is quite certain when or where it drew its first tortured breath. Historians only know that the first anguished squalls of the infant came rolling over the moors of Scotland in the fifteenth century. Golf cannot point to a legal father, such as baseball in the case of Abner Doubleday and basketball in the case of Dr. James A. Naismith. In fact, there is a question that golf was ever born at all. As some scientists contend in regard to man himself, the game may have just evolved.

Even the source of the name, which originally came out as "golfe" or "goff," has thrown researchers into a tizzy. Some attach to it a kinship with the German word "kolbe," meaning club. Others associate it with the Gothic word "kulban," a stick with a thick knob at the end. The majority opinion, however, is that "golf" is a Celtic form. In some old manuscripts, there are references to "golf-drum."

If you take the word of some historians, who are disinclined to give latter-day generations credit for anything of an inventive or creative nature, golf was first played by Adam in the Garden of Eden. The first man may have fashioned a club from an extra rib, which he drew from his apparently surplus supply, and amused himself by belting apples from one tree to another. This, of course, made Eve the first golf widow. Half in despair and half in boredom, she gorged herself on the forbidden fruit and every school child knows what happened after that.

The imagination was almost as rampant and the tongue was almost as firmly planted against the cheek of the researcher who traces the game's beginning to the cave man era.

Introduction

This book was from the beginning a labor of love. Looking back, I doubt that I would have undertaken the assignment if I had been able to envision the monumental effort that would be required. It would have frightened me away. Now I am happy it did not.

To a person whose job it was to keep abreast of this spiraling sport in reporting tournaments throughout the world, it was becoming increasingly difficult to put a finger on some important fact, an elusive record, or a leaf of legend on a moment's notice. Library shelves were crammed with wonderful books on golf, but they were between separate covers, and who could haul a library around from a tee in Tokyo to the Valley of Sin at historic St. Andrews?

The birth and the growing pains of golf in Britain were beautifully chronicled in the works of such historians as Horace G. Hutchinson, Bernard Darwin, H. Gardiner-Hill, Sir Guy Campbell, and Lord Brabazon of Tara, but to get a complete picture it would be necessary to haul the material around in a small truck. The same was true of American golf. Excellent histories were written by Harry B. Martin, Richard Tufts, Herbert Warren Wind, and Charles Price, but each presented a special phase of the game.

As for records, these were easily accessible. However, it was necessary to turn to the U.S. Golf Association publications for details on the U.S.G.A. Championships, such as the Open, the Amateur, the women's events, the Walker and Curtis Cup matches. For information on professional tournaments and the popular, lucrative tour, one had to delve into a separate pile of informative matter produced by the Professional Golfers Association. Neither of these bodies felt an obligation, naturally, to provide material on such an event as the Canada Cup and International Trophy matches. This had to come from the International Golf Association.

The reading market was becoming flooded also with books of instruction, biographies and autobiographies of the game's great personalities, past and present. What kind of a man was Harry Vardon, who had such a great influence on the sport in America? What about Willie Anderson, the transplanted Scot who won four of our Opens? And Francis Ouimet, Ben Hogan, Bob Jones, Arnold Palmer, and Jack Nicklaus? What about the pro tour: how did it start and grow? The ladies' tour, the U.S.G.A., the rules, golfing presidents—all interesting subjects—where do you find out about them?

It is physically impossible to cram the whole wide world of golf—its history, development, legends, personalities, events, and great courses and moments—between the covers of a single book, but in this instance one must admit we tried. The goal was to make this the most exhaustive, complete, and exciting book on the game ever written. It was not intended to be an encyclopedia, a cold recitation of facts and figures, but a document that comes alive with the magnificent men and women who made golf what it is today.

This book would not have been possible without the efforts of past historians whose works contributed so much to the background material and without the help of others who gave so generously of their knowledge and time. I am particularly indebted to the following persons: Joseph C. Dey, Jr., director, Don Weiss, director of publications, and Janet Seagle, of the U.S. Golf Association; Bob Russell, assistant executive director, and Don (Doc) Giffin, director of public relations, of the Professional Golfers Association; Fred Corcoran, tournament director, of the International Golf Association; Herb Graffis, of *Golfdom Magazine;* Leonard F. Wirtz, tournament director, and Mrs. Nan Berry Ryan, director of public relations, of the Ladies' Professional Golf Association of America.

My deepest gratitude goes, too, to the many players and personalities who responded so willingly to requests for details and experiences which helped bring life to the book.

WILL GRIMSLEY
New York, March 1965
March 1966

Contents

Foreword   vii
Preface   ix
Introduction   xi

PART ONE

1. The Mysterious Birth   3
2. Commoners and Kings   6
3. Evolution of the Ball   12
4. Evolution of the Clubs   18

PART TWO

5. The Early Scots: They Rocked the Cradle   27
6. The Bug Bites America   32
7. The Vardon Influence   38
8. Willie Anderson—Man of Mystery: The First Four-Time
        Winner   44
9. Francis Ouimet—Drama at Brookline   50
10. The Fabulous Haig   56
11. Gene Sarazen: The Bridge Linking Four Eras   64
12. Bob Jones: The Immortal Grand Slammer   74
13. Golf's New Age of Steel   84
14. Sam Snead: The Jinx King   94
15. The Miraculous Hogan   102
16. The Affluent Trailer Kids   114
17. Arnold Palmer—The Charger   122
18. Jack Nicklaus: "The Golden Bear"   132
19. The Women: The Babe Was Queen   145
20. New Faces of the Sixties   156

PART THREE

21. The U.S. Open: Golf's Most Prestigious Tournament   167
22. The British Open: "Grandpappy" of Championships—and
        other Foreign Events   174

23. The Masters   183

24. The U.S. Amateur: Rocked in the Cradle of Controversy   189

25. The PGA Championship—From Match Play to Medal   196

26. The Public Links Championship: Week-Enders Have
       Their Heyday   201

27. Women's Amateur: From Petticoats to Bermudas   204

28. The U.S. Women's Open Championship Started on a
       Shoestring   210

29. From Tykes to Old-Timers   214

30. The Ryder Cup   219

31. The Walker Cup   223

32. The Curtis Cup: The Women's International Series   228

33. The Americas Cup   231

34. The Canada Cup   233

35. World Amateur Team Championship: The Eisenhower
       Trophy   241

PART FOUR—*by Robert Trent Jones*

36. Ten Great Courses   247

37. Old Course at St. Andrews   253

38. Pine Valley   256

39. Merion Golf Club   258

40. Dorado   261

41. Pinehurst   263

42. Pebble Beach   265

43. Augusta National   267

44. Oakland Hills   269

45. Firestone   271

46. Bellerive   274

47. Other Great Courses   276

PART FIVE

48. Ten Shots that Rocked the World   281

49. The Ever-Changing Principles of Play   294

50. The U.S. Golf Association: Zealous Guardian of the "Spirit
       of the Game"   297

51. The Professional Golfers Association   301

52. The Ladies' Professional Golfers Association   305

53. The Tour: From Hamburgers to Cadillacs   307

54. The Golf Boom: Where Do We Go from Here?   311

    Appendix   315

    Index   321

PART ONE

Chapter One

The Mysterious Birth

According to this particular version, in the days before invention of the wheel, a cave man once was wandering idly over the hillside, swinging a knobby stick he had picked up along the way. Sighting a pebble, he gave the rock a whack and the rock bounded across the ground. The cave man followed the line and upon reaching the pebble sent it spinning again. On his third shot, the pebble accidentally fell into a cauldron skimmering on an oakwood fire.

The family dinner spoiled, the wife became furious. But the cave man was fascinated. He took his knobby stick, retreated to his original starting place on the hillside, and started peppering away at another rock. He spent frustrated hours trying to loft the pebble into the cauldron a second time, without success.

That evening, sitting around with friends guzzling goat's milk, our hero described his intriguing sports activities of the day. His friends became highly excited. They decided that on the following day they would find themselves a similar crooked stick and a rock and see how many swings it would take to knock the pebble into the cauldron. Later, the prehistoric sportsmen carved out straight, strong sticks and affixed flint heads to provide better loft. They sought round, smooth pebbles from the river bank. And that's how golf was born—or was it?

Far more plausible is the explanation preserved in the archives of the U.S. Golf Association's museum in New York. It has been ascertained that the Romans in the day of Caesar's empire played a game called paganica. Legionnaires, bivouacking on the open countryside while waiting for new areas to conquer, got pleasure out of hitting a ball stuffed with feathers with a bent stick. In the first century before Christ, Romans overran Europe, crossed the English Channel and occupied parts of England and Scotland. They did not withdraw until the fourth century after Christ. Historians assume that the invaders continued to knock around the feather balls and the sport infected the natives. The old Roman game of paganica, then, they say, was the forerunner of golf and kindred games played in Holland, Belgium, and France.

Although Scotland generally is credited with being the cradle of the game, there are some obstinate probers who persist in the theory that the pastime of the curved stick and small ball was first played on a large scale in the Low Countries. They attempt to substantiate their case with some drawings from Holland supposedly antedating the fifteenth century, when first references to the game were made in Scotland. One of these drawings showed an old Hollander leaning on a curved stick, bearing a striking resemblance to one of the earlier golf clubs. Another painting was that of a small girl with several heavy-headed clubs under her arms.

There is no question that a game quite similar to golf was played in Holland and northern France before golf made a formal

Dutch girl playing golf, from an unknown print believed dating to the Fourteenth Century.

appearance in Scotland. In fact, there were several such games, some of them still played by villagers in the hinterlands. At best, they can be called a no-closer relative to golf than a distant cousin. They are more kin to billiards, croquet, or hockey.

For years, the Dutch whiled away the hours with a pastime called "kolf." The name was much closer to the modern fairway sport than the formula of the play itself. The game was staged in a rectangular area, 60 by 25 feet. The floor was as smooth as a billiard table. A small stone wall about 2 feet high enclosed

the small playing field. At each end was a post about 5 inches in diameter and placed 10 feet from the end wall.

The contestants in this unusual sport used clubs about 4 feet long with straight shafts and heavy brass heads with a smooth-hitting surface. The ball was as big as a baseball, made of elastic and sewn with a fine wire. The object was to knock the ball from one end to the other, hit the post, and then bring the ball finally to rest as near to the wall as possible. The winner was the one who could negotiate the course, hitting both posts, in the fewest number of strokes. In case of a tie, the winner was judged by the closeness of his ball to the wall. The game actually was a combination of billiards and croquet. It required skill and touch rather than power. The carom was the thing.

Of much closer kinship to golf was a game called chole—"choulla" in Latin and "choulle" in French—which is mentioned in legal documents dating back to the 1350's. The sport was particularly attractive to the Belgians, peasants mainly, and they say if you look hard enough you can find some of them playing it even today.

Chole was a game fascinating in its simplicity. The tools of the trade consisted of clubs with large iron heads, not too dissimilar from the old-fashioned golf niblicks, and an egg-shaped ball made of beechwood. It was a gambling game, the fourteenth century predecessor of the dollar Nassau. The game could be played either by individuals, one to a side, or teams, three or four to a side.

In a two-man match, both players used the same ball. A course was agreed upon. There was a starting point and a finishing point—usually a tree, stone or gate post—perhaps a half-mile away. The object was to reach the designated spot and strike the tree, gate post, or whatever it was, in the fewest number of strokes.

This, in essence, is how the game was played.

First, there was an auction, a sort of rudimentary Calcutta pool. The player with the

4

smallest bid—let us say he chose six strokes—was given the chance to try it. The opponent was supposed to try to foil the effort. They did not scramble over a moving object, as in hockey. They hit a stationary ball, as in golf.

Bets were posted, then the game began. The competitor who wagered he could do it in six strokes hit off. He was permitted to play three shots before his opponent was given a chance at what was called the "dechole" or "hit back." The object of the opponent was to knock the ball so far in the opposite direction or send it up into such a treacherous hazard (into a ditch, behind a wall, or underneath a tree) that the other player would be unable to fulfill his auction and would lose the bet.

In the case of team matches, there would be players on the offense (trying to make the goal in a specified number of shots) and players on the defense (trying to prevent success of the project). They would hit alternate shots. This may have been the origin of the Scotch two-ball foursomes in golf, in which two players use one ball and take alternate swings at it.

That the game of chole was played in Belgium in the fourteenth century is substantiated by court records of the time. There were no sports pages in those days, but acts of violence and those fracturing the law were recorded with meticulous care. One of the reports referred to an argument in which one chole player bashed another across the skull with an iron-headed club, thus proving that while techniques and equipment may change with the passing of the centuries human nature remains the same.

The French had a game called *pell mell,* or *jeu de mail.* It was a blood brother of Belgium's *chole,* if not an ancestor. Players took crooked sticks and batted wooden and feathered balls across the countryside, playing for a tree stump or an overhanging hoop. They counted strokes and had their own peculiar ground rules but, as far as is known, they did not dig a hole and try to climax their round with a putt. This is golf's one distinguishing feature from its kindred sports.

French Marquise on the links, from a 1780 sketch.

Perhaps the cave man did play a Neanderthal version of the fairway game. Who knows? Maybe the shepherds on the hills around Palestine actually used their long crooked sticks for tiffs with an invisible par. Caesar himself may have taken a few practice swings while all Gaul was divided into three parts. Nevertheless, such theories must remain in the realm of pure fancy; there is no concrete proof to back them up.

Archaeologists have uncovered no crude cudgels with flint heads which might provide a link with the Dark Ages and the centuries that preceded them. The glass cases in the golf museums contain only sticks with stiff shafts and variously shaped knobby heads, such as used in Scotland in the fifteenth century.

5

Chapter Two

Commoners and Kings

On March 6, 1457, an act of Parliament of King James II sternly warned Scotsmen "that fut ball and golfe must be utterly cryit dune." So far as is known, this is the first authentic historical reference to the game. It indicated that the sport already had a firm foothold in Scotland, where it probably had been played a century or more without arousing official notice, and that authorities were becoming greatly alarmed over the strange fad which was taking the people's interest away from archery. So golf, as well as football, was placed on the prohibition list.

This was the period before firearms had come into general use. The bow and arrow were the chief weapons of warfare. Also, the neighboring English, who were constantly at odds with the Scots, were supposed to be superior archers. Because of this and the constant fear of invasion, there was a royal decree that all male citizens should spend a certain period of their leisure time brushing up on their marksmanship. When the subjects started showing an interest in other pastimes and neglecting their archery, the king usually clamped down either by prohibiting the diversionary sport, as in the case of golf and football in this instance, or by lengthening the hours of archery practice.

It is interesting that most of the early allusions to golf in Scotland and England dealt with royal deterrents aimed at discouraging the sport. There were laws against playing on the Sabbath. Later, these laws were amended to prohibit golf on Sundays during "sermonses." Tariffs were imposed on golf balls imported from Holland.

The 1457 Parliamentary Act fell on deaf ears. The Scots were a hardy, individualistic and stubborn breed. They continued to hack away over the heather and dunes with their knobby sticks and feather-stuffed balls. This flagrant defiance of authority resulted in stiffer action by Parliament in 1491. A law was passed that not only fixed a fine and imprisonment for anyone caught playing the game but also imposed a fine and jail sentence for anyone on whose property the violators were found.

The newest edict met with strong opposition, not only from the common burghers, who suddenly were denied a favorite form of recreation, but also from the nobility. The issue was carried directly to King James IV, who succeeded to the Scottish throne in 1488. Many of the men around the king argued that golf was a wholesome, honorable game which not only should not be banned but should be encouraged for the welfare of the people. James is said to have insisted that it was a ridiculous sport, requiring neither strength nor skill, and properly should be abandoned.

The story goes that some of the nobility sympathetic to the sport invited the king out on the castle lawn to see for himself. James reluctantly acquiesced. One of the leather-covered balls was placed on the turf and the king indulged in a few royal swings. He had

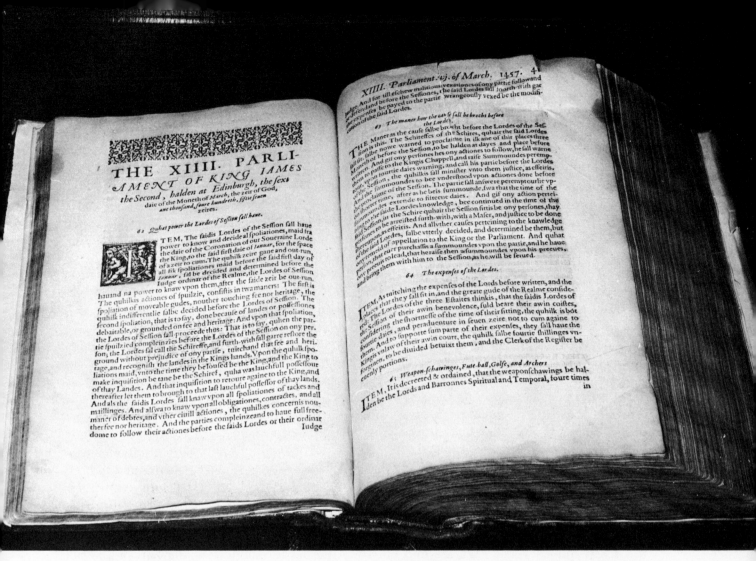

This first mention of golf, or "Golfe," in the Articles of Parliament, in the reign of King James II in the year 1457, shows that the game was a deeply rooted pastime in the Fifteenth Century and considered a threat to the defense of the realm. Instructions to the king's sheriffs were to arrest anyone playing it.

little luck. The balls he did not miss completely were dribbled only a few yards. Proud and determined, James came out the next day and tried again. The bug had bitten. The king became a devotee and a fair player before he was slain in the Battle at Flodden in 1513 while invading England.

The law was not immediately rescinded but it became only a few meaningless words. With royalty playing the game, the plebeians felt no obligation to adhere to the edict. The game increased in popularity. It was played by royalty and the gentry as well as the tradesmen.

James V (1512–1542) found time between his personal feuds with the Earl of Angus and his war with Henry VIII of England to play at Gosford in East Lothian. There he set up a private links and spent many pleasant hours competing with his favorite golf companion,

the Earl of Wemyss. James V was so particular with his private course that he permitted only wooden-headed clubs to be used.

His daughter, Mary Queen of Scots, was reared in the tradition. She learned to play at an early age and continued the sport when she was sent away to school in France. There, students carried clubs for her and she referred to them as "cadets." The pronunciation of "cadet" in French is "cad-day" and many historians believe this is the antecedent to the now popular term, caddy, meaning club-carrier.

It was during Mary's reign—in 1552—that the famous St. Andrews course in Scotland, recognized as the birthplace of golf, came into existence. The Queen played openly, drawing sharp criticism from her many enemies. She played both at St. Andrews and in the fields beside Seton. Critics accused the queen of stepping outside her castle door and taking some practice swings with a golf club shortly after her husband, Lord Darnley, was murdered.

The Royal Family's devotion to the game was unbroken with the ascension of King James VI, who took over the English throne as King James I. Grandson of James V and son of Mary Queen of Scots, James was credited with introducing the sport to England.

James and a few of his blue-blooded courtiers rode south into England for a holiday of stag-hunting, a popular sport of the day. After a short time, the aristocratic companions of the king became bored and decided they would like some diversion. They wanted to play some golf, as they did back in Scotland. They petitioned the king, who did not need much persuasion. A seven-hole course was laid out on the sandy ground of Blackheath Common, 8 miles from the heart of London.

History does not record how James and his courtiers got the necessary equipment to play. Whether they had clubs strapped to the sides of their horses and feather balls tucked away in their saddlebags is not known, although this seems quite unlikely. We are told only that the royal gentlemen struggled around the improvised layout with "hockey-shaped sticks and feather balls." James himself never was a good player, but he was an avid devotee. He played the game with enthusiasm and vengeance.

The date of this particular episode was 1608. The people of Royal Blackheath contend that James and his courtiers were instrumental in setting up the first official golf club and that the title "mother of golf" should be applied to Blackheath and not to the famed Royal and Ancient Club of St. Andrews, which did not come into being until 1754.

James I apparently continued his devotion to the game. Ten years after the expedition to Blackheath, he issued an order placing an embargo on feather golf balls imported from the Netherlands and gave a 21-year lease for the making and marketing of balls to James Melvill, a student at St. Andrews University.

Both of James I's sons—Henry Prince of Wales, the elder, and Charles I, the younger—took up the game and figured in interesting anecdotes handed down by golf historians.

James, who died at an early age, was practicing his swing at school under the watchful eye of the schoolmaster. The prince warned the schoolmaster that he should stand farther back. As James lifted the club, a schoolmate cautioned: "Beware that you hit not Master Newton." The prince, thinking the schoolmaster was out of earshot, raised his hand and said: "Had I done so I had but paid my debts."

Charles I was playing a round on the links at Leith when news was brought to him of the Irish Rebellion. Sportsmen still like to speculate about the king's reaction. Did he break off the match immediately, toss down his clubs, and rush to face the latest emergency, or did he resolutely hole out?

James II, son of Charles I, had a riotous career. As the Duke of York, he escaped to France during the civil war of 1648 and entered the army of Louis XIV. Later, he enlisted in the service of Spain. He married Anne Hyde, daughter of the Earl of Clarendon. He returned to England in 1682 and succeeded to the throne on the death of his brother, Charles II. A victim of the Bloodless Revolution, he went into exile and died there. Through it all, he played golf.

The one-time king of England, Scotland, and Ireland, who was a regular at the Leith Links, is credited with having a role in the first international match, a sort of forerunner to the present Walker Cup and Ryder Cup duels.

While he was Duke of York and Lord High Commissioner, two English noblemen in his entourage persisted in arguing that golf was an English, rather than a Scottish, game, apparently basing their contention on James VI's visit to Blackheath some 75 years earlier. The Duke stoutly defended Scotland as the true cradle of the sport. Finally the dispute became so heated that it was decided the issue should be settled on the golf course. The two

English noblemen would play the Duke and any other Scot of his choice. The match was designed to put the English-Scottish argument to rest.

The Duke made a thorough investigation of the golf-playing abilities in the area and finally came up with a shoemaker as his partner. The cobbler's name was John Patersone. The man had been born and reared in the tradition of the game and had been good enough to win the local championship. Principally through the skill of the shoemaker, the Duke and Patersone gave the English pair a thorough trouncing. The Duke was so pleased that he gave the cobbler a handsome bonus and a coat of arms.

Years later, an old man used to sit around the shops at Edinburgh and tell how he once carried the Duke's clubs. The man, a clubmaker named Andrew Dickson, related how it was his custom to run out ahead of the players and check where the balls landed. If true, he probably was the first fore-caddy. Even with the royal blessing, golf continued to encounter obstacles. Church authorities, who had considerable power and influence, did not object to the pursuance of this healthful exercise on weekdays, but considered it a sacrilege when citizens took to the links on the Sabbath.

Two of Scotland's leading golf personalities of a later period—Horace G. Hutchinson, British amateur champion in 1886–1887, and Sir Guy Campbell, architect, player, and member of the rules committee in the early 1900's—produced valuable research in tracing golf through this period of its growing pains.

Through pressure from the clergy, the Town Council of Edinburgh passed a resolution in 1593 forbidding play on Sunday. Town records show that John Henrie and Pat Rogie were prosecuted for playing on the Leith Links "during sermonses." A man named Robert Robertson had to sit in the seat of repentance at Perth in 1604 for similar desecration of the Sabbath.

There was an insertion in the official ledger of January 30, 1621, which said: "David Hairt —The quhilk day David Hairt, prenteis to Gilbert Banhop wrycht, confest prophanatione of the Sabbath in playing at the goff in the park on the Sabboth aftirnone in tyme of preaching; and therefore is ordenit to pay . . . ." This may sound like so much gibberish in present-day language, but it was obvious David stepped on some sacred toes and had to pay for it.

On April 27, 1651, complaints were lodged against five men—James Rodger, Johne Rodger, Johne Howdan, Andrew Howdan, and George Petersone—for playing on Sunday. A week later, all five, after confessing they had profaned the Sabbath, were forced to make public repentance.

Golf, in its infancy, was a casual, pleasant pastime. The first links were laid out along the coastline of Scotland, where the receding sea left sandy wastes, later transformed into gently rolling, grass-covered dunes, ridges, and knolls. It was unnecessary to build artificial hazards. Mother Nature herself was the architect and she laid out courses on the British Isles that have endured for centuries—a challenge to the best of the game's shotmakers without any help from man.

At first, the courses were very narrow and limited in the number of holes. The same holes were used by both the outgoing and incoming players, creating mild traffic jams at times. The incoming players were always given priority. It was a violation of the social graces to play without a coat.

It was the practice even in the earliest times, to carry several clubs. The memoirs of the Marquis of Montrose, harking back to the late 1620's, tell of the Marquis purchasing a set of six clubs while having some old ones mended. The Marquis must have been a real links addict. There are references to his stopping at Leith on a journey to buy two golf balls for 10 shillings and also to his playing golf on the day before his marriage to Mistress Magdalene Carnegie.

Golf became primarily a game for club members. The Royal Blackheath Club was started in 1608, on a whim of James I, as

The Golfers, a grand match played over St. Andrews course Dec. 20, 1830, from an engraving by Charles E. Wigstaffil.

previously related. The Honourable Company of Edinburgh Golfers, or the Company of Gentlemen Golfers, was started in 1744 by a small group accustomed to playing on the Leith Links. The president was Duncan Forbes of Culloden, who became famous as the man who tried to put down the Clan uprising in 1745.

The Company played over the five holes at Leith for 45 years, later moved its activities to the Musselburgh Links, and acquired a big plot of land near Gullane for construction of a championship course now known as Muirfield.

It was this group of enthusiasts who conceived and promoted what must have been the first tournament competition. The Town Council of Edinburgh put up a silver club, valued at 15 Scottish pounds, to be presented to the winner. The entry fee was 5 shillings. The players were to go out in pairs or threesomes and the one who won the most holes was to be declared the victor. In case of a tie, the leaders were to compete in a play-off round. The winner was to be designated the

Captain of Goff, with privileges to oversee disposal of the booking money, settle disputes among the members, and serve as superintendent of the links. The tournament was played and was won by an Edinburgh surgeon, John Rattray.

The Leith golfers apparently were a gay and fun-loving lot who, like millions of their twentieth-century successors in the fairway sport, considered the game just a short cut to the nineteenth hole. They said some players acted as if they were in a funeral procession and looked more like a parcel of love-lorn shepherds with crooks in their hands than a band of jovial fellows who should be having a good time. It is said that the Leith sportsmen were wont to close the day with "copious libations of pure and unadulterated claret."

On May 14, 1754, some 22 noblemen and gentlemen formed the Society of St. Andrews Golfers, later known as The Honourable Company of the Royal and Ancient Club. They adopted 13 articles for the game's first official code of rules. These rules form the nucleus of standards accepted throughout the

10

world today. One of the first rules was that a ball could be removed from water or watery filth, redropped, and played with the loss of one stroke. Another said the golfer must play honestly for the hole and not for the opponent's ball.

Despite the crudeness of the equipment, the crooked sticks, and the feather balls, scoring was remarkably good. James Durham of Largo won the silver club at St. Andrews in 1767 when the course was thick with heather and win by shooting a 94. The average winning score at the time was 100 to 105, but the course was not then stretched to its full and formidable length. In 1849, playing with the feather ball, Willie and Jamie Dunn shot a 92 while Allan Robertson and Tom Morris, Sr., registered a 93 in a team match over the old St. Andrews course. It was a remarkable feat.

Ship's officers from Scotland or England are supposed to have brought golf to Canada as early as 1850 and shortly afterward small, three-hole courses popped up in Montreal and Quebec. The United States, destined later to dominate the sport, was slower getting infected with the tantalizing "bug." The United States traces its introduction to the sport to 1888, but that is another story.

Chapter Three

Evolution of the Ball

When King James IV of Scotland and his courtiers sneaked out of the castle for an illegal Saturday afternoon of "golfe" at the turn of the sixteenth century, their object was to bang away at a small, round piece of leather stuffed with feathers. The feather ball was the standard missile of the game for at least four centuries, starting with the time the sport apparently was played on a popular scale around 1440, until 1848.

Some of these relics are on display at the museums of the Royal and Ancient Golf Club of St. Andrews and the United States Golf Association in New York. The U.S. Golf Association also has compiled a thorough account of the transition of golf equipment, tracing it from the feather ball period (1440–1848), through the gutta percha era (1848–1901) to the machine-made, rocket-like ball of the present day.

Golf came hard back in the old days when it was struggling for a foothold in the social and recreational scheme. Not only did it have to buck royal prohibitions, but, even where it was possible, there were equipment snags. Everything was made by hand. This was slow, meticulous work. The market was not flooded with clubs and balls.

Feather balls thus became something of a luxury. The best ball makers could produce only about four a day. These sold for up to 5 shillings apiece, or, in bulk, a pound a dozen. Whether computed in English or Scottish pounds, this was quite expensive. For some, it was equivalent to a week's wages.

First, there was the tedious task of processing the leather covering. The leather first was softened with alum and water and then cut into four, three, or two pieces. These were stitched together with waxed threads outside in and then reversed. A small hole was left in the leather. Through this hole were stuffed boiled goose feathers.

This may sound like child's play but it was an intricate and exhausting procedure, requiring the skill of a master craftsman. The ball-maker had to hold the cover in his hand in a recessed ball-holder and push the feathers through the hole with a stuffing rod. This was a tapering piece of wrought iron 16 to .20 inches long with a wooden crosspiece, which the ball-maker braced against his chest. An awl was brought into use in the latter stages of the operation.

It took a bucket of feathers to make one ball. After the leather cover had been stuffed until it could hold no more, it was stitched up. Then the ball was hammered hard and round and given three coats of paint.

It was almost impossible to get a perfectly round feather ball. Even if one did, the ball was soon knocked out of shape or cut by the impact of the club. During this period, wood-headed clubs were used almost exclusively because of the damage to the ball by an iron. In wet weather, the balls tended to become sodden and fly apart. At best, a player was lucky to play two rounds with one ball.

In the reign of James VI, the Scots bought their balls from Holland, forcing James to

FEATHER BALL

About 1810

Donor - T. Suffern Tailer, Jr.

FEATHER BALL

About 1845

Donor - T. Suffern Tailer, Jr.

A GOURLAY BALL
MADE PRIOR TO 1850
BY DOUGLAS GOURLAY

DONOR: THE ROYAL MUSSELBURGH GOLF CLUB
EAST LOTHIAN, SCOTLAND
PRESENTED IN 1953

FEATHER BALL

About 1835

Donor - Robert Cunningham

FEATHER BALL

About 1845

Donor - T. Suffern Tailer, Jr.

Feather golf balls, vintage of 1810–1845, on display at Golf House.

invoke a prohibitive tariff. In 1603, James appointed William Mayne to be the royal club-maker and in 1618 he gave James Melvill exclusive ball-making rights at 4 shillings per ball.

By the middle of the eighteenth century, several prominent ball-makers had established themselves in Scottish communities. The most prominent perhaps was the Gourlay family of Leith and Musselburgh. The patriarch of the family was Douglas Gourlay of Leith. His son carried on at Musselburgh. It became fashionable to play with a "Gourlay" ball.

Another leading ball-maker was Allan Robertson of St. Andrews, the son of Davie Robertson. The latter was renowned as the tutor of Old Tom Morris, regarded as the greatest player of his day. Allan Robertson turned out 2,456 feather balls in 1844. He bitterly fought the introduction of the gutta percha ball and once sharply rebuked Old Tom Morris for playing with the revolutionary pellet. As a result of this argument, it is said, Old Tom Morris left St. Andrews and refused to return until Robertson died in 1859 at the age of 44.

Robertson's pique was short-sighted and unnecessary. It was inevitable that progress and man's ingenuity would come up with a ball which cost less, lasted longer, flew farther, and went truer than the old "featherie." This came with the introduction of the gutta percha ball, the first of which is believed to have been made by the Reverend Dr. Robert Adams Paterson in 1845.

Gutta percha is a concrete juice produced by various trees, found particularly in India and other parts of the Far East. It has the property of becoming soft and impressionable at the temperature of boiling water and of holding its shape when cooled. It is not affected by water except at boiling temperature.

The idea of using this material for the making of golf balls came from the gutta percha packing around a black marble statue of Vishnu which had been sent from India. This discovery had a tremendous impact on

the game and the statue now is enshrined at St. Andrews University. The first balls were produced under the name "Paterson's Patent."

The "gutties," as they were called, were much easier to produce than the "featheries." They were simply a single lump of gutta percha, molded into proper shape—not much dissimilar to a hard rubber ball. With the introduction of the "gutties," with their low cost and long-lasting qualities, more players turned to the game.

Gutta percha was shipped from overseas in long, round rods about 1½ inches in diameter. With the aid of a gauge, each rod was sliced into small pieces like a roll of sausage— each piece to make a ball of the desired size and weight. The piece was softened in hot water, rolled on a flat board, lined to simulate the seaming of a feather ball, painted and then placed on a rack for several weeks to season.

Originally, the balls were smooth. Then it was discovered that the smooth ball ducked in flight. To correct this, makers started putting nicks in the ball with the thin end of a hammer. This created "dimples," a feature which never has been abandoned.

The first gutta percha balls were made entirely by hand. Later iron molds, or ball presses, were introduced. The gutta percha could be placed into these molds for the manufacture of uniform balls. Earlier in the era, a number of coats of paint were put on each ball. When it was found that too much paint filled the indentions or markings, the coats were reduced to two.

The gutta balls were about the size of the United States ball, 1.68 inches in diameter, but often varied slightly in weight. The balls were marked 26, 26½, 27, 29, etc., designating pennyweights in the troy weight scale. Twenty pennyweights equal an ounce.

The gutta balls became famous through brand names or the names of their makers. The best-known balls of the time carried the brands of Old Tom Morris, Robert Forgan, and the Auchterlonies. A few of the names familiar to the old golfers were the Eureka, Melfort, White Melfort, White Brand,

14

Henley, O.K., Ocobo, A. 1, Park's Special, and Agrippa.

Shortly after the gutta attained widespread popularity, an ingenious inventor came up with a rival that was called the putty ball and labeled the Eclipse. Nobody knew its ingredients exactly but it was said to contain a cork filling and India rubber. Players found it would not carry as far off the tee but really took off once it hit the ground. Also, it had good wearing qualities. But it did not make the grade. By the end of the 1890's, it was off the market.

The gutta percha had free rein until the turn of the century; then, as the feather ball before it, fell victim to progress. A Cleveland man named Coburn Haskell decided that a livelier ball could be produced. He solicited the aid of Bertram G. Work of the B.F. Goodrich Company at Akron, Ohio. In 1898, Haskell came up with a ball made from winding rubber thread under heavy tension around a solid rubber core.

Haskell's rubber ball was covered with black gutta percha, lined lightly by hand, and painted. The paint tended to fill in the indentations, a problem experienced earlier with the gutta, and the fault was not rectified until Dave Foulis, a Chicago professional, hit on the idea of putting them in a mold used for making the "gutties." The result was bramble markings which improved the flight of the ball.

The rubber balls were placed on the market in 1899, but they were not an immediate sensation. Golfers felt they could hit the new balls about 25 yards farther off the tee but found difficulty controlling them around the greens. They were, if anything, too lively. They soon got the nickname, "bounding billies."

Arguments over the relative merits of the gutta and rubber balls continued until 1901, when Walter J. Travis won the U.S. amateur championship with a Haskell ball from an Agrippa mold. He putted so sensationally that all complaints about the rubber ball's jumpiness on the greens soon disappeared. It was

not long afterward that the gutta became passé.

By this time, the machine age was beginning to flower. It no longer was necessary to make balls tediously by hand in the professional's shop. Machines could turn them out in mass production, increasing their availability and reducing the cost. A.G. Spalding & Brothers, a sporting-goods manufacturer in Chicopee, Massachusetts, leaped into competition with B.F. Goodrich in making rubber golf balls. In 1903, Spalding got a license to produce the Spalding Wizard. Later the company developed a hard, tough cover made from balata, a gum from the bully tree.

Then began the mad race of manufacturers to come up with the better ball. It was found that the liveliest ball was one that was wound the tightest. This placed added premium on materials and machines. The first threads used came from the wild rubber of the Amazon River basin. Later, plantation rubber was refined enough to be used. Efforts were made to get machines that could wind the thread to the greatest possible tension without snapping it.

There were endless experiments with the core. A small sac of water was substituted for the solid rubber core. Then lead was used, but this was found to be dangerous when the ball was opened. Then came a fling at zinc oxide, but it was discovered that the pigment tended to unbalance the ball. In the Twenties, solutions involving glue, glycerin, and water were put into the first-line balls. In the 1950's and 1960's, many of the top professionals were playing a ball with a steel center.

Indentations became important. Early rubber balls were made with the bramble and reverse mesh markings of the gutta ball. In 1908, an Englishman named William Taylor reversed the markings on his molds and produced the dimple effect, in contrast to the bramble. The mesh proved a natural aftermath.

The first rubber balls were light and large. They weighed 1.55 ounces and were 1.71 inches in diameter. Also, they were inclined to float. With no regulations governing size and weight, manufacturers battled to find the best combination. Finally, around 1915, both the size and the weight had diminished to the 1.62-ounce and 1.62-inch ratio.

However, experiments on both sides of the Atlantic Ocean continued and the ball proved to be the one area in which the game's two powerful ruling bodies—the Royal and Ancient of St. Andrews and the United States Golf Association—could not see eye-to-eye. While agreeing on a universal code of rules, each sanctioned a different size ball. Going into the 1960's, Americans were playing a ball 6/100 of an inch larger than that used in Britain and in many foreign countries following Royal and Ancient standards. There always has been an argument, it seems, over what constitutes the proper size.

Both the British and Americans were playing the 1.62-ounce and 1.62-inch ball when, in 1931, an American committee headed by Herbert Jacques came up with what it called "a better and pleasanter ball for the greatest number playing the game." The ball measured 1.68 inches in diameter and weighed 1.55 ounces. This came to be known as the "balloon ball." But Jesse Guilford, the old Boston siege gun who won the National Amateur in 1921, had another name for it. He called it the "Three L ball—larger, lighter, and lousier."

The U.S.G.A. stuck grimly to its guns and the next year issued a statement which said: "The average golfer has discovered he can make shots with the new ball which were beyond his control with the old. He has found no loss of distance—he is continually playing from better lies, and he is amazed to find scores averaging lower. Women golfers are playing better with the new ball."

Suddenly, in 1932, without notice, the U.S.G.A.'s committee on better golf balls reversed itself: "A careful study of the 1.68–1.55 ball has been made," the committee said in a solemn and apologetic report. "The first balls on the market were oversized and substantially underweight which, combined with generally unfavorable weather, brought a storm of protest. . . ."

Complaints against the "balloon ball" were enumerated: (1) it did not have sufficient weight to hold the course or bore into the wind; (2) on the putting green, it was too easily diverted by the irregularities of the surface when its power was spent, (3) it failed generally to measure up to requirements.

On January 31, 1932, the United States adopted what it considered the perfect ratio and this became the standard ball. The rules specified that it should weigh no more than 1.62 ounces avoirdupois and should measure no less than 1.68 inches in diameter. The British did not follow suit. They stuck with a ball of the same weight, 1.62 ounces, but smaller. The Royal and Ancient rules specified the British ball could not be less than 1.62 inches in diameter.

The difference in the two balls—6/100 of an inch—appeared infinitesimal. However, there was a marked difference in the way the two balls played. While the Americans argued that their ball was the "most pleasurable" for most players under all conditions, the British insisted that the smaller pellet was more effective and more practical for the gusty crosswinds and head-winds of the old seaside courses in Scotland and England.

Taking a conciliatory attitude, the Royal and Ancient asked British players and those of the Commonwealth countries—Australia, Canada, New Zealand, etc.—to try the plumper American ball for a few months and then make a report. They did. The reaction was negative. "Nobody liked the bigger ball," an R&A spokesman said. "The sentiment was overwhelming for our own."

There was one bizarre twist to the whole affair. Under the wording of the rules of the two countries, the British ball became illegal in the United States because the U.S. statute set a minimum of 1.68 inches. On the other hand, the American ball could be played at any time in Britain because the R&A rules held the ball "could not be less than 1.62 inches." It said nothing about the ball being bigger.

A rather incongruous situation developed. When American players such as Ben Hogan, Sam Snead, and Arnold Palmer competed in the British Open Championship, they had the option of playing either ball. On the other hand, when Commonwealth players such as Henry Cotton of England, Peter Thomson of Australia, and Gary Player of South Africa teed off in the United States Open, they were compelled to play the fatter American ball.

No such inequities prevailed, however, in international competitions such as the Ryder Cup, Walker Cup, and International Canada Cup matches. By agreement between the two big rules-making bodies, competitors were permitted to use either ball. Almost invariably, they chose the smaller British ball.

American players contended that the U.S. ball was more maneuverable and easier to finesse around the greens but that the British ball could be hit straighter and farther off the tee. Some estimated that the smaller ball was good for 20 to 30 extra yards on the drive—with or without the wind. In competition, no one was willing to concede this advantage.

Gene Sarazen said the smaller ball drove and putted better. Sam Snead said on a fast green he preferred to putt the British ball because "it ducks into the hole while the bigger stays out." Jerry Barber, the wee, 140-pound Californian who won the American Professional Golfers Association championship in 1961, said the smaller ball helped the big hitters. C. Alec Hill, former British Walker Cup player and one-time chairman of the rules committee of the Royal and Ancient, had an answer: "Why penalize athleticism?" Peter Thomson, the great Australian stylist who won the British Open crown five times,

refused to play the rich American pro tour because he could not play the bigger ball.

Manufacturers continued efforts to create a ball with superior rocket power, but they were constantly under a restraining hand of the militant rules makers. Quite obviously, super golf balls could be developed, but the men of the U.S. Golf Association and the Royal and Ancient realized that a free hand could make a mockery of the game.

In 1941, the U.S. Golf Association installed a testing device at its New York headquarters. Another contraption was used for testing golf balls outdoors. The rule was passed that the velocity of the ball should be not greater than 250 feet per second when measured on the U.S.G.A. apparatus.

In the 1950's, some manufacturers became overly zealous in their advertisements and told the world their assembly lines were putting out golf balls which would shoot through the air as if powered by jet propulsion. "Guaranteed to go 20 yards farther than any other ball," boasted one advertisement.

Each time these wild claims were made or there was the slightest suspicion of nonconformity, the balls were confiscated by the U.S.G.A. They were placed in the testing machine, an awesome collection of nuts, bolts, wires, and flashing lights. The balls were shot through a barrel at a screen and judged by an electric eye. Lights flashed. Needles jumped. The velocity of the balls was measured much in the way a cardiograph probes the heartbeat of a man.

If the ball passed the test, it was approved. If it flunked, it was outlawed. "The velocity of the ball shall not be greater than 250 feet per second on our machine," the U.S.G.A. said. "There is no super ball."

Chapter Four

Evolution of the Clubs

During the latter part of the nineteenth century, an Oxford University professor, upon being introduced to the social fad then sweeping the British Isles, described golf as "the art of putting little balls into little holes with instruments very ill adapted to the purpose." No more succinct or appropriate commentary could have been made on the primitive aspects of the implements with which early devotees battled the gorse, heather, and whin of the seaside courses.

Relics of the game's swaddling-band days, carefully preserved in the museums of the Royal and Ancient Club of St. Andrews and the U.S. Golf Association, are a source of wonder that the pioneer practitioners were able to strike the ball with the power and skill which history shows that they did. The wood clubs were long, whippy sticks with oversized leather grips, greyhound necks and faces that resembled the heads of a snake. The irons were rudimentary—a slab of crude metal attached to a wooden shaft. The putters at first were all wooden, from the top of the shaft to the end of the striking surface.

No effort was made to fit a club to an individual. Tall men played with short clubs, often having to stoop to make contact. Short men played with long clubs, creating the virtual situation of the club swinging the man, rather than vice versa. The earliest clubs were made in an upright position, forcing the player to stand practically on top of the ball when taking his stance. This was the cricket influence. Many of the early golfers were converted cricketers. It took them years to get away from the cricket bat grip and the cricket swing.

The first club-maker of any renown was William Mayne of Edinburgh, who received a Royal Warrant as club-maker and spear-maker for James VI in 1603. An old notebook of that period tells of payment for repairs on "play clubis," "bonker clubis," and an "irone club," proving that the golfer's desire for variety and specialization is not a strictly modern concept. Mayne was followed by Andrew Dickson of Leith and Henry Mill of St. Andrews. Dickson boasted of having made clubs and even served as fore-caddy for James II when the latter was the Duke of York. Mill also operated during the Stuart era, but there is no record that he ever held a Royal Warrant.

It is quite possible, although not certain and not subject to proof, that some of the rudimentary clubs still in existence came from the hands of these craftsmen.

Among the oldest clubs known is a set of six woods and two irons now on display in the so-called Big Room, overlooking the home green of the Troon Golf Club in Scotland. These relics were found in a walled-up closet in an old house at Hull. Also discovered in the closet was a copy of a Yorkshire newspaper, dated 1741. The clubs must have been made several years previously.

All eight of the clubs have shafts made of ash. All except one of the woods and one of

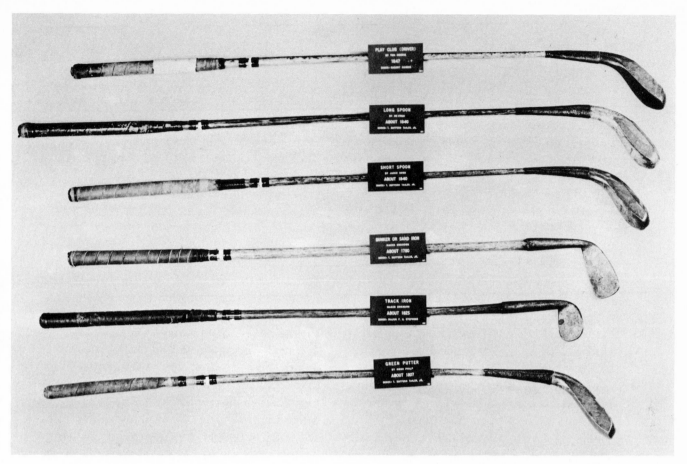

These were the primitive implements with which golfers battled par in the middle of the Nineteenth Century. *Left to right,* they are the play club (driver), long spoon, short iron, bunker or sand iron, track iron (for getting the ball out of wagon tracks) and green putter. Golf House exhibit.

the irons are without grips of any kind. The grips on the two clubs are large and heavily padded. The wood clubs have long, broad heads. They are leaded and boned, with the lead extending from near the toe to two-thirds of the way to the heel. The iron clubs have broad faces, square toes, and heavy, nicked sockets.

Club-making began to thrive in the latter part of the feather-ball era. One of the most famous artisans was Simon Cossar of Leith, who held an appointment as official club-maker for the Company of Gentlemen Golfers. He was followed by Douglas McEwen and Hugh Philp, who became known as the Chippendale and Heppelwhite of the trade.

McEwen was born in the tradition. His grandfather, James, a wheelwright, started the family business in 1770 at Leith. James had a son, Peter, who carried on the trade and married into the Gourlay family, the famous feather-ball-makers of Musselburgh. Douglas

McEwen made his club heads from small cuts of hedgethorns, planted horizontally on sloping banks so that the stems grew at an angle at the root. This created a natural bend at the neck. The cuts were split, shaped, and trimmed with a handsaw. The thorn heads were never varnished or stained but were rubbed with red keel for a beautiful, natural finish.

Philp, born in 1782, was a carpenter in St. Andrews who did such an outstanding job repairing clubs for the golfers that in 1827 he was appointed club-maker for the Society. Like McEwen, he used hedgethorn for the heads as well as apple and pear. Most of his shafts were of ash. He became so well known and his business thrived to such an extent that he was compelled to add an assistant, James Wilson. The pupil mastered the art of the teacher so well that for years afterward players were unable to tell the difference between a Philp and a Wilson product.

19

Naturally, only a few of the more fortunate were able to avail themselves of the work of these craftsmen. They say that Sandy Herd, the 1902 British Open Champion, cut jointed stumps from the woods around St. Andrews to make rough club heads. He practiced with balls made of champagne corks weighted with nails. Harry Vardon, the famed British stylist, learned the game in his native Jersey with home-made clubs hewn from oak branches and blackthorn. The blackthorn shafts were so rough and carbuncled from knots, the story goes, that Vardon could not hold the club with the palms of his hands—as was customary in those days—but slid his thumbs down the shaft and held the club lightly in his fingers to avoid blisters. This is said to have been the origination of the famed Vardon grip.

By the middle of the nineteenth century, clubs had come to be divided into four groups —drivers, spoons, irons, and putters.

There were two kind of drivers principally —the "play club," with a flat face and no loft, designed to hit a ball which was teed up or on safe ground, and the "grassed drivers," slightly lofted to lift the ball from a hazard or a downhill lie. Horace Hutchinson, the British amateur champion back in the mid-1880's, described wood clubs of the time as "stout, stubborn and bull-headed."

After the heads were fashioned from thorn, apple, pear, or beech and properly leaded and boned, they were glued to the shafts, originally made of ash and later of hickory. They were secured with tarred twine. Then they were equipped with big, unwieldy grips made of stuff strips and covered with leather. The grips were nailed to the shaft and bound with tarred twine.

The original grips were so bulky and slippery that players carried a coal dust product in their pockets and applied it periodically when their hands became sweaty. The practice was similar to that of bowlers applying chalk to their fingers or billiards players chalking their cue stick at a later time, but it was a messy necessity and rough on clothes.

Spoons during the feather-ball period were of four types. There were long spoons, middle spoons, short spoons, and baffing spoons. The "baffy," or baffing spoon, short and stiff with a laid-back face, was the club used for pitching to the green. It later was replaced by the lofting iron.

Subsequent additions to the wood club family were the brassie and the wooden niblick. The brassie got its name from a brass sole placed beneath the little strip of horn and designed to play off roads and hard lies without injuring the head of the club. The wooden niblick was made with a small head so that it could dig into a rut and more easily cut through heavy grass or moss.

It was during the latter part of the nineteenth century that an enterprising clubmaker named Henry Lamb introduced a driving club which, instead of a flat face, had a bulge in the center. A stand-out golfer himself, he contended the departure gave him greater distance. Most of the other players of the time were skeptical. They insisted that a ball had to be hit perfectly to achieve full value of the innovation. They said a ball hit on the heel would have a tendency to go to the right and one hit on the toe would veer left. Many years later, club designers adopted Lamb's lead to an extent by putting a slight outward curve to the face of the driver.

Because of the fragile nature of the feather balls, which were chopped up and cut at the seams by bladelike sticks, the heavy emphasis was on wood clubs instead of irons prior to the advent of the gutta. But irons were made and used, although not on the broad scale that followed introduction of the gutta percha and later the rubber ball. There were three serviceable irons—the driving iron, the cleek, and the bunker iron.

The driving iron was not much different from its more refined and more streamlined descendant, the No. 1 iron. It had a long, stiff shaft and a heavy head. There were several varieties of the cleek, a club thick in the upper edge of the blade. There was an approaching cleek, good on pitch-and-run shots, and a putting cleek, different only in its shortened shaft and flat facing of the blade. The sand iron, as used by the early devotees, is not to be in any way identified with the sand wedge, which made a revolutionary bow decades later. It was a heavy driving iron with a laid-back face, much like a mashie-niblick which replaced it.

For years, golfers played with wooden putters. It was not until putting surfaces became greatly improved and a dead-eye putting wizard named Bob Fergusson, from Musselburgh, astounded friends with his success with a metal blade that the iron putter came into use. It was conceded that a ball stroked with an iron blade gripped the ground better and ducked into the hole. Even so, some teachers recommended that golfers carry two putters—one of wood and one of iron. The wood putter was to be used over rough terrain; the iron putter when the going was smooth.

The gutta percha ball, introduced in 1848, wrought other significant changes. Club-makers had to discard old techniques and install fresh ones to keep pace with the changing game. The gutta ball was harder and put more strain on the clubs. As a result, the woods had to be made with shorter, fatter heads. To impart more resiliency, thorn was discarded entirely, and the softer apple, pear and beech woods were used. Leather insets were placed on the faces. Because the gutta ball was less fragile, iron clubs increased in number and variety.

While two or three clubs may have been sufficient for commoners and kings back in the fifteenth century and five or six for players later in the feather-ball era, such abbreviated sets were inadequate for the fairway artisans as the sport grew in popularity. During the late stages of the gutta period, just before the end of the nineteenth century, a player did not feel well-outfitted and capable of coping with any emergency with less than eight clubs. That was the average set. Some carried as few as six, others as many as ten.

The set was picked from a list of some 13 varieties, including: woods—driver, bulger-driver, long spoon, brassie, middle spoon, short spoon, wooden putter; irons—cleek, midiron, lofting-iron, mashie, niblick, and iron putter. Willie Park, Jr., is said to have used 10 clubs in winning the British Open championships of 1887 and 1889. They were a bulger-driver, straight-faced driver, spoon, brassie-niblick or brassie, wooden putter, cleek, iron, mashie, iron-niblick, and iron putter.

The mashie was regarded as a hybrid weapon—a cross between the niblick and the iron. Whereas the niblick was considered a workhorse tool, made for coarse work and designed to dig out of obstacles, the purpose of the mashie was to "pitch the ball dead to the pin." Horace Hutchinson described the lofting iron as "fascinating, most coquettish, feminine without doubt, delightful on occasion, exasperating and untrustworthy. So full of moods and tenses."

Young Tom Morris was one of the players who saw the advantage of iron clubs for a majority of the difficult tasks on the golf course and he was able to manipulate them with rare skill. He won four British Open crowns before he died prematurely at the age of 24 in 1875. Doubters were convinced by Young Tom's impressive performances. There was a rush to replenish sets with appropriate irons.

Many of the club-makers shifted easily from the feathery to the gutta period. Douglas McEwen lived until 1896 and passed the family guild on to a son, Peter. At St. Andrews, James Wilson, the protégé of Hugh Philp, took in his nephew, Robert Forgan. Other outstanding club-makers included the Andersons and Auchterlonies of St. Andrews, the Simpsons of Carnoustie, Ben Sayers of North Berwick, and Willie Park of Musselburgh. Old Tom Morris was a greenskeeper and a professional at Prestwick before he moved to St. Andrews, where his name became a legend.

Robert Forgan was a visionary, enterprising individual credited with making numerous innovations. It was he who produced the bulger-driver and the ebony putter. He developed the method of driving in the pegs holding the bone to the soles of wooden heads at a slant. He took a leading role in popularizing hickory for the use instead of ash.

Hickory first made its way to Scotland in the form of ballast, which reached Dundee from Russia over the Baltic. This happened around the middle of the nineteenth century and no one recognized the wood as possible ideal material for golf clubs. Later bolts of hickory intended to be converted into shovel and axe handles began moving up the Clyde to Glasgow. The wood came from the Cumberland Mountain area of Tennessee in the southern part of the United States.

History fails to record the name of the intrepid gentleman who had the first golf club shaft fashioned from one of these hickory poles. One was made. It fell into the hands of Forgan, who saw its potentiality. It was light, strong as steel and tough as pig iron. Water or dampness had no effect on it. It would not warp when varnished and oiled. The hickory first was seasoned, split into 1½ inch squares, then cut and planed down to the size desired. It made a perfect shaft.

As techniques improved, the clubs took on a smarter, sharper look. The cumbersome, sledge-hammer grip disappeared, and was replaced by a smaller, neater, and more practical grip. The irons began to look like precision implements rather than an unfinished slab of heavy metal. The woods lost their long, awkward heads for stubby, powerful hitting areas. The principles of club-making, still largely handcraft with the aid of a few shop devices, remained basically unchanged.

The heads of the wood clubs were cut out of a block, filed, spoke-shaved, chiseled, gouged, leaded, boned, glass-papered, sometimes stained and treated with a hare's foot dipped in a mixture of oil and varnish. The depth of the club heads increased from five-sixteenths of an inch, as used by Allan Robertson when he shot a 79 at St. Andrews in 1858, to one inch and then to two inches.

Iron heads were hand-forged from a bar of mild iron. Then they were heated, hammered, emery-wheeled, and polished. The involved process was climaxed by piercing the socket for the rivet and then nicking it. Shafts for wooden clubs were glued onto the head and reinforced with tarred twine. Shafts for the irons were finished with a prong to fit into the socket and holed for the iron cross-rivet. The grips, strips of untanned leather, were wound spirally over a cloth foundation, bound with twine, and varnished.

The improved clubs and the livelier gutta percha ball produced remarkable gains in scoring. Young Tom Morris shot a 77 at St. Andrews in 1869, breaking Allan Robertson's record 79. The first British Open Championship at Prestwick, Scotland, was won by Willie Park, Sr., with a 36-hole score of 174. Young Tom Morris won the same tournament over the same course ten years later with 149.

This is the type of equipment Americans saw when the sport was introduced in the United States in the 1880's. The United States' first championships were played in 1895, three years before the invention of the rubber ball and six years before its acceptance.

The advent of the rubber ball occurred after the Industrial Revolution. As the parade moved into the twentieth century, the sun began to set on the individual club-maker and factories took over.

The harder rubber ball brought about the use of persimmon and later laminated club heads. Shoe-last machines were used on an increasing scale. Splicing became outmoded. Sockets were bored in the hosels and shafts were inserted instead. Faces of the iron clubs were deepened to meet the challenge of the livelier ball and were machine-lined to increase the spin of the ball in flight. Hard insets were put on the faces of wooden clubs.

Hand-modeling of woods and hand-forging of irons quickly became a lost art. A Dayton, Ohio, company—the Crawford, McGregor and Canby Company—started turning out wooden club heads instead of shoe lasts. Foundries began converting drop-forging processes to iron heads. In Chicopee, Massachusetts, a designer was experimenting with steel rods for shafts.

Steel shafts were legalized by the U.S. Golf Association in 1926. The Royal and Ancient, which does nothing impulsively, followed suit three years later. Names of clubs went out of fashion. They became so numerous that they had to be numbered instead—No. 2 wood, No. 3 wood, etc., and irons from 1 through 10, plus the putter. Clubs became so specialized that some of them were numbered in fractions, such as 7½ iron, 5½ iron, etc.

Macdonald Smith resisted the steel invasion for years. While manufacturers were seeking a perfect steel shaft, the old pro continued producing hickory-shafted clubs at a plant in Tennessee. Also he played them long after fellow professionals had shifted to steel.

The first experiments with steel were unsuccessful when it was proved the perforated shaft, developed by Allan Lard in Chicopee, Massachusetts, was not an improvement on hickory. The locked-seam shaft was little better but the answer came when a seamless shaft of high carbon steel which could be heat-treated and tempered was finally produced by the Union Hardware Company of Torrington, Connecticut.

Clubs of every description hit the market and it became fashionable to play with matched sets. Old-timers resented the trend. They believed the true test of golf was in making a variety of shots with one club by playing half shots, three-quarter shots, lofts, pitches, and pitch-and-run shots. They accused the new breed of buying their shots in the shops, saying they had one swing and many clubs.

The situation reached its most ludicrous heights in the early 1930's. In 1934, Lawson Little, playing in the British Amateur at Prestwick, had so many clubs in his bag that the caddy asked to be paid extra money.

On January 1, 1936, the U.S. Golf Association passed a rule limiting the number of clubs that may be carried in a bag to 14, saying "The multiplicity of clubs tends toward mechanization of the game." In 1939, the Royal and Ancient passed a similar edict.

The Royal and Ancient was not always so timid about taking the initiative on such matters. The General Electric Company of Schenectady, New York, inspired by the inventive craze of the early part of the century, put out an aluminum headed putter with a shaft attached near the center instead of at the heel. Walter J. Travis of New York used the novel implement in winning the British Amateur Championship in 1904. The R&A later declared the club illegal.

GOLF CLUBS: NEW NUMBERS, OLD NAMES

Woods

No. 1—Driver	No. 3—Spoon
No. 2—Brassie	No. 4—Cleek

Irons

No. 1—Driving Iron	No. 6—Spade Mashie
No. 2—Midiron	No. 7—Mashie Niblick
No. 3—Mid Mashie	No. 8—Lofting Iron
No. 4—Mashie Iron	No. 9—Niblick
No. 5—Mashie	No. 10—Putter

When Jock Hutchinson won the British Open in 1921 with deeply slotted faces on his pitching clubs, the Royal and Ancient imposed a ban. In 1924, the U.S. Golf Association imposed a regulation governing markings which became effective in 1924. Horton Smith, the American professional, used a revolutionary sand wedge designed by E. M. MacClain of Houston, Texas, back in the 1920's. The club had a concave face. The U.S.

Golf Association banned the principle of concavity in 1931.

However, Gene Sarazen developed a different type of sand wedge—a heavy-bladed club with a straight face—and used it effectively in winning the British and American Opens in 1932. The golf fathers put the club under a microscope, found nothing unfair in its character, and gave it unqualified approval. The result: The club has become a standard weapon for bunker play and short shots to the green.

The game has undergone many transitions in equipment but not out of the eagle eye range of the two powerful bodies which rule the sport, the Royal and Ancient Club of St. Andrews and the U.S. Golf Association. It is their determination, they say, to preserve the original form of the game—and they have done it.

PART TWO

Chapter Five

The Early Scots: They Rocked the Cradle

A block from the main street in the little town of St. Andrews, Scotland, there stands an old structure of smoky-gray stone. It is not much to look at. It is drab, dirty-looking, lacking any architectural elegance or distinction. It might well pass for a railroad terminal in some obscure western American outpost. It is the clubhouse of the Royal and Ancient Club of St. Andrews.

Cold and aloof, the aged building stands alone—monumentally if not majestically— with the sea whipping up white caps at its back and in front of it a chain of dunes and ridges, knolls and hollows stretching like a thumb between the Firth of Forth and the Firth of Tay. This is the famous Old Course.

If there is mystery about where and when the game of golf drew its first tortured breath of life, there is none about where it was nurtured through its growing pains and guided to healthy maturity. Old St. Andrews may not have been the actual birthplace of the sport, but there is no question that hers was the hand that rocked the cradle and hers was the maternal eye that watched over it through the rocky period of adolescence.

She is still the doting parent. She peers from behind the blinds of those old gray walls and zealously guards the conduct of the now full-grown offspring. In conjunction with the U.S. Golf Association, the Royal and Ancient Club writes the rules, interprets and enforces them. The Royal and Ancient conducts the major British championships and oversees the British role in such international events as the Walker Cup and Curtis Cup matches. The ancient clubhouse off the Firth of Tay may not be a castle, but no one disputes that it is the capital seat in the broad kingdom of golf.

Other clubs could boast of earlier origins— such as Royal Blackheath outside London, where James I and his bored courtiers played the game as early as 1606, and Leith, where the Company of Gentlemen Golfers organized and drafted a set of rules in 1744. Other clubs could boast of outstanding players—such as Prestwick, where Old Tom Morris first

Old Alick, a professional in the early Nineteenth Century and official hole-cutter for the Royal Blackheath Golf Club, established in 1766.

mastered the game and passed on his knowledge to his son, and Musselburgh, which produced the great Willie Park. But inevitably all roads led to St. Andrews. The Old Course became the most famous of the links and in 1834 its position as the focal point of golf became official when King William IV granted the Society of St. Andrews Golfers the title of Royal and Ancient.

One of the great early figures of the game was Allan Robertson, prominent ball-maker whose career spanned the changeover from the feather ball to the gutta percha era. An obstinate man, he vigorously resisted the new and livelier missile and did everything in his power to discourage its popularity.

At the time, Robertson not only was the most successful ball-maker in St. Andrews but he semiofficially held the position of professional at the club. They say he bribed the

caddies to turn over to him all the gutties found on the course so that he could burn them. Once, with a small gallery of golfers looking on, he teed up a gutta percha ball and then purposely topped it. This was proof, he contended, that the guttie would not fly. He had a bitter quarrel with Tom Morris, who came over from Prestwick to work in his shop, because Morris insisted on playing the gutta percha ball. They parted company, and Morris ultimately set up a shop of his own—one that still bears his name and overlooks the eighteenth hole at St. Andrews' Old Course.

No one ever really found out how good a golfer Allan Robertson was. An intense rivalry was built up between him and his former assistant, Tom Morris, but repeated efforts to get the pair together in a money match were unsuccessful. Morris's supporters insisted that their man was ready but Robertson repeatedly ducked the confrontation. Robertson was an unbeaten champion, they insisted, only because he refused to face up to the few creditable rivals at hand.

This criticism was not entirely fair. It is true that Robertson, although a beautiful stylist, lacked the power of some of his contemporaries. Nevertheless, even his most vociferous detractors had to admit that he had a masterful short game and a marvelous touch around the greens. He was a wizard with the cleek. He was the pioneer of precision iron play. He was the first man to break 80 over the Old Course at St. Andrews. His 79, with the feather ball and the crude implements of his day, was a remarkable feat.

The Old Course at St. Andrews and the other links where the game got its start were a severe test of a man's stamina, skill, and patience. The seaside layouts were the handiwork of nature, originally sandy wastelands where the tides had flowed and ebbed and birds had flocked by the thousands, producing fertilizer and vegetation. Thick, coarse grass cropped up over the dunes, gullies and hollows which formed natural hazards. Rabbits and other wild life once inhabited the area. Heather, whins, broom, and some small trees

Allan Robertson, one of Scotland's golf pioneers.

Old Tom Morris, He helped rock the cradle. From a 1903 etching.

took root and became a shelter for the animals.

These courses have remained little changed through the years but marked improvement has been made, particularly in the putting surfaces. The Old Course once occupied such a narrow strip—hemmed in by the arable land on the west and the mass of whins on the east—that until the middle of the nineteenth century there was room only for single greens—first eleven and then nine. Players on the incoming and outgoing nines used the same greens, with the homeward bound given priority.

The greens were extremely rough and variable, nothing like the fast, marble-top surfaces available to the stars of the twentieth century. However, they offered one advantage. The holes for the cups were dug into the earth naturally, without the tin cones. As players dug their hands into the holes to retrieve their balls and to pluck sand to tee up for the next drive, the edges became worn away. The more wear, the larger the target.

In those formative days, golf was a fiercely competitive sport. In Scotland, almost everybody played—the shopkeeper, the squire, the army colonel, and the college professor. At first, there was little differentiation between professional and amateur. There usually was a heavy bet hanging in the balance in every foursome. Almost every shot was a crucial one. Feelings ran high.

Two of the most sought-after players for foursome play were Willie Park and Tom Morris. Both were long hitters, measured by the standards of the day, but Park was believed to lack stamina. Park came from Musselburgh, whose members were intensely jealous of St. Andrews, and vice versa. Morris established himself at Prestwick before moving into Robertson's shop at St. Andrews.

The practice was for the foursomes to set out about 11 o'clock in the morning and play two rounds without intermission. At St. Andrews, players stopped at the fourth hole—the Ginger Beer hole—for a short rest and some refreshment on the second round. Betting on these matches always was brisk, both among the players themselves and the townspeople. There was invariably a good-sized, argumentative gallery on hand.

In early British golf lore, no informal matches created a greater stir than those be-

Mustaches and heavy wool jackets were the golf styles of the early Nineteenth Century, as shown in this photograph of a man driving at St. Andrews.

tween Allan Robertson and Tom Morris, on the one hand, and the Dunn brothers, Willie and Jamie, on the other. The latter two, products of Musselburgh, were among the first of the salaried professionals, moving later to England's Royal Blackheath Club where their salaries ranged from 7 to 17 shillings—or less than $3—a week.

In the middle of the nineteenth century—the late 1840's—the Dunns played Robertson and Morris a series of matches which started at Musselburgh, moved to St. Andrews, and finished at North Berwick. Playing on their home course at Musselburgh, the Dunns rolled up a lead of 13 holes, principally because Robertson was not in the best form. Robertson and Morris rallied, however, and finally pulled out the match at North Berwick after being four down with eight holes to play. Sensationally, they won six holes in a row to win, two up. If such a match had taken place 100 years later, the players would have been subjected to suspicion for "dumping." If they had been horses, they would have been given saliva tests.

Competition of this sort was on an informal basis until 1860, when the call went out to all golfers that a 36-hole stroke play tournament would be staged at Prestwick. The prize: a belt, later designated the Belt, with a capital "B," to become the personal property of any man able to win it three years in succession.

The first tournament was won by Willie Park with a score of 174. Thus he became the first British Open champion. The battle for the Belt continued for 11 years. Park won two more times, in 1863 and 1866. Old Tom Morris captured four titles, in 1861, 1862, 1864 and 1867, but he never was able to string three of them together. This was a feat to be reserved for his son, Young Tom Morris, who won in 1868, 1869, and 1870 to retire the Belt.

After Young Tom had walked off with the prize, there was a year's suspension of the tournament. The Open Championship was resumed in 1872 at Prestwick, with Young Tom making it four in a row, and the next year the tournament began rotating among the three major clubs—Prestwick, St. Andrews, and Musselburgh. It was not until 1892 that the British Open was extended to 72 holes.

Young Tom was a golf prodigy—the Bob Jones of his era. He attracted attention and began playing matches when he was just 13 years old. He had just turned 18 when he captured the British championship for the first time in 1868. He dazzled golfers of the time with his superb shot-making. He won the Belt with scores which his contemporaries did not believe possible. In 1868, Young Tom recorded 157 for 36 holes—13 shots better than the score with which his father won the tournament over the same course the year before. In 1869, he fired 154. In 1870, he shot a then phenomenal 149. His superiority was reflected in the fact that in the three championships he won Young Tom had an average nine-stroke lead over the tournament runner-up.

At the time of these championships, Prestwick's course consisted of 12 holes, which were played three times around. The courses then, as now, had no par figures, as Americans know them. Conditions—principally the gusty winds and rain squalls that blew in from off the sea—determined scoring, but a perfect score over Prestwick's 12 holes was fixed at 49. Young Tom's rounds in 1870 were 47, 51, 51—regarded as quite phenomenal.

Young Tom Morris was a bold, aggressive player, having qualities associated a century later with Arnold Palmer. He was a smooth, graceful swinger but he disdained style for hitting power. He put all he had into his tee shots. Old-timers recalled with a chuckle—and perhaps a bit of excusable exaggeration—that Young Tom could break the wooden shafts of his clubs merely by waggling them. The younger Morris had a faculty for getting into trouble and out of it with a minimum of penalty. He was a tremendous iron player and a superb, pirate-bold putter who pointed his left toe at the hole and stroked the ball off the

Golf lovers still make pilgrimages to the grave of Young Tom Morris, one of Scotland's early greats.

toe of his right. The young man's fame as a golfer spread quickly. When a subscription was raised among golf clubs to erect a monument to Tommy, even those in England kicked in generously.

It was only natural that the game played with such passion at St. Andrews, Prestwick, and Musselburgh should spread and infect other areas. A Scot general from St. Andrews, visiting in England, was responsible for the formation of Royal North Devon and Westward Ho, the first seaside course in England, in 1864. A year later came the Wimbledon Club, composed of members of the London Scottish Rifle Volunteer Corps. In 1869, the Royal Liverpool Golf Club, with its links at Hoylake, emerged, certainly unaware of the titanic role it was to play ultimately in the world of golf. An old Scot schoolmaster provided the inspiration for the Royal St. George's Club on Sandwich Bay in 1887. Less than 10 years later, similar clubs sprang up in Ireland and Wales.

Scot professionals were much in demand. The number of devotees of the game mushroomed. Golf was on its way to becoming a big-time sport—and a multimillion-dollar business.

31

Chapter Six

The Bug Bites America

On one of the walls at Golf House, head-quarters and museum of the United States Golf Association in New York, there hangs the portrait of a dour gentleman, sitting stiffly in a straight-backed chair. He has a handle-bar mustache and long sideburns. He is snappily attired in a red jacket, checkered vest, knickers and high stockings. A small cap sits rakishly atop his head. Around his throat is draped a white bandanna. In his right hand he is gently cradling a golf club—an old-fashioned cleek or a mashie.

He is John Reid, "the father of American golf." Many people had a role in helping introduce and popularize the sport in the New World, but it was this transplanted Scotsman from Dunfermline who is credited with establishing the first permanent golf club in the United States and thus sowing the seed which in a few decades was to produce the most powerful golfing nation in the world.

The golf "bug" was not quick to bite in the new land. While there is evidence that the game was introduced to these shores as far back as the latter part of the eighteenth century—undoubtedly brought over by Scottish regiments—it failed to take root until some 100 years later. In fact, golf got a firm foothold in Canada before it was formally accepted by sportsmen in the United States.

There were many reasons for the delay. The early climate of a young, pioneer nation just beginning to flex its muscles was not perfectly suitable. Most of the people were absorbed with the task of hewing out a new life for themselves. They liked sports, but of a more robust nature—such as horse-racing, prize-fighting, and that new game attributed to a man named Abner Doubleday, baseball. They had little time for leisure and they saw little sport or physical challenge in the pastime of knocking a little white ball around an open pasture with a long-handled stick. They regarded it as a stupid sport for the fat, aged, and idle rich. Then, when sports might have started getting popular, the country was rent by the Civil War.

Research of the period immediately following the Revolutionary War has uncovered newspaper references to "golf clubs" and "golf greens" but no records of golf competitions. The clubs apparently were purely social—designed for dining and dancing—and use of the word "golf" was of no significance.

A Charleston, South Carolina, newspaper, the *City Gazette,* dated October 13, 1795, carried notice of an anniversary party of the Golf Club to be held at a place called Harleston's Green. A similar ad in the same paper two years later referred to the organization of the "South Carolina Golf Club." The Savannah (Georgia) Golf Club has in its archives an invitation to a Golf Club Ball, dated December, 1811, and newspaper advertisements announcing Golf Club activities for a period

John Reid, Father of American Golf.

up to around 1830. If, however, anybody took the trouble to play golf, it is still a mystery.

Canadian golf historians report that the game was brought to that Dominion as early as the 1850's by ship's officers from Scotland. Three-hole courses popped up in Montreal and Quebec, and on November 4, 1873, the first club was formed in Montreal. This ultimately became the Royal Montreal Golf Club and preceded the first established golf club in the United States by 15 years.

John G. Reid had first seen golf played when he was a young boy growing up in Dunfermline. Memories of the mushrooming sport on Scotland's seaside links stayed with him when he moved to America, settled in Yonkers, New York, and worked himself up to an executive position with an iron foundry. He had an affinity for all sports, being particularly adept at shooting and tennis, and it was only natural that as his time for leisure increased, Reid's thoughts should drift back to the favorite sport of his former homeland.

In 1887, Reid learned that his good friend and fellow Scotsman, Robert Lockhart, was returning to Britain on a business trip. While over there, why not pick up a set of golf clubs and some golf balls, Reid suggested to Lockhart. Lockhart thought it was a swell idea. He became so entranced with the mission, in fact, that he arranged his itinerary to take him to St. Andrews and to the shop of Old Tom Morris, the Scottish professional whose name was almost synonymous with the game itself.

Lockhart ordered a set of six clubs—driver, brassie, spoon, cleek, sand iron, and putter—plus two dozen gutta percha balls. Since the order could not be filled on the spot, he directed that the equipment be delivered to his home in New York.

It was in dead of winter, with temperatures at the freezing point, when the shipment arrived. Lockhart was so excited that he took the clubs and balls out to an open area on the Hudson River and put them through a preliminary test. Then he delivered them to his friend Reid.

Reid had fully intended to wait until spring to unveil his surprise to his small and select coterie of friends. But when the holiday of Washington's Birthday, February 22, 1888, broke clear and mild, he was unable to suppress his enthusiasm. He got together a few of his cronies and took them to a Yonkers cow pasture. Three short holes were laid out and cups dug with the head of one of the irons. Thus emerged the first golf course ever built in the United States.

The first photograph taken of golf in the United States. Scene is the Yonkers cow pasture which became the St. Andrew's course.

In this historic golfing party, in addition to Reid, were John P. Upham, Henry O. Tallmadge, Harry Holbrook, Kingman Putnam, and Alexander P. W. Kinnan, making six in all. Since there were not enough clubs to go around, Reid and Upham squared off in a friendly match and the other four formed the gallery. Thus golf got its humble beginning in America.

Shortly afterward, the New York area was virtually paralyzed by one of the severest blizzards of all time and the ground was first covered by snow, then frozen, and later turned into a sea of mud by the spring thaws. For a period of weeks, golf was unthinkable. The little band of par-fighting pioneers had no choice except to hibernate and await both more agreeable weather and the additional equipment ordered from Scotland.

Until the new clubs and balls arrived, the sextet took turns using Reid's six clubs and gutta percha balls. Great care was taken that none of the treasured balls be lost. Even so, it soon was discovered that the original three-hole layout in Reid's private cow pasture was wholly inadequate. The group took over a larger plot of land, some 30 acres located at North Broadway and Shonnard Place, belonging to John C. Shotts, a German butcher. They laid out a rough course of six holes, with bumpy greens about 12 feet in diameter. They never bothered to get a lease from the butcher or pay him rental. They simply played—and there was no squawk from Shotts.

Before the summer was well under way, additional clubs and balls came from Scotland. The original group of Reid and his friends became golf addicts. They played at every opportunity but always came out in force on Sundays. Strollers stopped to watch their antics in wonderment. They were scoffed at by some onlookers and were sharply criticized in the neighborhood pulpits for desecrating the Sabbath. It was almost as if history had rolled back the pages to Scotland in the seventeenth century.

On November 14, 1888, Reid gave a dinner party attended by four other of the golfing regulars—Tallmadge, Holbrook, Putnam, and Upham. During the course of the festive evening, Reid proposed that the group set up an organization to regulate their new-found activity. "Ayes" echoed around the dinner table. They decided to call their body the St. Andrews Club of Yonkers, naming it for the famous old club in Scotland. Reid was elected president, Upham secretary-treasurer. Lockhart and Gilbert Turner were elected to membership. Later the club took in J.C. Ten Eyck, S.H. Fitch, E.I. Loiselle, Kinnan (who was in that Washington's Birthday sixsome) and Colonel Heermance. "For Men Only" was put aside briefly. On March 30, 1889, Upham teamed with Mrs. Reid and Reid partnered Miss Carrie Low in a precedent-setting mixed foursome match. Upham and Mrs. Reid won by 1 and one-half holes, the group having agreed that halved holes should count one-half point.

In the spring of 1892, the club was confronted with a menace that was to haunt bigger and more lavish layouts later in the golf boom of the twentieth century—expanding residential development. The City of Yonkers announced plans to extend Palisade Avenue north, bisecting the six-hole course. Reid and his cronies were forced to move a half-mile up the road to a 34-acre apple orchard. They laid out a new six-hole course among the apple trees. A large tree beside the home green became the parking place for jackets, picnic lunches, and liquid refreshment. The Yonkers golfers became known as "The Apple Tree Gang."

Their ranks grew and their good times increased proportionately, but our hardy fairway pioneers had trouble finding a permanent home during these formative years. In 1894, at the insistence of the younger members, the club moved to a new site at Grey Oaks on the Sawmill River Road and in three days carved out a nine-hole course over the hilly terrain. Three years later, recognizing the need for a full 18-hole layout, the St. Andrews Club transferred to its final location at Mt. Hope.

While they laid the cornerstone for golf in the United States, members of the "Apple Tree Gang" did not have the sport to themselves for long. In Middlesborough, Kentucky, an industrial iron center, a group of Englishmen in 1889 completed a nine-hole course and formed the Middlesboro Club, which claimed the distinction of being the second such club organized in the country. By 1894, six years after the first shots were hit in Reid's Yonkers cow pasture, there were courses of six and nine holes in Paterson, Lakewood, New Brunswick, and Montclair, New Jersey; Tuxedo, Newburgh, White Plains, and Long Island, New York; Newport, Rhode Island, Greenwich, Connecticut, and Chicago, Illinois.

One of the game's early driving forces was Theodore A. Havemeyer, the so-called "Sugar King" and prominent member of Newport, Rhode Island, society, who was first exposed to golf while holidaying in the French resort of Pau. For years he tried in vain to interest his friends in the new sport. Finally, in 1890, he built a nine-hole course at Brenton's Point in Newport, a summer colony for such millionaires as Cornelius Vanderbilt, Oliver Belmont, and John Jacob Astor. The Newport Golf Club was formed and Havemeyer became the first president.

Duncan Cryder, another transplanted Scotsman with a deep-seated love for the game, is credited with taking golf out of its primitive, cow pasture setting in the United States and giving it a look of some respectability. In 1889, he and two Long Island friends, W.K. Vanderbilt and Edward S. Mead, commissioned Willie Dunn, a well-known Scottish architect and professional, to construct a 12-hole course on the eastern end of Long Island. The area chosen was 4,000 acres along Great Peconic Bay in Southampton. Indians from the Shinnecock reservation were used as laborers. In June 1891, it was unveiled—the first real golf course in America. Shares were sold at $100 apiece, a club house was erected, and Shinnecock Hills became the nation's first duly incorporated golf club.

If John Reid is the father of American golf, then Theodore Havemeyer and Duncan Cryder must be recognized as legitimate "uncles" and a lady named Miss Florence Boit must go down as the game's favorite "aunt." She became interested in golf in Pau, France, and when, in 1892, she visited her uncle, Arthur Hunnewell, in Wellesley, Massachusetts, she brought along her clubs and some golf balls. She attracted attention by practicing her chipping and putting on the Hunnewells' spacious front lawn.

By incorporating a couple of neighbors' lawns, it was possible to lay out a seven-hole pitch-and-putt course, which turned into a weekend gathering place for people in the community. Among those intrigued by the new sport was Laurence Curtis, who recommended that golf be added to the program of The Country Club in Brookline, Mass. The suggestion met with immediate approval and a six-hole course was built, with little idea at the time that The Country Club was destined to become one of the landmarks of the game.

The country's first 18-hole layout was built in Chicago, and it was a monument to the vision and driving force of a single man, Charles Blair Macdonald.

Macdonald was the son of a wealthy Chicago business executive and of Scottish descent. At the age of 16, he was sent to St. Andrews University in Scotland for schooling and, while there, was introduced by his grandfather to the famed Royal and Ancient Club. He played with Young Tom Morris, one of Scotland's leading golfers, and he himself developed into a performer of exceptional skill.

Upon returning home, Macdonald built a tiny, seven-hole course on the lawn of John B. Farwell's estate in Lake Forest, Illinois, and sold the game to his chums at the downtown Chicago Club. In 1892, the Chicago Club built a nine-hole course on a stock farm in suburban Belmont and, under Macdonald's constant prodding, added another nine holes in 1893. Not content with this accomplish-

Old Tom Morris, Sr. and golfers at St. Andrews, 1860s.

ment, the Chicago Golf Club fashioned a new 18-hole layout in a beautiful, 200-acre setting in Wheaton, 25 miles from Chicago. This became one of America's great championship courses, comparable to some of the top layouts in Britain. By 1900, there were 26 golf courses in the Chicago area.

Macdonald, a big, stubborn man and a purist in the observance of old British golf traditions, became the center of numerous controversies growing out of the sport. He took an unwavering attitude about rules, course design and the conduct of the game. He cultivated numerous critics.

The headstrong man from the Midwest figured prominently in the first competitions staged in the United States.

In the summer of 1894, the Newport Golf Club sent out open invitations to amateurs and professionals to compete in September for the championship of the country. The idea was intriguing to the game's new converts.

Twenty players teed off in the 36-hole, two-day medal play event. Macdonald was heavily favored. However, after shooting an opening 89 the Chicagoan blew to a 100 and the tournament was won by W.G. Lawrence, a Newport player, with 188. Macdonald fumed. He said such tournaments should be decided by match, rather than medal, play.

A month later, the St. Andrews Club announced plans for a match play championship. Macdonald was one of the 28 players from eight clubs who showed up. He battled his way into the finals and then, after playing Laurence Stoddard even through 18 holes of the final round, he lost the sudden-death playoff by slicing his tee shot into a corn field. Macdonald's excuse this time was that he had been ill.

Bickering over the outcome of these two tournaments may have resulted in the formation of what was to become the United States Golf Association. At any rate, there were increased demands for a national body which could establish rules, standardize play, run tournaments, and serve as a court of appeals.

A general meeting of golf clubs was called for December 22, 1894. Delegates from five clubs showed up. They represented St. Andrews of Yonkers, New York; The Country Club of Brookline, Massachusetts; the Newport (Rhode Island) Golf Club, Shinnecock Hills of Southampton, New York, and the Chicago Golf Club. Theodore Havemeyer, the sugar tycoon, beat out Reid for the honor of being the first president of the Amateur Golf Association of the United States, later to become the U.S. Golf Association. Henry O. Tallmadge was named the first secretary. The new association later announced plans for the first National Championships, the Open and Amateur, to be staged during the same week in October, 1895, at the Newport Golf Club. Macdonald defeated Charles E. Sands, 12 and 11, in the final round to become the first official U.S. amateur champion.

The handful of men who gave the game its start in the United States could not possibly have imagined the kind of giant their baby would grow into in the next three-quarters of a century.

Chapter Seven

The Vardon Influence

Every time a golfer wraps his hands around the shaft of a golf club, the chances are nine out of ten that he applies the light finger hold known as the overlapping grip. Although there are departures, this has become the universally accepted method of gripping a golf stick. It is not new-fangled or revolutionary. It is generations old, tracing back to the latter part of the nineteenth century. It is the Vardon grip, certainly popularized if not actually conceived by a Jerseyman—Harry Vardon.

One of the most coveted honors sought by American professionals is that which goes yearly to the tournament player achieving the best scoring average on the Professional Golfers Association tour. The award carries the name of the same one-time British star. It is the Vardon Trophy.

Harry Vardon was one of the giants of British golf at the turn of the century. He won six British Open Championships—more than any other man—between 1896 and 1914. He crushed the outstanding players of his day in challenge matches. He became a model for style and skill. Yet his influence was not confined to the tight little islands where the game was pioneered.

Vardon made two extended visits to the United States, where the sport was just beginning to take root, in 1900 and 1913, and returned for a brief farewell appearance at the age of 50 in 1920. He won the U.S. Open Championship on his first visit and tied for the title on his second, losing to young Francis Ouimet in the famous playoff at The Country Club in Brookline, Massachusetts. He played in several cities. Wherever he showed, Vardon attracted thousands who marveled at his fluid, graceful swing, and then went home and tried to duplicate it. Generations later, neophytes of the links were still being told by their elders, "This is how Vardon did it."

Even Bob Jones, who became the greatest of America's champions, fell under the magic Vardon spell.

Jones was just a tyke of 11 when Vardon and his friend, the hulking, mustachioed Ted Ray, visited Atlanta in 1913 on their exhibition tour. The two British greats played a match at Atlanta's East Lake course with Stewart Maiden, the Scottish-born East Lake professional, and another Atlanta pro, Willie Mann.

Bobby recalled in later years that the occasion made a tremendous impact on his young mind. He said he followed every shot with wide-eyed wonder and Vardon became something of his personal idol. Jones was impressed by the brute power of Ray, a huge man who dug tremendous divots out of the earth and almost knocked the cover off the ball with every drive, but he was attracted more to Vardon, who swung with such effortless grace and rhythm that it was like watching a symphony.

Jones said he was thrilled seven years later, when, at the age of 18 and now an established star in his own right, he was paired with Vardon in the National Open at Toledo. By this time, the always neat and distinguished-looking stylist from Jersey had added a few pounds. He was gray around the temples and he had effected a light mustache. But the unbroken rhapsody of his swing remained the same.

It was during this tournament that the famous British champion made his first comment on the young American's game.

With an easy shot to the green, Bobby tried a pitch and topped the ball miserably.

"Mr. Vardon did you ever see a worse shot than that?" Jones asked.

"No," Vardon replied, with typical British candor and succinctness.

Bobby, a trifle flustered, let it go at that. It was an incident he never forgot.

Although most Americans regarded Vardon as the almost flawless stylist, the British wizard received no such carte blanche acclaim from contemporaries in his own country. Bernard Darwin, who represented Britain in international matches from 1902 through 1924 and who served as captain of the Royal and Ancient Club, said he was puzzled rather than attracted by the pronounced lift of the club on Vardon's back swing. He also noted that Vardon's right elbow was "inclined to wander at its own sweet will." J.H. Taylor, one of Vardon's keenest rivals, described the latter's style as "ungainly" and said the lift in the backswing violated principles of accepted orthodoxy.

Nevertheless, even Vardon's severest critics ultimately had to agree that the great champion's swing became a model of beauty. Some contended that Vardon smoothed out his swing in his later years. Others said he never changed it but golf observers grew to accept it—with its obvious defects—because of Vardon's astounding achievements.

Although a man of moderate size, Vardon had tremendous power off the tee. He was a fine iron player and, although he himself argued otherwise, a sound putter. His real forte, however, was the full brassie shot. On the long par 5 holes and the par 4's into the wind, Vardon frequently laced the ball up to the hole with two prodigious wood shots while others were using two woods and a pitching iron to get the same results. It proved a big advantage.

Vardon faced formidable competition in Britain, particularly from J.H. Taylor and James Braid. They were the awesome triumvirate of the era. With only a year separating their ages, they scrambled among each other for honors and dominated the game from 1894 until the start of World War I. Taylor and Braid each won five British Open titles, one less than Vardon. Of the 21 British Opens contested between 1894 and 1914, the triumvirate collected 16 of them.

Taylor won the championship in 1894 at Sandwich and in 1895 at St. Andrews and tied for the title in 1896 at Muirfield before losing to Vardon in a play-off. He had a unique flat-footed style, with both feet firmly planted on the tee, and a short, quick swing. He was remarkably straight on his drives, however, and was one of the boldest and most talented iron players of the era.

Braid worked as an apprentice joiner at St. Andrews and Edinburgh and built up a reputation as a good amateur before he took a job as club-maker in the Army and Navy Stores. He drifted inevitably into golf and first attracted attention in the 1897 Open at Hoylake, where he finished second to Harold Hilton by a stroke. It was not until 1901 at Muirfield that he finally crashed through to the title, but he seemed to like the taste of it. He won 5 in the next 10 years. Braid had a wonderful temperament—absolutely impervious to pressure and outside distractions. He was a good driver, excellent iron player, but a poor putter. He tried desperately to cure his putting ills by changing clubs and techniques, but he never whipped the problem.

Vardon came into the world the same year that Young Tom Morris captured his third straight Open title and retired the Belt.

40

Harry was born May 9, 1870, in the little village of Grouville in Jersey. His father was a gardener. He came from a big family—six boys and two girls—and he was the fourth oldest of the boys. The two younger brothers, Tom and Fred, also became golf professionals and Tom worked for years in the United States.

Harry was a thin, frail-looking youngster but had an aptitude for sports. At first, his ambition was to excel at cricket but later he turned his attention to football. He became quite good at the sport, and later, after establishing himself as a tournament golfer, he played with and captained the Ganton football team.

Young Vardon was seven years of age when a group of sports enthusiasts selected a section of common land in Grouville and laid out a golf course, inciting the wrath of the conservative and highly religious tenant farmers in the area. Despite opposition, the intruders got a permit from the parish constable and set up a headquarters in a neighboring house which was rechristened the Golf Inn.

Shortly, the new links were a beehive of activity. Golfers came over from England to try the course. The people of Jersey were intrigued but unexcited over the innovation. All the youngsters of the locality were enticed to become caddies. Among these was Harry Vardon. At first, the youths carried out their club-toting duties with disinterest. Then they were hit by the fever. They wanted to take a fling at the game themselves.

Since the course was off-limits to the caddies and since none of them had clubs, balls, or money, Vardon and his friends—most of them seven and eight years old—improvised ingeniously. They found a vacant lot and constructed their own miniature course with four holes measuring about 50 yards each. They made teeing grounds and smoothed out small areas of grass for greens. They still lacked balls and clubs. For balls, they decided to use big white marbles known as taws, about half the size of a regulation golf ball. They made their own clubs. First, they cut a thick branch from an oak tree, sawed off a few inches, and then trimmed the piece until it was shaped like the head of a driver. The shafts were made of good thorn, white and black, and affixed to the head by boring a hole with a hot poker.

Vardon displays the left hand grasp of the club in the Vardon grip that became the standard.

The youngsters actually became quite adept at making clubs. When the oak heads began to chip and crack, the heads were sheathed with tin. The tin-headed clubs became known as brassies. They say that the shafts of these primitive clubs were so rough that they produced callouses on the palms of the hands. Thus Vardon, to escape these blisters, effected the light, finger grip. In this fashion—fact or fiction, take your choice—the famous Vardon grip was born.

Because Vardon and his companions worked or went to school during the day, they often did not get a chance to play except at night. Vardon recalled later that some of the best matches among the half-pint practitioners were played at night by the light of the moon. Four of the boys would go out and engage in a stroke play competition, with a few marbles put up as stakes. To prevent loss of taws, one of the players was sent ahead as a sort of fore-caddy to listen for the thud of their fall. After the three had driven, they would move forward and the lookout would return to the tee to take his shot, thus inviting all sorts of skullduggery in the dim light. If the player, upon reaching his ball—or taw—found himself in an unfavorable position, Vardon said, it was not at all unusual for him to give his ball a gentle kick, unbeknownst to his rivals, and thus improve his lie.

Later, the youngsters inherited old, beat-up gutta percha balls and damaged clubs from members for whom they caddied. The boys often repaired and refitted the hand-me-down clubs with their own primitive, hot poker methods, but the end result was never completely satisfactory. The clubs never lasted. Occasionally, one of the caddies would be given an undamaged club as a reward for strict application to duty. This was cause for celebration. Each of the boys would have to get a swing or two with the new stick.

During his caddying days, Vardon made a habit of watching and copying the styles of the better players. Long after he had become a champion and achieved international renown, he acknowledged that his style was nothing more than a patchwork of the styles of men he had seen and admired. He did not pattern himself after any one individual, he said, but rather took a little from this one and a little from that one until his swing was actually a composite of many players. His approaching, chipping, and putting also had mixed parentage. He never took a lesson in his life.

Because his family was large and his father's means were limited, young Harry had to quit school and start work at the age of 13. He became a gardener and played golf with his employer, a stuffy army major who gave him some of his old clubs. He joined a working-men's club and at 16 won his first prize—a vase given for a members' tournament which lasted six months. Meanwhile, his interest in golf was intensified by the success of his younger brother, Tom, who had entered a club-making shop at St. Anne's-on-the-Sea and had finished second in a tournament at Musselburgh.

Harry was 20 years old when, through Tom's influence, he got a job as greenskeeper and professional at a new nine-hole course in Ripon, near Harrogate. Because there were few good players at Ripon, Vardon moved shortly afterward to another nine-hole course at Bury. Here, there were several top-class golfers, especially amateurs, capable of giving Harry a good game. Vardon's reputation as a golfer spread throughout the area and friends arranged a match with Alexander Herd of Huddersfield—a 36-hole test, home and home. It was Vardon's first professional match. So nervous he could hardly hold a club, Vardon was smothered. Chagrined by his humiliating defeat, he vowed he never would tense up in a match again. They say he did not.

Vardon played in his first British Open Championship in 1893, at the age of 23, at Prestwick, finishing far down the list. The next year at Sandwich he came in fifth and in 1895 at St. Andrews he tied for ninth, the title both times going to his friend, J.H. Taylor. Vardon finally crashed through at Muirfield in 1896, tying Taylor for the Championship

The amazing Harry Vardon, winner of six British Open titles, was 61 when he played in the Open at Carnoustie in 1931. Tommy Armour won it.

had left his golf in America. Others said—with greater justification—that Vardon was simply the victim of putting jitters.

Vardon, in describing his lean years immediately following his victory in the Open in 1903, openly admitted that the latter was the case. He said he completely lost his putting touch. His confidence on the greens was shaken. This was a theory later expounded by the great Ben Hogan, who insisted that a golfer's legs were not the first to go in advancing age but rather the nerves on the putting green. Vardon said he got to the point that he felt a cold chill every time he walked up to a short putt. He did not mind the 5- and 6-footers. He dreaded putts of 3 and 2 feet and he said he feared the 2-footers more than the 3. Even in his later years, Vardon said he lost little or none of his power off the tee and none of his steadiness with his irons. Yet his confidence on the greens was shattered, resulting in failure after failure.

Nevertheless, the phenomenal British master came back to win his country's Open Championship again in 1911 at Sandwich and an unprecedented sixth time in 1914 at Prestwick, beating out J.H. Taylor by three strokes on the latter occasion.

Vardon still had enough of his old wizardry left at the age of 43 to return to America in 1913 and tie Ted Ray and Francis Ouimet for the U.S. Open Championship. It was immaterial from the standpoint of Harry's host of admirers that he lost in the play-off to the young American ex-caddy, Ouimet. It was a tremendous effort by the Grand Old Man of British golf.

Vardon returned home from his American excursions with the warning that golf in the United States was on the ascendancy and soon would be challenging Great Britain for supremacy in the sport. The Yanks, he said, were a zestful, enthusiastic lot and John Bull would be wise to keep his trophy cabinet tightly locked.

Which made Harry Vardon more than a great champion and gentleman. He was a prophet, as well.

with a score of 316 and then capturing the play-off. He took pride in the fact that in the 36-hole play-off he did not three-putt a single green. When he failed to hole the ball, he stuck it stone dead to the cup.

This was significant because Vardon's ability as a putter came up for considerable discussion later in his career. After winning three of the following seven British championships and capturing the U.S. Open title in 1900 on his first try, the brilliant stylist fell into a dismal slump. Some contended that he

Chapter Eight

Willie Anderson—Man of Mystery: The First Four-Time Winner

Nine months before Bob Jones was born, a stone's throw from the East Lake course in Atlanta, Georgia, a Scotsman named Willie Anderson won the United States Open Golf Championship. Seven years before Ben Hogan saw the light of day in a humble blacksmith's home in Dublin, Texas, this same Willie Anderson put the finishing touches on his fourth open victory, thus setting a record which both Jones and Hogan later were to duplicate but no man was to surpass.

Willie Anderson remains one of the men of mystery in American golf. Early historians thought so little of him as a golfer, even while he was collecting Open championships in clusters, that they did not see the necessity of probing into his background. They were much more impressed with Willie's good friend, Alex Smith, another Scotsman who came from a well-known golfing family in Carnoustie, and a pair of amateurs who captured the nation's fancy in the early part of the century, Walter J. Travis and Jerome D. Travers.

Thus Willie's early background—his boyhood, his introduction to golf, the circumstances surrounding his migration to America—is lost in the shadows of obscurity. He may have contributed to his own anonymity in history by his peculiar personality. Scotsmen as a breed are renowned for their reticence, but Willie Anderson carried this tradi-

tional trait to a ridiculous extreme. He was dour. He was introverted. He seldom spoke a word—on the golf course or off it. As a result, even his closest friends—and he had some, most intimate of whom perhaps were the Smith brothers, Alex and Willie—knew little or nothing about his personal life.

Anderson played in the third Open Championship in 1897, registering from the Watch Hill Club. Golf observers should have taken note of him right then, but they did not. Relatively unnoticed in the field of 35, the quiet Scotsman shot 79–84—163 over the Chicago Golf Club in Wheaton, Illinois, and missed the championship by a single stroke. The title went to Joe Lloyd, an English professional who worked at the Essex Country Club in Manchester, Massachusetts, in the summer and in Pau, France, in the winter.

One fact became obvious as Willie pursued his bid for tournament prizes—either through his own choice or that of his employers, he had trouble finding a permanent job. Until he finally got located with Apawamis Golf Club in Westchester County, New York, Anderson showed up every year for the Open with a different club affiliation.

In 1898, he represented Baltusrol in Springfield, New Jersey, and finished third behind Fred Herd and Alex Smith. The next year, the tournament was at Baltimore, and Anderson, registering from New York, fin-

Willie Anderson

ished fifth. In 1900, when Harry Vardon won, Willie was still farther down the list, tied for eleventh and signing in from the Oconomowoc Club.

The breakthrough finally came in 1901. At that time, Willie was employed by the Pittsfield (Massachusetts) Country Club. There were 60 entries in the field at the Myopia Hunt Club in Hamilton, Massachusetts. After double rounds on two days, Anderson found himself tied with his old friend, Alex Smith, at 331—to this day the largest score ever to lead the National Open. In the 18-hole play-off, Anderson shot an 85 and Smith an 86.

Anderson and Smith, while the closest of companions, were exact opposites both in personality and in their approach to the game.

Smith, credited with refining the swing of Jerome Travers, was a hearty, outgoing individual who seemed to look upon golf—even the tournament phase of it—as a big picnic. He played with a relaxed casualness, carrying on a constant conversation all the way around the course. He had a sharp wit. He was loaded with color. He played very fast, never dawdling over a shot. He almost putted on the run. In 1910, he blew an easy 3-foot putt that would have given him the championship. He laughed heartily at his mistake and then went out the next day and beat his brother, Macdonald, and Johnny McDermott in a play-off for the title.

Anderson was as reserved and serious as his best pal was uninhibited. He was actually grim in a match—a 1900 edition of Ben Hogan. He had no sense of humor. He was cold, calculating, and business-like. To him, golf was more than a game. It was a profession and a challenge. Once he teed off, he was like a tiger. He refused to let anybody or anything interfere with his concentration. Although he spoke only when necessary, he could be frigidly biting to anyone who disrupted his train of thought.

The silent Scotsman was not an impressive character, either in the way he looked or the way he played golf. He was of medium height, 5'10", and weighed about 165 pounds. He

had the pugnacious face of a prize-fighter, strong arms and shoulders, but at times there was a look of frailty about him. He usually wore a wool cap, which he kept pulled low over his eyes, baggy trousers, and a tweed jacket. His swing was far from classic. It was a flat swing, which got the job done with a minimum of mistakes, but which packed neither the fluid grace nor the power expected of great champions. Willie was a great admirer of Harry Vardon, whom he watched closely on the latter's visit in 1900, and attempted to pattern his game as much as possible after that of the stylish Englishman. Critics insisted that very little of Vardon's polish wore off. However, it should be noted that the year after he followed Vardon with such devotion Anderson won his first Open championship.

The second came in 1903. The site was the Baltusrol Club, where Willie had worked five years before. Now he was firmly entrenched at the Apawamis Club, had no worries about his security, and could concentrate on the championship. He did. Saying no more than two dozen words during the two days, Anderson started with a record 73 and tied David Brown for the title at 307. Again he proved himself an excellent play-off competitor. In the 18-hole play-off, he shot an 82 to Brown's 84.

Willie won his third Open and his second in a row in 1904 at the Glen View Golf Club in Golf, Illinois. This time, instead of starting fast, he closed like a whirlwind—a silent one. He fired a last round 72 for 303, which gave him the championship by five shots over Gil Nichols.

History was made at the Myopia Hunt Club, scene of Anderson's first Open victory, on September 21–22, 1905. Anderson put together rounds of 81-80-76-77-314—and beat out Alex Smith by two strokes. He had won his fourth Open (a feat not to be equalled until 25 years later) and his third in succession, an accomplishment no succeeding player —not even Jones or Hogan—could match.

Anderson's reign was broken the next year by Alex Smith. Willie finished fifth. Shortly afterward, it was discovered that Anderson had a lung ailment. He lingered a while and then succumbed to a premature death—one of the great but least appreciated and known of all American champions.

While Willie Anderson and Alex Smith were staging their titanic battles for Open honors, the terror of the more prestigious United States Amateur was a middle-aged immigrant from Australia, Walter J. Travis.

Travis was just a boy when his family moved to the United States from Melbourne. Coming from a sports-minded country, he was a good athlete. He played tennis, cycled, and swam. He shunned golf. To him, golf seemed like a game for old men and a waste of time. However, years later, on a visit to England, Travis took periodic strolls alongside a golf course. The more he watched, the more intrigued he became. When he returned to

Willie Anderson and Alex Smith

America, he bought a set of clubs and began playing with friends over the Oakland course on Long Island. The year was 1896. Travis was 35 years old.

The lean Australian, who wore a thick General Grant beard at first and puffed away constantly on a smelly cigar, was a stickler for perfection. He poured over golf manuals and instruction books. He studied techniques. Reasoning that half the game was played on the greens, he worked particularly hard to perfect a putting stroke. On his other strokes he concentrated on accuracy rather than length.

Two years after taking up the game Travis went to the semifinals in the National Amateur. In another two years—1900—he was National champion. The "Old Man," as he was known to his contemporaries, completely baffled his opponents. He did not appear to be a good golfer. He just nudged the ball off the tees. His long iron play was average. Around the greens, however, he was sheer dynamite. He was a deadly chipper, and he nonchalantly ran in putts from unbelievable distances.

In 1900, at the Garden City (New York) Golf Club, Travis won the low medal with 166 and defeated Findlay Douglas in the final, 3 and 2. He repeated as both medalist and champion the next year at the Country Club of Atlantic City (New Jersey) and in 1903 won the medal for the third straight time. But his bid for a third successive Amateur title was foiled by Eben Byers in the third round. He had to wait until 1903 to grab No. 3 and to settle his score with Byers, whipping the latter in the final at Glen Cove, New York, 5 and 4.

In 1904, Travis decided to make a bid for the British Amateur Championship, a title never won by anyone other than a Briton. The tournament was scheduled at the Royal St. George's Golf Club in Sandwich, a relatively short course, and Travis figured this would be his best chance for a victory. But when he arrived in Britain a couple of weeks in advance, he found himself in a terrible slump. Not only was his general game off the beam, but he had lost the secret of previous successes—his fantastic putting touch. Before the tournament, the former Australian shifted to a new set of clubs and borrowed a revolutionary putter from a friend—a mallet-headed putter with the shaft inserted at the center, later a source of bitter controversy. The putter had been designed by A. W. Knight of Schenectady, New York, and was christened the "Schenectady Putter."

The sudden slump proved to be only one of Travis's problems. The British generally took a cold attitude toward invaders and they developed a special animosity for Travis, who, wishing to concentrate on his golf, declined their official invitations to parties and receptions. The officials of Royal St. George's considered Travis' aloofness as an affront. Travis himself could not have cared less. Nevertheless, the situation proved unsettling. Travis was not permitted to practice with the good British players. He was assigned a cross-eyed, incompetent caddy.

Despite all the built-in distractions, Travis suddenly found his game just before the tournament started. With the British galleries pulling hard against him, he surprised even his critics by sweeping through the early rounds, principally on machine-like steadiness. Then in the semifinals he ran against Harold Hilton, rated the best amateur of the day on the strength of two British Open and two British Amateur triumphs. Old Man Travis is certain to get his come-uppance now, the British chortled. But he did not. Travis beat the off-form Hilton, 5 and 4, and went on to turn back Ted Blackwell in the final, 4 and 3. The British galleries failed to applaud. Some British officials termed the victory a "fluke" because of the unorthodox Schenectady putter. The putter was ruled illegal three years later by the Royal and Ancient Club of St. Andrews.

Travis, who shaved off his beard and later grew another one, continued to play golf until he was well in his fifties. Before he quit in 1915, he won the New York Metropolitan Amateur Championship, en route beating a young man named Jerome Travers. Travers was to become the next sensation of amateur golf.

Travers, unlike Travis, was born in the golfing tradition. He started swinging clubs when he was 9, played regularly at 13, became a pupil of Alex Smith at 15. He won the Intercollegiate Championship in 1904, at the age of 17, and scored a 7 and 6 victory over Travis in the Metropolitan in 1905. Young Jerry won the Metropolitan in 1906 and now seemed ready for greater things.

The sturdy, free-swinging young man reached voting age and golf maturity in 1907.

He won the first of his four National Amateur crowns by defeating Archibald Graham, 6 and 5, at Cleveland, Ohio. He repeated in 1908 in Garden City. He passed up the tournament in 1909 and 1910 and lost in the third round in 1911 to Harold Hilton. In the meantime, he made an ill-fated bid for the British Amateur in 1909, losing in the first round.

Young Travers reasserted himself in 1912, beating Chick Evans 7 and 6 for his third title at the Chicago Golf Club, and repeated in 1913 at Garden City. He established himself as one of America's great amateur players of all time.

Chapter Nine

Francis Ouimet—Drama at Brookline

In the nineteenth century, it was the custom of Boston gentlemen to take weekend rides on horseback to the country. They usually stopped at a friend's estate or an inn for a respite before starting the long homeward trek.

A few of the riders decided it would be desirable to set up a private stopping place where sportsmen might relax, refresh themselves, and indulge in recreational activities. In 1860, 70 men proposed the establishment of a club. Outbreak of the Civil War thwarted the idea and the play was shelved until 1882, when The Country Club was organized.

The original invitation to prospective members was that the project should include a comfortable club house, restaurant, bowling alley, lawn tennis courts, and a track for race meetings. Golf was not mentioned by the founders. Nevertheless, a six-hole course was laid out in 1893. This layout, hewn out of a forest over a natural rolling terrain, ultimately was expanded to include 27 holes divided into nines named Clyde, Squirrel, and Primrose.

From these rudimentary roots grew The Country Club of Brookline, Massachusetts—proudly retaining the capital "T," since it considered itself the first such club of its kind —destined to become an historic landmark in American golf.

If the Royal and Ancient Club of St. Andrews is the birthplace of British golf, then The Country Club at Brookline cannot be denied as the spot where the sport in the United States, while not actually born, got its great awakening.

Until 1913, when the annual U.S. Open Golf Championship was assigned to The Country Club, golf in America was considered a snobbish, panty-waist pastime indulged in only by the elderly and the idle rich. The best players were mainly English and Scottish. When the overseas stars consented to play in an American tournament, it was not a question of whether a Briton would win but rather which one.

So it was in September, 1913. The dates of the U.S. Open were changed to permit the participation of the two great British professionals, Harry Vardon and Ted Ray. The field included other notables, such as England's Wilfred Reid, France's Louis Tellier, and such rising American pros as Johnny McDermott, Mike Brady, and Tommy McNamara, but none figured to match strokes with Vardon and Ray.

Vardon was the stylist, a man of fluid grace and power—a picture golfer with the sensitive touch of a safe-cracker around the greens. Ray was a hulking 200-pounder who cared little for form but who threw all his tremendous strength into his shots. He was the longest hitter of his day, the reigning British Open champion at the time. Vardon won five British Opens.

50

The least of American threats to this mighty one-two punch of British—a 100 to 1 shot by modern betting standards—was the frail, 20-year-old gardener's son who lived across the road from The Country Club and who learned the game by toting clubs at 28 cents a round. His name was Francis Ouimet. His father, an immigrant French-Canadian, did not understand golf and thought it a waste of time. His mother thought it was too strenuous for her thin, hollow-cheeked son.

After the first 36 holes of the 72-hole medal play competition, it was no surprise to find Vardon and another Englishman, Reid, out front at 147. Ray, exploring the course's underbrush with his wild, booming drives, was two shots back, followed by MacDonald Smith and Jim Barnes, a pair of transplanted Scotsmen. Nobody paid much attention to Ouimet and another 20-year-old youngster from Rochester, Walter Hagen, who were tied at 151.

At the end of the third round, Vardon and Ray were out front as expected but they had strange and unanticipated company. Young Ouimet, the ex-caddie, had shot a creditable 74 over the rain-drenched course and had moved into a 54-hole tie with the two British

Francis Ouimet and his caddy, Edward Lowery, walk down a fairway at The (cap T) Country Club in Brookline, Massachusetts, en route to victory in the 1913 United States Open.   **U.S. Golf Association**

stars at 225. Excitement ran high at The Country Club but no one dared let hopes soar out of bounds. The neighborhood kid could not be expected to pull off such a miracle, Brookliners said.

Ray came slogging in with a final round 79 for 304. Shortly afterward, Vardon, his usually reliable putter gone sour, came home with a matching 79 for a two-way tie. The threats of Mac Smith, Barnes and Hagen drowned, one after another, on the soggy old course and only Ouimet was left with a chance—a faint one—to overtake the leaders.

Francis, showing no sign of tension although he acknowledged later that his nerves were strumming like guitar strings inside, came to the thirteenth hole needing two birdies on the final six holes to gain a tie. He was walking a tightrope. A bogey—a stroke over par—would certainly cook his goose.

A deafening roar went up when Ouimet chipped in from off the green to get a birdie at the thirteenth. Now he needed only one more birdie. He parred the long fourteenth and scrambled to stay even at the fifteenth and sixteenth. Two holes to play. At the dogleg seventeenth, Ouimet hit a good drive and put his approach 20 feet past the pin. It was a tough sidehill putt but Francis gave the ball a solid whack and the ball, as if guided by some unseen hand of destiny, rolled into the cup. The crowd's guarded optimism suddenly exploded into wild pandemonium. Ouimet needed only a par 4 on the final hole to tie.

A picture of cool determination, the Ouimet boy hit a good drive into the fairway, sent his approach to the front of the green and chipped 5 feet short of the cup. History was riding on the next stroke—a difficult putt surrounded by tones of pressure—but the reed-thin youngster in the checkered cap never wavered. He gave the line a quick, cursory look, strode up to the ball and knocked it into the back of the cup. He had tied Vardon and Ray for the Open championship.

It seems reasonable to assume that a young, fuzz-faced kid, going out the next day to face two of the world's greatest golfers, might

spend the evening tossing in sleeplessness and munching nervously on his fingernails. Not Ouimet. He recalled that he went to bed early, slept well, and awoke the following morning to find rain beating against his window pane.

Although he may not have been gripped by tension, he nevertheless was not unaware of the importance of the occasion. "I realized I was just an amateur," he recalled later. "I played golf for fun. I considered professionals as something like magicians who had an answer for everything. I felt I was in the play-off by mistake."

Ouimet arrived at the first tee of The Country Club, accompanied by his 10-year-old caddy, Eddie Lowery, who played hooky from school to carry Francis' clubs. Lowery, later a successful San Francisco automobile dealer, sponsor of such well-known golfers as Ken Venturi and Harvie Ward and an official of the U.S. Golf Association, related years afterward that his principal duty, in addition to lugging Ouimet's cheap canvas bag, was to keep his client on a level psychological keel by reciting fixed lines. Before each of Ouimet's shots, the half-pint caddy in the white sailor hat was to mutter: "Take your time—you've got all day" and "Keep your eye on the ball."

Ouimet said he got himself into a perfect frame of mind. He decided to concentrate on each shot, play it for all it was worth, and then forget it—good, bad, or indifferent. "It was a wonderful mood to get into," he said. "I was numb."

The numbness appeared to be transferred to the tense, breathless crowd as the play-off match went to the nine-hole turn, still all square. The first important break came at the tenth, where Vardon and Ray both three-putted and Ouimet got down in par 3 on the 140-yard hole.

It was here that the intense pressure must have begun to seize the two visiting giants of the links, while falling off the bony shoulders of the former Brookline caddy. Both Vardon and Ray must have been haunted by the question: "What if I should lose to this strip of a youngster?"

At the fifteenth, the long, over-the-hill hole, the big, mustachioed Ray hit a spectator's derby with his drive, pitched into a bunker, took two blasts to get out and wound up with a double bogey 6. This put him four shots back of Ouimet and three behind Vardon. At the dog-leg seventeenth, Vardon hooked his drive into the thick, knotty rough, played into the fairway and used his third shot to reach the green, two-putting for a 5. Ouimet, inspired by this opening, knocked in an 18-foot putt for a birdie 3. Now he had a 3-stroke lead.

This disastrous turn shook the great Vardon. On the final hole, he blew a double bogey 6 and it did not matter that Ray, completely out of the picture, rallied with a birdie 3. Seemingly poised and unshakeable, young Ouimet laced his drive up the middle, hit his second to the green 18 feet from the pin, and sent his approach putt to within 4 feet.

As Ouimet confidently measured the final putt, he looked a picture of tremendous calm to the tense gallery, but he recalled later: "For the first time, I thought about the cham-

pionship. I couldn't get my breath. The green began heaving beneath me. I couldn't even see the hole."

He putted. The ball hit the back of the cup. Francis Ouimet was the new Open golf champion of the United States. He had fired an amazing 1-over-par 72 under the most trying of conditions and had won a play-off from two of the game's greatest stars. Vardon finished with a 77, Ray 78.

The hilarity at The Country Club over the neighborhood boy's historic triumph swept like wildfire throughout the rest of the country and abroad. The story was front-paged in the nation's newspapers and talked about on streetcorners, in clubs, in drugstores and in drawing rooms. Ouimet became an overnight national hero. Golf emerged as a game for the common man. Its popularity boomed.

An English journalist caught the spirit of the event when he wrote: "There will never be another like it. When we are old men, little golfing children will ask us to tell them again the romantic story of the 20th of September in 1913."

There was nothing in Ouimet's modest beginning to indicate that he some day would be one of the immortals of American golf.

The front page of *The Boston Traveler* on September 20, 1913 reflects the impact of Francis Ouimet's victory over England's Harry Vardon and Ted Ray for the 1913 U. S. Open Championship. The feat helped popularize golf in America. Ouimet, *center,* is shown with his play-off victims, Vardon, *left,* and Ray, *right.*

FRANCIS OUIMET'S RECORD

U.S. Open Champion: 1913. (Tied for second, 1925.)
U.S. Amateur Champion: 1914, 1931. (Runner-up, 1920; semifinalist 1923, 1924, 1926, 1927, 1929, 1932.)
French Amateur Champion: 1914.
U.S. Walker Cup team: 1922 through 1936; captain, 1936 through 1949.
Walker Cup record: Singles, won 4, lost 2, halved 2. Foursomes, won 5, lost 3.
Elected original member of Golf's Hall of Fame, 1944.

Francis was born May 8, 1893, in an outlying thinly populated area of Brookline, a Boston suburb. While he was in grade school, his father moved the family to a house across the street from The Country Club, one of the most exclusive if not the poshest on the Eastern coast. He was 11 when he followed his older brother, Wilfred, into the club's caddy ranks. The rules strictly forbade caddies to play on the course, but Francis and Wilfred often sneaked in some stolen practice shots when the pro, Alex Campbell, was not looking.

The younger Ouimet quickly became infatuated with the sport. He acquired an old mashie and later a brassie in exchange for balls which he had found on the course. Frequently he would get up at 5 o'clock in the morning and sneak out on the course for some practice until he was chased by the greenskeepers. On weekends, he and friends would spend all day at a public nine-hole course at Franklin Park.

Francis worked in a dry-goods store to get enough money to pay entrance fees in tournaments. In 1910, at the age of 17, he tried to qualify for the National Amateur, scheduled at The Country Club, and failed. He tried the National Amateur again —without success— in 1911 and 1912, but he went to the finals in the Massachusetts State Amateur in 1912 and won it in 1913. In 1913 also, after winning the Open, he qualified for the first time for the National Amateur and went to the semifinals before losing to Jerry Travers.

Ouimet won the first of his two National Amateur crowns in 1914 at Manchester, Vermont, beating Jerry Travers in the final, 6 and 5, and that same year captured his first international title—the French Amateur. There was a 17-year victory drought before the tall, angular Bostonian crashed through to his second Amateur championship by defeating Jack Westland, 6 and 5, at Chicago in 1931.

During this long, lean period, Ouimet qualified for the U.S. Amateur tournament 13 times. He reached the semifinals six times and the finals once. In three of the semifinals—1924, 1926, and 1927—he bowed to Bob Jones, whom he called "the greatest golfer who ever lived." Chick Evans beat him in the last round of the 1920 Amateur at Roslyn, Long Island, 7 and 6.

He remained the true amateur, playing the game for fun and never letting it take a dominant role in his life. As a result, he never was able to add a second Open victory. After finishing fifth in 1914, he did not make another strong bid until 1925 when he finished in a second place tie with Johnny Farrell, a stroke behind Jones and Willie MacFarlane.

Ouimet played in more Walker Cup matches than any other man. He served with the United States' international team as an active competitor from 1922 (when the series with Britain was launched) through 1934. In 1936, he took over the role as nonplaying captain and held this post until 1949, when he asked to be relieved.

On May 1, 1951, Ouimet was accorded the highest honor Britain can bestow upon a personality in connection with golf. He was elected captain of the Royal and Ancient Golf

First American to be elected captain of the Royal and Ancient Golf Club of St. Andrews, Francis Ouimet plays in on September 19, 1951. The old gray club house is in the background as the Bostonian hits an 180-yard drive off the first tee.

Club of St. Andrews in Scotland. Bedecked in a red coat, he played himself "in" by striking the ball off the first tee at the famous old links where the game is supposed to have been born.

He was the first non-Briton elected to the post. The Duke of Windsor in 1922 and the King of England in 1930 had been among the previous St. Andrews captains.

A scholarly, soft-spoken man, Ouimet epitomized the ideals of amateur golf set up by the U.S. Golf Association. Richard S. Tufts, former president of the U.S. Golf Association, said of him: "A thorough sportsman, modest, always considerate, a true amateur with the highest personal standards, he has always been devoted to the best interests of golf." One of his pet projects was the Francis Ouimet Caddy Scholarship Fund, providing caddies with funds for a college education.

Friends like to relate this story as an example of Francis Ouimet's extreme modesty:

After his victory in the National Open in 1913, Francis was approached by a 70-year-old Brookline golf enthusiast, who said, "Well, Francis, now that you've won the championship, I don't suppose you'll find time to play with me any more."

"What are you doing next Tuesday afternoon?" young Ouimet asked.

Chapter Ten

The Fabulous Haig

During the 1913 United States Open at Brookline, where Francis Ouimet fired the "shot heard 'round the world," golf got its formal introduction to another personality destined to make an indelible mark on the game—although such an idea seemed far-fetched and ludicrous at the time.

He was a slender young man of 20 who, although making his first important tournament appearance, moved around the locker room of The Country Club with the cocky air of an established champion. His dark hair was slicked down on his head. He wore a striped silk shirt, a red bandanna around his neck, white flannel trousers and white buckskin shoes with red rubber soles.

The flashily dressed youngster recognized Johnny McDermott, the defending champion, sitting at one end of the locker room. The brash newcomer strode up to the champion and extended his hand.

"You're Johnny McDermott, aren't you?" he said. "I'm W.C. Hagen from Rochester and I've come to help you boys take care of Vardon and Ray."

McDermott was speechless. Finally, he managed a condescending smile and acknowledged the interruption. Titters came from the pros who were within earshot.

There was nothing humorous about the situation to W.C. Hagen, the professional's assistant at the Rochester Country Club, who had astounded his bosses by asking for time

off to play in the Open. He was deadly serious in his intentions.

No one was snickering when the cocky kid from Rochester moved within two shots of the great British stars, Harry Vardon and Ted Ray, after three rounds, and caught them with five of the final 18 holes to play. Then Hagen took a triple bogey 7 at the fourteenth hole and finished with a 307—just three shots back of Vardon, Ray, and Ouimet, who tied for the championship later won by Ouimet in their historic play-off.

If he could have saved those three shots at the fourteenth, the rookie from Rochester might have had a role in that great drama.

Instead, he had to be content with a tie for second place with MacDonald Smith, Jim Barnes, and Louis Tellier. Boston papers listed him as "W.C. Hagin."

"I'll be back and show them," vowed a determined Walter Hagen. "They'll spell my name right the next time."

They did—the next time, and the next, and the next.

Walter Charles Hagen became the king of golf professionals when Bob Jones reigned as amateur emperor in the Golden Era of Sports. The fabulous Haig—as he became universally known—strode the world's fairways with a majestic flourish for a quarter of a century, collecting national championships, entrancing galleries, amassing and spending a $1,000,000 fortune.

56

Walter Hagen, *right,* was a slender, dapper man of 29 when he gathered with Jock
Hutchison, Bob MacDonald and Charles (Chick) Evans on the tee at the U. S. Open
Championship at Skokie, Illinois, in 1922.

He played with caddies and kings, and
treated both alike. He kept presidents, maha-
rajahs, and princes waiting at the first tee. He
was a companion of titans of the financial and
business world. He called them all—royalty
or commoners—by their first name. He defied
and tore down many of golf's stuffiest traditions.

The flamboyant mashie master played on
five continents and captivated them all. He
won 11 national championships, 2 less than
the immortal Jones, and set a record of 4
successive U.S. professional titles which may
never be equaled. He was professional golfers'
champion—PGA—five times.

He won the U.S. Open Championship, regarded as the world's premier test of amateurs
and pros, in 1914, and repeated in 1919. He

followed this with four British Open crowns
(1922, 1924, 1928, and 1929), and added the
national championships of France (1920),
Belgium (1924), and Canada (1931). Seven
times—between 1927 and 1939—he served as
captain of the U.S. Ryder Cup forces against
Britain's top professionals.

In marathon matches billed as for the unofficial championship of the world, he scored
one-sided victories over Cyril Walker in 1924,
Bob Jones in 1926, Gene Sarazen in 1927, and
Johnny Farrell in 1928. Perhaps no triumph
gave the Haig greater satisfaction than that
over Jones in a 72-hole match in Florida.

"Everybody was acclaiming Jones as the
greatest golfer in the world and saying I was
second best," Hagen recalled later. "It
rankled me a bit, so I got a friend, Bob

Harlow, to arrange the match—36 holes over Bob's course in Sarasota and 36 over my course in St. Petersburg.

"I had an 8-hole lead leaving Sarasota and went on to win, 12 holes up with 11 to play. It was my greatest thrill in golf." It was also the worst beating ever absorbed by Jones. The Haig brought a princely charm, a ready wit and sartorial elegance to the game. He revolutionized wearing apparel on the golf course. His suits were the wooliest, his cashmeres the fleeciest, his shirts the silkiest, and his shoes the swankiest that could be obtained.

Tall and handsome, with his dark hair always impeccably brilliantined, he lived as lavishly as he dressed in the wild, easy-spending era known as the Roaring Twenties. He was a heavy spender who tossed $20 tips around as if they were chicken-feed. Occasionally, he would turn over his entire winning check to his caddy.

"You're only here for a short visit," Hagen once said in enunciating his credo. "Don't hurry. Don't worry. And be sure to smell the flowers along the way."

Hagen missed few of the flowers.

It was not the least unusual for him to attend an all-night party and then, after a brief shower, take the course for an important championship match. Once the Haig, late for a match, rushed to the first tee, still wearing a tuxedo, white tie, and patent leather shoes.

Walter Hagen, *right*, had reason to beam in this picture with his rival, Bob Jones, *left*, whom he beat in a 72-hole challenge match in 1926 by the score of 12 and 11.

Hagen was beginning to add pounds but losing none of his flair for flashiness in 1933 when this picture was taken with Abe Mitchell.

He teed off without removing his satin-trimmed jacket, and shot a 67.

He astounded staid Britons by showing up for the British tournaments in a limousine, replete with chauffeur and footman, and three trunks loaded with his lavish attire, including lemon-yellow gloves and spats.

When Hagen showed up at Deal in 1920 for the British Open Championship, he was shocked to learn that the club house was off limits to professionals—because they were not regarded as gentlemen. A stiff club secretary with a waxed mustache directed him to the golf shop, where professionals were compelled to dress.

Hagen found the pro's shop small, dirty, and inadequate, so he rebelled. He ordered his big, black limousine parked daily at the front door of the club house. "We'll use my car for a dressing room," he told the club secretary. The Haig used his footman as a fore caddy. His chauffeur met him at the eighteenth green after each round with a polo coat.

The club resented this circumvention of tradition, but had no means of preventing it.

From Deal, where he finished a disappointing fifty-fifth, Hagen went to Paris for some fun and the French Open. There, he and George Duncan, the British Open winner, led a strike against the club-house ban on professionals and refused to compete unless the restriction were lowered. Faced with almost certain collapse of their tournament, the French aristocrats had to yield. The British soon followed suit. Hagen was credited with erasing the ancient barriers.

Hagen shook up the British and French galleries by wearing apparel the richness and colors of which would shame a peacock. At Deal, his favorite ensemble consisted of a black sleeveless pullover sweater, white silk shirt, black tie, white flannel knickers, grey stockings, and black and white shoes. On another occasion, he was called a "symphony in blue and brown."

The Haig got to the point that he bought white flannel trousers in gross lots. When a pair got soiled, he did not go to the trouble of having them cleaned. He gave them to bell-hops and hotel employes as tips.

"He is in golf to live, not to make a living," one contemporary said of Hagen.

In order to live on the scale he desired, Hagen had to play golf for a living. He earned more than $1,000,000 from the game and spent it as fast as he collected it. For all his frills and Fancy Dan propensities, he was a keen competitor on the golf course. He hated to lose. His theory was that second- and third-place finishes meant nothing. His aim always was to finish first. He gambled to win, not caring how far down the ladder failure of the bold stroke might toss him. For him, it was all or nothing. He was a go-for-broke guy.

Hagen may have been cut from the same mold that three decades later produced Arn-

59

old Palmer, the Pennsylvania strong-boy who fascinated galleries with his great clutch performances. The Haig was not much of a stylist. He swayed and threw too much body into his drives. As a result, he was erratic off the tees. He was often in trouble—the inveterate scrambler, the inveterate gambler. Yet he had the rare faculty of pulling off the big shot when it was needed. Tremendous with the short irons, possessing a wonderful touch around the greens, and a superb putter, he was ever a threat. He was a "climax" player.

"Walter has the touch of the jeweler's scale," Tommy Armour once said. Another critic said the Haig had the ability to boil three shots into two. South Africa's Bobby Locke acknowledged that he acquired his rare putting skill from studying Hagen. "He was the world's greatest putter," Locke said.

Hagen was more than a fine craftsman. He was a fairway psychologist. Call it gamesmanship or what you will, he was not averse to using guile to win important matches.

He often unsettled his adversaries by remarking loudly after placing his ball at the first tee: "Well, who's going to be second?"

In the final of the PGA championship at Salisbury, Long Island, in 1926, he began conceding 4- and 5-foot putts to his opponent, Leo Diegel, who accepted this generosity with amazement.

However, late in the match, when pressure began to mount, Diegel was faced with a simple 22-incher. He looked at Hagen, expecting another concession. Hagen simply turned his back and stared off in another direction.

Diegel's poise suddenly became unhinged. "There must be a roll," he said nervously to his caddy. He putted, and missed. Hagen won the match, 5 and 3.

On another occasion, Hagen, playing in a professional tournament, had a ball lying 15 feet from the cup while his opponent was half that distance away. The Haig broke into a grin.

"What's so funny?" the opponent asked.

"I was just thinking," Hagen replied, "how much harder your putt will look after I make mine."

Hagen putted, and made it. His opponent missed.

In the 1919 Open at Brae Burn in West Newton, Massachusetts, Mike Brady was already in with a score of 301 when Hagen came to the final hole needing a birdie 3 to win. He hit a beautiful midiron shot to the green, putting the ball hole high 8 feet from the cup. Hagen called Brady out of the club house to watch the crucial putt. Brady stood there, shaking in his shoes, while the Haig putted—and missed by half an inch.

In the 18-hole play-off the following day, Hagen got his opponent fuming quickly by remarking: "Mike, I notice you've got your sleeves rolled up. You should roll them down so the gallery won't see your muscles quivering." Hagen won the play-off by a stroke, 77 to 78.

Hagen often under-clubbed himself purposely, inveigling his opponent also to use the wrong club and hit short. Hagen realized that with his phenomenal finesse around the greens, this would give him a tremendous advantage. At other times, when out in front on the fairway, he would select an iron from his bag as if preparing for the next shot. His opponent, noting Hagen's selection, would choose a similar club and hit well short of the green. Whereupon, his ruse a success, Hagen would put the iron back in the bag, draw forth a wood and proceed to loft the ball to the center of the green.

All the world was a stage to the great Haig, and he never missed a cue.

Once he stroked a long, $3,000 putt and tossed his putter to the caddy while the ball was still rolling. The ball dropped.

In the 1926 British Open at Royal Lytham and St. Anne's, Hagen came to the final hole needing an eagle deuce to tie Bob Jones for the title. Confidently, he boomed his drive down the middle of the fairway, leaving himself a full iron, 150-yard approach to the hole.

Hagen's classical follow-through, in the U. S. Open at Scioto Country Club, Columbus, Ohio, 1926.

With that familiar brisk, confident stride, Hagen walked toward the green area and asked that the flag be removed from the hole. Officials standing around the green were astounded. They didn't understand Walter's request. "The flag," Hagen insisted. "I want the flag removed."

Then, while the large gallery held its collective breath, Hagen returned to his ball and hit an astounding shot which almost dropped into the hole.

It was immaterial that the ball bounded over the green; Hagen took a six and finished third. He had relieved pressure from his own shot by diverting the crowd's attention to the flag stick. He had given his old rival, Jones, quite a start. "I wouldn't have been surprised if the ball had gone into the hole," Jones commented afterward.

Hagen astonished British galleries by yelling to the Prince of Wales, who later as King Edward VIII gave up the throne of England and became the Duke of Windsor: "Hey, Eddie, hold that flag, would you, please?"

Hagen was born December 21, 1892, the second of five children and the only boy. His father, William, was a blacksmith in the car shops of East Rochester, earning $18 a week. Both his father and mother were of German stock.

When he was five years old, Walter began playing with a discarded golf stick left at his home by Andy Christy, a local professional. Later Christy gave him some old golf balls and Walter created such havoc around the modest Hagen homestead that he had to move to his father's cow pasture.

"I would herd the cows all in one spot where I had made a hole, so they could eat the grass and make a close putting surface," Walter recalled later.

He started caddying at nine, hanging around the pro shop of the Country Club in Rochester. He swept floors, polished clubs, and stole a few practice shots when nobody was looking. Still, golf remained a secondary attraction to the rapidly growing blacksmith's son. Walter's real love was baseball. He concentrated on pitching. He developed a good curve ball and change of pace. He worked on his speed and control. He dreamed of a major league career.

Hagen continued to caddy during the week and to play baseball on Sundays. He also went to school three nights a week, worked part-time as a garage mechanic and a wood-finisher. By the time Walter reached 15, Andrew Christy, the pro at the Country Club, needed an assistant. Walter got the job. Before long, he was shooting regularly in the 70's.

In 1912, Andrew Christy left the Rochester Country Club for another pro job and Hagen, although just 19, was asked to be Christy's successor—a head pro's job at $1,200 a year, plus what he could pick up giving private lessons. Thus big-league baseball lost a pitching prospect. The Philadelphia Phillies were ready to sign Walter to a contract. But young Hagen had made up his mind—his future lay in golf, not on the diamond.

After missing out by three strokes in his tournament debut in the U.S. Open at The Country Club in Brookline in 1913, Hagen came back the following year and won the title at Midlothian in Blue Island, Illinois. Playing in a rakish straw hat, he opened with at 68, slumped to rounds of 74 and 75, and then held off a strong challenge by amateur Charles (Chick) Evans, Jr., to win with a score of 290. Evans was just a stroke farther back.

Hailed as the bright new star of professional golf, Hagen went into a temporary slump after his Open victory and some began to term him a flash in the pan. It was not until five years later, in 1919, that Hagen reasserted himself by winning his second Open at Brae Burn.

In 1920, he played in his first British Open at Deal, finishing fifty-fifth with an average 82 score. The following year, at St. Andrews, he finished sixth and in 1922 at Sandwich he finally won his first big international victory.

WALTER HAGEN'S RECORD

U.S. Open Champion: 1914, 1919. (Runner-up, 1920; third, 1935.)

British Open Champion: 1922, 1924, 1928, 1929. (Runner-up, 1923; third, 1926.)

PGA Champion: 1921, 1924, 1925, 1926, 1927. (Runner-up, 1923.)

Belgian Open Champion: 1924.

French Open Champion: 1920.

Canadian Open Champion: 1931.

Ryder Cup Team Captain: 1927, 1929, 1931, 1933, 1935, 1937, 1939.

Ryder Cup Record: Singles, won 3, lost 1; foursomes, won 4, lost 0, 1 halved.

World's Low-Scoring Record: 62, Belleair, Florida, 1921. (Later beaten by Mike Souchak, 60, and Sam Snead, 59.)

Unofficial Championship of World: Beat Cyril Walker in 72-hole match, 17 and 16, in 1924.

Unofficial Championship of World: Beat Bob Jones in 72-hole match, 12 and 11, in 1926.

Unofficial Championship of World: Beat Gene Sarazen in 72-hole match, 9 and 8, in 1927.

Unofficial Championship of World: Beat Johnny Farrell, 3 of 5 matches, in 1928.

Thus, in three years, Hagen had moved from fifty-fifth to sixth to first in the hallowed British event and had become the second man in history to take the cup from British shores.

His name was to appear on the big trophy no less than four times. He won again in 1924, 1928, and 1929, finishing as runner-up in 1923 and third in 1926.

Hagen won the first of his five PGA crowns in 1921. Then in 1924 he started his amazing string of victories, capturing the title in the rugged match play event four consecutive years. No other golfer has been able to win more than two in a row.

In taking four consecutive championships, Hagen won 22 straight individual matches, a record. He was finally stopped by Leo Diegel in the second round at Baltimore in 1928. He won 40 individual matches over the years in PGA competition.

Finally, in 1940, nearing 50 and with his once-brilliant skills dulled by high living, the Haig made an attempt at a come-back in the 1940 PGA tournament at Hershey, Pennsylvania. It was his last try. He stored away his clubs and retired.

"I couldn't stand the thought of probably shooting an 80," said the proud fashion-plate from Rochester.

Chapter Eleven

Gene Sarazen: The Bridge Linking Four Eras

On April 6, 1963, an unusual third-round pairing in the Masters Tournament attracted the bulk of the 30,000 gallery at the Augusta National Golf Club. One of the players was Arnold Palmer, the defending champion, seeking an unprecedented fourth title, and the recognized No. 1 professional in the world. Placed with him was Gene Sarazen, the redoubtable squire from Germantown, New York, 61 years old, the ageless link to the game's adolescent days. It was not merely the matching of the old master with the new that made this particular tandem intriguing. They were tied with the same score after the first 36 holes of the tournament—147.

Sarazen's deeply tanned face could not help breaking into a pleased smile as he heard the comments rippling through the crowd packed around the first tee:

"Same old Gene—he never changes."

"Looks no different than he did 25 years ago."

"The Peter Pan of golf."

"He's like Ol' Man River—he just keeps rolling along."

It was immaterial that Gene's stubby, piano legs began to show signs of strain on this third straight day of competition and he fell off his amazing early pace. However, he had made one significant point. For one round, or for two, Sarazen was still able to match strokes with the best players in the world.

This son of an immigrant Italian carpenter became one of the remarkable wonders of the wonderful world of golf. He played with Harry Vardon and Ted Ray, the great British stars, in the swaddling days of hickory-shaft clubs. He carried on a fierce international rivalry with Bob Jones and Walter Hagen in the Golden Twenties. He battled the Guldahls, Hogans, Sneads, and Middlecoffs in the period before and after World War II. Then, when Palmer and the powerful Jack Nicklaus burst upon the scene in the 1960's, Gene was still in there, swinging away. Age and growing business responsibilities cut his big-time tournament competition to a minimum, but he still could be seen at the Masters, the seniors' events, and periodically at other tournaments. He never ceased to be a marvel to those who followed the sport.

Sarazen was a golfing anachronism—a link with the past whose fabulous career spanned not two, not three, but four distinct eras of the game. He was a sturdy, unwavering bridge between Vardon and Nicklaus. He was both an anachronism and a contradiction. He effected the attire of the 1920's. His sharp, incisive mind was attuned to the Jet and Space Age.

While other golfers changed to slacks and short-sleeed sports shirts, Sarazen stuck to knickers and turtle-neck sweaters. They became a trademark. Even as he moved into his

64

sixties, Gene continued to walk with a quick, springy step. His coal-black hair, with hardly a strand of gray, was slicked down on his head. He never lost his enthusiasm. He talked golf as he played it—with a bubbling effervescence and defiance of convention.

If there was an old-fashioned flair in Sarazen's mode of dress, there certainly was nothing archaic about his golf philosophy. He was constantly shocking the conservative rulers of the game with his radical proposals. He insisted that putting was permitted to play too important a part in the sport—with generally around half the strokes of every score used on the greens—and suggested that the cups be enlarged from 4¼ inch diameter. The recommendation received an icy reaction. He argued that golf was becoming a game of sheer power rather than finesse. He proposed that courses be streamlined to about half their size, enabling businessmen to get in a full 18-hole round after office hours. He conceived and

Time seemed to stand still for Gene Sarazen, shown surveying a shot in a 1962 tournament at the age of 60.

popularized the sand wedge, which became one of the most important clubs in the golf bag.

Sarazen carried on a running campaign against slow, methodical play. He contended that it was ridiculous for golfers to study every shot meticulously and spend minutes before striking a simple 3-foot putt. Such habits, he said, tended to distract the other players and to dull the interest of the galleries. He did not mind how big the name that happened to fall in his line of fire. He struck out at Ben Hogan, Cary Middlecoff and Jack Nicklaus, three of the sport's slowest.

It was to Gene's credit that he practiced what he preached. He was one of golf's fastest, most impatient practitioners. If anything, he played too quickly for his own good. At times, they said it appeared that he virtually hit the ball on the run. He never fussed and fretted over putts. He walked up to the ball resolutely and gave it a quick, authoritative tap. Hit or miss, Sarazen engaged in none of the histrionics that became routine on the putting greens. He picked up the ball and strode briskly to the next tee.

Sarazen is joint holder of the speed record in the Masters. In 1947, he and George Fazio were first off the tee in the final round at Augusta. They played the 18 holes in one hour, 57 minutes. Gene shot a 70.

Undoubtedly contributing to Gene's knack for getting the job done quickly was his supreme confidence. This bordered on cockiness, and it was a quality he never permitted to grow dull. He was aggressive, pirate-bold, an architect of the "big moment" or the "big shot." He seemed to believe that some divine spark or inspiration would pull him through —and it frequently did.

Bob Jones recognized this rare trait when he once said of Sarazen: "Sarazen has ever been the impatient, headlong player who went for everything in the hope of feeling the timely touch of inspiration. When the wand touches him, he is likely to win in a great finish as he did at Fresh Meadow and Skokie, or in a parade as he did at Prince's, but if it

touch him not throughout the four rounds, the boldness of his play leaves no middle ground. When he is in the right mood, he is probably the greatest scorer in the game, possibly that the game has ever seen."

Sarazen rallied from four shots back in the final round in winning his first National Open championship at Skokie Country Club, Glencoe, Illinois, in 1922. Ten years later, he won the British Open at Sandwich with a record score of 283, 13 under par for the Prince's course and 5 shots ahead of the runner-up, Macdonald Smith. Then he returned home and added the U.S. Open title with one of the most phenomenal scoring streaks in golf history. Eight shots back with 28 holes to play, Gene blazed over the final 28 holes in 100 strokes in what Jones later described as "the finest competitive exhibition on record."

Sarazen's faculty for doing the sensational— and often the impossible—was demonstrated again in the 1935 Masters. He was counted out of the running when he came to the fifteenth hole of the final round. He needed three birdies on the four finishing holes— some of the toughest in golf—to tie Craig Wood, who already was in with 282. On the 485-yard, par 5 fifteenth, Gene crashed a good drive down the fairway and then holed out a 220-yard spoon shot for a double eagle that became the most talked-about shot in golf. With one prodigious blow, Sarazen had picked up his needed three strokes. He played the final three holes in par for his tie and the next day, still riding the momentum of his one spectacular shot, defeated Wood in the 18-hole play-off.

The brash, bold-shooting graduate from caddy ranks compiled a record that placed him among the game's immortals. In addition to his two U.S. Opens, British Open and Masters, he won three Professional Golfers Association titles—in 1922, 1923, 1933—when that tournament was a hazardous, gruelling match-play grind. He tied for another U.S. Open crown in 1940, losing to Lawson Little in a play-off, and missed by a single stroke in

1934. He was runner-up in the PGA in 1930 and medalist in 1931. He was runner-up in the British Open in 1928. He twice was winner of the PGA Seniors—in 1954 and 1958.

Sarazen is one of three men—Jones and Hogan are the others—with the distinction of winning the U.S. and British Opens the same year. Only he, Ben Hogan and South Africa's Gary Player have been able to win all four of the major professional championships—the U.S. and British Opens, the PGA and the Masters. Sarazen played on six Ryder Cup teams (in 1927, 1929, 1931, 1933, 1935, and 1937), winning four and drawing one of his six individual matches. In the PGA tournament, he set a record of individual matches won, a total of 53.

Sarazen was born in a two-family house in the workingmen's district of Harrison, New York, on February 27, 1902. His father, Federico Saraceni, who wanted to be a priest but who had to turn to carpentry when his parents died in his native Italy, had immigrated to America in search of a fortune. The Saracenis lived in four crowded upstairs rooms—father, mother Adela, an older sister Margaret, and Eugene.

Young Gene was an industrious youngster. He helped with the family's meager finances

Spectators follow the flight of the ball as Gene Sarazen drives off in the 1932 British Open at Sandwich.

by selling magazines, running errands for neighbors, and picking fruit for three cents a quart. He was eight years old when he first heard about golf. His mother came home from a shopping trip one day with the report of a neighbor's son, Fred Biscelli, who was serving as professional, caddy master and greenskeeper at the Larchmont Country Club. "He makes a lot of money," Mrs. Saraceni told her young son, "and he needs boys to carry the sticks for the rich people." Gene could hardly wait to rush over and ask Biscelli for a job.

It was hard at first. Gene could hardly lift the heavy bags. He did not know a jigger from a brassie. However, he managed. Proudly, he brought home 45 cents to show for his first day's work—25 cents for caddying 18 holes plus a 20-cent tip. He worked three years at Larchmont, gaining in size and knowledge, and then in 1913, at the age of 11, he switched to the larger Apawamis Club, where he heard there was a chance to make more money. Apawamis, like Larchmont, was not far from Gene's home, in Westchester County, about 20 miles northeast of New York City.

It was in 1913 that a young Boston caddy, Francis Ouimet, astounded the golf world by beating the two great British stars, Harry Vardon and Ted Ray, for the U.S. Open championship. This feat seemed to raise the stature of caddies everywhere and, at Apawamis, officials decided to let the club-carriers have a one-day tournament of their own over the course, where previously they had been barred. Gene played hooky from school to compete. He shot 105 and finished last.

Gene was 15 when he had to quit school and go to work as a carpenter's assistant because his father was wiped out in a business venture. Later the same year, the Saracenis had to move to Bridgeport, Connecticut, where Papa Saraceni got a job in a war plant. Young Gene continued as a carpenter's helper in another plant where he drilled holes in wooden racks for shells to be shipped to the Russians.

This added responsibility, plus a long siege of pneumonia, interrupted the youngster's association with golf but failed to dull his love for the game. Gene decided that he definitely wanted to make golf his career. His father objected strenuously. "It's a game for rich men," the elder Saraceni insisted. "Every young man should have a trade. You should stick to carpentering."

Gene was headstrong. "I'm going to learn how to make golf clubs," he said. "I'm going to learn how to teach. I'm going to play in tournaments."

He began hanging around a nine-hole course in Bridgeport called Beardsley Park. There he was befriended by a little dark-eyed Italian pro named Al Ciuci, later to become one of Gene's closest friends and a leading professional in the New York metropolitan area. Ciuci let the eager boy hang around the golf shop, fondle clubs, and, when business was slow, go out on the course to practice chipping and putting.

One afternoon, playing on the Beardsley course with Ciuci and two other golfers, Gene holed out on a 145-yard, par 3 hole and got a write-up in the local paper. "Eugene Saraceni scored a hole-in-one," the small item said.

Gene scanned the paper for hours. He read and reread the story, with mixed emotions. He liked what it said. He did not like the sound of the name: Eugene Saraceni. It did not sound crisp like Chick Evans or Jim Barnes. He decided that if he were going to become a golf champion he would need a simpler name. That night, he got out a blackboard and some chalk and began experimenting with the letters. Finally he hit upon the name he wanted: Gene Sarazen.

Although only 5'5" and 110 pounds, Sarazen was able to give the ball a tremendous wallop. Under the watchful eye of Ciuci, he improved steadily. Soon he was playing the nine-hole Beardsley Park course in 35 and

Gene Sarazen putting on the 18th hole for a victory in the Agua Caliente Open, 1930.

under and beating everybody around the place. In the late fall of 1918, at the age of 16, he moved to the Brooklawn Club on the outskirts of Bridgeport as an assistant to George Sparling. Even this did not satisfy the restless youngster. He realized that as long as he stayed near his home he always would be looked upon as an ex-caddy. When an assistant's job opened up at Fort Wayne, Indiana, he took it. Shortly afterward, he shifted again to a club in Titusville, Pennsylvania.

By this time, the young assistant pro was attracting some attention but hardly was setting the golf world on fire, as he fully expected he would do. He qualified for the National Open at the age of 18 in 1920, tying for thirtieth, and again in 1921, placing seventeenth. He got some headlines when he upset Jock Hutchison in an early round of the 1921 PGA and added to them the next winter when he won his first big tournament, the New Orleans Open. However, there was nothing to indicate he would be a factor in the National Open at Skokie in 1922, nothing except Gene's premonition—he was sure he was going to win it.

Sarazen started reasonably well, with a 72 and 73, but in the third round he took too many chances and wound up with a 75, which included eight fives on his card. At this point, he was four strokes back of the leaders, Bob Jones and Wild Bill Mehlhorn, and appeared to be hopelessly out of contention.

Gene hitched his belt, stuck out his square jaw and said to his playing partner, Johnny Farrell: "This is no time to be timid—I'm going for everything."

He ran in a 25-foot putt on the third hole for a birdie and sank from 15 feet on the fourth for another. His confidence now was booming. Sarazen hit out on every tee, shot for the pin instead of the green and went boldly for every putt. He bogeyed the tenth but got the shot back at the eleventh, then played six straight pars to the final hole. At the seventy-second, a 485-yard hole, Gene used a driver for his second shot off the fairway and sent the ball to the apron of the

green. He got down in two for a closing birdie and a total of 288. Jones, finishing later, took 289, Mehlhorn 290 and Walter Hagen 291. Sarazen had his first national championship.

The brash kid from Harrison had come of golfing age, and Titusville was too small for him. Widely sought for exhibitions, he took to the road. He basked in the new-found spotlight, and loved every minute of it. He won the 1922 PGA, challenged Walter Hagen to a 72-hole match for the unofficial world's championship and whipped the Haig, 3 and 2.

After this early surge of success, Sarazen fell victim to the occupational hazard that strikes many young golf champions. First, he became lax and overconfident. Then, he started thinking. Whereas in the past he had merely put the ball down and hit it, he now began experimenting with his grip and his swing. Soon, he was completely confused.

He managed to win the second of his three PGA titles at Pelham, New York, but he was a bust in his first try at the British Open in 1923. He arrived at Troon, Scotland, hailed as the brightest new star of American golf. He was favored to win. But he opened with a lackluster 75 and used 14 strokes on the first two holes of the second round. On the second hole, he buried his drive in the face of a bunker in front of the tee and took two big whacks at the ball before he could get it out. He got a 9 on the hole, finished with an 85, and failed to qualify for the final 36 holes.

This started Sarazen's ten lean years, similar to Jones's seven years of want between 1917 and 1923 when the Grand Slammer almost despaired of ever winning a national crown. Sarazen, with small, stubby hands, changed from the interlocking to the Vardon overlapping grip and back again. He altered his swing almost every month. His putting touch failed him. He managed to win a few minor tournaments during this unhappy span, mostly in the New York area, but his game lacked the precision and confidence to hold up in major competition. Just when he felt he was getting his touch back, he would be felled by a round in the 80's.

70

Sarazen chips out of the rough on his way to
winning the British Open at Sandwich, England,
1932.

The break in the prolonged slump finally came in 1932, and it came with a loud explosion. It happened in the British Open, played over the flat, 7,000-yard Prince's course at Sandwich. Frustrated by a long series of disappointments and frustrations, Gene was willing at this stage to try anything, even the use of a grizzled, 60-year-old caddy named Skip Daniels whom he had fired in a clash of personalities five years before.

With the wily Daniels at his elbow, Sarazen opened with a 70, which gave him a one-stroke first round lead over Britain's Percy Alliss and Mac Smith. He tied the course record with a 69 on the second day and shot three strokes in front of the field. A third-round 70 increased this advantage to 5 shots and a pressurized closing 74 gave him the championship easily at 283, a tournament record.

Sarazen now definitely was back on the stick. He went to the National Open at Fresh Meadow on Long Island with greater confidence but a few misgivings. He had served as professional at Fresh Meadow between 1925 and 1930 and the tradition was that a player never won a tournament on his own course. Also, only one man, Jones, had ever won the British and U.S. Opens in the same year.

Gene's reservations seemed fully justified when he shot 74 and 76 for the first two rounds and needed 38 strokes for the first nine holes of the third. It was a different Sarazen who had played these first 45 holes. Perhaps he wanted the championship too badly. Again, maybe it was the ingrained respect for the course which he had picked up in his years of battling it. At any rate, Gene played cautiously. He shot for the fat part of the greens instead of the pins. Only excellent putting kept him alive.

The turning point came on the forty-fifth hole, the ninth hole of the morning third round. At this stage, Sarazen was 7 shots off the pace and a par on the ninth would give him a 39.

"I decided to chuck my dainty safety tactics," Sarazen recalled later. "I determined to go for broke, as the expression goes."

On the forty-fifth, a 143-yard hole, Gene laced a seven-iron 12 feet from the pin and sank his putt for a birdie deuce. Suddenly, the spark of inspiration of which Jones spoke came afire. Sarazen began hitting out on his drives. He boldly fired at the pins and disdained the dangers of the bunkers. On his putts, he was in the cup or 3 feet past—never short. He birdied three holes in a row—fourteenth, fifteenth, and sixteenth—and came home in 32.

Sarazen was still the relentless attacker when he teed off for the climactic final round in the afternoon. His reward was a final round 66 and a score of 286, which gave him his second Open title by three strokes over Phil Perkins and Bobby Cruickshank.

Here's how the final 28 holes were played in 100 strokes:

Hole	Par	Sarazen
45	3	2
46	4	4
47	4	4
48	3	3
49	4	4
50	3	2
51	4	3
52	5	4
53	4	4
54	4	4
55	4	4
56	4	5
57	4	3
58	3	2
59	5	5
60	4	3
61	4	4
62	4	4
63	3	2
64	4	4
65	4	4
66	3	3
67	4	4
68	3	3
69	4	3
70	5	5
71	4	4
72	4	4

GENE SARAZEN'S RECORD

National Open Champion: 1922, 1932. (Tied for title in 1940, losing to Lawson Little in playoff, 73 to 70; runner-up in 1934.)

British Open Champion: 1932. (Runner-up, 1928.)

PGA Champion: 1922, 1923, 1933. (Runner-up, 1930; medalist, 1931.)

Masters Champion: 1935.

Winner of World's Unofficial Professional Championship: 1922, defeated Walter Hagen, 3 and 2, in 72-hole match.

PGA Seniors Champion: 1954, 1958.

Ryder Cup Member: 1927, 1929, 1931, 1933, 1935, 1937. Record: foursomes, won 3, tied 2, lost 2; individual, won 4, tied 1, lost 1.

Holds Record Most PGA Matches Won: 53.

Sarazen added his third PGA crown in 1933, missed the Open by a single shot in 1934 when Olin Dutra won, and then, in 1940, at the age of 38, tied Lawson Little for the Open championship at Canterbury in Cleveland, losing in the play-off, 73 to 70. It was Gene's last serious bid for one of the major championships, although his enthusiasm and determination kept him active for years afterward.

Gene never contended he had a secret formula for longevity. "Good golf, as I see it," he explained, "is simply a matter of hitting good shots consistently. A player can do this for many years after he has passed his physical peak, if his swing is fundamentally correct."

Written instruction is helpful only in spelling out fundamentals, Sarazen said. Golf champions are made by practice and playing. If the amazing squire had a secret for his staying powers in the game, associates said, it was simply this: The boyish enthusiasm that fired him back in Harrison, New York, never lost its glow.

Chapter Twelve

Bob Jones: The Immortal Grand Slammer

In the summer of 1913, while the golf world was acclaiming Francis Ouimet's victory in the U.S. Open at Brookline, the bug was just beginning to bite an 11-year-old youngster in Atlanta, Georgia.

His name was Robert Tyre Jones, Jr. He had been given a sawed-off cleek and three battered golf balls when he was five years old. He and his neighborhood pals had improvised a five-hole course in his front yard. He had followed his mother and father around the East Lake Country Club course. He had even played in some junior tournaments. But his interest in golf remained casual. He liked fishing and baseball better.

Then, one day, he shot his first 80 over the man-sized East Lake course. The year was 1913. Bobby had a match with his schoolboy rival, Perry Adair. He won the match but, more importantly, he shot an 80—a legitimate 80.

He could not wait to show his father. He raced across the course to where the elder Jones, Robert P. Jones, was playing. Without saying a word, Bobby proudly stuck out the clumsily-penciled scorecard. The father looked at it and beamed. He grabbed his son and gave him a big hug. It was at this moment that Bobby Jones decided he wanted to be a golf champion.

If Ouimet's triumph over Britain's Harry Vardon and Ted Ray at Brookline took golf from its stuffy country-club atmosphere and gave it to the common man, then it remained for Bob Jones to send the sport skyrocketing to unprecedented popularity.

He was the fairway giant of the fabulous Golden Twenties that spawned such sports heroes as Jack Dempsey in boxing, Babe Ruth in baseball, Bill Tilden and Helen Wills in tennis, and Earl Sande in horse-racing. Jones was young, good-looking, clean-cut—the typical All-American boy. He had a flawless style. Although an amateur, he faced and consistently beat some of the greatest professionals the game has known—such as Walter Hagen, Gene Sarazen, Tommy Armour, Macdonald Smith, Harry Cooper, and Leo Diegel.

Between 1923 and 1930, he amassed 13 national titles—five U.S. Amateurs, four U.S. Opens, three British Opens, and a single British Amateur. In the last nine years of his career, he played in 12 Open championships—nine American and three British—and finished first or second in 11 of them. Jones personally considered the latter feat superior to his Grand Slam.

However, it is the Grand Slam for which Jones will be forever renowned. In 1930, he climaxed his career by winning the U.S. Open and Amateur, the British Open and Amateur —an unparalleled sweep of the major championships in a single season. Two months later—on November 17, 1930—he announced

Bob Jones

his retirement from competitive golf in order to make a series of instructional films. He was only 28, at the peak of his career. What would have happened had he chosen to continue? The thought defies imagination. Probably he would have added at least a dozen more national crowns to his gaudy collection.

Bobby Jones was born March 17, 1902, not in the golfing tradition. His father was a good baseball player at the University of Georgia, good enough to get a Brooklyn contract upon his graduation. But the grandfather—Robert Tyre Jones, for whom Bobby was named—was a straight-laced gent who frowned on such a frivolous profession. He would have none of it, so Bobby's dad pursued his career at law.

Bobby's first memory of golf went back to the summer of 1907, when his family moved to a boarding house near the East Lake course in Atlanta. The five-year-old youngster could look out his window and see East Lake's rolling fairways. He could see players whacking away at the ball with their sticks. Jones, looking back on these scenes, said he never remembered a wave of inspiration or anything similar—not even when another boarder gave him his first club. His mother and father became devotees, however, and soon Bobby found himself trailing them around the course.

There never was an indication, though, that young Robert was cut out for an athletic career. He had an oversized head and a frail body. From babyhood on he had been troubled with a digestive ailment that forced him to eat soft foods until he was five. This did not dwarf the lad's industry. Shortly after acquiring his first golf club, Bobby constructed his first course in front of his house. He and his friends played by the hours.

Bobby was six when he won his first tournament—a six-hole event for the neighborhood kids arranged as part of a birthday party. One of Jones's victims was long-tressed Alexa Stirling, a playmate who later won the women's national championship three times in a row. Bobby's trophy was a silver cup 3 inches high. He proudly displays it beside the extravagant silverware won in his international triumphs.

Bobby's interest in the sport was intensified when a young Scotch professional named Stewart Maiden came to East Lake to succeed his brother, Jimmy. Young Jones dogged the heels of the new pro and soon began trying to copy Maiden's graceful, effortless swing. He mastered it to such a degree that club members commented on the similarity of his and the professional's form. Bobby beamed.

As Bobby grew older and bigger, his golf scores became proportionately smaller. In 1911, at the age of nine, he won his first championship, a junior tournament at the Atlanta Athletic Club. At 13, he won two club championships and two invitation tournaments away from home against some of the South's top amateurs. The next year, 1916, he won three such invitation affairs and captured the Georgia state title. Southern golf circles began to buzz over the sensational Georgia schoolboy.

Young Jones was just 14 when he invaded Philadelphia's Merion Cricket Club in the late summer of 1916 for the National Amateur. He now stretched 5′4″ and weighed 165 pounds. The green youngster created quite a stir when he led the field in the first round of qualifying with a 74. Although he blew to an 89 on the second round, he won two matches before bowing to the defending champion, Bob Gardner, 5 and 3.

Spectators at the 1916 Amateur remembered Jones as a lad with a perfect swing and an ungovernable temper. Bobby ranted when he missed a shot. Occasionally, he tossed a club in disgust. He was sharply criticized by the press for his deportment. Jones gradually learned to harness his emotions, but he was doomed to a series of bitter disappointments before he finally was to establish himself as the king of golf.

As it developed, Jones was destined to suffer through "seven lean years" before enjoying his "seven years of plenty." Many have attached this Biblical reference to Jones's career.

Bob Jones was a hefty swinger at 14.

He became a leading golf figure, widely sought for exhibitions. He won the Southern and other regional titles with regularity. Yet when he came to a national event, something always happened to derail him.

His next U.S. Amateur venture was at Oakmont in 1919. Jones beat Bob Gardner, this time in an earlier round, and went on to the finals, where he bowed to Davison Herron of Pittsburgh, 5 and 4. He lost 18 pounds during the rugged week.

The year 1920 found the 18-year-old Georgian a wiser but thinner man. He had grown 6 inches and lost 20 pounds but streamlining brought no more success. He won the Southern again and made his debut in the National Open at Toledo. Four strokes off the pace at the end of the third round, Jones blew up on the last round and finished with 299. This gave him eighth place behind the winner, Ted Ray. Bobby won the qualifying medal in the National Amateur that same year at Roslyn, New York, but lost to Ouimet in the semifinals.

In 1922, Jones made his first trip to England as the 19-year-old baby member of the Walker Cup team. He helped Uncle Sam win the trophy from the British but in the British Amateur at Hoylake he lost in the fourth round. In the British Open at St. Andrews, he picked up in disgust after blowing a hole in the third round.

Returning home, Bobby improved in the National Open, finishing fifth at Columbia Country Club in Washington. The winner was Jim Barnes with 289. Jones's jinx trailed him into the National Amateur at St. Louis where, after two hot rounds, he lost to Willie Hunter, the British champion.

By this time, Jones was beginning to worry a great deal over his failure to win a major title. He knew everyone expected him to be a champion, but he was not one. Comments he heard around the club houses and locker rooms troubled him. "That Jones boy has everything," they would say, "but he can't go in the clutch." Actually, this was an unfair appraisal. Jones was no quitter. He played some of his most brilliant golf under championship pressure only to lose through an unlucky break or to fail because somebody got red hot. It seemed that Bobby always was running into someone on a phenomenally torrid streak.

Young Jones had other ideas on the matter, a philosophical outlook which blunted somewhat his disappointment over repeated failure to win the big ones. "Every tournament has somebody's name on it," he once said. "No matter how well you play, the fellow whom the fates have picked will win out. The ball just falls that way." This was a philosophy which did not desert him even after his fortunes changed. He always contended he lost many tournaments he should have won and that he won many he should have lost.

Bobby had a leg operation early in 1922 but it did not impede his golf. He went on to the National Open at Chicago and finished in a tie for second behind Gene Sarazen. However, he was still improving in the Open—from eighth to fifth to second. Next time perhaps, he consoled himself, it might be all the way. But a sickening doubt rose to haunt him. At Brookline, in the National Amateur later in the year, he received another jolt. He met Jess Sweetser, the ultimate tournament winner, in the semifinals, and Sweetser clobbered him, 8 and 7.

Seven years, eleven major tournaments and still not a victory—that was Jones' lamentable story at the end of 1922. He was, nevertheless, the biggest name in amateur golf. Although never a winner, he still was regarded as the best. Fans flocked to see the chunky Georgian with the fluid, one-piece swing.

Meanwhile, Jones had been graduated from Georgia Tech, and enrolled at Harvard, where he was seeking his M.A. degree. He was a busy young man of 20, but he found time to practice and point for his next big championship try—the National Open at Inwood on Long Island.

Inwood, scene of the 1923 Open, was a tough par 72 with tight, gun-barrel fairways and plenty of distance, favoring the long, straight hitter. In practice rounds, Bobby was horrible, spraying his tee shots and barely breaking 80. Nevertheless, he fired a 71 for the first round and found himself only a stroke off the pace set by Jock Hutchison. He fell a shot farther back with a second round 73. After 54 holes, with a round to play, Jones was ahead with 220, followed by Bobby Cruickshank with 223 and Hutchison with 224.

Then Jones began pressing. Instead of playing cautiously for pars, he tried to land the knockout punch with birdies. His game cracked. He shot 5-5-6 on the last 3 holes, which had a 4-4-4 par, and finished with 76 for 296.

Bobby was disconsolate. "I didn't finish like a champion," he said to his longtime friend, sports writer O.B. Keeler. "I finished like a yellow dog."

Cruickshank sank a 7-foot putt on the final hole to tie for the lead at 296 and force a play-off with Jones for the title. Bobby was given a reprieve.

In the exciting 18-hole play-off, only 3 holes were halved. The two came to the final hole where the day before Jones almost had blown the championship by taking a double bogey six. The match was square. This time Jones did not falter.

After Cruickshank had hooked his tee shot onto a road that snaked through the course, Bobby got off a good drive which faded to the short rough on the sun-baked turf. Cruickshank played his second safe, 50 yards short of a yawning lagoon guarding the green. Now the choice was up to Jones. Should he play it safely for a tie or gamble for victory? Jones strode to the ball with quick, sure steps, jerked a midiron from his bag, made one sweeping look at the assignment, and swung. The crowd let out a tremendous roar.

Jones's shot tore 200 yards through the air, dropped lightly to the green, and dribbled 6 feet past the cup. Shaken, Cruickshank hit his pitch over the green and into a bunker. He had to settle for a 6 and 78. Jones had an easy 4 for 76 and he at last was the Open champion of the United States.

77

There was a moment of high frenzy among Bobby's supporters. Stewart Maiden, the Carnoustie pro from whom Bobby copied his grooved swing, bashed a new straw hat over a neighbor's head. Friends swarmed around the 21-year-old champion, who, too dazed to be elated, groped for the club house.

Jones said later he did not remember any of it. The first conscious thought he had, he said, was: "I've won a championship. At last, I've won a championship." He acknowledged that his morale was wearing thin at this point. If this one had not come off, he said he might have been tempted to give up tournament golf.

Thus, it was a seasoned and confident young man of 21 who went into the National Amateur later that year at the Flossmoor Club in Chicago, Although heavily favored, Jones was eliminated in the second round by tall Max Marston of Philadelphia, who went on to beat Sweetser in the finals.

The National Open in 1924 was at Oakland Hills Country Club, near Detroit. Jones used 300 strokes around the long, wind-swept layout and finished second behind Cyril Walker, a fragile little pro who had 297. Bobby, however, returned to Merion, the scene of his debut at 14, and won the U.S. Amateur impressively, defeating George Von Elm in the finals, 9 and 8. It was the beginning of a colorful rivalry between the two great amateurs. But, for Jones, the year 1924 had even greater significance. It was the year he married his childhood sweetheart, Mary Malone.

Bobby had proved he could win championships but he had not fully shaken his runner-up jinx. In the National Open at Worcester, Massachusetts, in 1925, he finished in a tie with lank Willie Macfarlane and lost by a stroke in the double-round play-off. He retained his amateur crown at Oakmont, scene of his 1919 final round defeat, by overwhelming a hometownsman, Watts Gunn, 8 and 7.

In 1926, Jones returned to England—a trip he had looked forward to for five years. He was determined to make the British forget the brash youngster of 19 who had folded in the 1921 British Amateur and quit in disgust in the Open. He played brilliantly in the Amateur at Muirfield, Scotland, but lost a sixth-round match to the sub-par shooting of Andrew Jamieson, 4 and 3. He figured in two victories which helped Uncle Sam win the Walker Cup at historic St. Andrews and then he journeyed to St. Anne's-on-the-Sea for the British Open.

It was in qualifying for the British Open at nearby Sunningdale that James shot what he always considered his finest round in competitive golf. He toured the long, treacherous layout in 66—6 under par. He did not have a 5 or a 2 on his card. British golf critics acclaimed it the best round ever shot on the Isles.

Here's Jones' card:

Par out	554	344	434	–36
Jones out	444	334	434	–33
Par in	544	353	444	–36–72
Jones in	434	343	444	–33–66

The Open itself was something of an anti-climax after that. Jones won it with a score of 291. Hagen, who started torridly, and Von Elm finished in a tie for third behind Al Watrous. The British forgot the Bobby Jones of 1921 and took a new Bobby Jones to their hearts. The name always was spoken with a degree of reverence in the golf-minded islands.

Jones came home to a ticker-tape welcome, a parade down Broadway, and a speech at New York's City Hall, but his mind must have wandered to Columbus, Ohio, where the Scioto course was being manicured for the National Open. The strong-nerved Atlanta robot, attracting the bulk of the galleries, took a hefty 79 in the second round but rallied to win with 293. His bid for a U.S. double failed when he was beaten in the final of the Amateur at Baltusrol in New Jersey by his old rival, Von Elm, 2 and 1. Von Elm became the last man to beat Jones in a 36-hole match in major competition and the only one to take the Atlantan's number over that distance in the last seven years of Bobby's career.

In 1927, Jones was mixing iron shots with law books and his studies at Emory University were encroaching on his golf practice. The staleness showed at Oakmont, where Bobby finished eleventh in the U.S. Open, his worst ever in the event, but he whipped his game into shape in time to win both the British Open and U.S. Amateur. He fired a record 285 to capture the British Open at St. Andrews by 6 strokes. He swamped Charles (Chick) Evans, 8 and 7, in the finals of the National Amateur at the Minikahda Country Club in Minneapolis. He played 224 holes in the two events in 17 strokes under par.

If Jones's growing championships had begun to take on a checkerboard look, it was due to the fact they had followed a checkered course. Going into 1928, he had won five national championships in a row but had failed to bracket the two big U.S. titles in a single season.

In 1928, Bobby, now busy with a budding law practice, passed up a return trip to Britain and confined himself to the two major American championships. In the Open at sprawling Olympia Fields, near Chicago, he dissipated an early lead with a last round 77, tied Johnny Farrell at 294, and lost the 36-hole play-off. He retained his amateur title, however, by lacing Phillip Perkins, 10 and 9, in the last round at Brae Burn Country Club, West Newton, Massachusetts.

Jones caught up with the pros again in 1929 after they had stopped him two years in a row. He won the National Open at Winged Foot in Mamaroneck, New York, sinking a spectacular putt on the seventy-second hole to tie Al Espinosa at 294 and gain a play-off, which he swept easily. He was surprised in the opening round of the National Amateur at Pebble Beach, California, by an unknown youngster named Johnny Goodman, from Omaha, who won, one up. Goodman later won the National Open in 1933, becoming the only amateur besides Jones to turn the trick since 1916.

Bob Jones drives off the first tee in a 36-hole play-off for the U. S. Open Championship at Winged Foot in Mamaroneck, N.Y., in 1929. He beat Al Espinosa, shown in white cap at the right, by 23 strokes.

Early spring practices in 1930 convinced Jones, who was long on premonition, that he was headed for an outstanding season. He was hitting the ball better than ever in his life. He was brimming with confidence. But he never dreamed, he said later, that he was headed for a Grand Slam.

As captain of the U.S. Walker Cup forces, he was given another shot at the British Championships. The British Amateur, the only major crown that had escaped him, brought Jones to a reunion with the famed old St. Andrews course, which he said he at first underrated but later had learned to love. Bobby squeaked through some early matches and then conquered Roger Wethered, 7 and 6, in the finals.

Some 25,000 fans went mad. Jones was pushed through the milling, shouting mob by a cordon of policemen and convoyed to the club house, nearly a mile away. Weary but pleased, Bobby turned to some friends and said with a wide grin: "I'd rather have won that tournament than any other in golf."

In the British Open at Hoylake, Bobby stepped off with rounds of 70 and 72 for an early lead but faltered with closing rounds of 74–75 for 291. He went to the club house to sweat out the late finishers. Leo Diegel and Macdonald Smith both made strong challenges but fell two strokes off the pace. Jones sailed home with half of his Slam.

America's golf fever was spurred to a new pitch when the game's great gathered at Minneapolis' Interlachen course for the U.S. Open. Ten thousand fans swarmed the narrow fairways under a hot June sun to see if the amazing amateur could make history.

Bobby sent pulses pounding when he played the first round in 71, a stroke back of

Police give Bob Jones protection from exuberant British crowds after his victory in the 1930 British Amateur at St. Andrews, one of the legs of his Grand Slam.

A smiling Bob Jones receives congratulations from his final round victim, Roger Wethered, after the British Amateur Championship in 1930.

Macdonald Smith and silver-haired Tommy Armour. At the halfway point, Horton Smith led with 142 and Jones was tied with Light-horse Harry Cooper at 144. At least 10 pros were in the running. Jones uncorked a blistering 68 in the third round and moved 5 shots ahead of the field. He had to sink a 40-foot putt on the final hole for a slumping 75 and a score of 287. That was good enough to win by two shots over Mac Smith, with Horton Smith third.

If Jones's fatalistic attitude about golf tournaments ever wavered, it received a real bolstering from an odd incident during the second round at Interlachen. It was the renowned episode of the "lily pad shot."

On the ninth hole—a par 5, 485-yard dog-leg with a small lake in front of the tight, well-

Bob Jones, *left*, and Gene Sarazen, *right*, are among those who gathered in New York in 1953 to honor Ben Hogan for his feat of winning the British Open.

trapped green—Jones went for the green with a spoon on his second shot. It was a shot he had made several times in the past without mishap. However, on this occasion, he half-topped the fairway wood shot and the ball whizzed toward the water. The ball hit on the surface about halfway across, took a surprising kick onto the other side of the bank, and hopped up just short of the green. Spectators contended the ball hit a lily pad.

"It looked like a drowned ball for sure," Jones recalled later. "It would have meant a six or a seven and would have cost me the tournament. It was perhaps the luckiest shot I ever played in a championship."

The U.S. Amateur, fourth leg in Bobby's bid for a Grand Slam, was played at Merion, in the suburbs of Philadelphia. Jones was razor-sharp. He defeated Canada's Ross Somerville in the first round, 5 and 4, and trounced another Canadian, Fred Hoblitzel, 5 and 4, later in the day. He walloped Fay Coleman, 6 and 5, and his old Walker Cup teammate, Jess Sweetser, 10 and 9, to gain the finals.

Eighteen-thousand fans turned out for the climactic round, sending Jones against Gene Homans. Bobby was unbeatable, Homans was nervous and it was a cakewalk for the stroke-making robot from Atlanta, 8 and 7. That was golf's one and only Grand Slam. Thus, the Merion Cricket Club became a landmark in the fabulous career of Bobby Jones. It was there that he played in his first national championship at the age of 14. There, he won his first amateur title at 22 and at 28 he closed the book with the greatest collection of championships ever crammed into a single season.

Francis Ouimet called Jones's secret "perfection in style and spirit." "He was absolutely perfect," Ouimet said. "It was discouraging and monotonous the way he hit practically every shot exactly as it should be hit. If he had come along 15 or 20 years later, he still would have been the best."

"The record book is the true barometer of greatness," said Fred Corcoran, the man who built the professional tour into a $1,000,000 enterprise. "Show me a man able to win 13 national championships in the space of seven years and I'll show you an equal to Jones."

Walter Hagen said: "If I were asked to vote for the greatest golfer of all time, I'd have to mark my ballot for Bobby Jones."

82

BOBBY JONES'S RECORD

U.S. Amateur Champion: 1924, 1925, 1927, 1928, 1930. (Runner-up in 1919, 1926.)
U.S. Open Champion: 1923, 1926, 1929, 1930. (Tied for the title in 1925 and 1928 but lost in play-offs.)
British Open Champion: 1926, 1927, 1930.
British Amateur Champion: 1930.
Walker Cup Competition: Won five matches, lost none.

O.B. Keeler, the Atlanta sportswriter who covered all of Bobby's major triumphs and who became known as Jones's Boswell, said it was competitive instinct—and not shotmaking ability—which set Jones apart.

"Competitive golf," Keeler said with a mischievous gleam in his eye, "is played mainly on a 5½-inch course, the space between the ears. This is where Jones excelled."

JONES'S SECRET: THE FREE BODY TURN

Bobby Jones was the golfing stylist in the purest sense. His swing was described as "poetry in motion." The expression became hackneyed because there was no better means of description. There was never a kink or jerky motion as he took his stance, brought the club back, swung, and followed through. The movement simply flowed. He was indeed the picture golfer.

Jones often told intimates that if there was one secret of his success it was the free body turn. He teed up the ball a bit farther forward than most players—opposite his left arch. His feet were closer together than in the stance used by most of his contemporaries. This gave him the freest, fullest body turn.

Bobby contended that the backswing and downswing should be blended so perfectly that they would form one continuous movement rather than two distinct movements. On the backswing, he executed a full rotation of the trunk to the right, keeping his head stationary and using his spine as an axis. On the downstroke, the trunk was unwound with the left side becoming a focal point. It was not unlike winding a coil spring and then unleashing it with all its power.

He kept his left arm firm on the backswing, lifting the club directly over the right shoulder as if intending to bash the ball into the ground, cocking the wrists and lifting the hands and arms straight up to the normal top-of-swing position. Then the weight was shifted from left to right and gradually back to left again as the club started on the downswing. The right hand moved into position to unleash its power. Then there was the follow-through, hands high and the weight transferred to the left side.

A Scot writer once described Jones's style in this fashion:

> Mr. Jones stands over the ball just as if he were engaged in ordinary conversation. There is no straddling of legs, no tying of muscles into a knot, no extravagant poses, nothing to suggest that he is thinking of or doing anything in particular. . . . Of the millions of golfers in the world, I do not suppose there is another who swings a club back so smoothly or so sweetly.

Chapter Thirteen

Golf's New Age of Steel

The retirement of Bob Jones in 1930 ended an era in golf. It closed the door on the amateur as a dominant factor in big-time tournament competition and opened the portal to a new "Age of Steel." The fancy of the golf public was snapped up quickly by a succession of professional precisionists, who, playing with custom-fashioned, steel-shafted clubs, proceeded to make a mockery of Old Man Par. Par no longer was a standard of winning golf. It took birdies to survive on the rugged, mushrooming professional tour.

After Jones, one other amateur managed to overpower the tough professional opposition and win the U.S. Open. He was Omaha's Johnny Goodman, who came out of nowhere to capture the title in 1933 at the North Shore Country Club at Glen View, Illinois. But it was a single, isolated, and perhaps lucky stab. The jealous pros reassembled their ranks and rebuffed every succeeding amateur challenge. Significant of the trend was the 1963 National Open at The Country Club in Brookline, Massachusetts, where, for the first time in history, no amateur qualified for the final 36 holes.

During the decades that followed Goodman's triumph, the amateurs mustered a few potent threats. They produced outstanding stars who came close in the big Open competitions, such as the National Open and the Masters, but none bulled through. The cause of the amateur was sabotaged by the lure of easy gold on the pro circuit. As soon as an amateur reached the stature where it appeared he might seriously challenge the pros, he almost inevitably took the leap into the money ranks. This happened to W. Lawson Little, Jr., the powerfully-built Californian who dominated the amateur game in the mid-1930's. Dr. Cary Middlecoff, the intense, nervous dentist from Memphis; Gene Littler, Arnold Palmer, and Jack Nicklaus.

There is certainly a touch of irony in the fact that while golf received its stimulus as a tremendous spectator sport through the efforts of two amateurs—Francis Ouimet, with his sensational Open victory in 1913, and Bob Jones, with his incredible record climaxed by the Grand Slam—it remained for the pros to tap the till of the game's burgeoning popularity and reap the financial profits.

A big, thick-necked Boston promoter, Fred Corcoran, was one of the first to recognize the gate appeal possibilities of the fairway sport. As tournament manager of the Professional Golfers Association, he sold the pro tour as an attraction to the major cities around the country and built it from a struggling $135,000 venture in 1934 to a business that netted more than $600,000 for the barnstorming pros in 1949. Under his impetus, the figure soared into the $2,000,000-plus bracket in the 1960's.

Nevertheless, during the period immediately following Jones's retirement, the pros themselves failed to produce one performer who clearly eclipsed the rest. Gene Sarazen

Bob Jones and Horton Smith. Smith, first winner of the Masters in 1934, excited golf galleries after Jones' 1930 retirement.

Regarded as one of the great match players of all time, Lawson Little demonstrates his power in this follow-through.

was still among the best, although in the twilight of his career. The fans had several day-to-day heroes: the amateur, Lawson Little, Jr.; Paul Runyan, "Little Poison," they called him; Johnny Revolta; Denny Shute; Craig Wood; and Ralph Guldahl. But the game temporarily suffered from the lack of the "big guy," the dominant personality.

Little, a bull-shouldered, long-hitting athlete from Stanford University, came closest to emulating Jones's feats as an amateur, but his climb to the pinnacle of the sport was frustrated by his inability to crack the pros. A dogged competitor and superb match player, he reveled in head-to-head combat. He could not generate the same kind of fierce fire when he squared off against such inanimate and intangible objects as the course itself and par in the medal play tournaments.

Little pulled off one of the game's incredible, unparalleled feats when he won both the British and U.S. Amateur titles in 1934 and repeated in 1935. This fantastic "double double" was unmatched even by the great Jones. During the course of the four tournaments—from Prestwick in Scotland to The Country Club of Brookline, Massachusetts, in 1934, from St. Anne's in England to the Country Club of Cleveland in 1935—the burly, curly-haired Californian won 31 consecutive matches, 25 of them over the ever-hazardous, 18-hole route. It was a performance which some observers rated comparable to Bob Jones's Grand Slam.

Little, son of an army doctor stationed for a period in the Orient, was a humorless, ruthless fighter on the golf course. He had a rare faculty for absorbing adversity—patches of

86

bad luck or bad golf—without wavering, and then snapping back with double intensity. He neither asked nor gave quarter. He was merciless when ahead, twice as dangerous when behind.

A powerful driver and one of the sport's real craftsmen around the greens, he fell into the category of what Ben Hogan later termed the "shot manager." He made a thorough study of every hole on the course. He thought out every shot, often drawing criticism from his opponents because of his slow, deliberate play. He refused to be hurried. He prided himself on being able to outthink his rivals.

Scotsmen for years talked about the unmerciful beating which Little gave James Wallace, a 30-year-old Troon carpenter, in the final of the 1934 British Amateur at Prestwick. The sensational Wallace had eliminated no less than five Walker Cup players en route to the last round and figured to give the big, curly-haired Yank a close battle.

Little knocked in an eagle at the third hole, went on to shoot a blazing 66, 5 strokes under the course record, and put his dazed rival 12 holes down at the end of the morning round. The American continued his pressure in the afternoon, birdieing three of the first five holes to close out the match at the twenty-third hole, 14 and 13. In the 23 holes played, Little had only one bogey—a 5 at the seventh hole in the morning—and had twelve 3's on his card. Wallace was left in a near state of shock. He did not know what had hit him.

Little turned professional in 1936. He never gained giant status among the money boys, although he had one tremendous spurt to beat Gene Sarazen in a play-off for the National Open crown in 1940 at the Canterbury Club in Cleveland. Then, as in the case of many others, his fire flickered out.

One by one, golfers captured the imagination of the expanding flock of fans. They glittered for a while, then faded. They seemed to lack the constancy and durability which made men such as Jones, Hagen, and Sarazen great champions.

Denny Shute, a serious, determined professional from Cleveland, put Professional Golfers Association championships back-to-back in 1936 and 1937, played on half-a-dozen Ryder Cup teams and twice was runner-up in the U.S. Open, losing to Byron Nelson in a play-off in 1939. But he never was able to establish himself as Mr. No. 1.

Horton Smith, a slim, handsome professional out of Joplin, Missouri, with a flair for immaculate dress and unbelievable birdie putts, grabbed a large and loyal following who saw in him a logical successor to Jones as the Emperor of Golf. The "Joplin Ghost," as he was called, created a sensation as a 21-year-old rookie in 1929 when he won 7 tournaments and finished second in 4 others on the winter and spring tour. He justified the faith of his fans by winning the inaugural Masters Tournament at Augusta, Georgia, in 1934 and taking the title a second time in 1936 by chipping in from 50 feet on the fourteenth hole and dropping long putts at the fifteenth and seventeenth of the final round. However, he never broke through in the big prestige championships, the Open and the PGA, although like the ageless Sarazen and in defiance of failing health he continued to play occasional tournament golf after reaching age fifty.

Jimmy Thomson, a husky, blond Scottish immigrant, won wide renown as the longest hitter in the game, booming drives that often soared 300 yards; but the closest he came to winning the National Open was in 1935 at Oakmont, Pennsylvania, where he finished second to dark horse Sam Parks, Jr. Harry Cooper was rated one of the best of the tournament pros in the late 1920's and 1930's, consistently ranking among the leaders in both money winnings and scoring averages. However, he lacked the faculty for coming through in climactic situations. He three-putted the next-to-last green in the 1927 Open at Oakmont when he appeared to have the title in the bag and ultimately lost a play-off to Tommy Armour. He missed by two shots in 1936 when Tony Manero won at Baltusrol in Springfield, New Jersey.

More successful but less lasting was Ralph Guldahl, a tall, stoop-shouldered Texan with an ungraceful swing, who won consecutive National Opens in 1937 and 1938, an achievement accomplished in the past by only three men—Willie Anderson, Johnny McDermott, and Bob Jones (later duplicated by Ben Hogan). In 1937, Guldahl fired a final round 69 and edged out Sam Snead for the title at Oakland Hills in Detroit with 281, an Open record. At Cherry Hills in Denver the next year, he rallied from four strokes back of Dick Metz with another brilliant closing 69 to win by six strokes. It was the largest winning margin in 17 years. Guldahl added the Masters in 1939. Then, mysteriously, he lost the key to his game and had trouble breaking 80. Frustrated and broken in spirit, he disappeared from the tournament circuit.

Meanwhile, as Hitler's goose-stepping legions poured over Europe and applied the torch to World War II, the interest of the golfing public was stirred anew by the emergence of a small knot of professional precisionists, who, in their grim struggle for supremacy, launched an unprecedented assault on scoring records.

The hard core of this new breed was a group of sinewy, leather-tough Texans who were closely tied in age—Ben Hogan, Byron Nelson, Lloyd Mangrum, Jimmy Demaret, and Harold (Jug) McSpaden—joined by a colorful, sweet-swinging Virginia hillbilly, Samuel Jackson Snead.

Hogan, Nelson, and Snead quickly established themselves as the "Big Three." Hogan and Nelson were keen rivals. They had grown up together as caddies in Forth Worth and had been battling each other on the links, tooth and toenail, since they were schoolboys. Most of the nation's golf fans were divided into Hogan or Nelson supporters. Hogan is the best, stoutly argued one of the factions. Nelson can kill him, contended the other. Meanwhile, everybody loved Snead. He had a captivating backwoods personality, immune to polish, and he had a picture swing which drew thousands to his gallery in every tournament—win, lose, or draw.

The argument between Hogan and Nelson partisans never was satisfactorily settled. The two men, although separated by only seven months in age, never came face-to-face while both were at the peak of their careers, Nelson played his finest golf during the war years when he was exempt from military duty because of hemophilia (a "bleeder"). Hogan reached his greatest heights in the early 1950's after Nelson, aching in bones and weary of tournament pressures, had gone into semiretirement.

Nelson, son of a Fort Worth merchant, was christened the "mechanical man." He clicked off pars and birdies with such monotonous ease that his performances tended to be dull

Ralph Guldahl, man of mystery. What happened to his game after successive U. S. Open victories in 1937 and 1938?

Lloyd Mangrum, Byron Nelson and Vic Ghezzi in the locker room at Canterbury in Cleveland, Ohio, after Mangrum won a three-way play-off for the 1946 United States Open Championship.

and boring. He seldom scrambled. A good driver, he grooved his shots down the middle of the fairway, missed few greens, and putted adequately, if not sensationally. He lacked the exciting recovery proclivities of Snead—he never needed them—and the grim attacking qualities of Hogan, who was like a dour tailor sewing a funeral shroud for his adversaries.

Lord Byron first attracted attention at the age of 22 when the tour cut through Texas in 1934. He outshot the big name players through the first two rounds before suddenly waking up to his position in the San Antonio Open and immediately afterward finished second to Craig Wood at Galveston. The pros began to regard him with respect when he managed to better than break even—without

winning anything of importance—on the circuit in 1935 and 1936.

Nelson, cool and imperturbable, moved solidly into the big-time in 1937. He overtook a slumping Ralph Guldahl and captured the first of his two Masters crowns. Byron went into a temporary slump in 1938 but snapped out of it the following year when he won the prestigious North and South and Western Opens and climaxed his surge with a victory in the National Open at Spring Mill, outside Philadelphia. Profiting from Sam Snead's fabled blowup eight on the final hole, Nelson tied Craig Wood and Denny Shute at 284 and then survived a double play-off. Shute fell first when Nelson and Wood tied at 68. Nelson shot a 70 to beat Wood by 3 strokes.

89

The "mechanical man" won the first of his two PGA crowns in 1940, beating Sam Snead 1 up in the 36-hole final at the Hershey (Pennsylvania) Country Club. He lassoed his second Masters in 1942, outscoring his old rival, Hogan, in a play-off. He still had not hit the pinnacle of his shot-making efficiency.

This came in the two-year period of 1944–45. Fighting raged in Europe and in the Pacific. The U.S. Golf Association suspended its national championships. The tour continued, with Government encouragement, because it was figured to be a booster to home morale, a release from the wartime pressures. It is true that competition on the circuit was on the thin side, with men like Hogan, Demaret, Mangrum, Craig Wood, and Horton Smith in the service, and that many of the courses had been barbered and softened. Yet playing conditions were no different from those of the

Byron Nelson, who dominated the game in the early 1940s, blasts out of a trap during one of his 11 successive tournament victories in 1945.

Jimmy Demaret puts out on the final hole in winning the first of his three Masters championships at Augusta in 1940.

prewar and postwar periods. It was difficult to downgrade the performances of Nelson and his close friend, McSpaden (the latter rejected by the armed services because of a sinus condition), who dominated the circuit as the "Gold Dust Twins."

Nelson did most of the dominating, and picked up the major share of the gold dust.

In 1944, Lord Byron won seven tournaments, including the All-American and Red Cross Opens, was medalist and runner-up in the PGA Championship, and wound up as the year's leading money winner (the payoff was in war bonds) with $35,055. He scored an amazing average of 69.67 for 85 rounds and won the coveted honor of being voted "Athlete of the Year" by The Associated Press.

In 1945, Nelson sent records toppling like ten-pins. He won a total of 19 tournaments, an all-time high, 11 of them in succession.

Byron's phenomenal winning streak was snapped at Memphis by an amateur, Freddie Haas, who became the first simon-pure in nine years to take a circuit tournament. Nelson, a man who acknowledged that despite his cool exterior he suffered internal pressure pains every time he walked to the tee, appeared relieved that his string was broken. "Every tournament was getting tougher—I couldn't keep a thing on my stomach," he said. No other player had been able to put together more than three victories in a row.

Nelson's triumphs included the PGA Championship at the Moraine Country Club in Dayton, Ohio. After tieing Johnny Revolta for the medal at 138, Byron proceeded to wade through his opposition despite an aching back which he said made him feel "a hundred years old." His toughest battle was with Mike Turnesa in the second round and

91

he had to put an eagle on top of Mike's birdie at the thirty-fifty hole to win, 1 up. He finally beat Sam Byrd, the former Yankee outfielder, in the championship round, 4 and 3. Nelson closed the year with an average of 68.33 strokes for 120 rounds—an unbelievable performance—and money winnings of $52,511, both records. Again he was named "Athlete of the Year."

Nelson's amazing 1945 sweep was not an empty one in any sense of the word. Snead and some of the other top professionals who had been in uniform had drifted back into the tournament grind, with the easing of war tensions. Hogan, whose military assignment permitted him to keep his golf game from going rusty, showed up periodically in his lieutenant's uniform to renew the tense rivalry with his long-time adversary from Fort Worth.

Immediately after Byron's string was broken at Memphis, Nelson and Hogan came to grips in the Knoxville Open at Holston Hills. Nelson won by 10 strokes over Byrd. Hogan was 11 shots back of the winner. At Nashville, Ben showed flashes of his old form, shot an opening round 64 at Richland and won with a 19-under-par 265. Nelson missed by three shots. Nelson won at Spokane and Hogan hit back at Portland with sizzling rounds of 65-69-63-64 for a record 261. Two weeks later, at Seattle, Byron topped this with rounds of 62-68-63-66—259, winning by 13 strokes and leaving a dazed Hogan 20 shots in the rear.

So it went—the two Texans battling each other like a pair of jungle cats. It was inevitable that such a blistering pace could not continue. Something had to give.

Shortly afterward, Nelson, always bothered by a chronic stomach ailment, retired to his small cattle ranch in Roanoke, Texas.

The door to golf greatness was just opening for Ben Hogan.

Byron Nelson relaxes after winning the Red Cross Open in 1945.

Chapter Fourteen

Sam Snead: The Jinx King

Sam Snead won more than 100 tournaments, competing against some of the greatest players the game has ever known. He captured championships on three continents. He earned close to $500,000, more than any man except Arnold Palmer, on the tough professional tour. In a fabulous career that spanned more than a quarter of a century and saw golf soar to new heights of popularity, this colorful hillbilly from the backwoods of Virginia became a national symbol of club-swinging perfection. Although he was a contemporary of such greats as Ben Hogan and Byron Nelson and was still active during the rise of Palmer and Jack Nicklaus, he was rated by fellow professionals as the finest striker of the ball who ever lived. He was the idol of the galleries. Yet, generations hence, when students of the sport are looking back on this booming era, the single most significant fact standing out in his record will be a negative one. The checkmark beside his name will carry the notation:

"He never won the Open."

Snead was one of those unfortunate individuals—bountifully blessed but partly damned—destined to become stepchildren of the golfing fates. They apparently are born under an adverse sign. They are given untold talent. They are equipped with the shots and temperament of champions. They are permitted a taste of greatness and then, while they are hungering for the juicy plum necessary for complete satisfaction, they are denied it. The perfectly-hit shot drifts into a bunker. The ball takes a crazy bounce on the fairway.

The critical putt, flawlessly stroked, fails to drop. After a brilliant performance, a tournament appears certainly won. Then some outsider emerges from nowhere on a burst of sudden birdies and steals away with the big prize. So it was with Snead, and others to a varying degree, in the case of the blue ribbon championship that is every tournament golfer's goal—the U.S. Open.

Snead, a bitterly disappointed man, nevertheless became hardened to his repeated failures to crash through to this one coveted title and reconciled himself to his fate. He was, he reasoned, just a victim of the whim of the gods. The more golf he played, Sam said, the more convinced he became—as Bob Jones always theorized—that a man's name is inscribed on the championship roll by an unseen hand before the first ball is ever placed on the opening tee.

"It gives you the eeriest feeling sometimes, like you don't have anything to do with the way a tournament comes out," Snead remarked once, in reminiscing about his fluctuating fortunes. "I've won many a tournament I knew I had no business winning. Everything just went right—a ball would carom off a tree into the fairway or bounce out of a bunker. A long putt would roll into the hole just when I needed it. Then, on the other hand, I've seen tournaments snatched right out of my hands when by all rights they should have been mine. It's destiny."

If Sam's own experiences had not been enough to convince him that golf is a fickle, unpredictable game, then certainly he could

Sam Snead

have confirmed this belief in reviewing the tragedies of fine players before him who suffered a similar fate. Most conspicuous examples belonged to Macdonald Smith, Leo Diegel, and Harry Cooper.

The Scot-descended Mac Smith was a superb golfer in the hickory-shaft era before and just following World War I. Harry Vardon, the great British star, looked at him on one of his visits to America and called him the best shot-maker he had seen in the New World. Mac Smith hit the ball with a clean, crisp stroke. He was an excellent putter and apparently had an ideal temperament. He seemed completely devoid of nerves. He allowed nothing to interfere with his concentration.

He was a gawky, loose-jointed boy of 20 in 1910 when he came to the seventy-first hole in the U.S. Open at the Philadelphia Cricket Club, needing only pars on the final two holes to clinch the championship. Instead, he finished in a tie with his older brother, Alex, and Johnny McDermott at 298, and, his spirit shaken, made a miserable showing in the play-off. Alex Smith won with 71. McDermott shot 75, and Mac Smith 77.

This set a pattern for Mac Smith's big-time career. He continued to play superlative golf. He won a good share of the tournaments. The major prestige championships, however, eluded him. Nine times in the U.S. and British Opens he finished within three shots of the winner. He could not crack the barrier.

It was exactly 10 years after Mac Smith's first disappointment in the Open that Leo Diegel borrowed the script and then proceeded to set out on a similarly checkered and heart-breaking career. Unlike the imperturbable Mr. Smith, Diegel was an intense, highly sensitive individual whose nerves usually were as taut as guitar strings. Thus, he was very erratic. When he was on his game and rolling, he was virtually unbeatable—a man who did not need to give quarter to Walter Hagen or Bob Jones. Then again, he could strike a psychological landmine and his fine game would blow up in his face.

Diegel should have won the first National Open in which he played. This was the 1920

Open at Inverness in Toledo. Through the first three rounds, he was only one shot back of the leader, Harry Vardon. When the British star blew sky high with the gale winds that swept the course, Diegel had his chance. However, with the championship ripe for plucking, he shot a final 77—using 40 strokes on the incoming nine—and fell into a four-way tie for second place, one shot back of the winner, Britain's Ted Ray.

On seven other occasions in major championships—the American and British Open—Diegel came close to taking the title. Always something thwarted him. In the 1925 Open at Worcester, Massachusetts, he needed to play only even par on the final six holes to take the crown. He soared nine strokes over. In the 1933 British Open at St. Andrews, he faced a similar situation, needing to shoot only one-over-par on the final five holes to clinch the championship. He three-putted the final two holes, missing from less than 3 feet on the seventy-second with the putt that would have given him a tie.

The same frustrations dogged the heels of Lighthorse Harry Cooper, a lean, sharp-featured Texan of British birth. He had the 1927 Open at Oakmont in his pocket but three-putted the next-to-last hole from 12 feet, finished in a tie with Tommy Armour and lost the play-off by 3 strokes. Nine years later at Baltusrol in Springfield, New Jersey, the personable, easy-going Cooper led through the first three rounds and posted a then-record score of 284 apparently to nail down the championship. He was being congratulated in the locker room when an obscure professional named Tony Manero came charging down the stretch with a closing 67, which gave him the title at 282. Cooper was the nation's top tournament golfer in 1937—low scorer and leading money winner—but the Open championship continued to stay out of his reach.

Samuel Jackson Snead's career followed the pattern of these unlucky predecessors almost as if it had been fashioned by a prewritten script. Like Mac Smith, Diegel and Cooper, Sam suffered early disappointments, seeing

Open championships disintegrate before his very eyes when he seemed to have them firmly in his grasp. As time went on, memory of these "near hits" grew in magnitude, and, although Snead himself vigorously denied it, created a mental block that only compounded his failures. For a while, the sweet-swinging Virginian apparently pressed too hard. By the time he had learned to look upon the Open as any other tournament, it was too late. He had lost some of his drive.

Sam was runner-up in the U.S. Open four times—in 1937, 1947, 1949, and 1953. He tied for the title in 1947, losing in the play-off. None of the other major professional championships escaped him. He won the Professional Golfers Association crown three times—in 1941, 1949, and 1951, when it was tough match play competition—and he was runner-up in the event in 1938 and 1940. He captured three Masters (in 1949, 1952, and 1954), whipping Ben Hogan in a play-off for his third crown, and he took the British Open in 1946

"Slammin' Sammy"—as he became known to idolatrous millions—became one of the game's captivating personalities. He traveled the world. He wore silk suits, cashmere sweaters, and $50 shoes, but city polish never wore off on him. He remained the perpetual hillbilly, completely devoid of affectation and full of droll backwoods humor. Every time his familiar straw hat (covering a balding pate) appeared on the course, crowds congregated. Even when he was not competition, Sam always attracted a huge gallery. People loved to watch him hit a ball.

Snead's swing was pure poetry. There was not a hitch. There was not a flaw. His magnificent tapering shoulders and piston-like arms moved as gracefully as a rippling brook, but the ball came off the clubhead like a cannon blast. Long and straight off the tee, he also was a tremendous iron player, and, despite his reputation to the contrary, a sound putter—more effective on the long ones than the short ones. If there was a weakness in his game, it was more mental than physical. Hit-

ting the ball came so naturally for Snead that he never had to think about it. Thus, he probably suffered from lack of good shot management.

Shot management—at least his own—was not a factor in the 1937 Open at Oakland Hills in Birmingham, Michigan, Sam's first and a bitter disappointment. Snead was a raw rookie of 25 who was just beginning to attract

Like the snap of a steel spring, Sam Snead's flawless style can be seen in this tee shot in the Goodall Round Robin Tournament in 1954.

attention on the tour. Playing superlative golf over the tough, testing course, he put four good rounds together and came to the club house the evening of the final day with a score of 283, just a shot over the Open record Tony Manero had set the year before. He looked like the certain winner. The press corps was scrambling around for biographical data on the spectacular hillbilly when Ralph Guldahl came in late with a closing 69 for a record-breaking 281 and the championship. It was a blow to young Snead. Historians later said if Snead had won this title—or the one in 1939—he probably would have gone on to a half-dozen Open Championships.

If Oakland Hills was a disappointment, Philadelphia's Spring Mill two years later was a heart-crusher—enough to drive a man to suicide. This was the scene of Snead's notorious eight, representing perhaps the biggest blow-up in major tournament history.

Sam came to the final hole—a 558-yard, par 5—needing only a par to win the championship outright and a bogey six to tie Byron Nelson, Craig Wood and Denny Shute. As he teed up the ball on the seventy-second, Snead did not know this, and he did not ask. He only knew that he had missed a 5-foot putt on the seventy-first hole and got a bogey five. He felt he had to gamble for a birdie on the closing hole. Mistake No. 1.

Snead hit his drive squarely but hooked the ball into some trampled rough where he had a lie on sandy soil. He was still 275 yards from home and there were some ugly traps up ahead in front of the green. The discreet move would have been to use an iron and make sure of getting the ball out and up. But no one ever accused Sam of being discreet. He decided to go for the green. Mistake No. 2.

He took a No. 2 wood with extra loft and whaled away. He hit the ball badly and it shot about 160 yards, falling into one of the sand traps where it was half-buried. The top of the bunker had been sodded with loose squares. Sam knew he could blast out safely with a wedge but he still was determined to reach the green, now 115 yards away. He called for

an eight-iron. Mistake No. 3. The ball went only about 4 feet and lodged between two sods. To get it out, Sam had to hit it with a sideswiping blow. The ball went 40 yards into another bunker. Snead's stomach turned a somersault. He had hit four shots and still was not on the green.

Snead, forced to stand on the side of the bunker, made a beautiful recovery, scraping the ball onto the green, 40 feet from the cup. He still could tie by sinking the putt. He went for it. The ball lipped the cup and spun 3 feet away. By now, Snead was glassy-eyed, in a state of near shock. He missed the 3-footer, then tapped the ball in for the most famous 8 ever made in golf.

In 1947, at the St. Louis Country Club, Snead sank a curling, 20-foot putt on the final hole to tie Lew Worsham for the Open championship with a score of 282. The 18-hole play-off was a slambang affair that went to the final hole all square. On the eighteenth, both players had good drives and approaches—Worsham landing in the frog's hair at the edge of the green and Snead on the green, 25 feet away. On his third shot, Worsham chipped within less than 3 feet of the hole. Snead putted, and the ball died just short.

Snead walked up and prepared to knock in his putt when Worsham suddenly interrupted him.

"Just a minute," Worsham said, "what makes you think you're away. Maybe I am."

Snead insisted—quite properly—that, under the rules, once a player had started to putt out he is entitled to finish.

In the confusion, the match referee, Isaac Grainger of the U.S. Golf Association, himself flustered, was called in to make a measurement. He found Snead's ball 30½ inches from the cup, Worsham's 30.

Snead had to putt. Rattled, his concentration broken by the incident, Sam missed. Worsham sank. Another Open had gone down the drain for the hard-luck Snead.

The boner for which Snead has been most roundly criticized was that which cost him the 1949 Open at Medinah in Chicago. He

needed only pars on the final two holes, relatively easy ones, to tie Cary Middlecoff, who had finished with 286. A birdie would have given him the title outright.

On the par 3 seventy-first, Snead's tee shot landed about 3 feet off the green in the short fringe grass. Sam faced the decision of whether to use a chipping iron or a putter. On shots of this type, there has been a growing tendency among the tournament pros to use the putter. There is less danger of scuffing the ball and leaving it short. Sam chose the putter. The ball bounced over the thick turf and rolled 8 feet past the cup. Then he missed coming back—a disastrous 3-putt green—and lost out by a single stroke.

In later years, Snead stoutly defended his choice of club on the hole. He insisted that under similar circumstances he would make the same decision again. His mistake, he said, was in not more closely examining the lie and noticing the necessity for more braking action.

Then came another golden chance in 1953 at Oakmont. Snead sank a long putt on the fifty-fourth hole and went to lunch only one shot back of a weary Ben Hogan. But, starting the afternoon final round, he hit his tee shot out of bounds on the first hole and wound up six strokes back of the victorious Hogan, although still in second place.

Old Sam never quit trying. A sturdy, strong athlete who neither drank nor smoked, he was a threat every time he teed up the ball. "I can still win the Open," he insisted, as he neared, reached and finally passed his fiftieth birthday. But his hopes—and chances—grew thinner with the years, and finally faded into nothingness.

Snead was born May 27, 1912, on a cow and chicken farm in Ashwood, Virginia, a few miles from Hot Springs. His mother and father, Harry and Laura Snead, were hardy mountain folk. He had four older brothers

Sam Snead follows the flight of the ball in the PGA Championship at Oakmont, Pennsylvania, in 1951, one of his three PGA titles.

and a sister. All the boys were good athletes, particularly Homer, the oldest, and Sam, the youngest.

Sam was a fast and shifty halfback in football. He was a good baseball pitcher. In basketball, he usually scored more points than the entire opposition combined. He could run 100 yards in 10 seconds flat. But he early had a real affinity for golf.

As a skinny tot, Sam shagged balls for his brother Homer who practiced driving in a pasture near the family home. He was seven years old when he cut a swamp maple limb with a knot on the end and carved a rough club face for his first golf stick. He swung it for hours at a time and practiced accuracy by belting rocks at fence posts 125 yards away. Later, he made himself a miniature course by sinking tomato cans around the farmyard. Hazards, he said, were a pump, a hayrake, an outhouse, and clucking chickens.

Snead played golf, along with other sports, at Valley High School in Hot Springs. Several colleges in the area sought to land the hillbilly phenomenon an athletic scholarship, but Sam was not interested. He had his mind set on golf.

He got a caddying job at The Homestead Hotel, a swank resort hotel in Hot Springs. Later he became an assistant in the pro shop at $25 a week. Stories of his golf prowess began to spread throughout the mountain area. Snead was 23, a handyman at the Cascades Inn in Hot Springs, when he attracted the attention of Fred Martin, golf manager of the Greenbrier Hotel in White Sulphur Springs, West Virginia, and became a full-fledged professional at the famous old club frequented by presidents, industrial tycoons, and financial barons. Thus began an association that continued through Snead's career.

The mountaineer stylist captured the West Virginia Open and the state PGA in 1936, firing a 61 in the latter tournament, and at-

Snead kicks up some dirt in disgust after flubbing a shot from the round in the 1962 United States Open at Oakmont.

Sam Snead didn't need to wear his cocoanut straw hat when he played in the Metropolitan Open at Bloomfield, New Jersey, in 1937.

tracted considerable regional attention by beating Lawson Little, Billy Burke, and Johnny Goodman in an exhibition at Greenbrier. Members of the club decided to back him in a fling at the professional tour.

Snead finished tenth in his first tournament at Miami, then moved to the Pacific Coast. He came in sixth in the Los Angeles Open, won the Oakland Open with rounds of 69-65-67-69 for 270 and added the Rancho Santa Fe Open, sponsored by Bing Crosby. By this time, the amazing hillbilly had caught the eye of Fred Corcoran, the PGA's tournament manager, who saw in Sammy a sure-fire stimulant for

the pro tour. Through Corcoran's promotional genius, the colorful, long-hitting Snead quickly became renowned throughout the golfing world. Fans swarmed to the courses to see him in action. He never disappointed. He lived up to his notices.

Slammin' Sammy won more professional tournaments than any other man—in excess of 100. For years, he was leader in the all-time money winning ranks, overtaken by Arnold Palmer when purses reached astronomical figures. In 1963, at the age of 50, he led the Masters tournament with four holes to play, but fell victim to an unruly putter and per-

SAM SNEAD'S RECORD

PGA Champion: 1941, 1949, 1951. (Runner-up, 1938, 1940.)
Masters Champion: 1949, 1952, 1954. (Runner-up, 1939, 1957.)
British Open Champion: 1946.
U.S. Open Runner-Up: 1937, 1947, 1949, 1953. (Tied for championship in 1947; lost by one stroke in 18-hole play-off to Lew Worsham.)
Leading Money Winner: 1938, 1949, 1950.
Vardon Trophy Winner (lowest scoring average): 1938, 1949, 1950, 1955.
Ryder Cup Member: 1937, 1947, 1949, 1951, 1953, 1955, 1959. Singles: won 5, lost 1; foursomes, won 4, lost 1.

mitted Jack Nicklaus to foil his bid for an unprecedented fourth title at Augusta.

Yet he could never win the Open.

SAM SNEAD'S RHYTHMIC SWING

Perhaps the main ingredient to Sam Snead's beautiful swing is what he calls the "perfect foot roll."

This calls for a pivot on the inside edge of the feet, particularly the inside of the right foot.

When he set himself on the tee, Snead dug in with his cleats on the inside edge of his right foot. He bent his knees, keeping them perfectly relaxed, and extended his posterior.

As the club came back, the right leg straightened, and, halfway through the backswing, his body shifted against the right foot. The left heel was well planted.

Upon contacting the ball, the inside sole of the right foot pushed against the resistance of the left foot.

Every movement was coordinated into one continuous, relaxed motion. There was never any tension.

Result: 300-yard drives, perfect control.

Chapter Fifteen

The Miraculous Hogan

On February 2, 1949, Ben Hogan and his wife, Valerie, were driving along a lonely Texas highway, en route from Phoenix, Arizona, to their Fort Worth, Texas, home. Suddenly, without warning, a huge transcontinental bus lunged out of the haze and skidded into the path of their automobile. Hogan, seeing a collision was inevitable, acted instinctively. He flung himself in front of his wife to try to shield her from injury. The heroic gesture probably saved both of their lives.

There was a screeching of brakes and then a sickening crash. The Hogan automobile was converted into an ugly mass of twisted metal. The impact drove the steering wheel through the driver's seat, like a spear from an angry hand. Thanks to Ben's quick thinking, Valerie escaped with only minor injuries. Hogan was not so lucky. He suffered a double fracture of the pelvis, a broken collarbone, a fractured left ankle and a smashed right rib.

Hogan was taken to a hospital in El Paso. Just when it appeared the game little golfer had weathered the crisis, thrombosis developed. In order to halt the clotting of blood, doctors performed a two-hour abdominal operation and tied off the principal veins in his legs, saving Hogan's life. However, his golfing future appeared certainly doomed.

"That's all for Hogan," a saddened sports world agreed generally. "He can never come back from this." Medical men could offer little extra hope. There was fear Ben might never walk again.

Such fear was ill-founded. It failed to reckon with the grim fighting qualities and flaming determination of the blacksmith's son to whom the word "can't" always had been like a red flag waved in front of the nostrils of a Brahma bull.

Hogan not only walked again, he played golf again. Furthermore, he won again—and again and again. He became the fairway Goliath of the Fifties, successor to Vardon and Jones, the one man able to awe and consistently overpower the tough breed who plied their trade on the professional circuit. He became a symbol—not only as a man of fortitude who fashioned an almost unbelievable comeback, but as one of the great all-time champions of the game. Golf's postwar era bore his indelible mark. It was "The Hogan Age."

To the National Open Championship he won in 1948 before the accident, Ben added three others—in 1950, 1951, and 1953. Half a dozen times he came within a shot or two of a fifth U.S. Open title, which would have projected him into a class by himself—beyond Willie Anderson and Bob Jones, the other four-time winners. He captured two Masters, setting the tournament low-scoring record in 1953, bettered 12 years later by Jack Nicklaus, and he won the Birtish Open in 1953 in his first and only try at this aged and honored championship.

His triple sweep in 1953—the Masters, U.S. Open, and British Open—was an unmatched

Ben Hogan

achievement which many golf authorities rated at least equal to Jones's Grand Slam. It was made in an era of much stiffer competition.

Hogan was a fine golfer before his highway smashup in 1949. He became a greater one afterward. It was as if new inspiration and a stronger psychological approach to the game had been sewn into his system with the same stitches that patched his withered legs.

The tight-lipped Texan came out of the accident a mellower man. He always had been a cold, detached, and at times mysterious "loner" on the tour. After his tragedy, undoubtedly moved by the sympathy and support of his millions of unknown followers, Ben made a strong effort to relax socially and defrost himself with occasional warmth. It was not easy. The iron rod of self-discipline and the deep-seated suspicion of outside influences, forged by years of adversity, did not bend easily. The hard crust the man had built around himself remained.

Newspapermen, including many friends of long standing, continued to find him hard to crack in locker room interviews and informal gab sessions. His closest golf companions—Jimmy Demaret and Claude Harmon were foremost of these—never managed to break through that cold, invisible wall.

Demaret once remarked facetiously that he could not understand why people thought Hogan was so taciturn. "When I play with him, he talks to me on every green. He turns to me and says, 'You're away.'"

"Those steel-gray eyes of his," another friend once remarked. "He looks at you like a landlord asking for next month's rent."

At Carnoustie, enamored Scotsmen christened him "The Wee Ice Mon." Tournament rivals on the circuit dubbed him "The Hawk." "The Hawk is coming," became a tournament watchword. It sent shivers up the spines of the pros. Demaret's personal term of endearment for Hogan was "Blue Blades." With the golf galleries that trudged in his wake, he acquired the reputation of being a sphinx, a robot, and a mechanical man.

If the automobile accident outside Van Horn, Texas, and the long months of agonizing recuperation added a touch of softness to the man's nature, they failed to douse the fierce competitive fire that burned inside him. Hogan's grim, merciless approach to the game never changed. Every rival was an enemy, a potential thief with designs on Hogan's gold and glory. Every golf course was a monster, to be slain like a big, flame-belching dragon. Par was a target to be shattered, like a flying disc from the blast of a shotgun. Ben fought them both—par and pro alike—with a relentless and angry zeal.

Hogan's attitude was reflected in a comment he made after winning the National Open Championship at Oakland Hills in Birmingham, Michigan, in 1951. Like most Open courses, Oakland Hills had been toughened for the tournament, but the architects had been overly conscientious. The fairways were so narrow, players complained, that they had to walk them single-file, Indian fashion. Fairway traps and heavy, wiry rough added to the tortures. The course became a veritable nightmare, so vicious that through the first three rounds none of the competitors—and they were the world's best—had been able to break par. No one was more frustrated than Hogan.

Finally, on his last round, Hogan shot a three-under-par 67, which brought him the championship. When he was handed the trophy at the presentation ceremonies, the usually reticent, reserved champion could not restrain a bit of exultation. "I'm happy," he said, "I brought the beast to her knees." It was like a victory chant from the throat of a modern Tarzan.

Overcoming apparently insurmountable odds became a grim game in the life of the stubborn Texan. When he was a young pro, just starting on the tour, Ben was plagued with an atrocious hook and well-wishers advised him to get in another trade. They warned he could never make a living at golf. Hogan corrected the fault. The world soon forgot the names of the men who offered the counsel. After the automobile accident, Hogan's obituary as a big-time competitor was written many times over. Each time Ben won another championship, someone would say: "That's the end—he can't do it again." He did.

After he had won the 1950 National Open at Merion, his first after the smashup, Ben happened to be in the club's washroom when he overheard a national sports columnist—not realizing the champion was within earshot—expounding to friends:

"Well, the Little Man has done it, and he might as well enjoy it. Now he has proved himself. He has been given a fat settlement by the bus company because of the accident. He's rich and contented. He'll never win another big tournament—mark my words."

Hogan, flushed and angry, confronted his critic. "You wouldn't want to bet on that, would you?" he demanded.

The writer was embarrassed but quick on his feet. "Certainly," he countered, "let's make it a dozen $10 ties."

Less than 10 months later, Hogan won the wager by capturing the Masters. Judging by subsequent triumphs, the columnist was fortunate Ben had not made it a parlay.

"People have always been telling me what I can't do," Ben once said. "I guess I have wanted to show them." This insatiable, almost fanatical urge to keep proving something to the world, and to himself, was a distinguishing feature of Hogan's success. He never denied that he liked to win.

Although he did not have the beautiful, fluid style of Snead, the boyish appeal of Jones, or the flamboyant color of Hagen, Hogan was a gallery favorite. By the thousands, fans flocked to Ben's heels for the pleasure of watching him meticulously bend a massive golf course to his will.

Hogan resented the nickname of "Bantam Ben" pinned on him by the sportswriters— "I'm 5'9" and I weigh 162 pounds," he said with chagrin. "If I were a fighter, I'd have to take on Sugar Ray Robinson (middleweight) or Archie Moore (light heavyweight)."

Nevertheless, on a golf course he gave the impression of being a much smaller man. Yet he presented a majestic figure, his shoulders slightly hunched, as he moved from tee to green looking neither to the left nor right. After the accident, Ben walked with a labored, stiff-legged step—not unlike the motion of a man on stilts. He never hurried. His familiar white cap was pulled low over his leathery, nut-brown face. His square jaws were like a vise. A cigarette dangled from tight, unsmiling lips. If his steely eyes wandered in the direction of the crowd, they looked without seeing.

There was deliberation and purpose in every move. He studied every shot meticulously and executed it with rare precision. You could almost envision gears grinding and wheels turning beneath that white cap as he surveyed each assignment. He was the paragon of conservatism. He became bold only when extreme measures so dictated. His formula was: Play the course and let your rivals play themselves.

During his hungry drive in the early Fifties, Hogan practiced for months getting ready for a big championship. It was his custom to get to the tournament scene as much as two weeks in advance. He subjected the course to scientific, microscopic study. He memorized the best placement positions on the fairways and the most effective approaches to the greens. Then he figured what score would be needed to win. This accomplished, he would fix the figure on some sort of intangible gadget in his head and then go out and try to shoot it, oblivious of the other scores—hot or cold—being shot around him. Associates marveled at how often Hogan would hit his predicted figure right on the head. "Management," Ben once said, "is 80 percent of winning golf."

"Management" was a problem for little Ben almost as far back as he could remember. He was born August 13, 1912, in the little town of Dublin, Texas. When he was 10 years old, his father, the village blacksmith, died, and his mother gathered up the family and moved to Fort Worth. Ben sold papers on street corners to help pay expenses. Later, when he was 12, he became a caddy at the Glen Garden Country Club, toting bags for 65 cents a round. It was his introduction to golf. He tasted tournament success for the first time when he was 15, tying for top prize in the club's Christmas Day caddy competition.

In spite of his wild hook and the misgivings of his friends, Hogan turned pro at 19 and, with $100 in his pockets, set out boldly to join the winter tour at Los Angeles. In a month, he was broke. He worked, saved, and tried again in 1933, with no better success. Discouraged but not disheartened, he returned home and spent the next three years working like a slave to refine his game.

The young professional's fortunes began to improve—but slowly. In 1936, he qualified for the National Open but failed to survive the 36-hole cut at Baltusrol in Springfield, New Jersey. He took perhaps the most important step of his life, marrying dark-haired Valerie Fox, and then rejoined the tour in 1937. His appetite was whetted but his pocketbook was not enhanced much when he finished third at Lake Placid and tenth in the Canadian Open.

Ben and Valerie hit the winter tour in 1938 with a cash balance of $1,400 and a million dollars' worth of hope. The reserve fund dwindled as Hogan moved from Pasadena to Los Angeles to Sacramento without winning an appreciable purse. The Hogans had exactly $85 to their name when they reached Oakland for the next tournament. On top of their other problems, a thief jacked up their car one night and made off with the two rear wheels and tires.

This brought the Hogans' situation almost to the breaking point. Ben and Valerie talked seriously of giving up the tour and going into another business. They decided Ben should take one final stab—at Oakland. The tournament would serve as the barometer of their future course.

"The night before that first round, I didn't sleep a wink," Hogan recalled later. "I knew how desperate our circumstances were. If I couldn't win any money in this tournament, we would be forced to sell the car and go back to Texas. I don't think I ever went into a tournament with more determination. I was forced to play every shot with the utmost concentration."

Hogan led the first round with a 66, finally finished the tournament in third place, collecting $385. "This probably was the turning point in my life," Ben said. The next two years were lean ones—he earned only $4,150 in 1938 and $5,600 in 1939, bare expenses— but Hogan had convinced himself he could lick the game. In 1939, he again qualified for the National Open and finished in a tie for sixty-second place. From then on, however, it was all uphill.

In the spring of 1940, Ben won his first tournament, the North and South Open at Pinehurst, North Carolina, and before the year was out he had his fellow pros buzzing. He won three other tournaments, tied for fourth in the U.S. Open, led both in money winnings ($10,656) and scoring averages. In 1941, he tied for third in the Open at Colonial in Forth Worth, five shots back of Craig Wood, and boosted his winnings to $18,358, the year's high. Success continued on a high scale in 1942. Hogan shot 280 to tie Byron Nelson for the Masters title, losing in a playoff. He won the Hale America Open, the wartime substitute for the U.S. Open, by firing a record-tying 62 in the second round, and he repeated as top-money winner ($13,143) and leader in the scoring averages. Midway in 1942, he entered the Army Air Corps as a lieutenant.

When Hogan returned to the circuit after the war, he was confronted with his old rivals —Nelson and Snead—and perhaps some doubts that he might be able to recapture his former No. 1 position. Nelson had been burning up the circuit during the war. Snead had attracted a huge following that was convinced that a man of such immense natural talent could not long be denied. Up to this point, Hogan had not won a major championship.

Byron Nelson and Ben Hogan have a 1945 reunion at the Glen Garden Country Club in Forth Worth, Texas, where both started as caddies.

This drouth was broken quickly. On August 25, 1946, at Portland, Oregon, Hogan defeated Ed (Porky) Oliver, 6 and 4, in the 36-hole final of the Professional Golfers Association Championship. If Ben's army of supporters had any doubts that he could regain his prewar touch, these were dispelled when Hogan shot to the top of money list again with earnings of $42,556 for 1946—regarded as a staggering total.

Two years later, Hogan captured the first of his four Open crowns at the Riviera Country Club in Los Angeles—"Hogan's Alley," they came to call it—by shooting four superlative rounds of 67-72-68-69 for an Open record 276.

The 1949 tour did not start auspiciously for the deliberate master from Fort Worth and he was headed home to do some refurbishing on his game when he was spilled onto that Texas highway. After the accident, Ben lay flat on his back for 58 days. When he was transferred to his home, he began a series of laps around the room—increasing them each day—to rebuild the strength in his legs. It was three months before he got outdoors and it was late August before he was able to pick up a golf club. In December, 10 months after the tragedy, he dared to play his first round. His legs covered from ankles to thighs with bandages, he went 18 holes with the aid of a golf cart.

106

There still was doubt—to all except Hogan—that he would ever play top-flight golf again.

In mid-January, 1950, the sports world was electrified by the report that Hogan had entered the Los Angeles Open at Riviera. It was the comeback test. Could he do it? It would take a miracle, everyone agreed. It seemed impossible.

On battered, faltering legs, Hogan trudged the first round in 73 strokes. Then he added a 69. On the third day, in the rain, he shot another 69. "The Little Man is coming," Snead said apprehensively, as he played the last round with a furtive look over his shoulder. Hogan showed signs of fatigue on the final day but he carved out another 69 and

tied Snead for first place with a score of 280. It was immaterial that the play-off, postponed by bad weather, ultimately was won by Snead. Hogan had written one of the most dramatic stories in sports and had proved his point—he could play golf again.

The sports world was tense and excited five months later when Hogan appeared at the Merion Club, outside Philadelphia, for the National Open. This indeed was the supreme test. The pressures and the 36-hole final day windup made the tournament one of the severest and most trying tests in sports.

Ben's battered legs stood up like stanchions of steel, although after each day's play he was forced to return to his room and put the

Hogan explodes out of a trap bordering a green in the 1950 Los Angeles Open, his first tournament after a near-fatal automobile accident.

Hogan, bundled in sweaters, holds the British Open trophy after his sensational victory at Carnoustie in 1953, completing his Little Slam of the U. S. and British Opens and the Masters.

injured members in traction to improve circulation. Hogan opened with a creditable 72, although eight shots back of Lee Mackey's record 64. He moved to within two shots of the lead with a second round 69, then finished with 72-74 for 287, which put him into a three-way tie with Lloyd Mangrum and George Fazio. A brilliant 69 in the play-off round smothered any remaining doubts that he would be able to regain his old throne.

In the ensuing major championships, the dark shadow of The Hawk lengthened. Hogan won the Masters in 1951, finishing with a 68, and two months later captured his third Open at Oakland Hills. Hogan's dynasty was shaken mildly in 1952 when Julius Boros won the Open at Dallas, but Ben stormed back in 1953 with one of the titanic performances of all time.

He won the Masters with successive rounds of 70-69-66-69 for 274, setting a tournament record. He won the National Open at Oakmont, outside Pittsburgh, with a comfortable 283, six shots better than runner-up Sam Snead. Then he fixed his sights on the British Open at Carnoustie.

Hogan had won every major championship in the United States, some several times over. He needed Britain's venerable championship to establish his position firmly at the pinnacle of all golf. In the old days, masters such as Hagen, Jones, and Sarazen had made regular forays to the Old World cradle of the game. Hogan and his contemporaries of the later era had felt no such compulsion and had been unwilling to make the sacrifice of missing the rich pro tour. So this was Ben's first try.

The Texas comeback marvel had captured the imagination of Britain's devoted golf fans

108

but not even the most romantic of them conceded him a chance at Carnoustie. Hogan faced not only a line-up of some of the world's greatest golfers but also conditions under which he had never played before. The course was hard, craggy and pock-marked. The greens, to use a Hogan term, were "like putty." The British ball was different— smaller in circumference. The weather was always foul—windy, rainy, and cold.

Draped in layers of sweaters and rain gear and feverish with a deep cold, Hogan shot an opening round 73, three strokes back of the leader, Frank Stranahan. A second round 71 put him two behind a pair of British Ryder Cuppers, Dai Rees and Eric Brown, as Stranahan faded. Hogan moved into a tie with Roberto De Vicenzo, the transplanted Argentine, after 54 holes with a 70 for 214. Golf-loving Scotsmen poured over the old course in droves to see the climax. The Wee Ice Mon obliged with a closing 68 for 282.

Now he had won the Masters, U.S. Open, and British Open in what he termed "my greatest year in golf." Hogan came home to a ticker-tape welcome up New York's Broadway and almost broke up with emotion on the steps of City Hall. "You want to cry," the man of steel said chokingly. "I owe it to God, and my wife, Valerie."

Hogan had one final, unfilled ambition. That was to win a fifth United States Open and thus move into a niche all to himself in this famed championship. It appeared that he had attained his goal in 1955 at the Olympic Club in San Francisco when he came in with a score of 287. However, a hollow-cheeked, little known pro from Iowa charged in late on a wave of birdies to tie for the title. Wrung of all emotion and fire, Hogan lost the next day's play-off, shooting a 72 to Jack Fleck's 69.

"I will never work this hard again to win a tournament," Hogan announced at San Francisco in a declaration of semiretirement. The prospect of a fifth Open never ceased to beckon him, however, and time after time he almost grabbed it only to have it slip away like a puff of smoke.

The welcome only accorded great heroes is given Ben Hogan with a ticker tape parade up Broadway July 21, 1953 after his return from his British Open victory at Carnoustie, Scotland.

In the 1956 Open at Rochester, New York, he needed only two pars on the last two holes to tie Cary Middlecoff. On the seventy-first hole, he froze on a 30-inch putt, backed off, and then missed. "My nerves are shot," he confessed. "It isn't the legs that go first, it's the nerves." At Winged Foot in Mamaroneck, New York, in 1959, he was in the thick of the fight until the final round when he faded and finished five shots back of the winner, Bill Casper. At Cherry Hills in Denver in 1960, he

Hogan went into semi-retirement in 1955 but continued to play in the Masters. He is shown teeing off in 1962.

was breathing down Arnold Palmer's neck until the seventy-first hole when a bold, gambling shot missed by inches and fell into the water. If the ball had stuck on the corner of the green where he aimed it, he might have had No. 5.

As he approached 50, Hogan sold his golf-club business for a small fortune and built a $200,000 home in Fort Worth. He announced he would continue playing in the Masters and the Open as long as he could walk.

An attack of bursitis and an operation slowed Ben down early in 1963, but he essayed a mild comeback by playing in the Thunderbird Classic at the Westchester Country Club in Harrison, New York. He managed to stay creditably close to par and even beat out his old rival, Sam Snead, by a stroke, but he found himself not equal to the birdie pressure of the Sixties.

"I just don't have the feel any more," Ben said sadly.

110

Hogan continued to be the master golfer from tee to green as he passed his fiftieth birthday, but he lost his nerves on the greens. Here he watches a putt go wide during the U. S. Open at Winged Foot in 1959.

BEN HOGAN'S RECORD

U.S. Open Champion: 1948, 1950, 1951, 1953. (Tied for first in 1955; lost playoff to Jack Fleck, 69–72.)

Masters Champion: 1951, 1953. (Tied for title in 1942 and 1954, losing playoffs to Byron Nelson and Sam Snead, respectively. Runner-up in 1946 and 1955.)

PGA Champion: 1946, 1948.

British Open Champion: 1953.

Ryder Cup: 1947, 1951, captain 1953.

Ryder Cup Record: Won 1 singles, 2 foursomes, lost none.

Leading Money Winner: 1940 ($10,656); 1941 ($18,358); 1942 ($13,143); 1946 ($42,556); 1948 ($32,112).

Vardon Trophy Winner: 1940, 1941, 1948.

Scoring Record, U.S. Open: 276, Riviera Country Club, Los Angeles, 1948.

BEN HOGAN'S $20,000 SECRET

When Ben Hogan was in his heyday, the undisputed king of the game, he confided to intimates that he had discovered a secret in the swing which was largely responsible for his tournament success. Fellow pros badgered him to pass along this priceless information. Hogan merely gave them one of his thin smiles and said, "Not yet, fellows—not until I'm ready to retire." There was wide speculation, but no one could solve the mystery.

Then, finally, in July, 1955, a month after little known Jack Fleck had squashed his bid for a fifth Open title at San Francisco, Hogan, having announced his semiretirement from big-time competition, decided to tell all. The cloak surrounding his famous secret was removed in a national magazine article for which Hogan reportedly was paid $20,000.

The mysterious maneuver, Ben revealed, was nothing more than a gimmick called pronation, a technique recommended by old Scottish pros years ago but later discarded as antiquated and unsound. The main value was to make the swing hookproof.

Hogan said he came upon the discovery quite by accident while trying to cure himself of a low, ducking hook—a malady most of the top pros are constantly fighting. With changes

HOGAN'S SECRET: After announcing retirement from big time competition in 1955, Hogan revealed the secret which he said made him a champion. The key to the secret was pronation of the wrists as shown in these drawings. The *left* drawing shows the position of his hands when he is not using the secret and the *right* the position when he is. The maneuver is executed before he reaches the top of his backswing. With a conventional swing Hogan's left wrist remains straight (*left*). Hogan's left wrist bends backward and inward forming a slight V when the secret is applied (*right*). The maneuver enabled Hogan to open the club face to the fullest and made it impossible for him to close it fast enough on the downswing to create a hook.

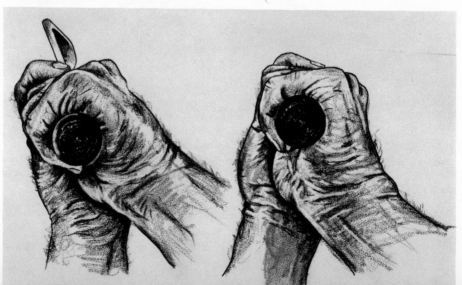

in his stance and grip, Ben could avoid the hook but he lost distance which he could ill afford to give away. Then he hit on the idea of pronation.

The change called for two adjustments. On the grip, he moved his left hand about one inch to the left so that the thumb was almost directly on top of the shaft. The second adjustment, which he called the meat of his secret, involved a cocking—an almost imperceptible twist—of the left wrist. The wrist was cupped gradually backward and inward on the backswing so that it formed a slight V at the top of the swing. This had the effect of opening the face of the club to the widest practical extreme at the top of the swing.

It is not, Hogan insisted, a difficult movement to master. On the backswing, the hands roll gradually to the right until the back of the left hand is facing almost straight up and the back of the right hand almost straight down. This opens the face of the club. On the downswing, the face of the club gradually closes and returns to its original position as impact is made with the ball.

Pronation in itself, Hogan said, did not prevent a hook but rather promoted it. It was when he coupled the idea with his two adjustments—the altered grip and the cocking of the left wrist—that Ben found the ball taking high, straight flight and, with a slight fade to the right, landing light as a feather. The result was that he got greater control without loss of distance.

Chapter Sixteen

The Affluent Trailer Kids

The retirement of Ben Hogan ended an era and opened up a new age in golf. By the mid-1950's, the touring professionals were playing for $50,000 and $100,000 purses every week instead of the meager $10,000 and $15,000 grab bags of earlier years. In addition, with the sport booming in popularity, there were numerous fringe benefits. Television producers jumped on the band wagon, and golf shows—both spot and contrived—mushroomed on the nation's screens. Manufacturers poured millions of dollars into the promotion of equipment and wearing apparel, and battled each other in the subsidization of the bright, new stars on the tournament circuit.

A new breed emerged. Instead of the former caddy, with his tattered bag and run-down heels trying to scratch out a bare existence, the businessman golfer took over the tour. He was college educated, a man who might have made a mark in any field. He was deadly serious and extremely conscientious. To him, tournament golf was like catching the 8:05 train for the office.

He drove to the course in a shiny limousine. He had a dozen pairs of shoes and wore the fanciest silks and cashmeres. His clubs were kept cradled in a rich leather bag. If a bit fastidious, he might even cover the heads of his wood clubs with mink or sable. The more successful carried along his own business agent or a coterie of lawyers to handle his myriad affairs. Champion or second stringer, he always went first class.

Perhaps no one was more impressed by these changing times than Fred Corcoran, the man who nursed the professional tour through its formative years as tournament director of the Professional Golfers Association and whose promotional genius turned it into a multimillion-dollar enterprise.

"In the old days," Corcoran recalled, "we could go to the Hollywood Plaza and get rooms for $3 a day. A roast beef sandwich with potatoes was 25 cents. Caddies cost $1 a round. You could live at Pinehurst on the American plan for $5 a day.

"In those days, you would see these young men in khaki trousers come in and sheepishly pay their small entrance fees. Few of them had decent equipment. They had beat-up golf balls and there hardly was a ten-spot among them. Now you see well-dressed businessmen golfers peeling off big bills as if they were chicken-feed."

Another throwback to the gay but hungry 1920's and 1930's, George Low, well-known scion of a family of professionals, found the contrast a quarter of a century later equally distracting.

"When I was on the tour," Low related, "a guy would win the first prize, and do you know what he would do? He would toss the whole check on the bar and say, 'Okay, fellows, let's drink it up.' And we did. Now what happens? These guys play a round of golf and chase to the practice tee where they work until dark. Then back at the hotel, do you

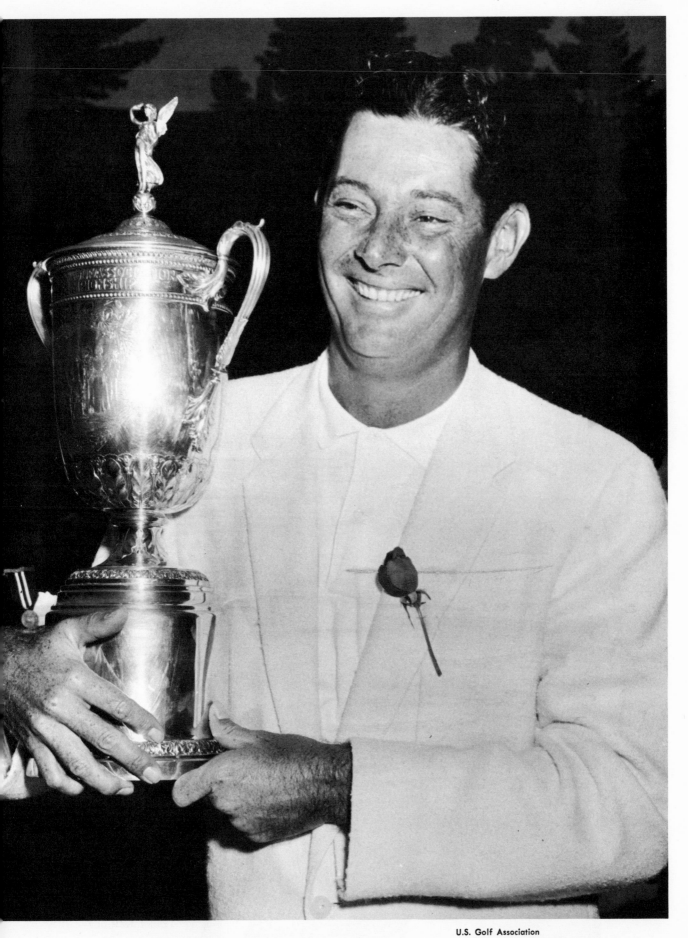

Dr. Cary Middlecoff holds the U. S. Open trophy, which he won in 1949 and 1956.

find them at the bar? No, sir. They're up-stairs, practicing putting on the rug."

Gene Sarazen dubbed them the Trailer Kids when many of them were following the circuit with wives and children in trailers—a fad, incidentally, which had only a brief life immediately after World War II. Sarazen un-hesitatingly agreed that these intent young precisionists were superior to the golfers of his own era, a period that included such masters as Bob Jones and Walter Hagen.

"They are young, strong, and confident," Sarazen said once, in assessing the golf picture in the middle 1950's. "They are the greatest hitters of the ball the game has ever known, playing with the most perfect equipment man can devise and on courses laid out to accent their tremendous power. They are college-trained, men of trigger judgment who can think under pressure. Many of them are ex-servicemen, afraid of nobody."

With Hogan out of the picture, a mad scramble began over his No. 1 position in professional golf. The strongest early bids were made by a taciturn, phlegmatic Navy veteran from San Diego, California, Gene Littler, and a barrel-chested former football player for Duke University named Mike Souchak.

Littler, a blond, good-looking young man of medium stature, joined the pro tour shortly after sinking a dramatic 18-foot putt on the final green for the National Amateur championship at Oklahoma City in 1953. He was an immediate pro success. He missed an 8-foot putt on the last hole, which would have given him a tie with Ed Furgol for the 1954 National Open championship at Baltusrol in New Jersey. He was the sensation of the 1955 winter tour. Self-taught, he had a fluid, one-piece swing which was the envy of his con-temporaries. The movement was so smooth and perfect in its execution that it appeared immune to flaw. Also, the Californian was blessed with an ideal temperament. "He listens without hearing," Sarazen once said, in predicting Littler would challenge the rec-ords of Jones and Hogan.

Burly Mike Souchak, former Duke University football player, was one of the affluent Trailer Kids of the 1950s.

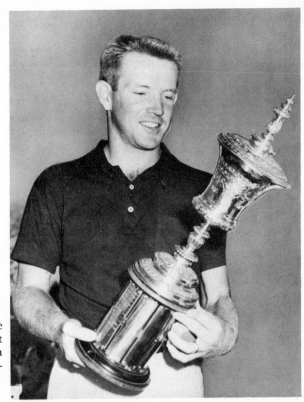

In the early 1950s, golf observers predicted Gene Littler would be one of the game's greatest. Gene lost his grooved swing for a while but came back to win the U. S. Open in 1961 at Oakland Hills in Birmingham, Michigan.

Souchak was a stocky slugger, 5'10", 210 pounds, with tremendous shoulders and arms. He hit his peak about the time Littler was making his strongest mark—in the mid-1950's. He shook up the golf world with a fantastic scoring binge in the Texas Open in the spring of 1955. Playing the Breckenridge Park course—concededly not a tough one but a recognized PGA test, nevertheless—he shot 9 holes in 27, a score once undreamed of, and had an 18-hole round of 60. This was a PGA record until Sam Snead came along a few years later with a 59 at the Greenbrier course in White Sulphur Springs, West Virginia. Mike won the Texas Open with a 72-hole score of 257, setting the PGA all-time record. Then, by way of showing that this performance was not merely a flash in the pan, he went out the following week and won the Houston Open with 273, having one round of 65.

Neither Littler nor Souchak fully measured up to expectations. Both remained sound golfers and consistently high finishers on the tour, but they were unable to seize a dominant position. Littler, impatient with his failure to reach quick success, tampered with his

once impeccable swing and fell into a dismal slump. "I always just put the ball down and hit it," he moaned. "I had no idea how to begin correcting it." Later, he recovered his groove, won the 1961 National Open at Oakland Hills in Birmingham, Michigan, and became a serious challenger again for pro honors. It was in the midst of his slump that he pulled off a rare feat—winning the rich Tournament of Champions at Las Vegas three years in succession, 1955, 1956, and 1957. Souchak, a tremendous hitter and one of the game's most popular performers, became a golfing bridesmaid: he often caught the bouquet but never managed to wed a big championship. Playing superbly, he tied for third in the U.S. Open in 1959 and 1960 and for fourth in 1961. He missed those three titles by a total of eight shots.

In addition to Littler and Souchak, the so-called Trailer Brigade of the 1950's included Jay Hebert, Billy Maxwell, Bud Holscher, Gardner Dickinson, Dave Ragan, Tom Lema, and Bob Rosburg. Arnold Palmer, who later was to emerge as the game's outstanding personality, was back in the pack at this time, just getting ready to make his move.

Many of these young golfers were able to stay on the tour through a syndicate plan borrowed directly from Wall Street. They made the tournament circuit on money provided by a patron or a group of friends with contracts to share in any prosperity the players might achieve. Lema, who served in the Marines during the Korean war, first was financed by Ed Lowery, San Francisco automobile dealer who launched Ken Venturi on a pro career, and later by a Sun Valley, Idaho, millionaire. Ragan made a deal with two Daytona Beach, Florida, businessmen who staked him to $12,000 a year for two years. Bill Casper got a $1,000 monthly allowance from a pair of financiers in Chula Vista, California, who shared in Casper's winnings. Ferree was backed by a Mobile, Alabama, steamship owner. Others had similar arrangements for staying on the tour.

The nickname of the Trailer Kids soon became obsolete. The young golfing tourists quickly gave up the mobile home arrangement and turned to sleek automobiles and commercial air travel in jumping from tournament to tournament. The mode of commutation failed to bring any greater success to the new, young breed. The period that spanned the fadeout of the great Hogan and the elevation of Palmer to the throne of golf was dominated by members of a group who called themselves "The Forgotten Middles," too young to be bracketed with the Hogan Era, too old to be associated with the misnamed Trailer Kids.

Julius Boros, a big, easy-swinging son of a Hungarian immigrant, interrupted Hogan's string of Open victories in 1952. Ed Furgol, an amazing cripple whose left arm was eight inches shorter than his right, crashed through in 1954 at Baltusrol and obscure Jack Fleck, from Iowa's corn country, beat Hogan in a play-off at San Francisco in 1955. Cary Middlecoff, the intense, highly nervous Memphis dentist, won his second Open crown at Rochester, New York, in 1956 and lost in a play-off the next year to handsome Dick Mayer at Toledo's Inverness Club. Terrible-

Consistent winners on the pro tour: Mike Souchak, Bill Casper, Bob Rosburg.

They called boyish Jackie Burke, Jr., "sophomore of the year for seven years." He's shown at the Masters, where he won in 1956.

tempered but rhythmic-swinging Tommy Bolt led every round in the sweltering heat at Tulsa in 1958. Bill Casper, Jr., put on a miraculous putting exhibition to win at Winged Foot in 1959—the year before Palmer crashed through at Denver.

Meanwhile, Middlecoff, Jack Burke, Doug Ford, and Art Wall, Jr., were starring in the Masters at Augusta. Burke and Ford added their names to the PGA championship roll, along with Chick Harbert, Dow Finsterwald and the Hebert brothers from Louisiana, Lionel and Jay. The big championships passed from hand to hand. No one was ready —yet—to establish himself as the undisputed king, in the tradition of Jones and Hogan.

Similarly, a serious amateur threat failed to materialize. Frank Stranahan, heir to a Toledo spark plug fortune, was one of those rare amateurs who never had to worry about ex-

penses. After World War II, he was able to concentrate on golf and follow the pro tour. Occasionally, he won one of the pro tournaments and passed up the cash. He won the British Amateur twice, in 1948 and 1950, but the American Amateur repeatedly escaped him, although he was generally recognized as the best amateur of his day. His greatest heartbreak came in 1950 when he reached the U.S. Amateur final at Minneapolis only to lose to Sam Urzetta, the janitor's son from Rochester, New York, on the thirty-ninth hole. Finally, discouraged by such repeated setbacks, Stranahan turned professional.

Harvie Ward, a graduate of the University of North Carolina, shot to the top in his field by beating Stranahan for the British Amateur title in 1952 and putting U.S. Amateur titles back-to-back in 1955 and 1956. Just when he was aiming at championship No. 3 and

119

Frail Art Wall, Jr., battled par and infirmities throughout a colorful but spotty career. He made more than 30 holes-in-one, won the Masters in 1959.

Doug Ford was one of the fastest and most controversial players on the pro tour. He won the PGA title in 1955, the Masters in 1957.

threatening to become the strongest amateur menace since Bob Jones, he drew a slap from the U.S. Golf Association for expense irregularities. Although it was a mild, innocent offense and the disciplinary action not too severe, Ward never recovered from the blow. He seemed to have no heart for golf after that.

Discouragement of another sort dulled the incentive of another promising amateur, Ken Venturi, a close friend of Ward's and like Ward a protégé of Ed Lowery, San Francisco automobile dealer. Venturi, with starting rounds of 66-69-75, seemed certain to become the first amateur to win the Masters championship in 1956 before he lost eight strokes to the ultimate winner, Jack Burke, Jr., on the final day. Four years later, now a professional, Venturi was trying on the green Masters' champion jacket for size when Arnold Palmer came charging in with one of his typical birdie finishes to beat out Ken by a single stroke.

Billie Joe Patton, a long-knocking, wise-cracking lumber executive from Morganton, North Carolina, led the Masters through the first two rounds and sank a hole-in-one on the sixth hole of the final round to finish only one stroke back of Ben Hogan and Sam Snead in 1954. Patton's unique knock for banging out of trouble and spicing every round with his drawling humor made him a standout showman, but he never scaled championship heights.

These were pinnacles on which had been placed reservation cards bearing two names: Arnold Palmer and Jack Nicklaus.

Chapter Seventeen

Arnold Palmer—The Charger

Golf, the orphan game born on the wastes and warrens of Scotland's wind-swept seacoast, moved into the world's comfortable parlors in the late 1950's and early 1960's. It was the Jet and Electronic Age. A flick of the television dial could bring the most picturesque courses and most exciting players into the living room—and TV sponsors and producers quickly capitalized on the appeal. Birdies and bogeys replaced cowboys and Indians as the Saturday and Sunday afternoon channels became choked with live and taped golf competitions.

To meet this new development, it was necessary that the game produce a hero. It did. His name was Arnold Palmer. He was a rugged, strong-faced son of a greenskeeper and professional in the little steel town of Latrobe, Pennsylvania, about 30 miles from Pittsburgh. A sturdy 165 pounds, he was built like a middleweight fighter with a thin waist and powerful tapering shoulders. He had hands like hams and arms like pistons. His boyish, deeply-tanned face ran the gamut of changing expressions. When concentrating, his brow became furrowed and his jaw tightened like a vice, a cigarette always dangling from his lips. When he rolled in a long birdie putt—which, his opponents grumbled, came distractingly often—his face broke into a wide grin. He carried on a running conversation with the gallery.

Personal magnetism, however, was only a fraction of Palmer's amazing appeal. It was his faculty for miracle finishes—dramatic spurts on the stretch holes which pulled victory from the jaws of defeat—which really captivated the public.

It got to a point that fans flocked to the big tournaments in mushrooming thousands, and millions of others hugged their television sets just to see another Palmer miracle. No matter how far he fell behind, these devoted disciples were convinced Arnie could pull it out. Fantastically, he often did—usually in the big championships where the money stakes and prestige values were high and everybody was watching. He became a legend. Just as the Lone Ranger could be expected to gallop up on his white charger and rescue the maiden in distress in the final reel, so Palmer could be counted on to salvage a tournament victory with a closing burst of birdies.

Thus, Palmer's following was not restricted to golf fans, people who admired him for the power of his swing or the precision of his putting stroke. Housewives addicted to the hanging-cliff soap operas, teen-agers and others knowing little or nothing about the game of golf joined his host of admirers which became known as "Arnie's Army."

"Arnie's Army" was an institution in itself, numbering thousands, perhaps millions. In increasing numbers, they swarmed to the tournaments to lend their moral support. Some carried signs proclaiming: "I am a member of Arnie's Army." Young ladies wore sweaters with "Arnie Baby" crocheted across the chest.

Arnold Palmer

Galleries were intrigued by Arnold Palmer's facial expressions. Here Arnie winces after missing a putt in a play-off with Jack Nicklaus for the 1962 U. S. Open title at Oakmont, Pennsylvania. Nicklaus won.

Most of them were loud and demonstrative, often embarrassing Palmer and creating problems during the course of play.

"It's very distracting," one prominent tournament player said. "These people have a regard for no one but Palmer. If he putts first, they break and run, stampeding for the next hole. They don't care how much they bother the other players."

It reached a point that Palmer was forced to putt last—even out of turn—out of deference to his playing companions. He often raised his hand and admonished the crowd, "Let the other players putt out, please." It did little good. Arnie's Army operated under its own rules, which were almost nonexistent. They needled Palmer's rivals, particularly Jack Nicklaus, whom they feared most of all. They ran and yelled like a pack of wild animals.

Palmer, appreciative of this intense loyalty, sought to harness his wild fan club, as one would tame a broncho. He copyrighted the name "Arnie's Army." He sent letters and official buttons to the members. Their enthusiasm, however, continued unabated. It was understandable. Their hero was a fabulous character.

Although he won the National Amateur in 1954 and his first Masters in 1958, Palmer did not really fire the imagination of the golfing public until the Masters of 1960.

In that one, Ken Venturi finished with a score of 283 and went to the little white club house to start trying on the traditional green champion's jacket for size and to get a briefing for the television interview. He seemed the sure winner, although a small knot of players was still on the Augusta National course, including Palmer.

Palmer failed to get needed birdies at the thirteenth and fifteenth, so he came to the seventeenth tee needing one birdie on the

Arnie's Army took to the air during the Masters Tournament in 1964 when a plane flew over the Augusta National course trailing the sign: "Go Arnie Go." Arnie went, winning his fourth Masters title.

final two holes to gain a tie. His chances were considered remote. These are two of the toughest finishing holes in big-time golf.

Palmer's drive was long and down the middle on the seventeenth, a 400-yard down-wind hole playing a par 4. He hit an eight-iron pitch to the green where the ball hit and sat down too quickly, leaving him a 25-foot putt. Twice Arnold lined up the putt and took his stance, only to step away when he became distracted by movement in the crowd. Finally, he tapped the ball firmly. The ball rolled toward the cup, seemed to hesitate a moment and then plop in. A birdie. Par on the closing hole would gain him a tie.

On the eighteenth, a 420-yard hole uphill and into the wind, Palmer decided to go for it boldly. He was shooting for a victory now, and not for a tie. He boomed his drive to the left, giving him a straightaway shot at the pin, set to the right on the lower deck of the massive green. He hardly hesitated as he punched a six-iron shot low into the teeth of the wind. The ball spun to the left and came to rest 5 feet from the cup.

With pressure tremendous and the eyes of millions watching on television screens, Arnold studied the putt carefully. He dropped a half-smoked cigarette to the green, hunched over the ball in that familiar knock-kneed stance and hit it. The ball hit the left-hand side of the cup and dropped. With birdies on the final two holes, Palmer had his second Masters championship. More than that, he now had a reputation he never was to lose as long as he was in his prime—the miracle maker of golf.

This blazing finish in a tournament renowned for the spectacular made Palmer the game's new "Golden Boy." He had the golf world at his feet.

"I won't be content," Palmer said afterward, "until I score a professional Grand Slam. My ambition is to win the Masters, the U.S. and British Opens and the PGA, all in a single year. I think it would be a greater achievement than Bobby Jones's Grand Slam in 1930."

The second leg was the U.S. Open at Cherry Hills in Denver, and it appeared that

124

the flame of Palmer's lofty golfing goal was destined to flicker away almost before it was fully lit. Big Mike Souchak got off to a blistering start with rounds of 68-67 while Palmer was scrambling around in 72-71. After a third round 72, Arnold's prospects were no brighter. He was seven shots back of the leader, Souchak, and there were 14 players between him and the top.

It looked like an impossible situation. It was the kind of spot that challenged Palmer—and thrilled "Arnie's Army."

"Go, Arnie, go!" they screamed, as players teed off for the final round in the afternoon. Arnie responded.

Palmer drove the first hole, a 346-yarder with an elevated tee, and two-putted from 20 feet for an opening birdie. On the 410-yard second, he holed out a 30-foot chip shot from off the green. He hit a wedge shot to within a foot of the hole on the third and sank a 20-foot putt on the fourth.

Four birdies in a row, and the crowd was going wild. Spirits fell when Arnie had to settle for a par 5 on the long fifth after catching a trap, but they revived quickly. Palmer nailed another birdie at the short sixth, sinking from 25 feet, and a wedge shot 6 feet from the pin brought still another at the 411-yard seventh.

At this stage, Palmer had played seven holes and birdied six of them. It was one of the most amazing spurts under pressure that the old game had ever known.

At the 230-yard eighth, Arnold dumped his tee shot into a trap, blasted to within 3 feet and then missed to take a bogey four. He scrambled for his par at the ninth, having to sink an 8-foot putt after hitting a six-iron shot over the green, then chipping long. But he turned in 30, equaling the lowest 9 holes ever shot in the Open, and he was back in contention. He played the incoming 9 in one-under-par for a 65, lowest score ever shot on a final round by the winner, for a 72-hole total of 280.

The hard-luck Souchak skied to a closing 75 for 283—three shots back. Both Ben Hogan,

trying for his fifth Open, and Jack Nicklaus, then an amateur, had a shot at the title but failed. Hogan, gambling for a birdie, missed the green by inches on the seventy-first hole and went into the water. Shaken, he took a triple bogey seven at the final hole to finish at 284. Nicklaus three-putted the thirteenth and fourteenth greens and wound up at 282, lowest score ever shot by an amateur in the Open. Palmer won by two shots.

From Denver, Palmer flew to the Centennial Anniversary British Open at historic St. Andrews in Scotland where he missed by a slender stroke in his bid to add a third jewel to golf's professional Quadruple Crown. He was making one of his patented rallies when a heavy rain-storm forced postponement of the last round and he finished as runner-up to Kel Nagle of Australia. Back home, he led the first round of the PGA at Akron, Ohio, but fell off the pace and the title went to Jay Hebert. He had missed his Grand Slam by an eyelash.

Palmer gets a kiss from wife, Winnie, after winning his second straight British Open Championship at Troon, Scotland, in 1962.

It's not a stampede, it's "Arnie's Army," the scrambling gallery which adopted Palmer as its hero.

Nevertheless, the image was established. Palmer held the patent for exciting comebacks. He was golf's birdie man. "The Charger," they christened him. Every time he teed up the ball, his fans came to expect the impossible.

In a play-off for the Masters crown in 1962, he fell three shots back of Gary Player, of South Africa, after nine holes, then birdied five of the first seven holes on the incoming side to win by three strokes. Proving he was human, he took a 12 on one hole in the Los Angeles Open, hitting two tee shots out of bounds before he ever put a ball into play. He had the 1961 Masters in his pocket only to blow up on the last hole, taking a double bogey six and losing by a shot to Player.

He won some and lost some, yet he went on to become the greatest money winner in the sport's history. His official winnings approached the $500,000 mark before he was 35. In 1963, although failing to win a major title, he set an all-time single season's mark by collecting more than $125,000; a figure later topped twice by Jack Nicklaus. Through other enterprises related to golf he pushed his yearly income to the $1,000,000 bracket, making him the No. 1 capitalist of the game.

He became the outstanding sports personality of his day—as well as the richest. He was writer, actor, teacher, business tycoon. Five lawyers, working for him almost exclusively, were needed to handle his business and financial interests. Two secretaries were hired full-time simply to answer his fan mail.

He set up his own company, which manufactured golf clubs, balls, shirts, slacks, shoes, and gloves. He headed 11 apparel companies with branches in Australia, Japan, and Europe. He was the largest stockholder in a chain of putting courses, had an interest in a number of driving ranges and owned a part of two swank country clubs. He owned his own printing company, an insurance agency, and investment firm. He produced golf carts, driving nets, and table-top golf games, all bearing his name.

He acted in the movies, took bit roles on television, produced and played in his own television show "Challenge Golf," cut instructional records, and endorsed a half-dozen items ranging from cigarettes to automobiles. He received as much as $5,000 for taking a bow on a TV show.

Palmer acknowledged that the pressure of his myriad business enterprises often affected his golf, but said he refused to let them steal away his principal interests and dedication.

"When I feel myself getting burdened with business, I just knock off, go back home and play golf with Pap," he said. "I think it's important to make money while you can, but my chief aim is to be the best golfer in the world. I won't let anything interfere with that aim."

"Pap" was Milfred (Deac) Palmer, Arnie's father, teacher, and severest critic, who started as greenskeeper and later became professional of the little nine-hole course in Latrobe where Arnold swung his first club shortly after he was big enough to walk.

"I don't think Deac ever once told Arnie that he thought he had made it," Arnold's mother once said, in describing the unique father-son relationship. "He's told me, but he would never tell Arnie—he wouldn't give him that much satisfaction."

"We argue and fight like cats and dogs," Arnold once said of his down-to-earth dad.

Born September 10, 1929, in Latrobe, Arnold Palmer was given his first golf club by his father when he was four. By the time he was seven or eight, he was playing golf regularly with some of the older boys who served as caddies at his dad's course and became a caddy himself when he was around 11.

"I couldn't wait to get out of school and get on the golf course," Arnie recalled later. "I hated to study, but nobody had to force me to work on my golf. I loved every minute of it. And even in those days, I hated to hit a bad shot. It made me feel awful."

Palmer later became caddy master at the club—"the worst I've ever had," Deac Palmer said—but he was constantly locking up the shop and sneaking out on the course to play. He worked around the course from 7 A.M. until noon, ate lunch and then worked in the shop until around 8 P.M. It was in the shop

Joy or anguish? It's hard to tell but it's really anguish after Arnold Palmer misses a 15-foot putt in 1963 Cleveland Open. Palmer won anyhow.

Wide World

that he learned to work on clubs—wrap the grips, hammer the shafts, and even shellac the woods. It was an art he never forgot nor ever became disenchanted with. While winning major championships, he often strode directly from the course to the shop and started hacking away at his clubs.

When he was in the seventh grade, he shot a 71 and won a local tournament. In 1946, he played in his first national championship—a junior event—but did not do well. The tournament was won by a youngster Arnold was to run into quite often later on the pro tour— Bob Rosburg.

Palmer later entered Wake Forest College but quit midway of his senior year after his closest friend, Bud Worsham, was killed in an automobile accident. Restless and on an impulse, he signed up for three years in the U.S. Coast Guard. For several months he hardly played golf at all. Then he was transferred to Cleveland where his interest in the game was revived by a group of friends who played regularly every week—rain, snow, or shine.

Arnold was 24 when he got out of the Coast Guard. He returned to Wake Forest, hoping to complete his education, but he pulled out again after one semester. "I just couldn't apply myself," he said later. He returned to

Cleveland where he got a job as a manufacturer's agent.

At this time, Palmer said he had no intention of ever playing golf seriously or of ever turning professional. In 1954, Arnold won the National Amateur at the Country Club of Detroit, beating Robert Sweeny 1-up in the final round. It was shortly after that, while playing in a tournament at Shawnee on Delaware, Pennsylvania, that he met Winnie Walzer, daughter of a Coopersburg, Pennsylvania, manufacturer. Within less than a week, he had proposed and the two were discussing plans for a honeymoon in England during the Walker Cup matches the following spring.

The more he thought about it, the more Palmer became convinced that if he planned to continue playing golf he should do it for money. He talked it over with his father, who himself always had had an ambition to play on the tour. He discussed it with Winnie, his bride-to-be. On November 19, 1954, he turned professional, signing a contract with a sporting goods company. He married Winnie during the Christmas holidays.

Palmer started his pro career on little more than a shoestring. Under Professional Golfers Association rules, he was ineligible to accept prize money from PGA-sponsored tourna-

Both Palmer and his caddy throw themselves into an act as Arnie's eagle putt rolls past the cup on the 13th hole in the final round of the 1964 Masters Tournament.

The strong features of Arnold Palmer are immortalized in bronze in this bust presented to the Golf House Museum. Arnie and wife Winnie examine the work with the sculptor, Eleanor Mellon.

ments until he had served six months' probation. However, he picked up $750 in a pro-amateur competition in Miami, and then went to Panama, where he tied Roberto de Vicenzo in a non-PGA event, collecting $1,300.

This was a stake. Arnold and Winnie bought an old trailer to be hauled around by their 1952 automobile and joined the tour on the Pacific Coast. Later they picked up a new trailer through a $600 loan from Winnie's parents. Palmer won enough money in non-sanctioned tournaments to keep the wolf away from the door until his probationary period was up. Success followed quickly. He was the leading money winner in 1958 with $42,607. Big paydays followed as a matter of regular course.

Three years after turning professional, the Palmers built a white ranch house overlooking the Latrobe Country Club course. There was an acre of romping room for their two daughters and a driveway large enough to accommodate their three limousines—a far cry from the second-hand trailer and jalopy with which they started their grand adventure.

While his last-gasp, pulse-pounding finishes may have been thrilling to Palmer's fans, they were little fun for the architect himself.

129

"People are always accusing me of purposely getting behind so that I can pull out of the hole," Arnold once said. "That's ridiculous. On those tight finishes, I bleed a little bit myself. If I had my way, I would win every tournament by 12 strokes."

Gene Sarazen said Palmer was a counterpuncher. "He's most dangerous when he's on the ropes, ready to be counted out," the old champion once remarked, in discussing the new.

"He's fantastic—he just seems to will the ball into the hole," said Jimmy Demaret.

One of the best insights into the course character of the Pennsylvania comeback wizard was offered by Palmer's long-time caddy at the Masters tournament, Nathaniel (Iron Man) Avery.

"It's let it go or blow it, all or nothing," Iron Man said in trying to describe Palmer's techniques. "This man don't know what it is to play safe."

The Negro bag-toter said he could always tell when Palmer was ready to make one of his fabulous charges.

"He tugs at his glove, jerks on his trousers, and starts walking fast," Iron Man said, "and then he turns to me and says, 'The game is on.'"

There apparently is a limit to the juices that can charge a man up for such unusual deeds.

Palmer started running into mild slumps, beginning in 1962. Then the slumps got bigger. Finally, like other golfers advancing in years, Arnie found himself fighting a war with his nerves.

Muscles aren't the first thing to go for the golf competitor, Ben Hogan always contended, it's the putting nerves. Palmer discovered this to be true.

"I haven't putted well since 1960," Palmer lamented during one of his slumps in 1963. "My game is better than it ever was from tee to green. I simply can't get the ball in the hole."

Usually when his game soured, Palmer returned to his home at Latrobe, Pennsylvania, and worked with his father. In a couple of weeks he would return to the tour good as new and start winning again.

This formula was not sufficient for the letdown that struck him early in the 1964 campaign and persisted through 1965. In April 1964, Arnie won his fourth Masters. Five weeks later he captured the Oklahoma City Open. Then the victory drouth began.

During the next 18 months, the frustrated Pennsylvania strong man won only one tournament—the Tournament of Champions at Las Vegas, April 29—May 2, 1965—and he failed miserably in his bids for the major championships.

During the 1964 season, he suffered a runner-up complex. He finished second in six tournaments and third in three, making enough money to finish only $81 back of leading winner Jack Nicklaus, but his slump went from bad to worse.

He tied Gary Player for the runner-up spot in the 1965 masters, won by Nicklaus, but could muster no serious charge in the other prestige events.

His bitterest disappointment came in the 1965 Professional Golfers Association Championship, played over his home course, the Laurel Valley Country Club. The PGA was the only major title Palmer had not won. Now in his own back yard, before thousands of his home folks, he was prepared to make the supreme effort.

Calamity struck quickly. On the first hole of the opening round, Arnie drew a two-stroke penalty for allowing the removal of some wooden railings that obstructed his shot. He finished the round with a one-over-par 72.

The nightmare came on the par-5 eleventh on the second round. Arnie pushed his drive into a bunker protecting the elbow of the long, dog-leg hole. He hit his second to the right, the ball rolling into a nest of stones at the bottom of a drainage ditch. Hitting from an awkward stance, he moved the ball only about 20 yards into some high rough. He plopped his fourth shot into a bunker, blasted out and was on the green in 5. He missed a tricky two-foot putt and got an apparent seven. However, it was later ruled that on his second shot from the nest of stones, Palmer had nicked one of the stones on his backswing. He was penalized two shots and given a 9 on the hole.

He rallied slightly for a 75 but shot 74 and 73 on the final two rounds for a 72-hole score of 294. He finished 14 strokes back of the winner, Dave Marr.

Most observers attributed Arnie's decline to the pressure of his growing business enterprises. Palmer stoutly denied it. "Golf is my life," he said. "I like to win. I am determined to win. No amount of money can change that."

ARNOLD PALMER'S RECORD

U.S. Amateur Champion: 1954.

U.S. Open Champion: 1960. (Tied for title in 1962, lost in play-off to Jack Nicklaus, 71–74; tied in 1963, finished third in three-way play-off with winner Julius Boros and Jacky Cupit with scores of 70, 73, 76, respectively.)

Masters Champion: 1958, 1960, 1962, 1964. (Runner-up in 1961.)

British Open Champion: 1961, 1962. (Runner-up in 1960.)

Leading Money Winner: 1960, 1962, 1963.

Vardon Trophy Winner: 1961, 1962.

Ryder Cup Member: 1961, 1963, 1965. Singles, won 3, tied 2; team, won 7, lost 2, tied 1.

Canada Cup Member: 1960, 1962, 1963, 1964. (Shared team title each year.)

Chapter Eighteen

Jack Nicklaus: "The Golden Bear"

Golf moved through the Spectacular Sixties to the tune of ringing cash registers pouring out their multimillion-dollar purses, the roars of record galleries, and booming drives which made birdies and eagles—not pars—the standard of tournament excellence. It became a brand new game. It was the age of brute strength. Style became passé. Sheer, unadorned power was the king. Every player—every one who succeeded, that is—was a home-run hitter.

Byron Nelson, his temples graying and his trim waistline showing the first faint signs of a bulge, stood near the eighteenth green at the Augusta National course during a Masters tournament in the early 1960's and sadly lamented the passing of an era.

"When Ben Hogan, Sam Snead and I were in our prime," Nelson said, harking back to the 1940's and early 1950's, "we were more conscious of style. We were careful how we looked. We took great pains to stroke the ball properly. We played position golf. We managed our way around the course, attempting to make every shot meticulously perfect.

"The modern players have thrown style out the window. All they think about is getting to the hole. They don't see anything but the flag. Their idea is to boom the ball out there as far as they can. They don't worry about how they look. Some of them, Arnold Palmer as an example, almost fall off the tee after they hit the ball. Trouble doesn't bother them. They figure they are strong enough to get out of it—and they usually are. They just slug away, going for birdies on every hole."

Representative of this new, young breed of home-run sluggers on the golf tour was a blond giant out of the Midwest named Jack Nicklaus. They called him the "Golden Bear." He drove the ball higher, straighter, and farther with more consistency than any player who had ever lived. He was a superb putter—exasperatingly slow but remarkably sure. He was a cold and calculating competitor, poised and mature beyond his years, even when he was winning national championships in his teens and early twenties.

No man, with the possible exception of Bob Jones, hit the game with greater impact. Nicklaus won the first of his two National Amateur championships at the age of 19. At 20, playing in the World Amateur Team Championship for the Eisenhower Trophy, he put together consecutive rounds of 66, 67, 68, 68 for a score of 269 over the Merion course outside Philadelphia—18 strokes better than Ben Hogan had played the same formidable layout 10 years earlier in winning the National Open. The same year, 1960, he shot the lowest 72-hole score ever recorded by an amateur in the U.S. Open.

The golf world was hailing this big, broad-beamed youngster as "another Jones" in the fall of 1961, after an overpowering performance in the American Amateur at Pebble Beach, California, when Nicklaus decided to turn pro. His pro debut was equally meteoric.

Jack Nicklaus

He won the National Open in his first try as a pro, beating Palmer in an 18-hole play-off for the 1962 title at Oakmont, Pennsylvania. At 22, he became the youngest player in 39 years to capture the blue ribbon championship of American golf. A few weeks later, he met Palmer again in a head-to-head duel and again whipped his powerful rival in a 36-hole battle for the $50,000 first prize of the rich, televised World Series.

If Palmer and members of Palmer's mushrooming "Arnie's Army" felt that Nicklaus was enjoying a streak of beginner's luck and would fall victim the next year to the inevitable sophomore jinx, they were doomed to disappointment.

If the "Golden Bear" completed his apprenticeship with the winning of the Open in 1962, then he finally matured in 1963 at the tender age of 23. He won the Masters at Augusta. Bothered by a hip ailment, he failed to qualify for the last 36 holes in defense of his U.S. Open crown at Brookline, Massachusetts, but he refused to be deterred for long. In the British Open at St. Anne's-on-the-Sea in England, he needed to par only the last two holes for victory, but instead took two bogeys and missed by a single stroke. He came home to win the Professional Golfers Association championship at Dallas. He defeated Julius Boros, Arnold Palmer, and Bob Charles in capturing the $50,000 first prize in golf's

It was Jack Nicklaus, *left,* who really threw the punch at Oakmont, Pennsylvania, where he beat Arnold Palmer in a play-off for the U. S. Open Championship.

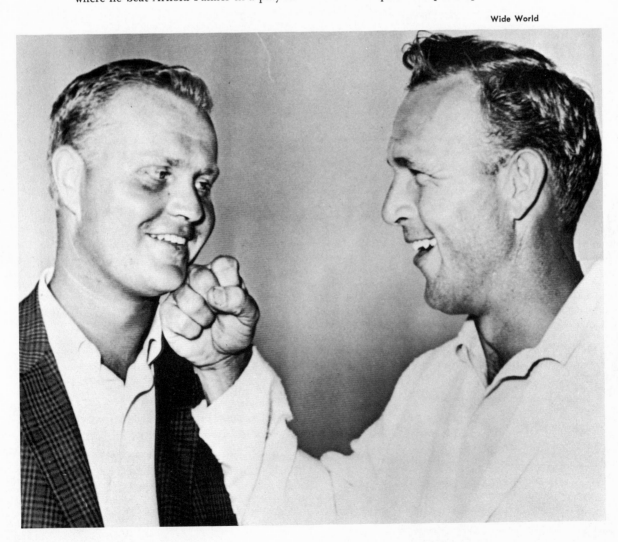

World Series for a second time. Then he climaxed his banner season by winning the Canada Cup International Trophy against leading players from 30 nations at Paris.

In less than two years, Nicklaus thus had been able to win all three of America's premier golf crowns—the Open, Masters, and PGA. Only three other players—Gene Sarazen, Ben Hogan, and Byron Nelson—had achieved this feat, but none at such a young age and in so short a space of time.

"Jack Nicklaus has reached his peak," commented Sam Snead in reviewing the youngster's 1963 season. "He has been playing top competitive golf since he was 14. No man can go to the trough that many times without having a lot taken away from him.

"So it is with Nicklaus. He has reached his plateau. I don't think he will get any better."

Snead's analysis was hardly out of his mouth before Nicklaus replied by beating out Palmer for the year's money winning honors in 1964 and then cracking Ben Hogan's 12-year record by winning his second Masters in 1965 with a phenomenal 17-under-par 271.

Bob Jones, originator of the Masters, called it "the greatest performance in golf tournament history."

Just when Arnold Palmer had shot his way to the pinnacle of the sport and appeared destined to dominate it for at least a decade in what loomed as the "Palmer Era," he looked over his shoulder to see the ominous and imposing shadow of the boyish behemoth from Columbus, Ohio.

It was an unsettling prospect. Here was a young man who could out hit Palmer almost every time off the tee, and keep the ball in the fairway. Furthermore, Nicklaus could rifle his iron shots at the pin and knock in birdie putts from across the green. He girded these physical attributes with an unshakeable, imperturbable temperament. "That big, strong, happy dude," Palmer once remarked with mixed admiration and envy. "He's ten years younger than I am and already has as much experience. He makes me feel like an old man."

Quick, early success proved one of Nicklaus' chief assets. Like Bob Jones, Walter Hagen, and Gene Sarazen, he reached competitive maturity at an early age. This kept him free of financial worries and the kind of complexes that haunt a man until he can win a major championship and prove himself. Some great golfers, such as Lighthorse Harry Cooper and Sam Snead in the case of the elusive U.S. Open, never shook off the nagging ghost. Hogan was 35 when he won his first Open, Palmer 30.

Nicklaus' other assets included his awesome harnessed power, a brilliant golfing mind, and excellent temperament, but he also had his liabilities. These were always at his elbow, threatening to push him back into obscurity should he ever relax his vigilance.

One of Jack's greatest problems was that of ballooning weight. He came from a German family which enjoyed good food. As a result, he carried on a constant battle with the scales. He was called "Blob-o" and "Whaleman" by his mates at Ohio State. The players on the pro tour immediately dubbed him "Ohio Fats." Nicklaus inwardly was offended by constant references to his size, but outwardly he took it in good grace.

On off season, Nicklaus, a six-footer, might let his weight get up to 220 pounds, with an inclination to get beefy around the hips and thighs, but on the tour a strict discipline and diet kept him down to around 200 pounds. "I am naturally big," Nicklaus insisted. "I feel stronger and play better at around 200 or 210 pounds."

As in the case of many finely tuned athletes, Nicklaus also suffered from a variety of physical ailments. His back gave him periodic trouble, forcing him to the sidelines for several weeks in the winter of 1962–1963 and striking him again just before the 1963 National Open. He treated cramps and tension of muscles with hydrocortisone and hot baths. He also had foot problems stemming from high arches. However, these minor aches and pains never seriously affected his game.

If Nicklaus had any faults, his fellow pros said, they were his tendency toward excruciatingly slow and methodical play and an apparent easygoing attitude. The latter might be interpreted to include lack of killer instinct. Both criticisms were subject to debate and grew weaker as Nicklaus' stature grew with tournament victory after tournament victory.

Nicklaus' relaxed, almost casual approach to the game was very deceptive. What some observers, including his rivals, interpreted as lack of fire and spirit proved in the long run to be tremendous, unbreakable calm. It was never possible to tell after one of Nicklaus' rounds whether he shot a 67 or an 80. He never blew up. He never, as was the habit of some headline competitors, rushed from the course in a huff without stopping to change his shoes.

The Columbus powerhouse resented suggestions that he lacked determination. "Competitive spirit is something inside a man," Nicklaus said. "People have entirely different makeups. Just because I don't jut out my jaw and jerk at my trousers doesn't mean that I have no desire. I think I want to win just as much as the next man. I can't help it if I don't wear my feelings on my sleeve."

If there was a jumpy nerve or an ounce of tension in Jack's hulking frame, it was never evident. Bob Jones became so keyed up before a major match that he was unable to keep food on his stomach. Hogan was a grim, taciturn butcher, jaws set like a vise as he chopped the course to pieces. Palmer was the chatty, wisecracking extrovert until he got one of his come-from-behind charges going. His lips tightened. His motions became jerky. He started moving fast between shots.

Nicklaus fit more closely into the Hogan mold. Not as sullen or intent as the Texas Hawk, he was a study in concentration. He ambled over the course in his traditional gray slacks, white turtleneck shirt and white cap without saying more than a couple of words. They said he looked without seeing and listened without hearing.

"I think he has a metal tube running from one ear to the other," Sarazen once commented of the young champion. "I've never seen a player who could shut himself off from all around him the way this fellow does. He puts himself in an invisible isolation booth."

On the course, Nicklaus may have been a frigid machine—phlegmatic and withdrawn. Off it, he was loose and relaxed, becoming the boy again. He had a good sense of humor, never dulled by a disappointing round. He talked excitedly in a high-pitched, squeaky voice, incongruous with his hulking size.

He never denied that he was a slow player, and he never apologized. "Golf is my living," he said once, retorting to criticism over his snail's-pace play. "Nobody tells me how to make my living."

Nicklaus followed the pattern of Hogan in walking off every course in practice rounds before a tournament and making a detailed chart of each hole. Whereas Hogan memorized desirable and undesirable positions and had the distances engraved on his photographic mind, Jack found it necessary to jot down landmarks and various yardages on a card which he kept stuffed in a rear pocket.

"It takes the guesswork out of golf," Nicklaus once explained. "I write it on a card because I'm not as smart as Hogan and can't remember it. Besides, I never saw the point in burdening my mind with all those details when it isn't necessary."

Before almost every shot, Nicklaus would haul out his chart and study his location. Sometimes, from the fairway, he would walk halfway to the green and back to his ball before executing the shot. This added to the slowness of his play and often to the exasperation of his opponents. He refused to be pushed or hurried.

Nicklaus was even more painstaking on the putting greens. He studied his line with the greatest of care. No obstacle, no hidden break escaped his close scrutiny. He hunched over the ball like a frozen grizzly bear—his head low and his knees together in knock-kneed

Nicklaus tosses his cap into the air after winning the 1963 Masters at Augusta.

fashion. He seemed to wait minutes—actually it was only seconds—before he brought the blade back. Then, playing the ball well forward, he struck it with a deftness and a gentleness that seemed out of keeping for a man of his heft and power. He was a bear with a feathery touch.

There was nothing gentle or feathery, however, about the way he tore into a ball off the tee. His drive was pure thunder, without lightning. There was nothing classic about the Nicklaus swing. It had none of Snead's fluid grace, Hogan's grooved crispness, or Nelson's rifle-like precision. It was sheer, explosive power that sent the ball screaming high and far into the air.

Because of his small, stubby fingers, Nicklaus employed the old-fashioned interlocking instead of the universal overlapping grip. He brought the club back stiffly, his head bobbing, and then uncoiled with his right knee forcing his left side out of the way and his right elbow flying away from his body. By no stretch of the imagination could it have been called a picture swing. But the impact was

like a thunderclap. The ball took off like a cannon shot. "I learned a long time ago not to worry too much about style," Nicklaus said. "My aim is to get the ball out there and keep it moving."

Jack Nicklaus was moving the ball almost from the day he was born—January 21, 1940, in Columbus, Ohio. The son of a prosperous and sports-minded pharmacist, his father, L. Charles Nicklaus, had played football, baseball, and basketball at Ohio State. He had taken a fling at pro football with the Portsmouth Spartans, had won the Columbus city tennis championship, and set two records on the municipal golf course, where he played on weekends.

It was only natural that Jack and his sister, Marilyn, born three years later, should become interested in sports. Jack played football, baseball, and basketball on the playgrounds and in school, but it was evident the first time he swung a club that golf was his game.

Jack was 10, a slender, tow-headed youngster when his father took him to the Scioto Club and put a set of clubs in the boy's hands. They played 9 holes, and Jack shot a 51. It was the highest nine he ever shot. "By the time he was 12, he was beating me regularly," his father said.

Young Nicklaus early caught the eye of Jack Grout, a tough Texan serving as professional at Scioto. Grout enrolled Jack in his junior classes and gave him special attention. "Hit the ball with all you've got and learn style later," the pro advised. That's what Nicklaus did.

Before he had finished his first year of golf, Nicklaus was shooting regularly in the middle 90's. He fired an 81 during his second year and started breaking 80 at the age of 13. Soon he was playing and beating most of the men members of the club.

Nicklaus was 15 when he qualified for his first National Amateur Championship and made the decision that changed his life. He was a member of his high school football team at the time and the dates of the Amateur conflicted with the grid schedule. Jack had to choose football or golf. He chose golf.

The 1955 National Amateur was played over the James River course of the Country Club of Virginia in Richmond, and it was a tournament Nicklaus probably never will forget. Bob Jones, who also had qualified for the Amateur at 15 and who went on to become one of the titanic figures of golf, was present at the tournament and he made a special point of watching the sensational prodigy from Ohio.

Nicklaus, playing Bob Gardner in the first round, happened to spy Jones in the gallery. His Adam's apple immediately leaped up in his throat.

"I was getting ready to drive off the eleventh tee when I saw Mr. Jones coming up the hill," Nicklaus later recalled. "I was one up after ten holes. I became so excited, I hooked my drive into the woods at the eleventh. On the twelfth, I sculled my approach over the green and on the thirteenth I really blew. I was so nervous I could hardly hold the club. I felt miserable. Then I saw Mr. Jones, who apparently had seen enough, take off for the club house."

Nicklaus had no reason to be embarrassed. Jones said later that while he had not seen the boy at his best, he was greatly impressed by his powerful swing and complete composure. Jones became one of Nicklaus' greatest boosters and even wrote a personal letter trying to dissuade Jack from turning pro.

At the age of 16, Nicklaus won the Ohio Open, beating some outstanding pros, and then set off on a brilliant amateur career. He qualified for seven National Amateur Championships, winning two of them—in 1959 and 1961.

It was the year 1959 that brought the long-hitting Ohio youngster into full blossom. Selected as a member of the U.S. Walker Cup team, he spearheaded a 9-3 victory over the British at Muirfield, Scotland, winning both his matches. He captured his first National Amateur title at the Broadmoor Golf Club in Colorado Springs, Colorado, beating the veteran Charles Coe in the 36-hole final, 1-up. In 30 matches played during the year, he was beaten only once.

In 1960, Nicklaus finished second in the National Open at Denver's Cherry Hills Club, his 282 placing him two shots back of the surging winner, Arnold Palmer. He failed to defend his Amateur crown when he dropped a fourth round match to Charles Lewis of Little Rock, Arkansas, 4 and 3, but he surged back with an overpowering performance in the World Amateur Team Championship at Merion. His 72-hole score of 269, 20 shots better than the next best total of the four-man American team, was rated one of the outstanding competitive performances of all time, by amateur or pro.

Nicklaus was a slender, crew-cut collegian when he won the second of his two National Amateur crowns in 1961.

Nicklaus made another strong run at the Open in 1961 at Oakland Hills in Birmingham, Michigan, shooting 75-69-70-70 for 284 and finishing three strokes back of the victor, Gene Littler. He swept to his second National Amateur title at Pebble Beach, California, playing the rugged seaside course in 20 strokes under par for the week and crushing Dudley Wysong, Jr., in the final, 8 and 6. Then he helped the United States retain the America's Cup with a victory over amateur teams from Mexico and Canada at Monterrey, Mexico.

It was shortly after the Mexican trip that Nicklaus, after long consideration and debate with himself, decided to turn professional. "I was in a real stew," Jack explained afterward. "I was trying to do three jobs at once. I was trying to get my degree at Ohio State. I was trying to keep up my insurance business. And I was trying to play golf. I wasn't doing justice to any of them. So I decided to concentrate on golf."

The decision brought keen disappointment to amateur quarters, since the powerful young man appeared to be the greatest amateur to come along since Jones, but there was no resentment. It was Jack's choice, and he made it with the conviction it was the best move for both himself and his family.

Nicklaus hit the winter tour in January, 1962, making his pro debut in the Los Angeles Open. Co-favored with Palmer and Gary Player, he finished in a tie for fiftieth place and collected $33.33. Tournament after tournament, he failed to live up to expectations

A lot of things come loose when Nicklaus pours himself into a shot. Here it's his cap after an approach.

but he was gradually edging up nearer the big money. His first big payday came when he finished second in the $100,000 Thunderbird Classic at Upper Montclair, New Jersey. The tournament was won by Gene Littler, who was to defend his title the next week in the U.S. Open at Oakmont.

At Oakmont, Littler stepped off to the first round lead but faded. Finally, after a real dogfight, Palmer and Nicklaus finished the regulation 72 holes tied for the title at 283. This necessitated an 18-hole play-off and provoked the unhappy comment from Palmer that later became famous: "I wish I were playing anybody but that big, strong, happy dude."

Since the match was played virtually in Palmer's backyard—only a few miles from Arnold's home at Latrobe, Pennsylvania—it was natural that the gallery of 10,000 should be predominantly pro-Palmer. It was more than that. It was actually hostile to Nicklaus. Arnie's Army was out in full force, and kicking up a storm.

Nicklaus took the lead at the first hole, which Palmer bogeyed, and, playing almost flawless golf, increased his advantage to four strokes through the eighth.

Arnie's Army was fit to be tied. "Go get him, Arnie!" "We're for you, Arnie baby!" the huge gallery yelled as it pushed and shoved over the massive course. Palmer became embarrassed and several times called upon his legion of fans to be more considerate and not break until Nicklaus had finished putting. The crowd paid little heed. It was enough to crack a lesser man. The composed Nicklaus never once showed a sign of pique or nervousness.

Neither did Nicklaus lose his poise when Palmer's putter suddenly got hot and the fabled Charger started one of his patented surges, cutting Jack's lead to a single stroke with six holes to play. Nicklaus refused to be budged and held on to win the play-off and the Open title, 71 to 74.

"I didn't get scared," Nicklaus recalled later. "I just told myself not to be an idiot.

When Palmer starts moving, most people get flustered and start making bogeys. I told myself just to keep playing my own game—and I did."

Nicklaus beat Palmer at his own game—that is, on the greens. Although rated the best clutch putter in the business, Palmer three-putted 10 greens over the 90 holes, including the 18-hole play-off. Nicklaus three-putted only once.

In the 1963 Masters, Nicklaus faced another pressure situation when, after leading at the three-quarter point, he saw his advantage suddenly disappear in a strong move by Sam Snead, who shot in front on the closing holes. Firing a streak of 18 straight pars over the third and last rounds, Nicklaus held on grimly to win by a stroke at 286.

Bothered by an aching hip, Nicklaus never got his game going in the 1963 Open at Brookline and failed to survive the 36-hole cut—the first time such a fate had befallen a defending champion. He recovered enough to compete in the British Open at St. Anne's-on-the-Sea and came to the seventy-first hole needing only pars on the final two holes to take the championship. He went bogey-bogey, however, and wound up a stroke back of Bob Charles of New Zealand, the ultimate winner, and Phil Rodgers.

Rushing home from England for the PGA Championship at Dallas, the Ohio strong-boy quickly got back in the groove. He won the PGA with rounds of 69-73-69-68 for 279, sinking a 30-foot putt on the sixty-ninth hole to stand off the pressure of young Dave Ragan and Australia's Bruce Crampton.

Nicklaus scored another significant triumph when he won the $50,000 first prize in the World Series at Akron, Ohio, for the second straight year. He put together steady rounds of 70-70 for 140 over the awesome Firestone Country Club course to win by a stroke over Julius Boros, the Open champion, who had 72-69 (141), and three over his old rival, Palmer, who shot 71-72 (143). Bob Charles, the British Open king, finished fourth.

Nicklaus climaxed his successful 1963 season by winning the individual championship and sharing team honors with Palmer in the Canada Cup matches at picturesque Saint-Nom-La-Breteche course on the outskirts of Paris. On the final day, with the last round reduced to 9 holes by a heavy fog, Jack unleashed a fantastic streak of 5 straight threes—birdieing 5 of the first 6 holes—in clinching the individual International Trophy with a 63-hole score of 237, 15 under par. "Fantastique!" blared French headlines, in tribute to the amazing young Yank.

The major titles escaped Nicklaus in 1964 but the money didn't and the slugger from Ohio climaxed a profitable year by coming from six strokes back to beat out Palmer for the individual championship in the Canada Cup matches at Royal Kaanapali on Hawaii's island of Maui.

Nicklaus' 72-hole total was 276 compared with 278 for Palmer, with whom he teamed for the Canada Cup Trophy.

If Palmer got a hint here that his golf dynasty was trembling under sledgehammer blows of his youthful rival, the message must

Nicklaus blasts from the sand on the second hole in the opening round of the 1964 Masters.

Nicklaus winds up and throws the ball down the fairway after putting out for his record victory in the 1965 Masters Tournament. His caddy beams.

have been brought home with chilling impact in the 1965 Masters at Augusta National.

This was the first important tournament of the year and golf followers poured in from almost everywhere to see the titanic battle between Palmer and Nicklaus over Georgia's flowering acres. Arnie's Army was never bigger or more vociferous.

The Army lost some of its enthusiasm when Gary Player of South Africa grabbed the opening round lead with a 7-under-par 65 but got its voice and stampeding energy back when Palmer pulled even with the other two members of the "Big Three," Player and Nicklaus, at the halfway point with 138.

At one stage in the second round it appeared that Nicklaus was headed for a collapse. Turning into Hell's Corner—the rugged stretch that includes the eleventh, twelfth and thirteenth holes—the Golden Bear took three straight bogeys.

While people were waiting for the thud that comes from a 210-pound man falling on his most generously padded section, Big Jack braked himself and ran in back-to-back birdies on the fifteenth and sixteenth.

This seemed to be all the impetus the big boy needed. The next day—a cloudless Saturday, April 10—he went out and figuratively tore the dreaded course apart with a 64,

141

which tied the one round record set in 1940 by Lloyd Mangrum.

Principally, the round left Jack's keenest rivals gasping for breath—Player five and Palmer eight shots back.

Nicklaus played the final round as casually as a weekend public links player out on a Sunday excursion with his wife. Nevertheless, he fired a final round 69 for 271 that clipped three shots off the proud record Hogan set in 1953.

The golf world was left aghast by the ease with which the powerful Nicklaus subdued a mighty course which had been described as

Nicklaus puts a little something extra into a putt on the first hole of the final round of the 1965 Masters, which he won with a record score of 271.

Wide World

the "Green Monster." Some observers called it the beginning of a new era. Others started talking about prospective scores in the 50's.

It was a victory of sheer power. In the four rounds, Nicklaus only used a wood once from the fairway. He played the long par five holes as if they were easy fours. On the fours, rated some of the most exacting holes in existence, he never used a club longer than a five-iron on his approach to the green. Much of the time he was flicking up a simple wedge shot.

He made it a new game. He went one stretch of 28 holes without a bogey. He had only one 3-putt green—that on the final round and on a par five hole where he 3-putted for his par.

"Palmer and Player played superbly," Bob Jones commented afterward, "but Nicklaus played a game with which I'm not familiar."

It appeared that a new era—the Nicklaus Era—was born in the game. Observers began talking about the necessity of remodeling courses to give them a chance against the awesome power of men like Nicklaus. They talked of future rounds in the 50's, with Nicklaus the chief perpetrator.

As honors piled up for the midwest giant, Nicklaus was asked one day if, like Palmer, he had his sights set on a professional grand slam—that is, winning the British and U.S. Opens, Masters, and American PGA all in a single year.

"I never think in terms of a slam or a sweep," Nicklaus replied quietly. "The tournament I am playing in is the one I want to win. And I want to win them all."

JACK NICKLAUS' RECORD

U.S. Amateur Champion: 1959, 1961.
U.S. Open Champion: 1962. (Runner-up in 1960 with lowest score ever shot by an amateur, 282.)
Masters Champion: 1963, 1965.
PGA Champion: 1963. (Runner-up, 1964.)
Winner, World Series of Golf: 1962, 1963.
Canada Cup: 1963, winner individual championship; teamed with Arnold Palmer for Canada Cup team crown.
World Amateur Team Championship: 1960, set 72-hole individual record with 269 at Merion Cricket Club, Ardmore, Pennsylvania.
Walker Cup: 1959, 1961. (Won four points, two team and two singles, never lost.)
Leading Money Winner: 1964, 1965.

Chapter Nineteen

The Women: The Babe Was Queen

From the day of its birth, golf apparently appealed to women as well as men. Proof of this is preserved in the works of Dutch master painters dating back to the sixteenth century and in faded records of the game. There is one portrait, dated 1505, titled "A Girl With a Golf Club," showing a small girl with a feather ball and primitive iron club. Another, tracing back to 1650, depicts a girl in a black beaver hat with an ostrich feather preparing to strike a feather ball on a rough links bounded by the sea and rocks. Mary, Queen of Scots, was criticized for playing golf on the fields of Seton shortly after the death of her husband, Darnley.

Early records preserved at the Royal and Ancient Club of St. Andrews show that the ladies were active on that aged course as early as 1810 and the Ladies Golf Club of St. Andrews was formed in 1867. The first mixed foursome match ever played in the United States was staged on the St. Andrews Golf Club of Yonkers course on March 30, 1889. The participants were John G. Reid, known as the "Father of American Golf," Mrs. Reid, John P. Upham and Carrie Low.

As time went on, more and more women took up the game. At first, as in the case of the men, the British women were dominant. But interest increased rapidly in America and by the 1920's the British ladies were beginning to develop a wholesome respect for their counterparts across the Atlantic. By the 1930's the pendulum had swung the other way and the United States emphasized its supremacy in the Curtis Cup matches, involving the best women amateurs of the two nations.

The ladies played well, but there remained a powder-puff quality about their game. Lacking the strength of men, they were unable to get great distance off the tee. They thus were compelled to make up strokes through delicate chipping and putting. This proved quite unappealing to the average fan, whose greatest delight comes from watching booming drives. Women's golf lacked public acceptance—that is, until the Babe came along.

The Babe was Mildred Didrikson Zaharias, recognized as the greatest woman athlete who ever lived. She could have excelled in any sport—and did in many of them—but she finally chose golf as her career. Interest in women's golf immediately skyrocketed. The big Texas girl belted the ball with the power of a man. She had a captivating personality. She was loaded with color. By the thousands, fans flocked to the courses to watch her play. It was her gate appeal that gave rise to and solidified the success of the Ladies' Professional Tour. She won every major championship, some of them many times over, and then, at the peak of her career, she was stricken with cancer. She died Sept. 27, 1956 at the age of 42.

Mildred Dickinson, of Norwegian extraction, was the daughter of a ship's carpenter who retired from the sea to live in Port Arthur, Texas, where the Babe and six brothers

Mildred (BABE) Didrikson Zaharias

and sisters were born. A tall, raw-boned girl, Mildred was a tomboy who never played with dolls. She liked to run and jump, play baseball and football, wrestle and box. She could do these things better than any boy in the neighborhood.

On July 16, 1932, the Babe, 18 years old, entered the National AAU women's track and field meet and Olympic tryouts at Evanston, Illinois, as a one-woman team representing an insurance firm in Dallas where she worked. Alone, the Babe won the team title with 30 points. Entering 8 of the 10 events, she won the 80-meter hurdles, baseball throw, shot put, broad jump, and javelin; finished second in the high jump, and fourth in the discus throw. She set three world records.

From there she went to the 1932 Olympic Games at Los Angeles where she became a sensation. She won the 80-meter hurdles and javelin throw. She tied for the gold medal in the high jump, only to be disqualified in the event for diving over the bar. This was a technique never before questioned. It later was legalized.

The Babe now was the toast of the continent. The newspapers and magazines were full of her exploits. Sports fans talked about her with the awe that had been reserved for such giants as Jack Dempsey, Babe Ruth, and Bob Jones. People wanted to see her. It was only natural that an enterprising promoter should seize on the opportunity to turn her professional and put her on tour. It was not long after the Olympics that the Babe signed for $3,500 a week.

She went on a tour of the vaudeville palaces, playing a harmonica and doing a tap dance. Soon tiring of this routine, she joined the House of David baseball team as a pitcher. She once pitched an inning for the Brooklyn Dodgers against the Phillies. Another time,

Babe Didrikson, the Dallas tomboy, was the heroine of the 1932 Olympic Games at Los Angeles. She set a women's javelin mark of 145 feet, 4 inches.

she struck out Joe DiMaggio. She worked out with the Southern Methodist University football team, won a fly-casting contest from leading male specialists, took up skiing, and even did some boxing.

The Babe turned to golf through the encouragement of Grantland Rice, the famous sports writer. Rice saw the Texas girl star in the Olympics, become an All-American basketball player and excel in softball, swimming and bowling. Convinced she could also become the best woman golfer in the world, Rice got the Babe to take up the game.

One of her first appearances was at the Brentwood Country Club in Santa Monica, California, shortly after the 1932 Olympics. Rice wanted to show her off to some of his skeptical newspaper cronies. The Babe, who had not had a club in her hand in more than a year, borrowed some shoes and a set of clubs from Olin Dutra. She easily broke 100, playing the back nine in 43. On the 523-yard, par 5 seventeenth hole, she hit two powerful woods into the wind and reached the apron of the green. She chipped close but missed her putt for a birdie. Her critical gallery was impressed.

In 1935, the Babe went on a nationwide tour with Gene Sarazen. She delighted galleries by smashing drives 250 yards, hitting

The Babe in action: Miss Didrikson, *second from the right,* goes over the last hurdle in winning the 80-meter hurdles in the 1932 Los Angeles Olympics.

Wide World

strong iron shots and clowning between swings. One of her tricks was to tee up her ball, walk back a few yards, and then saunter up and hit the ball without breaking stride. While her sheer power could get her through such exhibitions, she was not at this stage a finished golfer. Her short game needed refinement before she could become a factor in tournaments.

No one knew this better than the Babe herself. Determined to be the best woman golfer in the world, she settled down in California and worked for two years on her game. Then she ventured into tournaments. She was the standout gate attraction. She gave the ball a tremendous ride off the tee. She came up occasionally with some spectacular shots. But she lacked the rounded skill to compete with the more experienced players.

Refusing to be discouraged, she went back to the practice tee. She took lessons from Tommy Armour, one of the great teachers of the day. She practiced for hours at a time. Her hands became sore and raw. She soaked them in brine, bandaged them, and kept swinging. Her golf steadily improved.

Another event in 1938 helped change her life. She was playing an exhibition in Los Angeles and happened to be paired with a 300-pound professional wrestler named George Zaharias, known to mat fans as "The Crying Greek from Cripple Creek." The Babe and the Crying Greek hit it off from the start. They swapped banter and insults throughout the round, laughing up a storm, and decided to carry on at dinner. Shortly afterward they were married.

The Babe became a different woman. She wore lace and other frills. She started using make-up and having her hair done at the beauty salon. She took pride in her femininity. She cooked, sewed curtains and kept house. George worshipped her. Independently wealthy from large real estate holdings both in Denver and Florida, the big wrestler devoted his life to his wife and her golf career. He wanted her to be the best. He followed her around like a faithful St. Bernard dog.

As a professional, however, Mrs. Zaharias had no way to establish herself. There was only a handful of women professionals and they were restricted largely to exhibitions and clinics for sporting goods houses. The women's pro tour had not taken root. The major championships were the United States Women's Amateur and the British Ladies' Championship, open only to amateurs. In 1944, the Babe applied for reinstatement as an amateur and the U.S. Golf Association approved.

This made Mrs. Zaharias eligible for the National Women's Amateur Championship when that event was resumed after World War II. The tournament was played over the Southern Hills Country Club in Tulsa, Oklahoma, and the Babe was ready. She had kept busy during the war years by playing War Bond exhibitions. Eligible only for open tournaments, she won the Western Women's Open three times. She shot a 65 over the Brentwood course in Santa Monica. She had four rounds in the 70's over the tough Cypress Point layout. She played in the Southern California Open, the only woman competitor, and fired successive rounds of 74, 74, 74, 70 for 292.

Mrs. Zaharias was the center of attention when she teed up her ball in the match play Women's Amateur at Tulsa in 1946. The pressure on her was tremendous. The opposition was formidable, including such players as Maureen Orcutt, Mrs. Estelle Lawson Page, Helen Sigel, Dorothy Kirby, and Louise Suggs.

The Babe won her first two matches easily, beating Peggy Kirk and Betty Jean Rucker. She expected to have more trouble with her third opponent, Maureen Orcutt, but she took a four-hole lead through the first nine holes and won, 5 and 4, with a birdie deuce on the fourteenth hole. Hitting tremendous shots but scrambling at times, Mrs. Zaharias won over Helen Sigel in the semifinals, 3 and 2, and then crushed Clara Callender Sherman in the 36-hole final, 11 and 9, a record margin for the championship. The Babe went 5-up in the morning round with a fine medal score of 76 and sank a 9-iron shot from 120 yards for an eagle on the seventh hole of the afternoon round.

The victory in the National gave Mrs. Zaharias a tremendous psychological lift. Her confidence soared. Now she was convinced that no one could beat her. If she ever wavered in this thought, her gargantuan husband, George, was always at her elbow, whispering in her ear: "Babe, you're the greatest." During 1946 and 1947, this remarkable woman athlete piled up a string of 15 consecutive tournament victories. One of these was the British Ladies at Gullane, Scotland, in 1947. It was a title that never before had gone across the Atlantic.

The big, good-natured Texas girl became a favorite of the normally reserved and cool Scottish galleries. They thrilled to see a woman unleash such crackling, soaring drives. They delighted in her wisecracks and casual, uninhibited mannerisms.

A fan asked her during the British tournament: "How do you get such tremendous distance on your drives?"

"I just loosen my girdle and let the ball have it," the Babe replied.

Mrs. Zaharias, wearing faded blue slacks which she called her "lucky clothes," played brilliantly at Gullane. En route to the finals, she never was carried past the sixteenth hole and she won her semifinal match with Jean Donald, the Scottish champion, by the lopsided score of 7 and 5.

In the final, the Babe got off to a bad start but rallied to finish the morning round all square with Jacqueline Gordon. In the afternoon, the American champion turned on the steam. She won five of the first six holes of the afternoon round, knocking in an eagle at the twentieth, and it was a dazed Miss Gordon who finally surrendered, 5 and 4. Mrs. Zaharias discarded her slacks and put on a tight-fitting blue dress to receive the trophy as the first American ever to win the British Ladies Championship. Two months later, the Babe turned professional, accepting a $300,000 offer to make a series of movie shorts.

Principally through the gate appeal of this raw-boned daughter of Texas, women's golf immediately boomed. The girls swapped their long skirts and cumbersome blouses for shorts and practical skirts that hit about the knees. They smashed their tee shots like men. The low 80's no longer represented an adequate target for the fairer sex. Scores dipped into the low 70's and scores in the 60's were not uncommon as the ladies set up a distaff version of the professional tour and began barnstorming around the nation's major cities.

The Babe and her sharpshooting contemporaries inherited and embellished a game already rich in tradition.

Wide World

The inroads of cancer were already beginning to show when Babe Didrikson Zaharias got this kiss from her wrestler husband, George Zaharias, after playing in the All-America tournament at Tam o'Shanter in 1953.

The hardy men who pioneered the game on the seaside links of Scotland and the courses of England were not successful in keeping the pastime to themselves. The Ladies Golf Club was formed at St. Andrews in 1867. Similar clubs mushroomed about the same time at Musselburgh, Bath, Wimbledon, and Carnoustie. As far back as the 1890's, Britons were talking about the golf exploits of such women as Isette Pearson, Lady Margaret Scott, and Sybil Wigham.

It was amazing that they could swing a club at all, much less score creditably, considering the handicaps of their dress. The popular attire consisted of blouses with deep-starched collars and ties, military jackets, long tweed skirts with layers of petticoats underneath, and thick leather boots. A woman golfer in those days would not think of stepping up to the first tee without a stiff boater hat with braids of club colors around the crown.

The women became a bit more sensible about their styles after World War I—the period that saw the emergence of Britain's most famous woman golfer, Joyce Wethered. Miss Wethered, a tall, shy girl, learned the game from her brother, Roger Wethered, a captain of the Oxford team. She played with Roger and his friends, became a regular member of their party, and joined them in long and involved arguments over techniques.

She was pleasant, quiet, and unobtrusive. She seemed almost apologetic when she teed off in a match. But once on the course she became a veritable machine, swinging beautifully and striking the ball with crisp precision. Her chief rival was a rugged, powerful girl named Cecil Leitch, who crushed the ball with an awkward, unorthodox but effective swing.

Over a 15-year period, Miss Leitch won four British championships, two English, five French Opens, and the Canadian Open. Miss Wethered's career was packaged between 1920 and 1924 during which time she won the British women's title three times, the English title five. At the age of 24, Miss Wethered decided she had had enough of competitive golf. She retired, but not for good. She was lured back into action by the invasion, in 1929, of the great American star, Glenna Collett.

Like Babe Didrikson, Glenna Collett was a tomboy who could run faster, jump higher and throw farther than most of the fellows in her Rhode Island neighborhood. She was 17 when she drove her first golf ball, during a visit to her father's club, and became immediately interested in the game. She worked diligently but found progress slow. She began to improve when she started taking two lessons a week from the crochety pro, Alex Smith. By 1919, she was playing in club matches and some tournaments, largely with disheartening results.

In the careers of most tournament golfers, there is one shot or one match that often swings the pendulum from mediocrity to success. For Miss Collett, this turning point came in 1921, when, now 18 years old, she was paired against the great British star, Cecil Leitch, in the Berthellyn Cup competition at the Huntington Valley Club near Philadelphia.

Glenna went out with the intention of keeping the match close and not humiliating herself. Playing doggedly, she not only held her own but to the surprise of everyone came to the eighteenth hole leading her British rival, one up. Faced with a tough 10-foot putt to clinch the victory, she calmly knocked the ball into the cup. Her confidence soared.

Within less than a year after her important triumph over Miss Leitch, Miss Collett was the talk of women's golf. In 1922, she won the North and South, Eastern and the National Women's Amateur, beating Mrs. W.A. Gavin in the final, 5 and 4. Success continued in 1923 and 1924, but each of these years, although favored, she failed in the National. Her next National triumph came in 1925 at the St. Louis Country Club. She defeated Alexa Fraser in the last round, 9 and 8.

Glenna was beaten in the semifinals of the National tournament in 1926 by Virginia Wilson and was ousted in the second round the year after by Alexa Fraser. But in 1928, the tall, attractive girl from New England found the winning formula again and became the first woman golfer in modern times to win three United States championships in a row. She crushed Virginia Van Wie in the 1928 final at Hot Springs, Virginia, 13 and 12; defeated Mrs. Leona Pressler at Birmingham, Michigan, in the 1929 climax, 4 and 3, and repeated her victory over Miss Van Wie at Beverly Hills, California, in 1930, 6 and 5.

Beatrix Hoyt had won the women's National three times in a row back in 1896–98, and the gifted Alexa Stirling of Atlanta had sandwiched three straight titles around World War I, starting in 1916. However, none demonstrated the overwhelming mastery that came from the sticks of Glenna Collett. The 5'6", 125-pound Rhode Islander, married in 1931 to Edward H. Vare, Jr., of Philadelphia, gained the finals in 1931 and 1932, and then, in 1935, at the age of 32, won her sixth National championship at Interlachen in Hopkins, Minnesota, by beating Patty Berg, 3 and 2.

Miss Berg represented the new breed of women's golf in the United States—a group that later was to found the Ladies Professional Golfers Association and launch a successful pro tour patterned after that of their male counterparts. Patricia Jane Berg became a contemporary and the closest golfing companion of Babe Didrikson Zaharias. Patty was only 17—a chubby, pleasant Minneapolis girl

Friends and golfing rivals, Patty Berg and Babe Didrikson Zaharias at the Tam o'Shanter World Championship tournament in 1950.

with a shock of red curls—when she shot into the final round at Interlachen against Glenna Collett Vare.

For years, Miss Berg was not only the Babe's best friend but her toughest rival on the women's circuit. Patty gained the National Women's Amateur final again in 1937 at Memphis, losing 7 and 6 to Mrs. Julius A. Page, Jr., but she came back the next year at Wilmette, Illinois, to reverse the result, winning over Mrs. Page in the last round, 6 and 5.

It was the start of a fabulous career that saw Miss Berg win more tournaments as an amateur and professional than any other woman golfer, a total of 83 between 1935 and 1964. To her National Amateur crown, she added the National Open in 1946—having turned pro in 1940—seven Titleholders (the women's Masters), seven Western Opens, and four World's Championships at Tam O'Shanter. She was three-time winner of the Vare Trophy for lowest scoring average—1953, 1955, and 1956—and leading money winner of the LPGA in 1954, 1955, and 1957.

Miss Berg was just one of the formidable rivals with whom the great Babe had to contend.

Others included Louise Suggs, Georgia's little Miss Poker Face; the attractive Bauer sisters, Alice and Marlene; Betty Jameson, a tall, brown-eyed blonde from San Antonio, Texas; Beverly Hanson, a big, strapping girl from Fargo, North Dakota; Betsy Rawls, demure Phi Beta Kappa from the University of Texas; and later the "New Babe," Mickey Wright.

As long as her health prevailed and even when it began to fade, Babe Zaharias was queen of the fairways. She was the woman to beat in every tournament. Fans came out in droves to watch the fabulous Texan who could whack the golf ball with the power of a man.

She was leading money winner on the women's tour for four straight years—1948 through 1951. She won the Women's Open in 1948, 1950, and 1954. She was suffering from cancer—drawn and haggard but still putting

Babe Didrikson Zaharias, stricken with cancer, watches President Eisenhower demonstrate golf grip on a Cancer Society "sword of hope" at the White House in 1954.

on a bold front—when she teed off in the Women's Open at the Salem Country Club in Peabody, Massachusetts, in 1954.

On a bright July morning just prior to the opening of the tournament, the Babe was sitting on a small, green knoll at the Salem Country Club watching her opponents practice. She became fascinated by a long-legged, blonde-haired girl who was belting the ball for tremendous distances.

"Gee whillikens, get a load of that," she exclaimed to her husband, George, at her elbow. "I didn't think anybody but the Babe could hit 'em like that."

Four days later, Mrs. Zaharias, her face showing the strain of the dread disease, was paired with the long-hitting young girl in the final 36 holes of the tournament. She was astounded—and a bit hurt—to find herself often hitting behind her rival off the fairway.

The Babe went on to win her third Open with a score of 291 but she could not conceal her admiration for her companion, Mary Kathryn (Mickey) Wright of San Diego, California, just 19, who finished in a tie for fourth and won amateur honors with a score of 308.

"I don't know whether the Babe will be around five years from now," she told friends. "If she is, she'll have her hands full." The Babe often referred to herself in the third person.

It was a prophetic statement. On September 27, 1956, the superb woman athlete, after a courageous battle, succumbed to cancer in a Dallas hospital. Mickey Wright went on to become her successor—acclaimed by some as the greatest woman golfer who ever lived.

Miss Wright, a striking, willowy blonde who was 5'8½" tall and weighed 140 pounds, moved in almost immediately to take over the No. 1 position in women's golf. Like the Babe, she was a tremendous hitter, consistently outdistancing her rivals off the tee as much as 50 yards. She reached virtually all the women's par five holes in two shots and there were few par fours she could not play with a well-hit drive and a 6-iron. She regularly played irons to greens where the other girls were using woods.

If Mickey's game had a marked deficiency it was in her short game, particularly around the greens. Gene Sarazen once said that if Miss Wright had been as proficient in chipping and in blasting from sand traps as the men pros, she could have been a consistent money winner on the tour. "She can reach the area of the green in as few strokes as the best men professionals," Sarazen said. "She loses strokes on her short game."

Louise Suggs, who competed against them both, contended that Mickey got greater distance on her drives than the Babe. "Mickey got most of her tremendous distance on the fly," Miss Suggs said, "whereas the Babe hit a low rifle shot and depended mainly on the roll."

Mickey Wright was 11, even then a strapping girl of 5'8" and 145 pounds, when her father brought home her first set of clubs, a wood, two irons, and a putter. Mickey broke all four the first day swinging at the ball. Her father decided she had enough power to play the game. She broke 100 on a regulation course when she was 12 and by the time she was 13 she was shooting in the high 80's. She won the Southern California junior girls championship—her first tournament victory—when she was 14.

This was only the beginning. The next year she had a hole-in-one in an invitational tournament at the La Jolla (California) Country Club and she won a two-day tournament with

Mickey Wright throws down the flag after winning the women's Titleholders tournament at Augusta, Georgia, in 1961.

Mickey Wright, with her 1962 Titleholders trophy and cash.

Mickey Wright, hailed as the "New Babe," proudly holds aloft the U. S. Open Women's trophy after she won it for the fourth time in 1964.

a second-round 70. Two days before her nineteenth birthday, she fired a 68 to lead the first round of a tournament at St. Petersburg, Florida.

In 2½ years after starting tournament competition, Mickey cut her handicap from 25 to 4. She won the All America and "World" women's amateur titles at Tam O'Shanter in 1954, also gained the final round in the Inverness Invitational, won low amateur honors in the Ardmore Open, and was runner-up in the National Women's Amateur at the Allegheny Country Club in Sewickley, Pennsylvania. In that tournament, Mickey eliminated such established players as Dorothy Kirby, Mrs. Margarita de Maglione, and Polly Riley, before losing to Barbara Romack in the final round, which was carried over two days because of rain.

By this time, the statuesque, attractive California girl was fighting an internal battle with herself. She was undecided whether to continue her studies at Stanford University, aiming at a career as a psychologist or a doctor, or to take a fling at golf. Golf won. She turned professional in November 1954, and in 1956 she was voted the most improved player on the ladies' tour. From then on, success piled upon success until the entire recordbook of women's golf had to be rewritten.

In 1958, Mickey scored the "Big Double," winning both the Ladies' PGA and the National Open crowns in the same year, a feat she repeated in 1961. In the 1958 Women's Open at the Forest Hills Country Club near Detroit, Miss Wright set the tournament scoring record with a 290, erasing the mark set by Babe Zaharias at Salem, Massachusetts. Miss Wright bettered her own record with a 287 at Pittsburgh's Valley Country Club in 1961 and became the first woman ever to put two Open victories back-to-back. It was a feat which escaped the great Babe.

Mickey's remarkable career reached a high point in 1963, although she was denied a fourth National Open triumph. Of the 28

154

official tournaments in which she played, she won 13, surpassing the record of 10 tournament victories in a single year which she shared with Betsy Rawls. She won the Ladies' PGA for the fourth time. In the 28 tournament appearances, she finished among the top five 24 times, among the top ten in all but one. She collected $31,269.50 in official winnings, also a record and the first time any woman had gone over the $30,000 mark. She averaged 72.81 strokes per 18 holes for 95 rounds in taking the Vare Trophy for the fourth consecutive year. She became the first woman golfer to average better than 73.

She scored in the 60's 13 times—another record—with her best competitive round a 67 in a tournament at Dallas. She scored the only double eagle of the ladies' tour when she sank a three-iron approach on a 480-yard, par 5 hole at the Ogden (Utah) Country Club and

she made two holes-in-one. For her remarkable year, Mickey was named Woman Athlete of the Year in The Associated Press' year-end poll and was voted into the LPGA Golf Hall of Fame.

A modest, pleasant girl, Mickey Wright shrugged off suggestions that she was the game's "New Babe."

"Naturally I am flattered at being compared with Mrs. Zaharias," she said, "but I really don't think this is quite proper. The Babe was in a class by herself, and, as for me, I much prefer just being Mickey Wright. I have one ambition—and it may take 10 years or 15 years to reach it. That is, I want to be the greatest woman player in the world."

Mickey reached her destiny ahead of schedule. Then, in 1965, bothered by ulcers, she retired from big time competition, leaving a gaudy goal for those who came after her.

RECORD OF MRS. EDWIN H. VARE, JR. (GLENNA COLLETT)

U.S. Women's Amateur Champion: 1922, 1925, 1928, 1929, 1930, 1935. (Runner-up, 1931, 1932; medalist, 1921, 1922, 1924, 1926; co-medalist, 1931, 1934.)
Runner-Up, British Ladies' Championship: 1929, 1930.
Curtis Cup: 1932, 1936, 1938, 1948. (Captain, 1934, 1936, 1948, 1950.)

RECORD OF MRS. BABE DIDRIKSON ZAHARIAS

U.S. Women's Amateur Champion: 1946.
British Ladies' Champion: 1947.
U.S. Women's Open Champion: 1948, 1950, 1954.
Titleholders: 1947, 1950, 1952.
Vare Trophy Winner (Lowest Average): 1954.
Leading Money Winner: 1948, 1949, 1950, 1951.
Women's Golf Hall of Fame: 1951.

RECORD OF MICKEY WRIGHT

Runner-Up, U.S. Women's Amateur: 1954.
U.S. Women's Open Champion: 1958, 1959, 1961, 1964.
Titleholders: 1961, 1962.
Ladies' PGA Champion: 1958, 1960, 1961, 1963.
Vare Trophy Winner (Lowest Average): 1960, 1961, 1962, 1963.
Leading Money Winner: 1961, 1962, 1963.
Women's Golf Hall of Fame: 1963.

Chapter Twenty

New Faces of the Sixties

Moving into the 1960's, big time tournament golf found itself in the stranglehold of the powerful twosome—Arnold Palmer and Jack Nicklaus. Every time the ball was teed up in a major championship, they were listed as the favorites, in one order or another. This created complications on the professional tour. Sponsors considered their tournaments a bust unless the entry list included the highly publicized duo. Other players became bitterly resentful, contending that there were 20 or 30 men—not just two—capable of winning any major competition.

Nevertheless, the 20 or 30 usually did not win. Palmer won the Masters in 1958, 1960, 1962, and 1964; the National Open in 1960; and the British Open in 1961 and 1962. Nicklaus captured the U.S. Open in 1962, the Masters in 1963 and 1965, the PGA in 1963 and was runner-up in the British Open in 1963 and 1964, missing by a single shot in 1963. Palmer was the leading money winner in 1960, 1962 and 1963; Player, in 1961 and 1964 and Nicklaus in 1964 and 1965.

It took a little man in perpetual black from Johannesburg, South Africa, to crack the long Palmer-Nicklaus monopoly. Gary Player did it the way he subdued a golf course—coolly, methodically, patiently like a fairway undertaker.

The 5'7", 150-pound son of a mine supplier made his first trip to the United States in 1957 at the age of 21. He played in his first U.S. Open in 1958 at the Southern Hills Country Club in Tulsa, Oklahoma, and finished second to the winner, Tommy Bolt. It was then that the young South African announced to all within earshot his golf ambition.

"I have set four goals for myself," the youngster said, "I want to win the U.S. Open, the Masters and the American PGA, and I want to be the leading money winner on the tour. I don't expect to do them all in a single year. This is a long-range goal."

Player succeeded in reaching his plateau—and more. In 1961 he beat out Arnold Palmer and became the first foreign player in history to capture the Masters. He attained another rung the same year when he won official money honors with $64,450. He added the PGA, in 1962, at Aronimink Golf Club in Newtown Square, Pennsylvania. Then, in 1965, over the long and challenging Bellerive course in St. Louis, he completed his cycle by beating Australian Kel Nagle in a play-off for the U.S. Open crown—the first foreigner in 45 years to crash through.

After clinching the Open, the South African surprised everyone by announcing that he was giving his entire winner's purse back to the U.S. Golf Association to be used for charity—part to the Cancer Fund, part to the promotion of golf in America.

"I am doing it because I made a promise to Joe Dey (executive director of the U.S.G.A.) five years ago," Player said at the presentation ceremonies. "Also, I am doing it to try to repay America for its many kindnesses to me over the past few years."

His original blueprint did not include winning the British Open in 1959, the World Series of Golf in 1965 and the Canada Cup

GOLF'S BIG THREE: Arnold Palmer, Gary Player and Jack Nicklaus huddle on the putting green before competing in the 1962 World Series of Golf over the Firestone Country Club in Akron, Ohio.

individual and team prize at Madrid, Spain, also in 1965.

He became the third man in history to win the four major pro championships—Masters, U.S. and British Opens and the American PGA. The other two were Gene Sarazen and Ben Hogan. With all his globe-girdling, he found time to win the South African Open in 1956 and the Australian Open in 1957 and 1963.

Like Hogan, Player was a golfer who drained the ultimate from his physical assets. Slight in stature and conscious of his lack of

strength, he became a physical fitness addict. He watched his diet closely, concentrating on such strange food as wheat germ and dried fruit. He lifted weights and went in for a series of exercises. His arms became like piston rods, dangling almost to his knees. His hands were strong. He added as much as 20 and 30 yards to the length of his drives. He developed a sensitive and very effective putting touch. He became a smart, position player—almost a machine.

His ability to use accuracy and finesse to offset the power of such rivals as Arnold

157

Palmer and Jack Nicklaus, the other two members of golf's "Big Three" of the Sixties, was never better reflected than in the 1965 Open at Bellerive.

This awesome course was supposedly made for the so-called "home run hitters" and all except Palmer and Nicklaus were warned they would be making the trip to St. Louis only for the experience. The layout measured 7,191 yards, the longest course on which the Open ever had been played. It was threaded with streams and small ponds. The rough wasn't unplayable but hidden hazards lurked everywhere.

"I think it's a straight-hitters' course, and we foreigners are usually straight-hitters," Player remarked before the tournament.

Nagle took the first round lead with a 68. Player, starting erratically with three bogeys on the front nine, rallied for a 70. Palmer shot a 76, Nicklaus a 78.

Patient but unspectacular, Player surged to the lead with a second round 70 for 140 and added a 71 for 211 that put him two shots ahead of Nagle and Frank Beard at the 54-hole point. Shooting steadily and refusing to go for the big gamble, Player fired a final round 71 which tied him with Nagle at 282. He won the play-off by three strokes, 71 to 74. Palmer at 152 failed to make the cutoff. Nicklaus rallied slightly but couldn't muster a charge.

As golf moved into the windward leg of the Sixties, it became obvious that no single professional was ready to dominate the game completely. Nicklaus continued strong, setting the Masters record in 1965 and becoming the leading money winner for the second straight year, but he was able to win only one major crown. Player beat him in both the World Series and the Canada Cup.

Other players were clamoring for big pieces of the tasty golf pie. Tony Lema, a tall, handsome young man from San Leandro, California, with a touch of Walter Hagen in him, won the British Open on his first try in 1964 and almost repeated in 1965, blowing the last two holes to let the title go to Peter Thomson

Champagne Tony Lema blasts from a trap in the 1963 U. S. Open at Brookline, Massachusetts. He had a big year in 1964, winning four out of six tournaments, including the British Open, in a summer stretch.

of Australia for the fifth time. Ken Venturi came back from golf's graveyard to win the 1964 U.S. Open with a dramatic performance in the sweltering heat of Washington, D.C., only to have his hands go bad on him a few weeks later. An operation gave him new life after a pitiful try in the 1965 Open at Bellerive.

Bill Casper, long one of the game's best, found new life after losing 40 pounds because of food allergies. Rated the game's outstanding putter, Casper won the U.S. Open in 1959, twice led the Vardon Trophy standings for the best scoring average and seven times, between 1957 and 1964, finished in the Top Ten among money winners, six times in the first five.

Other threats included Bobby Nichols, a strapping six-footer from Louisville who won the PGA crown in 1964; Dave Marr, who succeeded him in 1965, and a reed-thin Puerto Rican named Juan (Chi Chi) Rodriguez. Although only 120 pounds, Rodriguez vied with Palmer and Nicklaus for distance off the tees. An uninhibited show-off, he captivated galleries and wound up with a faithful following which rivaled Arnie's Army; they called themselves "Chi Chi's Bandidos."

Until 1964, Venturi was one of the tragic figures in golf. As a youngster, he was acclaimed one of the sport's brightest prospects, the player most likely to inherit the mantle of the aging Ben Hogan. In 1956, as an amateur, he appeared to have the Masters championship in his grasp with a comfortable lead after three rounds. Then he blew to a final round 80 and Jack Burke, Jr., came from 8 strokes back to take it. In 1960, he was being fitted with the traditional green coat and interviewed as the new Masters champion when Palmer stole the title from him with phenomenal birdies on the last two holes.

This in itself should have been enough to wreck the spirit of the strongest man, but Venturi refused to fold. In his first four years on the pro circuit—1957 through 1960—he won 10 tournaments and in 1960 collected $41,230 in official winnings. Then suddenly

he went into a slump, aggravated by a pinched nerve that paralyzed his right side during the 1962 Palm Springs Golf Classic.

In 1962, he won only $6,951 in 27 starts on the circuit, little more than enough to pay caddy fees. The next year was worse. In 27 tournaments he picked up checks in only 8. Venturi's earnings amounted to a meager $3,848.

"I was so discouraged I was tempted to give up the game," Venturi said later. "I got to a point I was ashamed to show up at a golf course. I was afraid to shoot a good round. I knew a bad round was sure to follow. I was really at rock bottom."

Just before the sixty-fourth United States Open Championship in Washington, D.C., Venturi received a letter from a priest with a parish in Burlingame, California, near Ken's home. In effect, the priest, Father Francis Murray, told the hard-luck golfer: "Keep your composure. Don't let anything get you too elated. Don't let anything get you down. Keep an even pace and just ask God to let you do the best you can."

Venturi said these words were racing through his mind when he teed off at Congressional, a rank outsider lost in the shadows of such favorites as Palmer and Nicklaus. He still was just one of the pack when Palmer opened with a bristling 68, and the next day, when Tommy Jacobs fired a record-tying 64 for the 36-hole lead at 136, one stroke ahead of Palmer.

On Saturday, the day of the exhausting final two rounds, the huge crowd stormed out onto the steamy course in pursuit of Palmer and Jacobs, playing together, and left Venturi to struggle along in semiprivacy in the suffocating, 100-degree heat. Flying his irons straight at the pins and putting superbly, Ken played the front 9 in 30, 5 under par, on the morning round. On the incoming 9, he almost collapsed from the heat but managed to finish with an amazing 66, including birdies on the final 2 holes, which left him 2 shots back of the leading Jacobs but 2 ahead of Palmer.

His face was pale and his eyes glazed when Venturi went to the locker room. He gulped salt tablets and drank a glass of iced tea. He had no intention of failing to answer the call at the tee for the final round. While Jacobs and Palmer wilted under the intense heat and pressure, Venturi shot an even par 70 for 278, the second-lowest score ever made in the Open. Jacobs was second at 282. Palmer tied for fifth. Nicklaus finished twenty-third.

"Winning the Open changed my whole life," Venturi said later. "Instead of being embarrassed to show up for a tournament, I couldn't wait to get to the golf course. And my whole attitude became different. I never saw a trap. I never saw trouble of any kind. All I could see were the pins."

Lack of confidence was never one of the shortcomings of Tony Lema, who was a carbon-copy of Venturi in many other respects. He was of largely the same build—a 6-footer weighing 180 pounds. He possessed a classical swing. He was a brilliant iron player. But he was not scared of the Devil himself. He had a brashness, a cockiness reminiscent of the great Hagen and Gene Sarazen.

Lema turned professional in 1955 shortly after getting out of the Marines, worked as a club professional for two years, and then decided to strike out on the tour. His first five seasons were unproductive. He never won more than $12,000 a year in a game that is said to require $10,000 for bare necessities. Then suddenly, in 1962, he discovered the

Relief and happiness overtake Ken Venturi after he putts out for his historic victory in the 1964 U. S. Open at the Congressional Club in Washington, D.C. The triumph ended years of heart break and frustration for the San Francisco golfer.

Associated Press

Tony Lema, *right*, hobnobs with royalty after his British Open triumph in 1964. He and Fred Corcoran, *left,* tournament director of the International Golf Association, flank the former king of England, the Duke of Windsor.

winning formula and from then on he was on an escalator.

"It was just a case of getting a winning attitude," he said later. He finished fourth in the money list in 1963, collecting $67,112, and became the hottest player on the circuit in 1964.

Meanwhile, he chanced upon a publicity gimmick that was to add impetus to his growing popularity. Playing in the 1962 Orange County Open in California, Tony saw a large group of newspaper reporters drinking beer in the press room.

"Fellows, if I win this tournament," he said, "we'll all have champagne."

Tony won. Champagne flowed. Lema became known as Champagne Tony Lema. Every time he won a tournament after that, he bought champagne for the press room.

Lema's remarkable 1964 success could be traced to another incident. He was playing in the Oklahoma City Open in May when his

putting suddenly went sour. He was complaining about it in the locker room when Palmer happened to overhear him.

"Here's an old putter of mine I'm not using," Palmer said. "Try it." Whether mental or physical, Lema's confidence on the greens suddenly returned.

He won the Thunderbird in early June and repeated the next week in the Buick Open. Having won the Bing Crosby Tournament earlier, he became the first to win three tournaments on the 1964 tour. He finished twentieth in the National Open, which followed, but bounded back to beat Palmer in a sudden-death play-off for top prize in the rich Cleveland Open. He had won won three of his last five starts when he flew overseas for the one-hundred-fourth British Open at historic St. Andrews.

Despite his excellent record, Lema found himself an underdog again to Nicklaus, who had kicked away the title with bogeys on the last two holes in 1963. Normally, the Scotsmen take their golf very seriously and adopt a dim view toward any form of levity. The outgoing, wise-cracking but pleasant Champagne Tony immediately won their hearts and before the July weekend was over they were cheering him lustily.

Lema had never played a seaside course before. He had never used the smaller British ball. He was unfamiliar with St. Andrews, the craggy old course that had wrecked the hopes of champions. Loose and relaxed, Tony started with a creditable one-over-par 73 but on the second day fired a 68, with an eagle 2 at the twelfth on a 30-foot putt, for the halfway lead. His 141 gave him a 9-stroke bulge over Nicklaus, at 76-74 for 150.

Playing the morning third round, Tony got a jolt that should have sent him scampering for the North Sea. Striding to the sixth hole, he passed Nicklaus, who was just coming down to the thirteenth. Starting shakily, Lema had lost four shots to par on the first five holes. Nicklaus, on one of his fabled late charges, was four under par through No. 12. So Big Jack had picked up eight of the nine strokes he had trailed.

It was at this point that Lema showed a fortitude that endeared him forever in the estimation of the Scots. Instead of panicking, he set his jaw and proceeded to reel off five straight threes, three of them birdies. Nicklaus closed the round with a brilliant 66. Lema, completely unshaken, sank a 20-foot putt on the eighteenth for a 68. Nicklaus, for all his remarkable effort, had picked up only two shots. "That slams the door," a Scotsman was heard to remark. It did. Lema finished with a 70 for 279. Nicklaus, in second place, was five shots behind despite the two finest closing rounds (66-68) ever shot in the British Open.

True to his custom, Tony again sprang for champagne. The British, who do not like to see their Championship Cup taken overseas, were delighted.

Directly from St. Andrews, golf's international brigade moved to the American PGA

at the Columbus (Ohio) Country Club, where the spectators were divided into three groups, all clearly labeled with 4-inch buttons which could be purchased on the grounds for 50 cents. They were Arnie's Army (Palmer), Jack's Pack (Nicklaus) and Lema's Legion (Lema). Nobody was paying any attention to a tall, strapping young man from Kentucky, whose name—according to golf legend—already had been inscribed on the championship trophy. This old superstition of predestination in golf tournaments never got greater support than at Columbus. Bobby Nichols played like a man guided by unseen gods.

It was not the first time that fate had shown a special interest in Nichols. On September 3, 1952, Bobby, a promising football and basketball star at St. Xavier High School in Louisville, was critically injured when a car in which he was riding crashed at 107 miles an hour. Nichols was pulled from the wreckage with a broken pelvis, back injury, brain concussion, and severe internal injuries. For 13 days he lay paralyzed from the waist down. He was in the hospital 96 days.

While convalescing, young Nichols received a letter of encouragement from Ben Hogan, who almost died in a similar accident in the winter of 1949 but who came back against unbelievable odds to score his greatest triumphs. Bobby said his determination to be a golf champion was born right there.

Nichols, a 6'2", 200-pounder, attended Texas A. and M., worked in Texas oil fields, and turned professional in 1959. He failed to make expenses the first year (1960) but raised his earnings to more than $15,000 (1962). He was selected the most improved player on the tour in 1962, and in 1963 he made the Top Ten leading money winners for the second year in a row. Still, the big championships evaded him. Nichols was one of the longest hitters on the circuit. He had size and a good temperament. But he was very erratic, a scrambler who found it hard to put four good rounds together.

That was until the 1964 PGA. While the spectators were watching Palmer, Nicklaus,

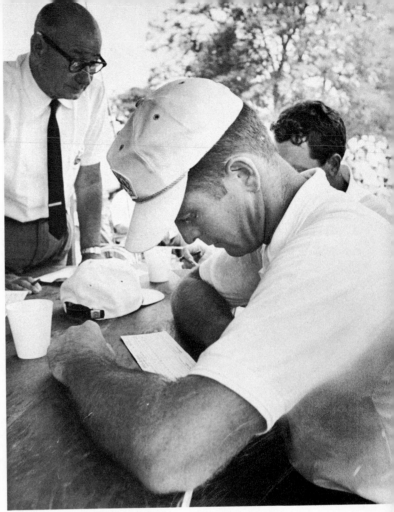

Bobby Nichols counts up the strokes after the final round of the PGA Championship at the Columbus (Ohio) Country Club in 1964. The total is 271 and that's good enough for the title.

and Lema, Nichols opened with a 64, a new single-round record in the tournament. He putted miraculously with a bargain-basement $5 blade he had picked up a few weeks before. He sank putts of 30, 20, and 15 feet, and knocked in the 8- and 10-footers as if they were routine.

He skidded on the second round to a 71 but held a one-stroke lead over Palmer. He protected that lead with a third-round 69, which saw him flail out of the rough on 9 of 18 holes and scramble from impossible positions to play the last 3 in 1-under-par. On the final day, Nichols knocked in a 35-foot putt for an eagle on the tenth hole and sank putts from 15 to 51 feet on 3 of the 4 finishing holes. He scored a record 271 for the championship.

"I wouldn't have believed it if I hadn't seen it myself," the 28-year-old Kentuckian remarked modestly afterward. He said he would spend part of his $17,000 prize money to erect a shrine to St. Jude, the patron saint of the impossible.

A similar shrine might be built in Puerto Rico by Juan (Chi Chi) Rodriguez, who, if not an architect of the impossible, proved at least a maker of the improbable. A mere wisp of a man, 5'7" and 120 pounds, Chi Chi consistently outdrove Palmer and Nicklaus, two of the biggest hitters in the game, and frequently sent the ball out farther than did big George Bayer, rated the sport's longest driver.

Chi Chi achieved his remarkable length through what he called his "secret," which he sold in paperback-booklet form to his admirers for $2. It was more than distance that drew the galleries and made him one of the biggest attractions on the pro tour. It was his flair for showmanship, which, while delightful to the fans, proved a source of controversy with his fellow golfers. Many of them resented his showboating and even reprimanded him for his antics.

Rodriguez, a snappy dresser, always played with dark sun-glasses. He effected bright

Juan (Chi Chi) Rodriguez of Puerto Rico, a little man with a big punch off the tee, became a gallery favorite in the mid-1960s. This was a typical reaction to acclaim in the Whitemarsh Open at Philadelphia.

colors, in the fashion of Jimmy Demaret, and an inevitable coconut straw hat, à la Sam Snead. When he sank a good putt, he often tossed the hat over the hole as if afraid the ball might leap out. Then he would do a catchy dance around the hole—half twist and half Latin.

This act always drew a round of laughter and applause from the galleries. Whereupon Chi Chi's bronze, thin face would break into a broad grin and he would wave and bow to the crowd.

The people loved it, but Chi Chi's golfing partners frequently were less amused. Palmer himself sharply criticized Rodriguez when the latter gave one of his wildest demonstrations as Arnie's partner in the second round of the 1964 Masters Tournament. "Showmanship is all right in its place, but Chi Chi sometimes carries it too far," Palmer said. "I told him so."

Rodriguez refused to be dissuaded, even by such important critics as Palmer and Nicklaus. He toned down his antics for a while, then resumed full scale. "My father always

taught me to tip my hat and bow when people are nice," Rodriguez said. "It's the polite thing to do. I love people. I have had so much sadness in my life, I try to make them happy."

The puckish Puerto Rican came from a very poor family, once carried three bags at a time in San Juan for as little as $1 a day. He turned pro in 1957, encouraged by Ed Dudley, pro at San Juan's Dorado Beach. The first years were lean ones but in 1963 Chi Chi won the Denver Open, his first tour victory, and picked up checks in 15 of the tournaments in which he played, collecting $17,674 for the year.

Rodriguez won his second tournament early in 1964—the Lucky International at San Francisco—and moved into the Top Ten among money winners. He climaxed his year by capturing the Western Open at Chicago. It was a two-man battle between him and Palmer, but the slender Puerto Rican never gave ground. On the last day, with Palmer driving at his heels, Chi Chi ran in birdies on three of the last five holes for his victory. He beat Palmer by the "Palmer Method."

164

PART THREE

Chapter Twenty-one

The U. S. Open:
Golf's Most Prestigious Tournament

The blue ribbon tournament in the world of golf—the toughest, the one carrying the greatest prestige and the one every golfer wants to win more than any other—is the United States Open Championship. Yet it was born an orphan, a sideshow to the first United States Amateur and throughout the early part of the century was overshadowed by the older British Open, which the Royal and Ancient Golf Club of St. Andrews smugly referred to as "The Open Championship," as if there were no other.

The first U.S. Open was played on October 4, 1895, the day after the ending of the three-day National Amateur, a carnival-like event that attracted the society set. The tournaments originally had been scheduled for September, but had to be postponed because of a conflict with the America's Cup yacht races, which were being staged off Newport, Rhode Island.

The site was a nine-hole course at the Newport Golf Club. Thirty-two golfers were attracted to the Amateur, whereas the Open enticed only 10 professionals and a single amateur. They played 36 holes in a single day—four trips around the Newport course.

Winner of the inaugural Open was Horace Rawlins, a 19-year-old English professional who had come to this country in January to serve as an assistant pro at Newport. Playing the gutta percha ball with crude hickory-shafted clubs, Rawlins turned in a score of 91-82 for 173 to win by two strokes.

Willie Dunn finished second at 175, followed by James Foulis and the lone amateur,

A.W. Smith of Toronto, tied at 176. There were five money prizes—$150, $100, $50, $25, and $10. Rawlins, youngest player ever to win the Open, also received a $50 gold medal for himself and the Open Championship Cup, which was to reside in his club until the next tournament.

The next Open shifted to an 18-hole layout, the Shinnecock Hills Golf Club in Southampton, Long Island, but it remained an anticlimactic sideshow to the Amateur. However, there was a sharp rise in competitor interest. Thirty-five entered and 28 finished the 36-hole tournament, played over a course that measured only 4,423 yards. Jim Foulis, the Scot professional who had tied for third in the inaugural event, won with a score of 78-74 for 152, with Rawlins finishing three strokes back in second place.

Foulis' home club, the Chicago Golf Club, was the site of the 1897 tournament, which this time was sandwiched between the semi-final and final rounds of the United States Amateur. Foulis could do no better than a tie for third, as the title went to Joe Lloyd, an English professional associated with the Essex Country Club of Manchester, Massachusetts. Lloyd, who spent his winters in Pau, France, fired scores of 83-79 for 162 to pace a field of 35. A young man named Willie Anderson, whose name later was to be inscribed four times on the Championship Cup, missed out by a single stroke.

The Open gained manhood and independence in 1898. It was divorced from the Amateur. It was extended from 36 to 72 holes,

Lew Worsham and Sam Snead examine putters after their play-off for the U. S. Open Championship in 1947, won by Worsham when Snead missed a short putt on the final hole.

following the example of the British Open. The tournament was awarded to the Myopia Club in South Hamilton, Massachusetts, a nine-hole layout. The event continued to be dominated by transplanted professionals from the Old Country. The winner was Fred Herd, a Scotsman from the Washington Park course in Chicago, who went around the nine-hole course eight times in two days with scores of 84-85-75-84 for 328.

The next two years produced historic developments. In 1899, Willie Smith, a Scotsman from Carnoustie who was employed as a pro at the Midlothian Club near Chicago,

won the tournament by the largest margin ever recorded—11 strokes. In 1900, the Open title went abroad for the first time, was won by the great Harry Vardon. The British stylist scored 79-78-76-80 for 313 and won by two strokes over his fellow countryman, J.H. Taylor, although he whiffed a ball on the final green.

Then began the era of Willie Anderson. The serious Scot, a pro at the Pittsfield (Massachusetts) Country Club, tied Alex Smith at 331, the highest ever recorded for a winner in the U.S. Open, in 1901 and captured the 18-hole play-off by a stroke, shooting an 85.

The rubber-core ball made its debut the next year and the livelier pellet was reflected in reduced scoring. For the first time, four rounds were played without an 80 or higher as Laurie Auchterlonie, from the Chicago Golf Club, won with 78-78-74-77 for 307. The tournament was beginning to grow in favor and interest. A record high of 90 entered and the prize money was raised to $970, with $200 going to the winner.

Meanwhile, Willie Anderson, whose name in later years was to be mentioned in the same breath with Bob Jones's and Ben Hogan's, had transferred to the Apawamis Club in Rye, New York. Playing at Baltusrol in Springfield, New Jersey, he became the first player to win a second Open when he tied David Brown at 307 and then won the play-off, 82 to 84, for the 1903 title.

That was not all the people were to hear of the reticent, business-like Willie. Anderson won again in 1904 at Golf, Illinois, and made

it four championships—three in a row—with a triumph in 1905 at the Myopia Hunt Club. His record of four Opens stood until Bob Jones duplicated it in 1930, to be matched 23 years later by Ben Hogan.

Through the first 15 years of the Open, the tournament was dominated by Scottish and English professionals who had taken teaching positions in this country, with a brief break when Harry Vardon took the trophy back to Britain in 1900. Home-born and home-grown talent was beginning to make itself felt, but it was not until 1911 that one of them crashed through to the championship.

That was Johnny McDermott, a brash former Philadelphia caddy representing the Atlantic City (New Jersey) Country Club. McDermott tied Mike Brady and George Simpson at 307 and won the play-off by firing an 80. By way of proving this victory was no fluke, McDermott repeated in 1912, putting together excellent rounds of 74-75-74-71 for

Ben Hogan tees off for his historic, par-breaking final round in the U. S. Open at Oakland Hills in Birmingham, Michigan, in 1961. The victory brought Hogan his third of four Open titles.

Julius Boros became the second oldest player ever to win the U. S. Open title when he captured his second Open crown at The Country Club in Brookline, Massachusetts, in 1963. At 43 years, 3 months, he was a month and a half younger than Ted Ray when the latter won in 1920.

294. Par for the Country Club of Buffalo, New York, course was 74 and McDermott was credited with being the first man to win the tournament with a sub-par score.

If McDermott's back-to-back triumphs were not enough to prove that Britain's dominance of the game was finally broken, then it remained for another former caddy, Francis Ouimet, to strike the telling blow. Britain's two veteran professionals, Vardon and Ted Ray, were heavily favored at the start of the 1913 championship over The Country Club course in Brookline, Massachusetts. No one paid the slightest mind to Ouimet, a scrawny, half-scared amateur of 20. However, at the end of four rounds, there was Ouimet tied with Vardon and Ray for the title at 304. National interest in the three-way play-off was tremendous. Newspapers carried the story in banner lines on the front pages. Fans anxiously awaited the result.

Ouimet's play-off victory, a 72 to Vardon's 77 and Ray's 78, created a national sensation.

Golf was no longer regarded as a society sport for the idle rich. It became a game of the common people. The number of entries for the Open soared, prize money gradually increased. The Open emerged as America's premier championship. Leading amateurs as well as the pros now sought the big prize, and they succeeded.

Jerome Travers, an amateur from Upper Montclair, New Jersey, won in 1915 and the next year, Charles (Chick) Evans, Jr., became the third amateur winner in four years. World War I forced suspension of the tournament in 1917 and 1918 and then followed the exciting era of Walter Hagen, Gene Sarazen, and Bob Jones. Hagen won his second Open in 1919, Sarazen burst through as a cocky, quick-playing, 20-year-old in 1922 at Skokie in Glencoe, Illinois, and the immortal Bob Jones, ending seven years of frustration, began his seven-year reign as King of Golf with an Open victory at Inwood in 1923. From that point until 1930, when he abdicated,

Emperor Jones was destined to win four Opens as well as five National Amateur titles, three British Opens, and the British Amateur.

The retirement of Jones ended the constant amateur threat in the Open, and the pros took over. They were a highly skilled breed who sharpened their games on the professional tour. The amateurs were unable to match their steady, week-in and week-out competition and gradually fell back into the "also-ran" category—with one exception.

Johnny Goodman, an amateur, won the tournament in 1933—the last to break the pros' tightening grip on the Championship Cup.

Lawson Little, a tremendous match play competitor, was a strong amateur threat in the 1930's but failed to win the Open until 1940 after he had turned professional. Jack Nicklaus turned in the lowest score ever scored by an amateur in the 1960 tournament at Denver, but had to be satisfied with second place after a record comeback by Ar-

Recovery shots enabled Julius Boros to beat Arnold Palmer and Jacky Cupit in a play-off for the U. S. Open championship at Brookline in 1963. Here Julius comes out of the hay at The Country Club.

Jack Nicklaus beams with his 1962 U. S. Open trophies.

nold Palmer, who made up a 7-stroke deficit in winning with a 280. Nicklaus won the Open in 1962, his first year as a professional.

After Jones, no single man dominated the Open until Ben Hogan, the grim Texas Hawk, came along in the late 1940's and early 1950's to win four championships in the space of six years. His first came in 1948 when he set the 72-hole scoring record with 276 at the Riviera Country Club in Los Angeles. An automobile accident almost shattered the career of the tight-lipped Texan in 1949 but, battling tremendous odds, he came back to win again in 1950, 1951, and 1953. He seemed to have an unprecedented fifth championship in his grasp at the Olympic Club in San Francisco in 1955 when little known Jack Fleck rallied with a burst of birdies on the final holes to tie Hogan at 287. Emotionally drained, tired, and intent on retirement, Hogan never got going in the 18-hole play-off, losing 69 to 72.

Hogan's dramatic comeback from the verge of death and the emergence of a new breed of gambling, long-hitting powerhouses, headed by Arnold Palmer and Jack Nicklaus, sent the game skyrocketing to new heights. A record

2,475 filed entry for the 1962 National Open and prize money reached the $100,000 mark. Instead of $100, which Horace Rawlins pocketed in the first tournament in 1895, the Open winner in the mid-1960's was picking up checks of $17,000 and better.

In 1965, the U.S. Golf Association changed the format of the Open to make it a four-day instead of a three-day tournament. Thus the double round on the final day, in effect since 1919 and long a feature of the British Open, was discarded. The 72 holes were played over four days—18 holes a day.

The incident of the year before at the Congressional in Washington, D.C., when winner Ken Venturi almost collapsed from heat exhaustion, was said to have been a contributing factor. The U.S.G.A. insisted that the change was made necessary by the increasing tendency toward slow play and the difficulty of cramming 36 holes into a single day.

Many old-timers criticized the move, contending it was dictated by a desire for the television dollar, and argued that the Open had been stripped of its one distinguishing feature. The action, however, was approved by a majority of the contemporary players.

172

HIGH AND LOW SPOTS OF THE U.S. OPEN

Most Tournaments Won: 4, Willie Anderson, 1901, 1903, 1904, 1905; Bob Jones, 1923, 1926, 1929, 1930; Ben Hogan, 1948, 1950, 1951, 1953.

Consecutive Winners: Willie Anderson, 1903, 1904, 1905; John McDermott, 1911, 1912; Bob Jones, 1929, 1930; Ralph Guldahl, 1937, 1938; Ben Hogan, 1950, 1951.

Foreign Winners: Harry Vardon, Britain, 1900; Ted Ray, Britain, 1920; Gary Player, South Africa, 1965.

Oldest Winner: Ted Ray, Britain, 43 years, 4½ months, 1920. (Julius Boros was 43 years, 3 months, 20 days when he won at Brookline, Massachusetts, in 1963.)

Youngest Winner: Horace Rawlins, 19, in 1895.

Smallest Winner: Fred McLeod, 108 pounds, in 1908.

Lowest Winning Score: 276, Ben Hogan, 1948.

Highest Winning Score: 331, Willie Anderson, 1901 (winner in play-off with Alex Smith.)

Highest 72-Hole Score: 393, John Harrison, 1900.

Highest 36-Hole Cut: 155, Olympic Club, San Francisco, 1955.

Lowest 36-Hole Cut: 147, Cherry Hills, Englewood, Colorado, 1960.

Biggest Winning Margin: 11 strokes, Willie Smith, 1899.

Longest Championship: 144 holes, won by Billy Burke after two 36-hole play-offs with George Von Elm, 1931.

Lowest Round: 64, Lee Mackey, Jr., in first round at Merion (Pennsylvania) Golf Club in 1950 and Tommy Jacobs, second round at Congressional Club, Washington, D.C., 1964.

Lowest First 36 Holes: 133, Mike Souchak, Denver, 1960.

Lowest First 54 Holes: 207, Ben Hogan, Riviera Country Club, Los Angeles, 1948.

Lowest Scoring Average (10 or more Opens): Ben Hogan, 71.90 for 70 rounds.

Amateur Winners: Francis Ouimet, 1913; Jerome Travers, 1915; Charles (Chick) Evans, Jr., 1916; Bob Jones, 1923, 1926, 1929, 1930; Johnny Goodman, 1933.

Lowest Amateur Score: 282, Jack Nicklaus, 1960 (finished second to Arnold Palmer's 280).

Most Times Runner-Up: 4, Sam Snead and Bob Jones.

Chapter Twenty-two

The British Open: "Grandpappy" of Championships— and other Foreign Events

On March 9, 1745, the record book of the Honourable Company of Golfers at Leith showed the following notation:

SILVER CLUB
Robert Douglas, writer in Edinburgh representing the Captain of Gentlemen Golfers, advises that several gentlemen of the County of Fife have contributed a Silver Club to be played annually on the Links of St. Andrews and he in their name desired to know what day would be most convenient for the Gentlemen Golfers to honour the Gentlemen of Fife with their presence on that occasion. It was the opinion of the Captain of Gentlemen Golfers present that Tuesday, 30th of April next, might be most convenient for them. . . .

The tournament was not played until May 14, 1754. A silver club with St. Andrew engraved on the head was set up as a permanent trophy. The following rules were established:

1. Any nobleman or gentleman or other golfers from Great Britain or Ireland may qualify by paying 5 shillings and signing in book lying in the house of Mrs. Williamson (not further identified) in St. Andrews.
2. Names marked "1, 2, 3, etc.," are placed in a bonnet and drawn by the signers, who are matched accordingly.
3. Players go out in order and a clerk shall mark each stroke each shall take on each hole.
4. When the "wholle golfers" have played 11 holes, they play in again to the Hole on the Hill, making 22. Afterward a scrutiny

is made of the clerk's book and the golfer who won the greatest number of holes (each player matched against all the others) is the victor.
5. Four crowns go to the winner.
6. Every victor must append a silver ball to the Silver Club for the year he wins and must give the Club lodging until a month before the next match is played.
7. Disputes must be determined by the other subscribers (golfers).
8. No coaches, chaises, wheel machines or people on horseback or dogs are allowed to go through the links.

The first winner was Bailie William Landale, a merchant in St. Andrews. Such was the forerunnner of the oldest championship in golf, the British Open.

The British Open, however, did not begin officially until 106 years later. The Prestwick Golf Club, on the west coast of Scotland 20 miles south of Glasgow, put up a Champion Belt which was to serve as a challenge prize to be competed for annually over the Prestwick course. The competition was to be at stroke play over 36 holes—3 times around the 12-hole layout. One of the specifications was that a player winning the Belt three times in succession should gain permanent possession.

The first Open was held in 1860. Eight professionals entered. The winner was Willie Park of Musselburgh, who had a 36-hole score of 174. Par for the 12 holes was figured at 49 by later historians. The British never recognized par as a measuring stick.

This dull, gray structure by the North Sea represents the seat of golf. This is the club house of the Royal and Ancient Club of St. Andrews, Scotland, where the game was cradled.

The first 11 Opens were staged at Prestwick, and this was known as the "Prestwick Era" or the "Morris Era." During this period, the entry ranged between 8 and 17, and the Morrises, father and son, dominated. Of the 11 championships decided between 1860 and 1870, Tom Morris, Sr., or Old Tom Morris, serving as pro at Prestwick, won the Belt four times—in 1861, 1862, 1864, and 1867. Then Young Tom Morris took over.

Young Tommy was just 13 when he attempted to enter an invitation tournament at Perth. The tournament officials insisted he was too young. However, they arranged a match with one of the outstanding local youngsters, William Greig, and Tommy played such impressive golf that his reputation soon spread throughout Scotland.

The younger Morris was 18 when he entered and won his first Open in 1868. There was no other champion for the next four years. Young Tom retired the Belt by winning again in 1869 and 1870, the latter year with the astounding score of 149—25 shots lower than Willie Park's winning total in 1860.

Many old-timers contended that Young Tom Morris, who died in 1875 at the tender age of 24, might well have been the greatest golfer who ever lived. In the three championships he won to retire the Belt, he averaged nine strokes better than the runner-up.

Young Tommy's sensational sweep and retirement of the Belt so shook up the promoters of the Open that they were unable to organize a tournament in 1871 and did not get back into business until 1872. Three courses—St. Andrews, Prestwick, and Mussel-burgh—decided to rotate the tournament among themselves, each hosting the event in successive years. They set up a permanent silver cup which could not be retired.

This system remained in effect through 1891. Scotsmen continued to monopolize the 36-hole competition. Young Tom Morris added his fourth straight title in 1872. Willie Park won No. 4 in 1875, 15 years after his first. Jamie Anderson of St. Andrews captured three in a row in 1877, 1878, and 1879, and Bob Ferguson of Musselburgh, borrowing a set of clubs for his first try, duplicated the feat in 1880, 1881, and 1882. Scottish complacency was rocked in 1890 when John Ball became the first amateur and the first Englishman to take the title. The Scots reasserted themselves the next year but already there had been dropped a hint of changing times.

In 1892, the burgeoning championship was expanded to 72 holes, thus establishing the pattern for future stroke play tournaments. It was decreed that single rounds would be played on each of the first two days, Wednesday and Thursday, and 36 holes on the final day, Friday, making the competition a test of endurance as well as golfing skill. Saturday was left open for play-off purposes. The British disdained playing sports on the Sabbath.

From the beginning, the British smugly referred to their championship as simply "The Open," in effect labeling it the championship of the world. It was not until the American Open in the 1920's began challenging the British event for prestige that it became necessary to qualify the name to "The British Open," although the proud Britons themselves never acceded.

The first 72-hole tournament in 1892 was played at Muirfield, the new home of the Honourable Company of Edinburgh Golfers. Muirfield replaced Musselburgh in the order of rotation. Later, other layouts, both in England and Scotland, were brought into the British Open sphere—first Royal St. George's in Sandwich, then Hoylake, Deal, Lytham and

St. Anne's, Troon and Carnoustie. Through all these shifts and changes, one traditional provision remained unaltered—that was that the Open always should be played on a seaside link. The British golf fathers always have insisted that seaside courses, with their freakish weather and close-knitted turf, provide the greatest test of a man's skill.

During these early years, the golf professional was held in disrepute by most of the British, who regarded him as a drunkard and a ne'er-do-well.

The Badminton Book, an early authority on British golf, described the professional this way:

> The professional, as we are now chief acquainted with him, is a "feckless," reckless creature. In golfing season in Scotland he makes money all the day, spends it all the night. His sole loves are golf and whiskey. He works at odd times—job work or time work—in the shops but he only does it when reduced to extremity. He can rightly earn seven [shillings] and six pence a day by playing two rounds of golf, or, if he does not get an engagement, three and six pence by carrying clubs. In the medal weeks, they pick up a little more and an extra shilling or two comes into the pockets on side bets which they make with little judgment but which they seldom pay if they lose.

The famous English triumvirate of J.H. Taylor, James Braid, and Harry Vardon is credited with putting respectability in the profession. They helped raise the professional from a ragged hanger-on to a reasonably well-rewarded performer.

Just as the period from 1860 to 1870 was the Prestwick Era in the British Open, so the years 1872 to 1891 became the Era of the English Invasion, with English players entering the tournament in increasing numbers, and 1892 to 1914 the Era of the Great Triumvirate—Vardon, Taylor, and Braid. In those 22 years just prior to World War I, which saw a five-year suspension of play, Vardon won six Opens, Taylor and Braid five each. In 1926, 32 years after winning his first Open, Taylor made a courageous effort at Royal Lytham and St. Anne's to keep Bob Jones from taking the Championship Cup to America. He shot a third-round 71, a score better than any of the four by Jones.

Jock Hutchison, a Scotsman who migrated to America, became the first overseas player to capture the crown when he defeated Roger Wethered in a play-off at St. Andrews in 1921. The first American-born winner emerged the next year. Walter Hagen, the flamboyant pro from Rochester, New York, who had finished fifty-fifth two years before in his debut at Deal, grooved his shots in the swirling winds at Sandwich and prevailed with an even 300. Thus dawned a new era in the British Open— the Era of American Ascendancy.

Of the 13 tournaments contested between 1921 and 1933, Americans won 12. The exception was 1923, when Arthur Havers, an Englishman, beat out Hagen by a single stroke. Hagen captured the title four times (1922, 1924, 1928, and 1929); Bob Jones won three (1926, 1927, and 1930); and the other championships went to Jim Barnes (1925), Tommy Armour (1931), Gene Sarazen (1932), and Denny Shute (1933), in addition to Hutchison's triumph in 1921.

After Jones retired with his Grand Slam in 1930 and Hagen went into retirement, the American bid for the Cup subsided. There was a big boom in tournament golf in the United States and the professional tour offered rich prizes almost every week. With caches of such gold at their fingertips, leading American pros were disinclined to make the long trip across the Atlantic and fight the bone-chilling winds and rains of the British seaside links for the meager financial reward, ranging between $2,000 and $4,000. Many of

Bob Jones drives from the sixth tee at the Old Course of St. Andrews where he won the British Amateur championship in 1930 en route to his Grand Slam.

Ben Hogan follows flight of the ball after chipping from the rough grass at the fourth hole in the third round of the British Open at Carnoustie, Scotland. Hogan's victory was one of the milestones of golf.

them could get that much for a casual exhibition.

As a result of the American snub, the British Open lost much of its importance. It no longer could be reckoned as a true world championship of golf and it definitely took a subordinate role to the United States Open and later the Masters at Augusta, Georgia. From 1934 through 1960, there were only two U.S. winners, Sam Snead won at St. Andrews in 1946, and Ben Hogan, making his first bid, pulled off his fantastic Triple Slam by whipping the bitter cold at Carnoustie in 1953. Dubbed the "Wee Ice Mon," the grim, business-like Hogan, who previously that year had won the Masters and American Open, captured the heart of Scotland.

Englishmen, with Henry Cotton setting the pace with three victories, dominated the British Open from 1934 through 1948. Then

came the Era of the Commonwealth, during which golfers from far-off Australia and South Africa monopolized the championship rolls. In the 12 tournaments from 1949 through 1960, the Cup went either to an Australian or to a South African 10 times. The string was interrupted only by Englishman Max Faulkner in 1951 and Hogan in 1953. South Africa won the title five times, four by the paunchy putting master from Johannesburg, Bobby Locke, and the other by Gary Player. Peter Thomson of Melbourne, Australia, matched Locke's quartet of victories, winning three in a row in 1954, 1955, and 1956, and Kel Nagle of Sydney beat out Arnold Palmer for the centenary championship at St. Andrews in 1960.

As the calendar moved into the 1960's, a giant tug-of-war developed among the United States' leading players for the honor of being

178

the No. 1 player in professional golf. Chief rivals were Palmer and Jack Nicklaus, the young power-hitter from Columbus, Ohio, who won the three major American titles—the Masters, Open, and PGA—by the time he was 24. Both Palmer and Nicklaus became exceptionally rich men through tournament winnings and allied business interests, and the size of a purse no longer became a deciding factor in their plans. Both realized—as did other top American pros—that the British Open, as the oldest and most revered of championships, still carried tremendous prestige.

Palmer, beaten out by a stroke at St. Andrews in 1960, stormed back to win the tournament in 1961 at Birkdale and repeat in 1962 at Troon. Shooting for the only major title that had escaped him, Nicklaus missed by a whisker in both 1963 and 1964. At St. Anne's on-the-Sea in England in 1963, Big Jack came to the seventy-first tee needing only to par the final two holes to clinch the crown. He went bogey-bogey and lost by a shot to Bob Charles, the left-handed New Zealander. In 1964 at St. Andrews, Big Jack finished with rounds of 66-68, the best closing rounds in the history of the hoary event, yet fell 5 shots back of the victor, Tony Lema.

Lema, a tall, good-looking stylist who had won three tournaments on the American tour in 1964, became the eleventh American to win the British Open. Playing a seaside course and the smaller British ball for the first time and refusing to waver under Nicklaus' tremendous pressure, the 30-year-old iron-master from San Leandro, California, carved out rounds of 73-68-68-70 for 279, only 1 stroke over the old course record. Both he and Nicklaus promised to be back.

The British Amateur began in 1885, a quarter of a century after the start of the Open. Thomas Owen Potter, honorary secretary of the Royal Liverpool Club, suggested a tournament "open to all amateurs," and immediately there was a question of eligibility. Douglas Rolland, a stonemason from Elie, filed an entry but later it was discovered that he had accepted some prize money previously in the Open. So he was disqualified.

Forty-four "gentlemen golfers" answered the call of the first tournament. A dark-horse, Allan Fullarton Macfie, was the winner, beating Horace Hutchinson in the final, 7 and 6. The event was so poorly organized that three players wound up in the semifinals, enabling Macfie to get a bye. The tournament was not officially recognized until years later, and Macfie was retroactively proclaimed the first British amateur champion.

In 1886, 24 clubs joined in buying a silver trophy and establishing what was regarded for years as the official championship, the first tournament to be played at St. Andrews. Horace Hutchinson, a flamboyant and exciting golfer with a loose swing, won the first of his two straight championships. However, he and all other British amateurs were forced to perform in the shadow of the great John Ball, hailed by many as the finest British amateur who ever lived.

Ball, the first amateur to win the British Open in 1890, captured eight British amateur crowns over a period of a quarter of a century. His first victory was scored in 1888 at Prestwick and his last in 1912 at Westward Ho!, the latter in an extra-hole match. Ball is credited with being one of the first to fly a shot straight at the pin. Pitch-and-run shots on the hard British courses had been the accepted technique.

American players failed to dominate the British Amateur as they did the Open. The reason was that because of the heavy expenses most of them were able to compete only on Walker Cup forays—every four years—when the travel costs were underwritten by the USGA.

Walter Travis, the Australian who moved to the United States and took up the game at the age of 35, was the first American winner. He already had won three of the last four U.S. Amateur crowns when he decided to take a shot at the British championship in 1904 at Sandwich. The Old Man, 43 years old, was resented by the British, who regarded him as

Gene Sarazen tees off in the 1957 British Open at St. Andrews.

an unwelcome invader, and he did little to assuage their bitter feelings toward him. As the tournament progressed, it developed into an international feud. Travis beat Harold Hilton, a two-time winner, in the fifth round, 5 and 4, and then eliminated Horace Hutchinson in the semifinals, 4 and 2. Against Edward (Ted) Blackwell in the 36-hole final, Travis piled up a 4-hole lead in the morning round. He started the afternoon round with a 7 but rallied his game for a 4 and 3 triumph that made him the first foreigner ever to win the British Amateur.

It was not until 22 years later—in 1926— that an American-born player was able to crash the barrier. He was Jess Sweetser, a brawny former Yale University athlete who four years earlier had cut down the great Bob Jones and three other former titleholders en route to the U.S. Amateur championship. He won the British Amateur despite the most trying conditions.

En route to Britain with the American Walker Cup team, Sweetser contracted a se-

vere cold on ship. Later this developed into influenza. The one-time Yale quarter-miler should have been hospitalized, but he insisted on playing. He was feverish. His sinuses were acting up. His diet was restricted to fruit juices and a few slices of beef. He got in only two practice rounds at Muirfield, site of the British Amateur. He played golf during the day and rushed back to the hotel to bed where he tried to revive himself with medication and massages.

Wheezing and sneezing and playing on little more than sheer courage, Sweetser battled his way to the semifinals where he encountered his toughest match of the tournament. In a rugged match, Jess and the Honourable W. G. Brownlow finished the regulation 18 holes all square and went 3 extra holes before Sweetser finally won the twenty-first. The final was anticlimactic with Sweetser winning 7 and 6 over Archie Simpson, a Scotsman.

The British Amateur was one of the most evasive titles for the immortal Bob Jones, who did not win it until 1930, the year of his

Grand Slam and retirement. Bobby beat Roger Wethered in the final at St. Andrews, 7 and 6.

Lawson Little, one of golf's finest match play competitors, captured successive titles in 1934 and 1935, winning the American Amateur the same two years with a phenomenal unbroken streak. Bob Sweeny, a smooth-swinging socialite from Palm Beach, Florida, brought the United States another victory in 1937 and two years later the Cup went to Charlie Yates of Atlanta.

American winners popped up on the championship rolls fairly regularly after that. Willie Turnesa, one of New York's famous golfing brothers, came through in 1947 at Carnoustie, and Frank Stranahan, heir to a Toledo, Ohio, sparkplug fortune, won in 1948 and 1950. Richard Chapman (1951) and Harvie Ward (1952) continued the United States streak, broken when Ireland's Joe Carr won in 1953. Joe Conrad, a sandy-haired Texan, was the next American victor, in 1955 at Royal Lytham and St. Anne's. Three years elapsed before Deane Beman of Bethesda, Maryland, pulled off another Yankee coup in 1959. In 1962, Richard Davies, an outsider from Pebble Beach, California, was the only one of 30 Americans to go beyond the fourth round. He went on to triumph at Hoylake, the thirteenth American to take the crown.

THE BRITISH LADIES' CHAMPIONSHIP

The British Ladies' Championship was born in 1893. In that year, the Ladies' Golf Union was formed at the Wimbledon Club and at the first meeting it was decided that a ladies' championship should be staged. The date was June 13, 1893, the site, Royal Lytham and St. Anne's. Thirty-eight women showed up for the event, including competitors from Ireland and France but none from Scotland.

It was a match play event. After three days of eliminations over St. Anne's nine-hole ladies' course, Lady Margaret Scott emerged as the victor. She defeated Isette Pearson in the final, 7 and 5, for the first of her three successive championships. A couple of Irishwomen, May Hezlet and Rhona Adair, were the chief thorns in the side of the English women during the early years of the championship. Miss Hezlet won three times and Miss Adair twice between 1899 and 1907.

Two English women, Cecil Leitch and Joyce Wethered, virtually monopolized the tournament during the era that followed World War I. Miss Leitch, daughter of a Fifeshire man, won her first British crown in 1914, the year before the Great War erupted, then added victories in 1920, 1921, and 1926. Miss Wethered, whose brother was Captain of Golf at Oxford, carried off the championship in 1922, 1924, 1925, and 1929. The tall, shy Englishwoman came out of retirement in 1929 to play at St. Andrews and stand off the challenge of a strong American invasion, headed by the formidable Glenna Collett.

Miss Collett, ultimately winner of six American Women's Championships and hailed as the Bobby Jones of her sex, never succeeded in getting her name engraved on the British championship roll. She was beaten in the final by Miss Wethered in 1929 and by Diana Fishwick, a poised 19-year-old English girl, in 1930 at Formby.

It was not until Mrs. Babe Didrikson Zaharias, the Olympic double gold medalist, made her invasion in 1947 that the United States was able to make a dent in the strong British front. Awing the British with her tremendous drives and her bold style of play, the Babe literally bulled her way to the finals and there crushed Jacqueline Gordon, 5 and 4, at Gullane.

Louise Suggs, the little shot-making machine from Georgia who was the complete antithesis of the Babe, gave America its second successive triumph in the British Ladies' Championship in 1948, scoring 1 up over Jean Donald at Royal Lytham and St. Anne's. Marlene Stewart, a Canadian, won the title in 1953, smashing Philomena Garvey in the last round at Porthcawl, 7 and 6. Margaret (Wiffi) Smith won at Sunningdale in 1956 and Barbara McIntire scored at Harlech in 1960. This was by way of reminding the British that the girls across the Atlantic still knew how to play the game.

OTHER EVENTS

Other countries held national championships but none of them gained the prestige of the two major golf-playing nations, Americans frequently crossed the border to take honors in the Canadian Championships, both Open and Amateur. Byron Nelson, who never played in the British Open, won the French Open in 1955 after he had gone into semiretirement. U.S. pros frequently traveled to the bottom of the world for the Australian Open, but only Gene Sarazen (1936) managed to get his name on the cup. Gary Player of South Africa beat out Arnold Palmer and Jack Nicklaus in 1962 and 1963.

HIGH AND LOW SPOTS OF THE BRITISH OPEN

Most Championships Won: 6, Harry Vardon (1896, 1898, 1899, 1903, 1911, 1914.)
Most Successive Championships: 4, Young Tom Morris (1868, 1869, 1870, 1872; no tournament in 1871.)
Youngest Winner: Young Tom Morris, 18, in 1868.
Lowest Winning Score: 276, Arnold Palmer, Troon, 1962.
Largest Winning Margin: 6 strokes, Bob Jones, 1927; Walter Hagen, 1929; Arnold Palmer, 1962.
First Foreign Winner: Arnaud Massy, France, 1907.
American Winners: Walter Hagen (1922, 1924, 1928, 1929); Bob Jones (1926, 1927, 1930); Gene Sarazen (1932); Denny Shute (1933); Sam Snead (1946); Ben Hogan (1953); Arnold Palmer (1961, 1962); Tony Lema (1964).

HIGH AND LOW SPOTS OF THE BRITISH AMATEUR

Most Championships Won: 8, John Ball, England (1888, 1890, 1892, 1894, 1899, 1907, 1910, 1912.)
First Foreign Winner: Walter J. Travis, Australian-born U.S. citizen, 1904.
American Winners: Walter J. Travis, 1904; Jess Sweetser, 1926; Bob Jones, 1930; Lawson Little, 1934, 1935; Robert Sweeny, 1937; Charlie Yates, 1938; William Turnesa, 1947; Frank Stranahan, 1948, 1950; Richard Chapman, 1951; Harvie Ward, 1952; Joe Conrad, 1955; Deane Beman, 1959; Richard Davies, 1962.
Biggest Winning Margin: 12 and 11, W.I. Hunter over A.J. Graham, 1921.
Longest Final Match: 38 holes, John Ball beat Abe Mitchell on second extra hole, 1912.

HIGH AND LOW SPOTS OF BRITISH LADIES' AMATEUR

Most Championships Won: 4, Cecil Leitch (1914, 1920, 1921, 1926); Joyce Wethered (1922, 1924, 1925, 1929.)
Most Successive Titles: 3, Lady Margaret Scott (1893, 1894, 1895); Enid Wilson (1931, 1932, 1933.)
First Foreign Winner: Mlle. Thion de la Chaume, France, 1927.
American Winners: Mrs. Babe Didrikson Zaharias, 1947; Louise Suggs, 1948; Margaret (Wiffi) Smith, 1956; Barbara McIntire, 1960.
Biggest Winning Margin: 9 and 7, Joyce Wethered over Cecil Leitch, 1922.
Longest Final Match: 38 holes, Moira Paterson beat Frances Stephens on second extra hole, 1952.

Chapter Twenty-three

The Masters

"This is the Mecca of the golf world," Gene Sarazen once said, in describing the Masters golf tournament at Augusta, Georgia. "It's like Port Said or Casablanca. It's golf's international market center. Everybody's here. Sponsors come to scout for young pro talent. Merchants push their wares. Everywhere you see little knots of people—in corners or in clusters under a big tree—talking million-dollar deals. Every important figure in the game—player, official, manufacturer, and devotee—may be found at the Masters. It's where East meets West."

Such was the romantic label put on the famed tournament by one of the game's most colorful and durable champions. Graphic as it was, Sarazen's description did not begin to give the full, broad picture of the Masters.

Born decades after the two big Opens—the British and the American—and lacking official championship status, the Masters nevertheless moved up astonishingly to challenge these old, established fixtures as the most prestigious test in golf.

To play in the Masters became the goal of golfers the world over. To win it was an honor every golfer coveted. Many gave it precedence over the U.S. Open, which became generally recognized as the premier championship of them all, and the ancient British Open, which in later years declined in stature if not in tradition. Certainly no other single tournament attracted the same spectator appeal.

After the Masters came into full bloom, various explanations were offered as to the reason for its amazing success. Undeniably, one of the major factors was the association of Bob Jones, the immortal Grand Slammer in whose head the idea first took root. The tournament was played on one of the world's most beautiful and exacting courses. It came at a perfect time of the year—just when the early flowers and craving for golf were beginning to sprout after the long winter hibernation. Held at the same site each year, it was perfectly organized. Through its invitation list, the tournament maintained a bridge with the game's romantic past without sacrificing anything to the jet-paced present.

The Masters exceeded the fondest dreams and imaginations of its founders: Bob Jones; Clifford Roberts, slender, bespectacled Wall Street investment banker; and the small circle

Biggest long shot ever to win the Masters, Herman Keiser, *center,* is flanked by Ben Hogan and Bob Jones after his 1946 victory.

of friends who became members of the Augusta National Golf Club.

It all started with a broad, rolling plot of Georgia farm country—and an idea of Bob Jones.

After completing his Grand Slam in 1930—that is, winning the U.S. and British Amateur titles and the U.S. and British Opens in a single year—Jones retired from big-time competition. He joined a sporting goods company, took a weekly show on radio, and made a series of instructional movie shorts. However, at the age of 28, he had no intention of completely giving up the game that had been his life. He confided to friends that it had long been his ambition to construct what he considered a perfect golf course, incorporating some of the great holes he had played throughout the world, and then to enjoy the game in privacy with close companions.

In Augusta, the home of Jones's wife, he had met Cliff Roberts, who occasionally vacationed there. They became close friends. Roberts became keenly interested in Jones's idea of a dream golf course in the heart of the Southland. The New York banker said he knew of a particular piece of property just west of Augusta which might be bought at depression prices. Jones was intrigued.

On a nippy December morning in 1930, Jones, Roberts and another friend, Alfred Bourne, a member of a prominent sewing machine family, drove to the site.

Jones took one look—and was smitten. "I knew instantly it was the kind of terrain I had always hoped to find," Bob said later. "I had been told, of course, about the marvelous trees and plants, but I was still unprepared for the great bonus of beauty it offered. Frankly, I was overwhelmed by the exciting possibilities of a golf course set in the midst of such a nursery."

The site was an old indigo plantation known as Fruitlands. In 1857, four years before the Civil War, a Belgian nobleman and horticulturist named Baron Prosper Jules Alphonse Berckmans had bought the land and turned it into a nursery. He planted magnolia seeds along a drive that led to his manor house. Near the house he also planted Spanish cork oak, Chinese fir and hedge. Throughout the area—365 rolling acres with clusters of stately pines—the baron let his horticultural instincts run wild. It became a veritable gar-

Presidential foursome at the Augusta National Club brought together, *left to right,* Byron Nelson, President Dwight Eisenhower, Ben Hogan and tournament chairman, Cliff Roberts, 1953.

den of azaleas, camellia bushes, redbud and dogwood.

Their minds made up, Jones and Roberts set about turning their dream into a reality. They contacted friends, mostly men of means, who shared their love of the game. They formed a holding company and mapped plans for the formation of a private club. Membership was selected on a national basis, with a maximum of 30 to come from the Augusta area. Initiation fee was put at $350 and annual dues at $60.

Thus the Augusta National Golf Club was formed. Jones was elected president. Fielding Wallace, an Augusta textile manufacturer, was assigned the task of acquiring the property. Alister MacKenzie, a renowned Scottish golf architect, was obtained to join Jones in laying out the course. Work began in the spring of 1931.

Both Jones and MacKenzie had definite notions about what constituted an ideal layout. Fortunately, there was no conflict.

A feature about which Jones was adamant was that the natural terrain and hazards of Baron Berckmans' beautiful nursery should be retained with a minimum of built-in effects. Jones objected to the so-called "penal" system of course design wherein the player is instantly penalized on an errant shot. He preferred what he called "strategic" design with few man-made hazards and broad, unencumbered fairways offering the golfer several lines of attack.

Jones believed a player should be rewarded according to the difficulty and daring of the shot and the skill of its execution. He also felt that extremely long par 5 holes were not a true test and there should not be any hole which could not be reached with two big, well-hit shots. At the same time, these par 5's should not be allowed to become easy birdie holes so hazards were planted near the green to discourage the swing-away, go-for-broke hitter.

So the design of the Augusta National course called for wide fairways, massive greens where pin position could toughen or soften the score, and a scarcity of traps. Whereas most championship courses had up to 200 bunkers—and sometimes more—Augusta's design called for only 22.

MacKenzie's requisites of the perfect golf course were that is should first of all be pleasurable to the greatest number of players. Like Jones, he believed that as much of the natural beauty of the land as possible should be retained and that the course should require strategy as well as skill to make it an interesting challenge.

The course was finished in the fall of 1932. A white Colonial club house was built, with a tree-lined approach and a circular driveway at the front and with a rear balcony overlooking the ninth and eighteenth greens. Ed Dudley was hired as the professional. The Augusta National Golf Club, with some 100 charter members, was born.

Architect MacKenzie looked over his handiwork and remarked, "The Augusta National represented my best opportunity, and I believe my finest achievement." He died shortly afterward, not living to see his and Bob Jones's creation become the center of the new golfing world.

Bob Jones beamed. The new course fulfilled his ideals. It offered a retreat for him and his friends. At first, the thought farthest from the mind of any of the select little group of members was that they should share this wonderful garden spot with anyone else.

When the final flagstick was planted in the hole in 1932, the country was in the grip of a great depression. Interest in golf had deteriorated, both because of the scarcity of the entertainment dollar and because of the absence of that magical figure who had given the sport a booming lift in the Twenties, Bob Jones. The professional tour was just getting its cleats into the ground. There was strong agitation to get a big tournament in the South —"Bob Jones's country."

Fielding Wallace, the Augusta textile tycoon who was a charter member of Augusta National, also was active in the U.S. Golf Association, which he later served as president. It was natural that when discussion of a Southern site for the U.S. Open arose, the name of Bob Jones's new course should be mentioned. The idea was presented to Augusta members—and quickly vetoed. If a tournament is held at Augusta National, they said, "we'll do it ourselves." Then came the automatic question: Why not?

The more they talked about it, the more Augusta members liked the idea. Finally, they were galvanized into formal action. Details were quickly worked out. It would be strictly an invitation affair. It would be 72 holes of medal play, one round a day on each of four days. It would involve the great and near-great of the game, past and present. The invitation list would include all past National Amateur and National Open champions still living, plus the top 24 finishers in the previous year's Open and other selected players.

The date for the first tournament was set— the final weekend in March 1934. Prize money, raised by tapping the members and asking for donations, was fixed at $5,000. Cliff Roberts, serving as tournament champion, wanted to call the tournament the "Masters." Jones objected. He thought the name too presumptuous. So the first tournament was labeled the Augusta National Invitation.

Another obstacle had to be overcome at the start. Roberts felt that, to insure the success of the event, Bob Jones himself should be a competitor. Jones said no. He had determined, after 1930, never to play tournament golf again. He wanted to stick to his guns, but Roberts was very persuasive.

"I pointed out to him," Roberts said later, "that, as host, he couldn't very well invite his golfing friends to come and play his course and then not play himself." He finally agreed that he at least would play until the tournament became established.

Eighty-eight invitations went out; 72 professionals and amateurs responded. Heading the list was the name of Robert Tyre Jones, Jr. High excitement swept the golfing world. Could Bobby, after four years of retirement, come back? Could he beat players like Paul

The recovery talents of wild, long-hitting Billy Joe Patton, North Carolina amateur, thrilled Masters galleries in the 1950s. Here Billy Joe sprays out of a creek on the 13th hole during the third round in 1961.

Runyan, Craig Wood, Denny Shute, Macdonald Smith, and Horton Smith? Few doubted that he could.

All eyes, of course, were on the fabulous Grand Slam king from Atlanta when the players teed off at 10 A.M. on Thursday, March 22. Bob had shot a 65 in practice but had played rather spottily in a pro-amateur event on the eve of the tournament opening. He was not very confident when he teed off with Runyan for his first round. The gallery numbered about 1,000, and everybody followed Jones.

Bob was a disappointment. Typical of those players away from steady competition for a long time, Jones showed loss of little of his old wizardry from tee to green, but he was erratic with his chips and he showed an unsteadiness of nerves in putting. Although he used a replica of his famed hickory-shafted putting stick, Calamity Jane, which had been donated to the Museum of the Royal and Ancient Club in St. Andrews, he 3-putted three of the last five greens and finished with a first round 76, 4 over par.

The opening round lead, with 70's, was shared by Emmett French, Jimmy Hines, and a handsome, 25-year-old pro from Missouri, who once had been nick-named the "Joplin Ghost" by sportswriter Horton Smith. Another stroke back at 71 were Walter Hagen, Craig Wood, Henry Picard, and Jimmy Golden.

Jones found no remedy for his putting problems on the second day—a cold, bone-chilling day with a brisk wind whistling through the pines. Again he 3-putted three greens, missing once from 12 inches, and recorded a 74. With a 36-hole score of 150, the Grand Slammer was 8 strokes back of Smith, who took over the undisputed lead at the halfway point with 70-72 for 142. Ed Dudley, the Augusta pro, fired a competitive course record 69 and went into a tie with Billy Burke for second place, one stroke back. Jones's horde of worshipful followers were beginning to despair.

Bob putted better on the third day but the best score he could salvage was a 72, and that was not enough. Smith continued to play exceptionally well, fired another even par 70 and led after 54 holes with 212. Closest pursuers were Billy Burke, with 213; Dudley and Wood, with 214; Runyan with 215; and Hagen with 217. Jones was out of contention, 10 shots off the pace.

Golf fans were filled with nostalgia, if not with hope, when Jones and Hagen, the two masters of sport's Golden Era, were paired for the final round. Hundreds followed them out of sheer loyalty and suffered heavily as Jones shot 72 and Hagen skied to a 77.

Meanwhile, an interesting battle developed for the first championship. Blond, good-looking Craig Wood finished early with a final 71 for 285. Then he sat back to see if anyone could better it. Runyan and Burke made bids, but fell back to 286. Big Ed Dudley dumped his tee shot into a ditch at the fourth and dragged home with a 74 for 288.

That left it all up to Smith, a late starter. Horton, shaky on the outgoing nine, nailed a birdie at the tenth and knocked in one from

Jack Nicklaus, the 1963 Masters champion, is draped with the traditional green champion's coat by the 1962 winner, Arnold Palmer. **Wide World**

10 feet for another bird at the seventeenth. Now he needed only to par the final hole to win by a stroke. He boomed a good drive up the fairway, sent his pitch onto the green 25 feet from the cup, and then calmly 2-putted for his 4. He was the first Augusta champion with 284.

The tournament became known as the Masters. In the second event, Gene Sarazen scored his famed double eagle on the fifteenth hole of the final round to tie Craig Wood at 282 and later win in a 36-hole play-off. The tournament became renowned for producing the spectacular. Sportswriters, who formerly covered from the upper back porch of the club house, soon became so numerous that special quarters had to be provided. By the 1960's, the number of accredited press, radio, and television personnel had soared to more than 1,000.

Roberts never disclosed attendance figures, but crowds attending Saturday and Sunday rounds were estimated to run between 40,000 and 50,000—the most ever to watch a major golf tournament. Fans poured in by air, rail, and highway, choking the city's hotel and eating facilities. No other single sports event, except perhaps baseball's World Series, received wider coverage.

In the space of a few years, the roll-call of Masters champions read like a "Who's Who" of golf. Horton Smith won his second title in 1936. Byron Nelson won his first in 1937 and repeated in 1942, beating Ben Hogan in a play-off. Jimmy Demaret, the man with the flamboyant wardrobe and delicate putting touch, became the first to win three Masters—1940, 1947, and 1950. Then Sam Snead matched him—1949, 1952, 1954—and later Arnold Palmer made it four—1958, 1960, 1962 and 1964. Hogan won in 1951 and 1953, the latter year setting the record 72-hole score of 274.

Hogan's record lasted 12 years. Jack Nicklaus added his name to the list of champions in 1963, becoming at 22 years and 3 months, the youngest ever to take the title, and then, two years later, shattered Hogan's record by three strokes.

Firing rounds of 67-71-64-69 for 271, he played the massive Augusta National course in 17-under-par for the four days, in a performance hailed as one of the greatest of all time in tournament golf.

MASTERS FACTS AND FIGURES

Tournament Record, 72 Holes: 274, Ben Hogan, 1953.

Best Single Round: 64, Lloyd Mangrum, first round, 1940; Jack Nicklaus, third round, 1965.

Nine-Hole Record: Front nine, 31, Cary Middlecoff, 1955; back nine, 30, Jimmy Demaret, first round, 1940.

Record First 36 Holes: 68–67—135, Byron Nelson, 1942.

Record First 54 Holes: 67–71–64—202; Jack Nicklaus, 1965.

Most Tournament Victories: 4, Arnold Palmer, 1958, 1960, 1962, 1964.

Oldest Winner: Ben Hogan, 1953, 40 years, 8 months; second oldest, Sam Snead, 1954, 39 years, 11 months.

Youngest Winner: Jack Nicklaus, 1963, 22 years, 3 months; second youngest, Byron Nelson, 25 years, 2 months in 1937.

Fastest 18-Hole Round: One hour, 57 minutes, Gene Sarazen and George Fazio, Final round, 1947.

Biggest Comeback: Craig Wood shot 88 in opening round in 1936, scored 67 in second—difference of 21 strokes.

Best amateur performance: Charles Coe, 281, in 1961, lost out by one shot to winner Gary Player. Ken Venturi, as amateur, was runner-up to Jack Burke, Jr., in 1956 and Billy Joe Patton missed by one shot when Hogan and Snead tied in 1954.

Longest Putt: 75 feet, by Cary Middlecoff for an eagle at No. 13 during the second round, 1955.

Chapter Twenty-four

The U. S. Amateur:
Rocked in the Cradle of Controversy

In the summer of 1894, six years after John Reid and his Apple Tree Gang had introduced golf to the United States, a group of enthusiastic members of the nine-hole Newport (Rhode Island) Golf Club decided it was time to hold a tournament to determine the best amateur and professional players. A date was set in September. Invitations were dispatched to the handful of golf clubs which had popped up on the East Coast and in the Midwest.

Most of the clubs were concentrated in the East, generally rough layouts of only nine holes. In New Jersey, there were courses at Paterson, Lakewood, New Brunswick, and Montclair. The St. Andrew's Club in Yonkers, where Reid and his cronies hit their first shots with clubs and balls from Scotland, moved to a six-hole, so-called "cow pasture" on Palisade Avenue and later transferred to the General Jacob Odell farm on the Sawmill River Parkway in Westchester County, New York. Tuxedo and Newburgh had courses and Long Island turned up with Shinnecock and Meadowbrook. Middlesborough, Kentucky claimed a course, built in 1889, and there was an active club in Chicago—the Chicago Golf Club.

Twenty players accepted the tournament invitation of the Newport Club. Outstanding entrants were Herbert Leeds, from Boston; Laurence Stoddard, representing St. Andrew's; and Charlie Macdonald, a highly-rated contender from Chicago. They were to play 36 holes, 18 holes on each of two days.

The confident Macdonald started with an 89 and seemed to have the tournament well in hand. However, on the second day he skied to 100, taking a 2-shot penalty when one of his drives landed against a stone wall that bordered the course. A member of the host Newport Club, W.G. Lawrence, won with a total of 188.

Macdonald refused to accept his defeat as official. He contended, for one thing, that the

Charlie Macdonald, the impetuous mid-Westerner from Chicago, as a controversial figure in the first U. S. Amateur Golf Championships. His stubbornness also helped start the U.S. Golf Association.

stone wall was not a legitimate hazard and that he should not have been penalized two strokes. Furthermore, he added, an amateur championship should be decided by match play, as in Great Britain, and not medal play. He insisted that the Newport tournament be ruled "no contest" and that another be staged on a match play basis.

The controversy created excitement in golf circles. Eastern golfers resented Macdonald's brashness and were eager to cut him down to size. It was inevitable that another tournament should be arranged right away. St. Andrew's took the initiative. Invitations were sent to 27 clubs for an October match play tournament to be held at the new St. Andrew's quarters on General Odell's Gray Oaks estate. Twenty-seven golfers answered the call for what was to be the first United States Amateur Championship.

Macdonald, an impetuous, restless man, swept through his earlier rounds, defeated Lawrence in the semifinals, and went into the last round against Laurence Stoddard, who was playing on his home course. The two finalists finished the 18-hole round all square. On the first hole of a "sudden death" play-off the first in American golf history—Macdonald drove into a muddy, newly ploughed field and lost the match.

Easterners delighted at seeing the temperamental Westerner get his come-uppance, and they immediately hailed Stoddard as the new national champion. Macdonald would have none of it. He was ill during the match, he insisted, and, besides, the tournament could not be regarded as a national championship because it did not have the sanction of all the clubs. Stoddard, he said, was nothing more than winner of a club tournament.

As a result of the Macdonald incident, a group of well-meaning golf leaders called a meeting for the purpose of establishing a recognized authority to oversee the conduct of the sport. The body would make and enforce rules, settle disputes, and organize tournaments. Thus the United States Golf Association was born.

One of the association's first acts was to arrange for a National Amateur Championship. The dates were October 1–3, 1895. The site was the Newport Golf Club, where Macdonald had been beaten in the first unofficial tournament. Arrangements were made for a one-day Open, to be held the day after the Amateur, largely as a sideshow.

The tournament drew 32 players, who went immediately into the championship bracket without having to qualify. The format was for 18-hole matches leading up to the final, which was to be contested over 36 holes. It turned into a gala social event with a round of parties every night.

The inevitable Charlie Macdonald, hated and feared by the Easterners, was back for another—and this time an unquestionably official—bid. Most of the other players were novices at the game. Willie Lawrence, who had handed Macdonald his first tournament setback, was not entered. Laurence Stoddard, who won at St. Andrew's, was eliminated in the early rounds. Playing confidently, Macdonald swept through to the finals, where he found as his opponent a young man named Charles Sands from Newport, who had been playing golf less than a year.

It was a rout. Macdonald piled up a 5-hole lead over the morning 18 holes and closed out the match early in the afternoon, 12 and 11. Now he was the true American champion and he had no complaints, only a determination to win the championship several more times. It was a goal he never reached. Frequently in contention, he was thwarted in all future efforts to take a second title.

In 1896, the Amateur was awarded to the Shinnecock Hills Golf Club in Southampton, Long Island. This was a layout designed by Willie Dunn, a Scottish professional and architect, for a group of wealthy Americans, including W.K. Vanderbilt, Edward S. Mead, and Duncan Cryder. Laid out along the Great Peconic Bay, the course at first consisted of 12 holes and later was enlarged to 18. In addition there was a special nine-hole course for the ladies.

The second tournament was dominated by H.J. Whigham, a foreign newspaper correspondent who attended Oxford University and learned his golf in England. Whigham won the qualifying medal with 86-77 when the field was cut from 58 to 16, then went on to defeat J.G. Thorp in the final round, 8 and 7.

The first American-born player to win the championship was H.M. Harriman of the Knollwood Country Club in White Plains, New York, who beat the defending champion, Findlay Douglas, in the last round.

During the early years, the Amateur was dominated by two men whose names were so similar they often were confused. One of them was Walter J. Travis, an Australian whose family moved to the United States when he was four years old, a dark-bearded man who did not take up the game until he was 35. The other was Jerome D. Travers, who began swinging clubs at the age of 9 on his father's Long Island estate and who was a seasoned competitor at 13.

Travis won the first of three Amateurs at the Garden City (New York) Golf Club in 1900, successfully defended his title in 1901 at Atlantic City, New Jersey, and captured his third and final title in 1903 at Glen Cove,

New York. In the 1903 tournament, the former Australian had to beat the largest field to date—128 players having been placed in the bracket in accordance with the format of the British Amateur.

Travers at this time was just a pink-cheeked boy in short pants hitting the ball between a flagpole and a big oak tree on his family's lawn. Taught by Alex Smith, a Long Island pro, young Jerome developed quickly. He was just 20 when he won the Amateur for the first time in 1907 at the Euclid Club in Cleveland. Although Travis won the qualifying medal, Travers repeated in 1908 at Garden City. There was a three-year hiatus, during which time the cup was carried to England by 42-year-old Harold Hilton, before Travers was able to pick up his string again, winning consecutively in 1912 and 1913.

Charles (Chick) Evans, Jr., of Chicago, who was destined to play in 50 Amateur Championships and win two of them, made his first appearance in 1907 at the age of 17. Bob Jones, who was to set a record of five victories, made his bow as a fuzz-faced boy of 14 in 1916 at the Merion Cricket Club in Haverford, Pennsylvania, where Evans finally crashed through to his first title.

Jones made it to the finals in 1919, as a 17-year-old, and captured the qualifying medal in 1920, but it was not until 1924 that he managed to battle his way to the championship after five futile tries. He smothered Francis Ouimet, 11 and 10, and George Von Elm, 9 and 8, at the Merion Cricket Club and repeated the next year with an 8 and 7 triumph over Watts Gunn. The immortal Bobby won again in 1927 and 1928 and climaxed his Grand Slam in 1930 with an 8 and 7 rout of Eugene Homans.

No one has come close to matching Jones's record in the Amateur. For a two-year period, 1934–1935, Lawson Little, a powerful hitter from Stanford University, set an amazing match play winning pace that even Jones did not duplicate, but it was a case of being short and sweet. In putting Amateur Champion-

Walter Travis came over from Australia, didn't take up golf until he was 35, yet won three National Amateur crowns.

Jerome D. Travers started playing golf at nine, had the finest instruction available, won his first Amateur at 20.

Walter Hagen, Francis Ouimet, Jess Sweetser and Gene Sarazen line up for a 1932 benefit match. The amateurs, Ouimet and Sweetser, beat the Pros, 1 up.

A rain-drenched crowd watches Jack Nicklaus hit his second shot on the 18th hole at Pebble Beach, California, where he beat Dudley Wysong, Jr., in the final of the 1961 U. S. Amateur Tournament.

ships back-to-back those two years, Little won 15 straight matches. Taking the British Amateur title the same two years and winning a Walker Cup singles match, he extended his string to 32 consecutive match victories.

Willie Turnesa, youngest of seven golfing brothers, won the championship twice, 10 years apart, in 1938 and 1948. Marvin (Bud) Ward was a double winner in 1939 and 1941. Harvie Ward, a talented North Carolinian playing out of San Francisco, appeared destined to become one of the nation's amateur greats when he captured the title in 1955 and 1956 but he drew a suspension from the U.S. Golf Association for expense account irregularities and the incident seemed to cut the heart out of his game. He never was a factor after that. Charlie Coe, a reed-thin Oklahoma City insurance executive, scored the most one-sided final victory in modern times by beating Rufus King at Rochester, New York, in 1949 and came back to win the title nine years later at the Olympic Club in San Francisco.

Golf fans were hailing burly Jack Nicklaus of Columbus, Ohio, as "Another Bobby Jones" when he swept to Amateur titles in 1959 and 1961—just when he was reaching voting age—but Big Jack succumbed to the lure of professional golf before the start of the 1962 season. He left his mantle to Deane Beman, a little, crew-cut insurance man from Bethesda, Maryland, who won the Amateur title in 1960 and 1963 and the British Amateur in 1959. Beman was one of the few leading amateurs who expressed no interest in the rich professional tour.

The U.S. Golf Association created a mild furore in 1965 by changing the format of the Amateur from match to stroke play. It had been a match play event since its beginning in 1895.

The move drew strong objections from such outstanding former champions as Francis Ouimet, who captained the Walker Cup team for many years, and Charles (Chick) Evans, who played in more Amateur tournaments than any other man.

"Match play is the heart of amateur golf," argued Ouimet. "Medal play is cold and impersonal. It is man against a course and a

193

Jack Nicklaus blasts out of the sand onto the 15th green in the final round of the 1959 U. S. Amateur at Colorado Springs, Colo. He beat Charlie Coe for the title, 1 up.

hundred rivals he may never see. In match play, it is two men, head to head."

Evans took a similar view. "When an amateur wants to play golf, he goes out and finds another fellow he can play," he contended. "Stroke play may be all right for the expert, the professional. Match play always has been the game of the amateur."

The U.S. Golf Association said the change was made because stroke play was accepted as the truest test of golfing ability. Another factor was the desire to keep the bulk of the field in tournament through the four days rather

than reduce the field to four and then two as in match competition.

The first Amateur as stroke play was staged September 15–18, 1965, at the Southern Hills Country Club in Tulsa, Oklahoma. The theory that the change in format would aid oldsters such as Defending Champion Bill Campbell, Charlie Coe, Bill Hyndman, Ed Tutwiler and Dale Morey, all Walker Cuppers in their 40's, was quickly dispelled. Collegians dominated the event and the title went to an outgoing 22-year-old University of Florida senior, Bob Murphy.

194

HIGH AND LOW SPOTS OF U.S. AMATEUR

Most Victories: 5, Bob Jones, 1924, 1925, 1927, 1928, 1930. Jerome Travers won 4: 1907, 1908, 1912, 1913.

Most Times Runner-Up: 3, Charles Evans, Jr., 1912, 1922, 1927; Ray Billows, 1937, 1939, 1948.

First American-Born Champion: H.M. Harriman, 1899.

First Foreign Winner: Harold Hilton, England, 1911.

Last Foreign Winner: C. Ross Somerville, Canada, 1932.

Oldest Winner: Jack Westland, 47, in 1952.

Youngest Winner: Robert Gardner, 19 years, 5 months, in 1909. Jack Nicklaus was 19 years, 8 months, in 1959.

Youngest Player to Qualify: Bob Jones, 14 years, 5½ months, in 1916.

Largest Winning Margin (18 Holes): 9 and 8. Harry Todd over Matthew Zadalis, 1941; Gerald Kesserling over Russell Brothers, 1950; Don Keith over Thomas Beck, 1958.

Largest Winning Margin (36 Holes): 14 and 13. Bob Jones over John Beck, 1928; Jerome Travers over George Crump, 1915.

Largest Margin, Final Match: 12 and 11. Charles Macdonald over Charles Sands, 1895. In modern times, 11 and 10, by Charles Coe over Rufus King, 1949.

Longest Extra-Hole Match: 10 extra holes, 1930, when Maurice McCarthy defeated George Von Elm on twenty-eighth hole at Merion Cricket Club.

Longest Final Match: 39 holes. Sam Urzetta defeated Frank Stranahan, 1950.

Most Appearances in Tournament: 50, Charles Evans, Jr., between 1907 and 1962.

Most Matches Won: 57, Charles Evans, Jr.

Chapter Twenty-five

The PGA Championship—From Match Play to Medal

When golf was taking its first awkward steps and even while it was developing into young manhood, the professional was regarded and treated as a second-class citizen. The country clubs and the major tournaments catered to the "gentlemen amateurs." In Britain, the professional was barred from the club house for years. He was viewed as part of the working help. Much of the snobbery carried across the Atlantic to the United States. In the early days, the United States Amateur Championship was the blue ribbon tournament. The Open, in which the pros were allowed to play, was nothing more than a one-day sideshow. The majestic Walter Hagen helped erase the barriers against the professionals in Britain. The Professional Golfers Association of America, formed in 1916, brought new dignity to a swelling number of golf teachers. It also gave the pros a tournament all their own—the PGA Championship.

Rodman Wanamaker of Philadelphia, who played such an important role in the organization of the PGA, also was largely responsible for the championship tournament. The department-store heir offered to donate a trophy, $2,580 in prize money and various medals, if the pros would conduct a strictly professional tournament along the lines of Great Britain's News of the World Championship.

On July 14, 1916, at a meeting in Garden City, New York, the Executive Committee of the newly formed PGA enthusiastically approved the idea. It was decided that the tournament would carry the ambiguous name of "The Championship of the Professional Golfers' Association of America." The winner would get a cash prize, a trophy, and a gold medal. A silver medal would go to the runner-up, and bronze medals to the semifinalists as well as to the low scorers in the qualifying rounds in each of the seven local sections.

The first PGA Championship was set for the Siwanoy Country Club in Bronxville, New York, October 10–14, 1916. Thirty-two players were picked through sectional qualifying, but there was one absentee, so a championship bracket of 31 was set up. Jack Dowling drew the bye in a blind draw. Pre-tournament favorites were Jock Hutchison, a 32-year-old Scot from St. Andrews, and "Long Jim" Barnes, a 30-year-old native of Lelant, Cornwall. They had finished second and third, respectively, in the United States Open, won earlier that year by the amateur, Charles (Chick) Evans, Jr.

All the matches were at 36 holes. Both Hutchison and Barnes swept into the quarter-finals without too much trouble. Hutchison won his first two matches by lop-sided 11 and 9 margins and then beat Cyril Walker in the round of eight, 4 and 3. Barnes coasted to 8 and 7 victories over his first two opponents before encountering Tom Kerrigan, who carried him to the thirty-fifth hole before bowing, 3 and 1. In the semifinals, Barnes faced

Willie Macfarlane and Hutchison opposed a cocky, 23-year-old youngster from Rochester, New York, Walter Hagen, whose name was destined to be written on the championship cup more often than that of any other man.

Barnes, playing excellent golf, crushed Macfarlane, 6 and 5, but Hutchison, the favorite, found he had a tiger on his hands in young Hagen. The Haig carried the match the full 36-hole distance but finally surrendered to the Scotsman, 2 up. The final was dramatic. Hutchison led through the early stages of the final match and it was not until the twenty-fifth hole that Barnes forged to the front for the first time. "Long Jim" lost his advantage temporarily at the thirty-first, but regained it on the thirty-third and went on to score a hard-earned 1-up victory. The English-born professional thus became the first PGA champion. He collected $500 in first-prize money, the Wanamaker Trophy, and for his permanent possession a gold medal.

The championship cup stayed in Barnes' cabinet for four years. No tournaments were played in 1917 and 1918, during World War I, and in 1919 "Long Jim" successfully defended his pro crown at the Engineers Country Club in Roslyn, New York. His final victim was the frail-looking, 108-pound Fred McLeod, who had won the National Open in 1908. The wee Scotsman started like a runaway stallion, firing a 37 for a 1-up lead after nine holes and then going two holes ahead by winning the tenth. Barnes, however, reversed the trend by winning the next five holes in a row and then went on to a 6 and 5 victory.

Hutchison, beaten in the finals of the inaugural tournament in 1916 and in the quarter-finals in 1919, finally made the grade in 1920. Even then he had to slip in through the side door, entering the tournament as an alternate after failing to qualify in the sectional test. The diminutive Scotsman won over J. Douglas Edgar, 1-up, in one of the event's most exciting finals. Hutchison led by 3 holes after 27 and went 4-up with a birdie at the twenty-eighth. Then Edgar, who had shot 278 for 72 holes in the Canadian Open in

1919 for what was called a world record, captured 3 of the next 5 holes. Hutchison barely hung on to win.

Hutchison's victory ended an era. The first three PGA tournaments had been dominated by men who migrated to the United States from the British Isles. In 1921, the great Hagen won at the Inwood Country Club in Far Rockaway, New York, becoming the first American-born professional to take the crown. He not only launched the "Era of Hagen," which was to see him win five titles and go to the finals another time in the space of seven years, but he also was to give impetus to a long-running American reign. After 1920, American-born professionals won in all but three years. The subsequent foreign victors were Tommy Armour, the Black Scot from Edinburgh, 1930; Australian Jim Ferrier, 1947; and Gary Player, the putting wizard from South Africa, 1962.

At Far Rockaway, Hagen, whose swashbuckling air and supreme confidence already had begun to shake up his fellow professionals, swept through the bracket like a tornado. He defeated Jack Forrester, 6 and 4; Tom Boyd, 6 and 5; John Golden, 8 and 7; Cyril Walker, 5 and 4; and finally "Long Jim" Barnes, 3 and 2. Against Barnes, the Haig fired a 69 in the morning round and added a 33 for the first nine holes of the afternoon. Barnes had no reply for such blazing golf.

When Hagen did not defend the title in 1922, Gene Sarazen, a cocky 20-year-old youngster just out of caddy ranks, took over. Brassier even than Hagen, the stocky son of Italian immigrants attacked a golf course and his adversaries with a zest that refused to be denied. He beat Emmett French, 4 and 3, in the final at Oakmont, near Pittsburgh. The next year, Hagen was his victim in the first extra-hole championship match. Playing at the Pelham Golf Club in Pelham Manor, New York, Sarazen led through the thirty-fourth hole but Hagen won the thirty-fifth and made a spectacular recovery from a trap for a halve at the thirty-sixth that sent the match into extra holes. At the thirty-eighth, Sarazen played out of a cluster of crayfish mounds and sent a shot to the green across a dangerous elbow to win with a birdie.

These two remarkable professionals, alike in many ways, went on to set all-time records in the PGA. The Haig's four successive titles (1924, 1925, 1926, 1927) never have been paralleled. In compiling this streak, Hagen won 22 consecutive matches—also a record—before finally losing to Leo Diegel at Baltimore in 1928. In all, he won 40 matches.

In 1924, at the French Lick Springs Golf Course in Indiana, the Haig won 2-up over Barnes. "Long Jim," four down after the morning round, cut Hagen's lead to a hole at the twenty-ninth but Walter refused to give ground. The next year, at Olympia Fields near Chicago, the Haig had to go extra holes to beat Al Watrous and Leo Diegel in the early rounds but in the final he crushed "Wild Bill" Mehlhorn, 6 and 5. Walter started with an eagle on the 515-yard, par 5 first hole and never lost his lead.

The Salisbury Golf Links in Westbury, New York, was the scene of Hagen's third victory in the string in 1926 and the final victim was that old antagonist, Diegel. It was a bad day for Leo. On the sixteenth hole, Hagen rolled a 35-foot putt to the lip of the cup. When Diegel went up to look at the ball, it dropped into the cup. Diegel promptly missed his putt. On the first hole of the afternoon round, Diegel hit an approach that skipped over the green to a spot underneath Hagen's parked car. When the car was moved, Diegel's ball was in a deep rut from which three swings were needed to dislodge it. Hagen won 4 and 3. The Haig had to battle from behind for his fourth straight triumph at Dallas in 1927 but he won on the final hole from Joe Turnesa when Turnesa's putt hung on the lip of the cup.

The bouncy, quick-playing Sarazen set a record for longevity and match play victories in the tournament. He played in 29 PGA Championships and won 51 matches, 11 more than Hagen. Sarazen won his third PGA

crown at Milwaukee in 1933, 10 years after capturing his second. His pride pricked by remarks that he was "all washed up," Gene battled his way to the finals and there scored a 5 and 4 victory over Willie Goggin. Twenty years later, the spry, ageless Gene was still showing them that he was far from being through as a top-flight competitor.

While no one has matched Hagen's five championships, only one other golfer has equalled the three compiled by Sarazen. That was the smooth-swinging Sam Snead, who won in 1942, 1949, and 1951. Snead's triumphs, however, were blunted by the fact that he suffered the most one-sided final defeat in the history of the championship.

The surprising rout of the renowned slammer from White Sulphur Springs, West Virginia, occurred in the 1938 tournament at Shawnee Country Club, Shawnee-on-Delaware, Pennsylvania. Snead's opponent was little Paul Runyan, a so-called "popcorn" hitter. Everyone expected the long-knocking, talented Snead to crush his frail opponent. It was akin to setting a bunch of cannons loose against air rifles.

Runyan, chipping and putting masterfully, fired a 67 at Snead in the morning round and took a 5-hole advantage. Even then, observers figured this was perhaps a fluke and expected Snead to recover in the afternoon. The tiny Runyan never gave the slammer a chance. He shot a 35 for the first 9 holes and increased his advantage to 7-up. He won the twenty-eighth and then closed out the match by halving the twenty-ninth. Snead was a badly beaten victim, 8 and 7—the largest margin ever recorded in a PGA championship round.

The first 15 years of the PGA championship—13 tournaments with 2 out because of the war—were dominated by six men. They were Jim Barnes (1916 and 1919), Jock Hutchison (1920), Walter Hagen (1921, 1924, 1925, 1926, 1927), Gene Sarazen (1922, 1923), Leo Diegel (1928, 1929), and Tommy Armour (1930). By contrast, in the 15 years from 1950 through 1964, there were 15 different champions, no repeaters.

PGA officials attributed this to the fact that the tournament was played on a different course in a different part of the country every year, giving all professionals a fair and equal opportunity. Since 1916, the PGA Championship was played in 22 different states, from Washington and Oregon in the West to Massachusetts and North Carolina in the East. Prize money rose from Rodman Wanamaker's original $2,580 to nearly $100,000.

Although the PGA produced many exciting matches through the years, the format failed to hold the interest of the public and, in the 1950's, the tournament began to lose some of its luster. In gate appeal it was running a poor third to the Masters and the United States Open, both 72-hole stroke play events. So in 1958, over the vehement protests of match play supporters, the old style was discarded and a 72-hole, 4-day stroke play competition was substituted. With the PGA choosing stronger courses and making a real test of the event, the pros' family championship quickly regained its lost prestige.

As long as players such as Hagen, Sarazen, Diegel, and Armour were getting into the finals, the interest of the public was maintained. In 1935, however, the championship bracket was increased from 32 to 64 players and 18-hole eliminations were installed for the early rounds. Under this procedure, the big-name players frequently were eliminated in the first or second rounds and the tournament sagged into an anticlimax with little-known personalities reaching the finals. The stay-at-home teaching professionals made the PGA Championship their yearly tournament outing and they usually came intent on picking off the scalp of one of the famous tournaments pros to impress their members back home. They often did.

In 1947, Ben Hogan, Sam Snead, Jimmy Demaret, and South Africa's Bobby Locke were eliminated in the opening rounds, leaving Australian Jim Ferrier to win the title with a 2 and 1 victory over Chick Harbert. Three years later, another "dark horse" final developed when Chandler Harper of Portsmouth, Virginia, defeated Henry Williams, Jr., 4 and 3, at Columbus, Ohio. In 1953, six former PGA champions fell in the first two rounds and the title went to Walter Burkemo, who beat little Felice Torza, a club pro, 2 and 1, at the Birmingham (Michigan) Country Club.

The first PGA stroke play championship was staged at Llanerch Country Club in Havertown, Pennsylvania. Dow Finsterwald, known as "Mister Conservative" on the pro tour, was the winner with a 72-hole score of 276. The slender Ohioan with the reputation for never taking a gamble fired a 67, 3 under par, for the first round. A 72 on the second day put him into a tie at 139 with Jay Hebert, who was destined to win the title two years later. Snead, shooting for his fourth PGA championship, wrested the lead from Finsterwald and Hebert after 54 holes with 207. Bill Casper, Jr., was second, a stroke behind, and Finsterwald lay in third place with 209. Finsterwald shamed his critics with bold, aggressive golf on the final day, shooting a 31 on the front nine and finishing with a 67, which gave him a two-stroke edge over Casper. Snead came in third with 280.

Bob Rosburg captured the 1959 crown over the Minneapolis Golf Club. Jay Hebert won at the tough Firestone Country Club in Akron, Ohio, in 1960. In 1961, at Olympia Fields outside Chicago, wee Jerry Barber sank putts of 20, 40, and 60 feet on the final three holes to tie Don January for the title, then fired a 67 to beat January by a stroke in the play-off. The year 1962 was Gary Player's year and in 1963 Jack Nicklaus, the "Golden Bear," won in Dallas' sweltering heat.

Nicklaus, at 23, thus joined such immortals as Gene Sarazen, Ben Hogan, and Byron Nelson as the only players able to win the three major American pro championships—the Masters, Open, and PGA.

Nicklaus was heavily favored when the PGA took its Championship to Jack's home town of Columbus, Ohio, in 1964, but his legion of supporters failed to reckon with the mysterious powers of St. Jude, the patron saint of the impossible. St. Jude was on the side of the young man from Louisville, Kentucky, Bobby Nichols, during that unbelievable weekend in July. Nichols, bouncing balls off tree limbs, slamming out of knee-deep rough and sinking 30- and 40-foot putts over elephant mounds, took the lead with a record of 64 on the first day and never looked back.

He led every round—a feat never achieved before in the PGA Championship and he stood off the pressure of the sport's most dangerous chargers. Jack Nicklaus and Arnold Palmer.

Using a bargain-basement putter, Nichols sank putts of 30, 20, 15 and 10 feet in getting 8 birdies on his opening round. He fired a 71,

1 over par, for the second round but held a 1-stroke lead over Palmer. On the third day, he drove into the rough on 9 of the 18 holes, slashed his way out of constant trouble, turned imminent double bogeys into birdies and matched Palmer's 69. Spectators were still waiting for the amazing young man from Kentucky to blow up when he knocked in a 35-foot putt for an eagle on the tenth hole, then sank putts of 18, 15, and 51 feet on the fifteenth, sixteenth and seventeenth holes for a phenomenal closing 67. The handsome, baby-faced Nichols was the new PGA champion with a new record score—271. Nicklaus and Palmer, the two men who were supposed to fight it out for the title, were 3 strokes back at 274.

HIGH AND LOW SPOTS OF THE PGA CHAMPIONSHIP

Most Championships Won: 5, Walter Hagen (1921, 1924, 1925, 1926, 1927.)
Most Tournaments Won: 29, Gene Sarazen.
Most Matches Won: 51, Gene Sarazen. Walter Hagen, second, 40.
Youngest Winner: Tom Creavy, 20 years, 8 months, 1931. (Sarazen was 20 years, 9 months old when he won in 1922.)
Oldest Winner: Jerry Barber, 45.
Most One-Sided Final in Match Play: 8 and 7, Paul Runyan over Sam Snead, 1938.
Longest Single Match: 43 holes, Johnny Golden over Walter Hagen, first round, 1932.
Extra-Hole Finals: Gene Sarazen over Walter Hagen, 1923; Paul Runyan over Craig Wood, 1934; Vic Ghezzi over Byron Nelson, 1941, all 38 holes.
Foreign Winners: Jim Barnes, England, 1916–1919; Jock Hutchison, Scotland, 1920; Tommy Armour, Scotland, 1930; Jim Ferrier, Australia, 1947; Gary Player, South Africa, 1962.
Most Consecutive Match Play Victories: 22, Walter Hagen, 1924–27.
Most Times in Finals: 6, Walter Hagen.
Most Times Runner-Up: 3, Byron Nelson (1939, 1941, 1944.)

STROKE PLAY RECORDS (STARTING 1958)

Best 72-Hole Score: 271, Bobby Nichols (64–71–69–67), 1964.
Best 18-Hole Score: 64, Bobby Nichols, first round; Jack Nicklaus, final round, 1964.
Best Score for 36 Holes: 134, Jerry Barber (69–65), 1959.
Best Score for 54 Holes: 204, Bobby Nichols (64–71–69), 1964.

Chapter Twenty-six

The Public Links Championship:
Week-Enders Have Their Heyday

The sensational victory of former caddy Francis Ouimet over the great British stars, Harry Vardon and Ted Ray, in the National Open at Brookline, Massachusetts, in 1913 changed the whole face of golf in the United States. Golf always had been considered a strictly society sport, played by the idle rich at exclusive country clubs. Now here was just a slip of a boy—scrawny, 20 years old, in baggy pants—who had at first tied and then won a play-off over two of the game's most noted players.

The story was front-page news throughout the country. The Boston boy's picture became familiar in every household. Drugstore clerks, bricklayers, and factory workers read the accounts with relish and deep national pride. It is not inconceivable that they said to themselves, "If this lad can do it, why can't I?" At any rate, there immediately was a sharp rise in the sale of golf equipment and balls. Popularity of the game soared. In no time at all, it had lost its image as a society sport. It became a game of the people.

As public interest in golf increased, heavier became demands for places to play. The country clubs, which nurtured the game through the early part of the century, were both expensive and largely exclusive—out of reach of the rank-and-file devotee. Municipal courses mushroomed. Every town of any size had at least one public course. The big cities had many, and they were usually crammed.

One of the first to recognize the importance of this new facet of the sport was James D. Standish, Jr., of Detroit, later president of the U.S. Golf Association. On February 1, 1922, Standish convinced the U.S.G.A. Executive Committee that a tournament should be set up for the public links golfers, growing in number and enthusiasm. They were ineligible for the National Amateur, restricted to players belonging to U.S.G.A. member clubs. Standish offered to establish a perpetual trophy.

The first Amateur Public Links Golf Championship was played over the Ottawa Park Course in Toledo, Ohio, on August 28–31, 1922. Standish, serving as chairman of the U.S.G.A. Public and Municipal Golf Course Committee, was made tournament chairman. The event was open to players not holding privileges of any course from which the general public was excluded.

To the surprise of the tournament committee, a total of 140 entries was received. All but four of these showed up for the 36-hole qualifying round to pick 32 players for match play eliminations. George Aulbach, a 19-year-old Boston University student, won the low medal with a creditable 70-69 for 139 score. Aulbach lost to Edmund R. Held, 19, of St. Louis on the twentieth hole of an overtime semifinal. Held went on to take the title—first winner of the Standish Cup—by beating another teen-ager, Richard J. Walsh, 18, of New York, in the 36-hole final, 6 and 5.

A team competition was added to the National Public Links when the second tournament was held at East Potomac Park in Washington, D.C., in 1923. The occupant of the White House at that time was Warren G. Harding, a handsome, white-haired man who had a keen interest in golf. The president frequently invited such players as Gene Sarazen and Walter Hagen to the White House. He served as an honorary member of the U.S.G.A. Executive Committee. President Harding donated a trophy for the team competition which became known as the Warren G. Harding Trophy.

The format of the tournament was unchanged—that is, it consisted of 36-holes qualifying at stroke play and matches among the low 32. Each city area was limited to four representatives, whose scores on the final 18 holes of qualifying were added to make up the team standings. Eighteen teams were represented at East Potomac Park, and Chicago was the first winner with a total of 311. Ray McAuliffe of Buffalo, New York, won the low individual medal with 76-77 for 153, and Richard Walsh, beaten in the inaugural 1922 final, captured the championship.

Thus the first two tournaments were won by youngsters who had not yet reached their twentieth birthday. In 1926, the title went to the youngest player ever to take the championship, Lester Bolstad, 18, a student at the University of Minnesota. Bolstad's final victim was Karl F. Kauffmann, a Pittsburgh stenographer, who came back the next year to start a string of three straight victories.

Kauffmann dominated the event during this three-year span, 1927 through 1929, as no player has ever done. He beat Bill Serrick of New York in the first extra-hole final at Cleveland in 1927, scored the most one-sided triumph (8 and 7) over Phil Ogden of Cleveland in 1928, and then in 1929, at the age of 30, became the first man to win both the low medal and the championship in the same year. Playing at the Forest Park Municipal Course in St. Louis, he captured the medal in a play-off and beat Milton Soncrant of Toledo, Ohio, in the tournament final. The Pittsburgh stenographer's reign ended on a bizarre note in 1930 at Jacksonville, Florida,

when he signed an erroneous scorecard in the qualifying and was disqualified.

Repeat winners in the Public Links were rare. The on-the-scene qualifying and the match competition proved a severe test and there was a steady improvement in the caliber of players that came off the municipal courses. Charley Ferrera, a San Francisco riveter, won the title in 1931 and 1933. There was not another double winner until Richard Sikes, a student at the University of Arkansas, put victories back-to-back in 1961 and 1962. When Ferrera won in 1931, he had the distinction of beating the youngest player ever to reach the Public Links final, Joe Nichols, a 15-year-old schoolboy from Long Beach, California.

The tournament got so big that in 1934, with 33 teams entered, the championship bracket was raised from 32 to 64 players. Two 18-hole rounds were played each day for the first two days, with both the semifinals and finals contested over 36 holes. David Mitchell of Indianapolis was the winner, beating Arthur Armstrong of Honolulu in the last round.

By the late 1930's, the system of unlimited city area qualification rounds was becoming unwieldy. Use of two courses was needed to handle the bulky field of 222 at Bethpage State Park in Farmingdale, New York, in 1936. Two courses also were necessary to accommodate the list of 247 starters at Cleveland in 1938. In 1939, the U.S. Golf Association instituted sectional qualifying, a format used successfully in both the National Amateur and National Open tournaments. Thirty-three sectional sites were chosen for the tournament at Mount Pleasant Park Golf Course in Baltimore and 2,401 Public Links golfers, the largest number to apply for any USGA championship up to that time, responded. One hundred and ninety qualified, 178 started, and the ultimate winner was Andy Szwedko, a 32-year-old Pittsburgh steel worker.

No tournament was held during the years of American involvement in World War II (1942–1945), but the resumption of play in

1946 at the Wellshire Golf Course in Denver produced an assortment of interesting highlights. The entry list was the largest ever recorded in an official U.S.G.A. competition, 3,586. Jimmy Clark of Long Beach, California, set an all-time qualifying record with 64-70 for 134, 8 under par. Smiley Quick, 37, of Los Angeles won the championship by beating Louis Stafford of Portland, Oregon, 3 and 2. As a result, he received a special invitation to compete in the United States Amateur at Baltusrol in Springfield, New Jersey, where he lost a 37-hole final match to Ted Bishop.

The Public Links Committee of the U.S.G.A. continued to experiment with the format. Another change was made in 1956. The number of sectional qualifiers was reduced from 200 to 150. A 36-hole qualifying round on the site was restored to cut the list to 64 for the match play championship. The defending champion was exempt from sectional but not from the Championship qualifying.

The tournament produced its first Negro champion in 1959 when William Wright of Seattle, playing with 12 clubs, won over Frank Campbell of Jacksonville, Florida, a former professional, 3 and 2. Wright, a student at Western Washington College of Education, played with only two woods, Two years later, Dick Sikes, a 21-year-old student at the University of Arkansas, carried his clubs all the way and captured double honors. He won the medal with 70-65 for 135, then flashed a blast-hot putter in sweeping to the championship. He repeated in 1963.

The state of California, with a large number of public courses and with a climate permitting year-around play, clearly dominated the tournament through its first three decades. California had the most individual champions, 11 men who won 12 titles, and the most team victories, also 11. On four other occasions, Californians were beaten in the finals. Los Angeles led all others in winning the Warren G. Harding Team Trophy, prevailing seven times.

The tournament was held on public courses in every year except one. The Miami Country Club was host to it in 1952.

HIGH AND LOW SPOTS IN U.S. PUBLIC LINKS

Youngest Winner: Les Bolstad, Minneapolis, 16 years and 3 months, 1926.
Oldest Winner: Verne Callison, Sacramento, California, 41, 1960.
Lowest Qualifying Score: 64-70—134, James Clark, Jr., Long Beach, California, 1946.
Lowest Team Score (Three Men, 36 Holes): 425, Dallas, 1959. Team members were Hal McCommas, Ray Patak, Gene Towry.
Largest Winning Margin, Final: 8 and 7, by Carl Kauffmann over Phil Ogden, 1928.
Largest Margin, Semifinals: 12 and 11, by Irving Cooper over Edward Hart, 1953.
Longest Extra-Hole Matches (One Round): 24 holes. R.A. Wimmer over A.B. Hadden, 1922; Gordon Hammond over Horace Henry, 1949; Leonard Pietras over Larry Lee, 1959.
Longest Final Match: 38 holes. Dave Stanley over Ralph Vranesic, 1951.
Most Extra-Hole Matches by One Player in One Championship: 4, Stanley Bielat, 1950.
Most Championships Won: 3, Carl Kauffmann.
Most Team Victories: 7, Los Angeles, 1933–34–38–39–46–50–60.
Most Times Runner-Up: 2, William Serrick, 1925–1927.
Medalists Who Won Titles: Carl Kauffmann, 1929; Wilfred Crossley, 1947; Richard Sikes, 1961.
Youngest Player To Reach Finals: Joe Nichols, 15, in 1931.

Chapter Twenty-seven

Women's Amateur: From Petticoats to Bermudas

One month and six days after the first official men's United States Amateur Golf Championship had been played over the nine-hole Newport (Rhode Island) Club in 1895, the ladies gathered at the Meadow Brook Club in Hempstead, New York, for their own fairway soiree. It was the inaugural U.S.G.A. Women's Amateur Tournament.

The date was November 9, 1895. Thirteen ladies turned out for the gala occasion. They all were attired in the golfing uniform of the day—hats, heavy leather boots, and layers of fabric that made it seem astounding that they were able to swing a club at all.

Long cloth or tweed skirts reached from their waists to their ankles. Underneath was an assortment of petticoats, also touching the shoe tops. Blouses with full-length sleeves had starched collars around which ties were draped. Over the blouse it was fashionable to wear a bright-colored jacket carrying the club emblem on the breast pocket. On the ladies' feet were heavy shoes, some wore boots with metal tackets. On their heads were broad-brimmed hats, held in place by hat pins or veils tucked under the chin. Around their waists were heavy leather belts with buckles.

Burdened with such handicaps, Mrs. Charles S. Brown of the Shinnecock Hills Golf Club in Southampton, New York, toured the course in the fewest number of strokes to become the first American woman golf cham-

Bustles, long skirts and hats were the biggest obstacles for ladies who played golf in the Nineteenth Century. This print shows the girls cavorting on the Minchinhampton Common.

pion. It was a rather casual one-day, 18-hole tournament. Nine holes were played in the morning. The ladies then took time off for lunch and played the final nine holes in the afternoon. The intermission was quite understandable. The ladies needed as many strokes for 9 holes as modern golfers do for the full 18.

Mrs. Brown had a 69 in the morning and a 63 in the afternoon for a total of 132. Miss N.C. Sargent of the Essex County Club in Manchester, Massachusetts, was runner-up, two strokes back at 134. The record shows that a Miss May Bird of the host Meadow Brook Club needed 173 swings to complete the 18 holes. She finished eleventh and last. Two of the starters picked up in disgust and failed to record their scores.

Before the next year's tournament, the ladies got together with officials of the U.S.G.A. and decided upon some changes. The event was to be converted to match play, with on-the-scene qualifying to determine a bracket of eight players. Twenty-nine, more than double the first year, teed off at the Morris County Golf Club in Morristown, New Jersey. The tournament was dominated by a 16-year-old schoolgirl, Beatrix Hoyt of Shinnecock Hills, whose name was to appear frequently in the championship rolls during the succeeding years.

Miss Hoyt won the low medal with a 95. Then she proceeded to sweep through her three matches, one by default, to take the championship, beating Mrs. Arthur Turnure in the 18-hole final, 2 and 1. The first champion, Mrs. Brown, did not compete.

In winning the inaugural Women's Amateur, Mrs. Brown received as a permanent possession a silver pitcher donated by Messrs. R.D. Winthrop and W.H. Sands, a prize that later was donated to the Museum at Golf House, headquarters in New York, of the U.S. Golf Association. A permanent trophy was established in 1896, with Miss Hoyt the first to have her name engraved on it. It was the gift of Robert Cox, a Member of Parliament from Edinburgh, Scotland, who helped design the Morris County course and who was a spectator at the second annual tournament.

Miss Hoyt repeated her triumph in 1897, again winning both the qualifying medal and the championship at the Essex County Club in New Jersey and made it a triple slam in 1898 at the Ardsley Club at Ardsley-on-Hudson, New York. After three sweeps in a row, the Long Island girl failed to take another championship, although she extended her medal victories to five straight by leading the qualifying in 1899 and 1900. She retired in 1900 at the age of 20.

Each year saw a sharp increase in interest and in the number of entrants. In 1898, 61 women registered, making it necessary to enlarge the championship bracket from 8 to 16. This was further broadened to 32 in 1902 when the entry list began to push 100.

After Miss Hoyt stepped from the picture, Genevieve Hecker of the Essex County Club put titles back-to-back in 1901 and 1902 and the Curtis sisters, Margaret and Harriot, later donors of the Curtis Cup, moved into prominence.

Margaret made her first appearance in the Women's Amateur in 1897 as a spindly-legged girl of 13, playing with only four clubs. In her first tournament, she qualified with 122 but had the misfortune of meeting the defending champion, Beatrix Hoyt, in the first round. Little Margaret was dispatched to the sidelines, 8 and 6. Miss Curtis reaped her revenge three years later when she met Beatrix in the semifinals of the 1900 tournament at Shinnecock Hills, Miss Hoyt's home course. This time Margaret prevailed on the twentieth hole of an overtime match only to lose in the final to Frances Griscom.

Margaret Curtis tied for the low medal in 1901 and 1902 and again in 1905 but failed to make another serious run at the championship until 1905 when she swept to the final round at the Morris County (New Jersey) Club. She lost on the final hole to Pauline Mackay. It was sister Harriot who first crashed through to the title, winning in 1906, but Margaret was destined for the greater success.

The next year at the Midlothian Country Club near Chicago, Margaret captured the medal and then dethroned her sister by whipping Harriot in the final, 7 and 6. Margaret was an all-around athlete who played tennis as well as golf. In the summer of 1908, she teamed with Evelyn Sears to win the Women's National Doubles championship and thus became the only American ever to hold national titles in the two sports simultaneously, although Ellsworth Vines developed into a leading professional golfer after retiring from tennis.

The Curtis sisters' dominance was interrupted temporarily when Dorothy Campbell of North Berwick, Scotland, came over in 1909 to add the American title to her British championship—becoming the first double title holder—and to repeat in 1910 after winning the Canadian. But Margaret Curtis snuffed out the foreign menace by crushing the Scottish star in the 1911 semifinals, 4 and 3, en route to the championship, and added her third and final victory in 1912 over her home course, the Essex County Club.

The annual entry list had soared over the 100 mark by the time Alexa Stirling, a magnificent irons player who was a contemporary and a neighbor of Bob Jones in Atlanta, came out of the South to sandwich three straight championships around World War I. Alexa was only 19 when she took her first title at the Belmont Springs Country Club near Boston in 1916. After a two-year suspension during the war years, the Georgia girl returned for victories again in 1919 and 1920. Participants and spectators at the 1919 tournament at the Shawnee Country Club, Shawnee-on-Delaware, Pennsylvania, were impressed by a 16-year-old girl from Rhode Island, Glenna Collett. They were to see a lot of her—and marvel more—in succeeding tournaments. She was destined to become the Bob Jones of women's golf, winner of six championships, three of them in a row; eight times in the finals and six times low medalist.

Miss Collett started her victory string in 1922 at the Greenbrier Golf Club in White Sulphur Springs, West Virginia. She won again in 1925, 1928, 1929, 1930, and 1935. She was 32 years old, a housewife married to Edwin H. Vare, Jr., of Philadelphia, when she defeated Patty Berg in the finals at Interlachen in Hopkins, Minnesota, in 1935.

The caliber of golf played by the women improved markedly in the years immediately following World War I, when Miss Collett was in her heyday. In the 1915 tournament, more than half the qualifiers failed to break 100 and an 85 was good enough to win the medal. A decade later, Mrs. Alexa Stirling Fraser won the low medal at St. Louis with a 77. Nine qualifiers shot 85 or lower. Women who shot in the low 90's failed to make the championship bracket.

The next player to dominate the Women's Amateur was Virginia Van Wie of the Beverly Country Club in Chicago, who won three consecutive championships in 1932, 1933, and 1934. Miss Van Wie started her string at the Salem Country Club near Boston by crushing Mrs. Vare, the former Glenna Collett, in the final, 10 and 8. By this time, the title round had been extended to 36 holes and Miss Van Wie, flashing brilliant golf, fired a 73 in the morning to build up an almost insurmountable lead. Miss Van Wie's third championship was won against an expanded field, the qualifying list having been raised in 1934 to 64.

The cup went overseas a third time in 1936 —the first time since Gladys Ravenscroft of England had won in 1913—when 19-year-old Pamela Barton added the American to her British Ladies' crown in 1936. The English girl defeated Mrs. John Crews, the former Maureen Orcutt, in the last round at the Canroe Brook Country Club in Summit, New Jersey.

Entry lists kept going higher and scores falling lower as the tournament moved through the 1930's into the 1940's. In 1939, the handicap limitation was raised to 8 strokes and 201 women, constituting the largest field to that date, filed for the championship at the Wee Burn Club in Noroton, Connecticut. Beatrice Barrett captured the low medal with a 74, set-

Mrs. Glenna Collett Vare won the U. S. Women's Amateur championship six times. This portrait hangs in Golf House, the U. S. Golf Association Museum in New York.

Mrs. Vare holds the Bob Jones Award, presented her by the U. S. Golf Association in 1965 for her contributions to the game.

ting the record, and seven players had scores under 80. The ladies were moving solidly into the 70's and fixing their sights on the 60's. Betty Jameson, a statuesque blonde from San Antonio, Texas, who later was to become a leading tournament professional, was the victor, winning the first of her two successive Amateur crowns.

World War II forced a three-year break in the tournament, which was resumed in 1946 at the Southern Hills Country Club in Tulsa, Oklahoma. Star of the show in Tulsa's sweltering September heat was the strapping, exciting Olympic heroine from Texas, Babe Didrikson, now signing herself as Mrs. George Zaharias. The Babe had turned professional after winning the 80-meter hurdles and the javelin throw in the 1932 Olympic Games but had applied for and received a return of her amateur status. Booming her tee shots down the fairway in a most unladylike manner and rifling her irons at the pins, she swept through

the championship bracket without once having to take a deep breath. She never had to go beyond the fifteenth hole and in the 36-hole final she crushed Mrs. Clara Callender Sherman, 11 and 9.

The Babe might have won a half-dozen Amateur crowns had she chosen to keep her nonmercenary status. But the lure of the pros proved too great and, after adding the British Ladies championship in the spring of 1947, she decided again to use her talents for making money.

The year 1949 saw another marked change in the format, made necessary for the constantly expanding entry list. Qualifying at sectional sites replaced qualifying on the scene. The size of the championship bracket again was doubled—from 64 to 128. The tournament continued to draw from overseas. Mrs. Jacqueline Pung, a portly Hawaiian housewife, became the first from those Pacific Islands to win the title when she prevailed in

1952. Four years later, Marlene Stewart, 22, of Fonthill, Ontario, took the championship cup to Canada for the first time by beating JoAnne Gunderson, a promising 17-year-old Seattle student, 2 and 1, at the Meridian Hills Country Club in Indianapolis. JoAnne was not long for the role of runner-up.

The next few years were to see a grim struggle between the long-hitting Miss Gunderson and the stylish, deadly accurate Anne Quast for the No. 1 position in women's amateur golf.

Miss Gunderson, just out of Seattle's Kirkland High School, turned on a spectacular streak of near-par golf and won the 1957 title with an 8 and 6 victory over Mrs. Ann Casey Johnstone, a 34-year-old Iowa housewife. The Seattle schoolgirl was only 8 strokes over women's par for the 127 holes she played.

The next year was Anne Quast's turn. The 20-year-old Stanford University senior from Marysville, Washington, defeated Barbara Romack in the final at Darien, Connecticut.

Miss Gunderson captured her second championship in 1960 but Anne Quast, who in the meantime had become Mrs. Jay D. Decker, matched it in 1961. Miss Gunderson played perhaps the best golf of her career, particularly in the final round, in winning her third title in 1962. In the 36-hole final at the Country Club of Rochester, New York, the strong girl from the Northwest fired a two-under-par 70 in the morning round, including eight threes, and routed Ann Baker of Maryville, Tennessee, 9 and 8.

As if engaged in a giant chess game and checking her rival's every move, Anne Quast snapped back in 1963 to grab her third Amateur crown, beating Peggy Conley, a 16-year-old high school junior from Spokane, Washington, in the last round.

She thus joined Miss Gunderson and five other players who were able to win three championships—each of them still only halfway to the fabulous Glenna Collett's record of six.

Joyce Wethered, one of Great Britain's outstanding woman players, is shown during a Curtis Cup match at Sandy Lodge, near London, in 1926.

HIGH AND LOW SPOTS OF U.S. WOMEN'S AMATEUR

Most Championships Won: 6, Mrs. Edwin H. (Glenna Collett) Vare, Jr.

Most Times in Finals: Mrs. Edwin H. (Glenna Collett) Vare, Jr.

Youngest Winner: Beatrix Hoyt, 16, in 1896.

Largest Winning Margin: 14 and 13, Mrs. Jay (Anne Quast) Decker over Phyllis Preuss, 1961.

Longest Final Match: 29 hours, 15 minutes, Barbara Romack over Mickey Wright, 1954. (Thunderstorm halted play after first 18 holes, match resumed the next day.)

Longest Extra-Hole Match: Mae Murray defeated Fay Crocker on the ninth extra hole (twenty-seventh), 1950.

Foreign Winners: Dorothy Campbell, Scotland, 1909-1910; Gladys Ravenscroft, England, 1913; Pamela Barton, England, 1936; Marlene Stewart, Canada, 1956.

Winners of British and U.S. Championships: Mrs. Babe Didrikson Zaharias, Louise Suggs, Barbara McIntire, Marlene Stewart, Dorothy Campbell Hurd.

First To Win Both British and U.S. Championships: Mrs. Babe Didrikson Zaharias (U.S. 1946, British 1947.)

Consecutive Winners: Beatrix Hoyt, 1896, 1897, 1898; Genevieve Hecker, 1901, 1902; Dorothy Campbell, 1909, 1910; Margaret Curtis, 1911, 1912; Alexa Stirling, 1916, 1919, 1920; Mrs. Edwin H. (Glenna Collett) Vare, Jr., 1928, 1929, 1930; Virginia Van Wie, 1932, 1933, 1934; Betty Jameson, 1939, 1940.

Youngest Semifinalist: Roberta Albers, 14 years, 8 months, 1961.

Chapter Twenty-eight

The U. S. Women's Open Championship Started on a Shoestring

Six professionals and 25 amateurs showed up for the first National Women's Open Golf Championship, played in Spokane, Washington, in 1946. It was an improvised event sponsored jointly by a budding and loosely knit organization called the Women's PGA and the Spokane Athletic Round Table. The two groups did a monumental job of promotion and managed to offer a purse of $19,700. It was to be many years before the prize money reached that figure again.

Patty Berg, the stocky, flame-haired plugger from Minneapolis, won the qualifying medal with 73-72 for 145, and then won the championship at match play, beating Betty Jameson of San Antonio, Texas, in the final, 5 and 4.

The inaugural tournament was the only one played at match play. The next year at the Starmount Forest Country Club in Greensboro, North Carolina, the format was changed to 72-hole stroke play. The winner was Miss Jameson but a pair of amateurs, Polly Riley and Sally Sessions, added a touch of excitement by tying for second.

Mrs. George Zaharias, the former Babe Didrikson, drew a large gallery of admirers and the curious to the Atlantic City (New Jersey) Country Club in 1948. The Babe, hailed as America's foremost woman athlete, had turned professional after winning two gold medals in the 1932 Olympic Games. She had been reinstated as an amateur, winning the Women's National Amateur in 1946 and the

British Ladies' Championship in 1947, and now had rejoined the professionals. She drilled her shots through gusty winds and heavy rains for a score of 300, which beat Helen Hicks by 8 strokes. The total purse was only $7,500, peanuts compared to the men's purses.

The Ladies' Professional Golfers Association supplanted the original organization and took over responsibility of the Open in 1949.

Patty Berg, one of the outstanding figures in women's golf, tries to urge a putt home during a 1960 Titleholders tournament at Augusta. That's Marjorie Lindsay in the background.

Louise Suggs, little Miss Poker Face from Georgia, sits amidst some of her many amateur and professional trophies.

This was Miss Suggs' year. Striding the fairways like a feminine Ben Hogan, playing every shot meticulously and grimly, she opened with a 69 and finished at 291, 14 strokes better than the runner-up, Mrs. Zaharias. The Babe came back the next year to duplicate the 291 score and win her second championship at the Rolling Hills Country Club in Wichita, Kansas. The runner-up was an amateur, Betsy Rawls, destined to become one of the leading women professionals during the next 15 years. The demure miss from Austin, Texas, wasted little time. She turned professional before the 1951 event and won the Open title at Druid Hills in Atlanta, Georgia, with 293.

Meanwhile, interest was increasing in women's tournament golf. The Babe was a magnetic gate attraction. The ranks of the lady professionals were being swelled by glamorous additions. The pretty Bauer sisters, Alice and Marlene, with their blonde hair and wide swings, joined the parade. Marilyn Smith, an attractive, effervescent girl from Topeka, Kansas, brought a sparkling personality to the game. Bettye Mims Danoff, Kathy

Cornelius, and Beverly Hanson added good looks as well as good golf.

In 1953, the ladies decided that the Open should have the official sanction of the U.S. Golf Association. This might add to its stature and enlarge public interest.

Fred Corcoran, the Boston Irishman who had been so successful in building up the men's tour in the 1940's, was taken on by the Ladies' PGA in an advisory capacity and urged to use his influence with the U.S.G.A.

In the spring of 1953, Corcoran, then in Atlanta with the women's tour, placed a telephone call to Joseph C. Dey, executive director of the U.S.G.A., and broached the subject of U.S.G.A. sponsorship.

"The U.S.G.A. would have to be given full authority in the conduct of the tournament," Dey said. "It could not share the responsibility jointly with the LPGA. The LPGA agreed to step out. The U.S.G.A. Executive Committee approved the project. The first official Women's Open, under U.S.G.A. jurisdiction, was staged June 25–28 at the Country Club of Rochester (New York). The event drew 17 professionals and 20 amateurs. Miss Rawls and robust Jacqueline Pung of Honolulu tied for the title at 302. Miss Rawls won the 18-hole play-off by firing a 71 to Mrs. Pung's 77.

Mrs. Zaharias, suffering from cancer which later was to take her life, made her final appearance in the 1954 tournament and won her third championship with a courageous performance. The player who later was to succeed her as the dominant figure in women's golf, Mickey Wright of La Jolla, California, played in the event as an amateur and tied for fourth place.

Miss Wright won her first championship in 1958, repeated in 1959, 1961 and 1964. Mickey's closest friend and traveling companion, Miss Rawls, won the championship in 1951, 1953, 1957 and 1960.

As an open championship, the tournament had no restrictions against foreign competition, and outsiders became a constant threat. Fay Crocker of Montevideo, Uruguay, won the title in 1955, two years after turning professional. Mrs. Marlene Stewart Streit of Canada, winner of the U.S., British, and Canadian championships, was low amateur in 1961.

The ladies shared in the general boom that sent golf enthusiasm skyrocketing in the 1950's and 1960's. Their ranks became larger, their tournaments richer, and their crowds multiplied. A criterion was the 1961 Women's Open at Baltusrol in Springfield, New Jersey. The total attendance was 9,592, more than 2,000 ahead of any previous turnout. The ladies were on their way.

Babe Didrikson Zaharias, skirt almost to her ankles, waves putter futilely at ball during the 1949 Women's National Open, won by Louise Suggs.

HIGH AND LOW SPOTS OF U.S. WOMEN'S OPEN

Lowest Winning Score: 284, Louise Suggs, 1952.

Lowest Amateur Score: 299, Anne Quast, 1959.

Highest Winning Score: 302, Betsy Rawls and Mrs. Jacqueline Pung, 1953.

Largest Winning Margin: 14 strokes, Louise Suggs, 291, over Mrs. Babe Zaharias, 305, 1949.

Lowest Single Round: 68, Betsy Rawls, 1960, and Fay Crocker, 1958.

Oldest Winner: Fay Crocker, 41 years old, 1955.

Youngest Winner: Mickey Wright, 23 years, 4 months, 1958.

Youngest Winner of Low Amateur Honors: Judy Torluemke, 15, in 1960.

Champions Who Led All the Way: Fay Crocker, 1955; Betsy Rawls, 1957; Mickey Wright, 1958.

Most Victories: 4, Betsy Rawls (1951, 1953, 1957, 1960), Mickey Wright (1958, 1959, 1961, 1964.)

Most Times Runner-Up: 3, Louise Suggs, 1955, 1958, 1959.

Winners of Both U.S. Amateur and U.S. Open: Louise Suggs, Mrs. Babe Didrikson Zaharias.

From Tykes to Old-timers

Unlike most sports, golf is a game with no age barriers. It is played by youngsters not yet in their teens and oldsters in their 70's and 80's still capable of shooting their age. Recognizing the broad interest in the game among both juniors and seniors, the ruling bodies of the sport have moved to stimulate this interest by providing regular tournament competition.

The Professional Golfers' Association of America was the first to act. It launched the PGA Seniors' Championship in 1937, setting up three age categories—Class C, 50–54 years; Class B, 55–59; Class A, 60 and over. The U.S. Golf Association established the Senior Amateur Championship in 1955 for men of member clubs who had reached their fifty-fifth birthday. Seven years later, in 1962, the U.S.G.A. had to do the same for the women, starting the Senior Women's Amateur Championship. The U.S.G.A.'s Junior Amateur Championship, for boys who had not reached their eighteenth birthday, was inaugurated in 1948, a year before the launching of a similar event for girls.

The seed for the PGA Seniors' Championship was planted by a Chicago brewing concern, with a commercial interest, and given root by a Minneapolis professional, Willie Kidd. The brewery approached Kidd with the idea of an old-timers' tournament and offered to donate $5,000 in prize money. Kidd was enthusiastic. He wrote letters to a number of aging professionals. Most of them were ex-

cited over the plan but none had an answer to the two big problems: Where do we get a course? Where does the financial support come from?

Kidd was not easily discouraged. He brought Grange Alves, Jack Jolly, and Captain Charles Clark into the picture and the four of them formed an unofficial tournament committee. They approached the Augusta National Golf Club in Augusta, Georgia, and received strong support from Bob Jones and Alfred Bourne. The Augusta National agreed to be host of the first tournament but it had to change its constitution which specified that only one event—the Masters—could be held on the site.

Bourne donated a trophy, which became a permanent prize for the senior 55 years and over who had the lowest score for the first 36 holes of the 72-hole tournament. The PGA stepped in with a $3,000 grant to get the project off the ground.

The first PGA Seniors' Championship was not an astounding success. Only 37 professionals showed up at the Augusta National Club. Jock Hutchison, an Americanized Scotsman who was runner-up in the first PGA Championship in 1916 and winner in 1920, became the first Seniors' champion. Still spry at the age of 53, Hutchison scored 76-75-72—223—for 54 holes and beat out runner-up George Gordon by 8 shots. The amazing old Scot came back 10 years later to repeat at Dunedin, Florida.

There were three former U.S. and British Open champions in the inaugural tournament. They were Fred McLeod, U.S. Open, 1908; George Sargent, U.S. Open, 1909; and Hutchison, who had won the British Open in 1921. Hutchison was the star attraction. Besides his British Open and PGA victories, he had won the 1920 Western Open and had tied twice for runner-up in the American Open.

Oldest player in the inaugural event was Val Flood, 72, of Shuttle Meadow, Connecticut. He was one of four contestants in the Class A, 60 and over group. Two others were Bert Way and Tom Clark. Way was a constant participant until he died August 11, 1963, 17 days before his ninetieth birthday. Clark succeeded him as the "Grand Old Man" of Seniors' golf. In 1964, at the age of 87, Clark won the 85-and-Over Division by shooting a nine-hole score of 56. It was just a token round. He had no competitors. McLeod captured the 80–84 Division with 52-45—97.

After the first year, is was decided that 54 holes were too much for the old-timers and the tournament was reduced to 36 holes. The PGA Seniors' Championship gained greater financial stablility in 1956 when the firm of William Teacher and Sons, Ltd., of Glasgow, Scotland, makers of Scotch whisky, took over the joint sponsorhip of the event and organized a World Seniors' Championship in which the American winner was matched against the best senior in Great Britain.

Many of the lasting names of golf were inscribed on the Seniors' trophy. Through the first quarter of a century, there were two triple winners—Eddie Williams (1942, 1945, 1946) and Al Watrous (1950, 1951, 1957). Gene Sarazen won in 1954 and 1958, and Paul Runyan, "Little Poison," was victor in 1961 and 1962. Sam Snead won in 1964 and 1965.

The tournament finally was enlarged to a 72-hole competition in 1963 at Port St. Lucie Country Club, Port St. Lucie, Florida. The winner was Herman Barron with 67-67-69-69—272, two strokes better than John Barnum. It was Barnum who gave Sam Snead the strongest run for it in the Twenty-Fifth Anniversary Championship over the West Course of the PGA National Club at West Palm Beach Gardens, Florida.

Snead, winner of more than 100 tournaments in his career, led every round in shooting 67-68-73-71—279. Barnum finished 3 shots back at 282 and third money went to E.J. (Dutch) Harrison, 285.

The U.S. Golf Association started the Senior Amateur in 1955 to meet, it said, "the remarkable growth of senior golf." Many senior organizations had been organized on district, state, and sectional levels, with the oldest, the United States Seniors' Golf Association, having a restricted membership of 850.

The first tournament was played at Belle Meade Country Club in Nashville, Tennessee, September 26 through October 1. Unlike its professional counterpart, this was a match play event. Some 128 players qualified in sectional trials and competed in 18-hole qualifying at the scene for a 32-man championship bracket. The tournament was open to seniors belonging to member clubs of the USGA and eligibility was limited to those holding handicaps of 10 and under. The tournament drew 370 competitors from 30 states and the District of Columbia.

The low medal was won by Martin M. Issler of West Orange, New Jersey, with an even par 72. The first Senior Amateur Championship went to J. Wood Platt, 56, of Bethlehem, Pennsylvania, who was 2 under par for 14 holes in overpowering George Studinger of San Francisco.

The following two tournaments offered a unique turn of events. In 1956, Frederick Wright, Jr., 58, of Watertown, Massachusetts, won the title by defeating J. Clark Epsie of Indianapolis in the final. A year later, the tables were turned and Epsie, 58, won a final round victory over Wright. Epsie became the first double winner when he captured the 1959 championship at the Memphis (Tennessee) Country Club at the age of 60. He did not, however, qualify as the oldest champion.

That honor went the year before to Thomas C. Robbins, 65, of West End, North Carolina, who defeated Johnny Dawson, 2 and 1, at Pebble Beach, California.

The first man to win consecutive Senior Amateur crowns was Merrill Carlsmith, a Hawaiian attorney. Carlsmith won over Willis Blakely of Portland, Oregon, in the 1962 final at the Evanston Golf Club in Skokie, Illinois. The next year, at the age of 57, he successfully defended his title by beating Bill Higgins of San Francisco at Sea Island, Georgia.

Interest in the tournament continued to mount. In 1960, there were 508 entries, some 50 percent more than had signed up for the original event five years earlier. Two years later the entry list numbered 525.

The inauguration of the Senior Women's Amateur Championship followed as a natural course. A number of senior women's associations had come into being but there was no single tournament open to members of U.S.G.A. clubs. The request to begin such a competition was approved by the U.S.G.A. Executive Committee in January, 1962. For every man, woman, and child there was a U.S.G.A. national championship.

The field for the Women's Senior Amateur was limited to 120 players, selected on the basis of lowest handicaps. The format called for 54 holes of stroke play, one round each day for three days, in three age categories: Group A—50 through 54 years of age; Group B—55 through 59; Group C—60 and over.

The first tournament was played October 17–19 at the Manufacturers' Golf and Country Club in Oreland, Pennsylvania. There were 96 entries and 91 starters. Maureen Orcutt of Englewood, New Jersey, a golf reporter for *The New York Times,* won the championship with a score of 80-80-80—240. She beat out the great Mrs. Edwin H. Vare, Jr., the former Glenna Collett, by seven strokes. Miss Orcutt had twice been runner-up in the Women's Amateur and had played on four Curtis Cup teams. She not only won the over-all crown but also the B-Group for players between 55 and 59 years of age. The A-

Group prize went to Mrs. Allison Choate of Rye, New York, and the C-Group title to Mrs. Theodore Hawes of Baltusrol, Springfield, New Jersey.

Mrs. Choate won a play-off with Miss Orcutt for the title in the second tournament in 1963. Playing at the Country Club of Florida in Delray Beach, Mrs. Choate rallied from 4 strokes back with 5 holes to play and sank a 25-foot birdie putt on the final hole to tie the defending champion at 239. The 18-hole play-off the next day followed the same pattern. Miss Orcutt led by three strokes with three holes to play but lost the advantage when she dumped an approach shot into a bunker on the sixteenth hole. The two tied again after 18 holes at 81, forcing a sudden death play-off. Mrs. Choate finally won with a birdie two on the fourth extra hole.

The U.S.G.A. was considering a championship for boys before World War II but it was not until January 9, 1948, that official approval came from the Executive Committee. It was decided to launch a Junior Amateur Championship for boys who had not reached their eighteenth birthday. The purpose, as enunciated by the Executive Committee at the time, was to "develop in the younger players a knowledge of the rules and background of the game and an understanding of the spirit in which it should be played."

The first Junior Championship was held at the University of Michigan, August 11–14. Of the 495 boys who entered, 128 qualified for the tournament bracket through sectional trials. Warren Higgins of Dallas was low medalist with a 69. The first Junior champion was Dean Lind, a 17-year-old high-school graduate from Rockford, Illinois, who swept through seven 18-hole matches. His final victim was a slender, handsome youngster from San Francisco, Ken Venturi, later to become one of the nation's leading amateur and professional stars and U.S. Open champion in 1964. An earlier round victim of Lind was a pudgy, 14-year-old boy, Mason Rudolph, from Clarksville, Tennessee, also headed for an outstanding career on the pro circuit.

216

The history of the Junior is crowded with names of players who later made their mark in big-time tournament competition. Rudolph came back as a 16-year-old in 1950 to win the title. He was succeeded in 1951 by Tommy Jacobs of Montebello, California, later a leading tournament pro. Rex Baxter of Amarillo, Texas, won the Junior at the age of 17 in 1953. Phil Rodgers was a semifinalist in 1955. Jack Nicklaus was a semifinalist in 1956 and a qualifier in the next four tournaments but he never managed to crash through to the title.

The Girls' Junior Championship was started in 1949 with a format similar to but on a smaller scale than that of the boys. Open to young ladies who had not reached 18 years of age and whose handicaps did not exceed 36, the tournament consisted of an 18-hole qualifying round at the scene and a championship bracket of 32, playing 18-hole eliminations. The starting field was limited to 120, accepted on the basis of lowest handicaps.

Like the Junior Boys' Championship, the girls' event proved a stepping-stone to a successful career in the game for many of the players. Victor in the first tournament at the Philadelphia Country Club was a captivating, blonde tyke of 15, Marlene Bauer. One of two pretty sisters who later were to draw galleries on the ladies' pro tour, the 5'3" Los Angeles girl, who had been playing since she was three, defeated Barbara Romack, a future Women's Amateur champion, in the semi-

finals and Barbara Bruning in the final. Miss Romack was medalist the next year at the Wanakah Country Club in Hamburg, New York, but the tournament finalists were two whom golf fans were to see and read about for years to come. Pat Lesser of Seattle, 1955 Women's Amateur champion, was the victor. Her victim was tall Mary Kathryn (Mickey) Wright of La Jolla, California, later to shatter all records as a touring professional.

Mickey finally won the Junior Girls' in 1952. She scored a 1-up final round victory over Barbara McIntire, another future Women's Amateur queen. The defending champion in this tournament, Arlene Brooks, was eliminated by a poised, smooth-swinging 14-year-old girl from Everett, Washington, Anne Quast. Miss Quast was to go on to win three National Women's Amateur crowns. Another three-time Women's Amateur winner, JoAnne Gunderson of Seattle, captured the Girls' Junior in 1956 at Toledo, Ohio.

Judy Eller of Old Hickory, Tennessee, daughter of a professional, accounted for two early records in the event. She became the first to win consecutive championships when she prevailed at Denver in 1957 and at Greenwich, Connecticut, in 1958. In the 1957 tournament, she participated in the longest final to that date by going 20 holes with Beth Stone of Mukogee, Oklahoma. The Tennessee girl ran in a 25-foot birdie putt on the second extra hole for her triumph.

HIGH AND LOW SPOTS OF PGA SENIORS' CHAMPIONSHIP

Most Championships Won: 3, Eddie Williams (1942, 1945, 1946); Al Watrous (1950, 1951, 1957).
Lowest 36-Hole Winning Score (1938–1953): 138, Eddie Williams, 1942.
Lowest 54-Hole Winning Score (1937, 1954–1957): 210, Al Watrous, 1957. (Bob Stupple also shot 210, lost in playoff.)
Lowest 72-Hole Winning Score (1958–1964): 272, Herman Barron, 1963.
Biggest Margin of Victory: 8 strokes, Jock Hutchison, Sr. (223), over George Gordon (231), 1937; Eddie Williams (138) over George Morris (145), 1942.
Winners in First Attempt: Jock Hutchison, Sr., 1937; Sam Snead, 1964.
Oldest Competitor: Bert Way, 89, in 1963. (Died August 11, 1963.)
Most Tournament Appearances: 24, Jock Hutchison, Sr.

HIGH AND LOW SPOTS OF USGA SENIOR AMATEUR CHAMPIONSHIP

Oldest Winner: Thomas C. Robbins, 65, in 1958.
Youngest Winner: Michael Cestone, 55 years, 9 months, in 1960.
Champions To Repeat: J. Clark Epsie, 1957, 1959.
Largest Margin, Final Match: 5 and 4, J. Wood Platt over George Studinger, 1955.
Closest Final Match: 20 Holes, Michael Cestone over Davis Rose, 1960.
Largest Winning Margin, Any Match: 8 and 7, Christopher Carr over J. Wood Platt, 1957; George Dawson over Dewey Bowen, 1959.
Longest Match: 24 holes, J. Clark Epsie defeated Larry Stage, 1959.
Lowest Qualifying Score: 71, J. Clark Epsie, 1958.

HIGH AND LOW SPOTS OF USGA JUNIOR AMATEUR CHAMPIONSHIP

Youngest Winner: Charles S. McDowell, 16 years, one month, 1961. (Mason Rudolph was 16 years, two months in 1950.)
Youngest Player to Qualify: Verner Stanley, 12, in 1952.
Largest Margin, Final Match: 6 and 5, Larry Beck over David Leon, 1957.
Largest Margin, Any Match: 9 and 8, Don Bisplinghoff over Eric Jonas, 1952; Ronald Wright over Gary Allen, 1959; Richard Meissner over John Diesing, Jr., 1962.
Longest Extra-Hole Match: 28 holes, Michael Eiserman over Patrick Honeycutt, 1960.
Lowest Sectional Qualifying Score: 60, Leo Jordan, Jr., over par 58 Santa Fe Hills in Kansas City. Over regulation par course: 66, by Jerry Fehr, 1950; Dale Lingenbrink, 1952.

HIGH AND LOW SPOTS OF GIRLS' JUNIOR CHAMPIONSHIP

Youngest Winner: Marlene Bauer, 15, in 1949.
Consecutive Victories: Judy Eller, 1957–1958.
Most Tournaments Played: 7, Margot Morton.
Largest Winning Margin, Final Match: 5 and 3, Margaret (Wiffi) Smith over Sue Driscoll, 1954; Judy Eller over Marcia Hamilton, 1959.
Longest Final Match: 20 holes, Judy Eller over Beth Stone, 1957.
Longest Match: 22 holes, Judith Mintz over Berridge Long, 1953.
Lowest Medalist Score: 74, Mary Mills, 1956; Roberta Albers, 1962.

Chapter Thirty

The Ryder Cup

In 1926, Samuel A. Ryder, a tousled English seed merchant, and a few of his golfing cronies were sitting around the club house at Wentworth speculating on the outcome of the impending British Open Championship at Royal Lytham and St. Anne's. They were particularly interested in the strong American team, headed by Walter Hagen and Tommy Armour.

"Why not get up a little informal match between the top U.S. and British professionals?" Ryder suggested.

"Bully idea!" the others exclaimed.

The proposal was put to representatives of both groups. Hagen and his companions leaped at the suggestion. The British agreed. The match was played at Wentworth—to the chagrin of the visiting Americans. The British scored a smashing victory.

The British won all four of the foursome matches. In the singles, only Wild Bill Mehlhorn of the Americans was able to get a victory. George Duncan clobbered the great Hagen. Losses were suffered also by Jim Barnes, who had come over to defend the British crown; Armour, Al Watrous, and Joe Kirkwood.

It was all in fun, and every shot was replayed later in the afternoon at a tea, at which Ryder was host.

"This was wonderful," George Duncan remarked, turning to his host. "It's too bad we don't have a match like this which is official."

"Why not?" said Ryder, reflectively.

Samuel Ryder was strictly a man of action. Back in the Eighties, as a nurseryman in his father's seed shop in the north of England, he proposed that seeds would sell better in penny packets. His father disagreed. So Samuel pulled up stake, moved to St. Albans, near London, and launched his own business with the motto: "Everything in a penny packet from orchids to mustard and cress." His business flourished. He became wealthy—and bored. A friend suggested that he take up golf.

Reared on music and cricket, Ryder at first spurned the idea, then relented. He employed a private professional and proceeded to tour the country, playing and watching golf. At the age of 51, he had a 6 handicap.

A golf devotee with almost unlimited resources to spend on his hobby, he reacted quickly to Duncan's proposal of an official match between the leading golf professionals of the United States and Britain.

The deed of gift was drawn up. A graceful gold trophy was set up by Ryder. The U.S. and British PGA organizations gave their approval. The Ryder Cup series was born—you might say, from a penny packet of seeds.

The first of the biennial matches was scheduled for the following June at the Worcester Country Club in Worcester, Massachusetts. The ground rules called for four foursome matches, in which players of two-man teams hit alternate shots, and eight singles matches, all over 36 holes. A point would be given for each victory—½ a point for each halved match.

Playing for blood this time and on home grounds, the Americans reaped pleasant revenge for their setback at Wentworth the year before. The Yanks won three of the four foursomes and took six of the singles, halving one and losing one, for a 9½ to 2½ rout. The only British winner in the individual competition was Duncan, who won 1-up over Joe Turnesa. Gene Sarazen drew with Charles Whitcombe. U.S. winners included Hagen, Mehlhorn, Johnny Farrell, Leo Diegel, John Golden, and Al Watrous.

The second match was played at Moortown, England, April 27–28, 1929. The Americans again took the lead in the foursomes, 2½ to 1½, and appeared headed for another one-sided triumph.

The story is told that Hagen, the American captain, cooked it up with his old rival, George Duncan, leader of the British, to arrange the pairings so that they would play each other. "Well, boys," the flamboyant Hagen told other members of the team, "that's a sure point for us."

Duncan must have got wind of the boast. The next day, the British captain smothered the U.S. ace, 10 and 8. Gene Sarazen was beaten by Archie Compston, 6 and 4. Farrell, Watrous, and Joe Turnesa also dropped decisions. The lone U.S. winners were Leo Diegel and Horton Smith, with Al Espinosa gaining a draw. The British won, 7 to 5.

Thus, the series was under way, played every two years with the site alternating between the two countries. Hagen led the Americans to victory in 1931 at the Scioto Country Club in Columbus, Ohio, but the British came back for a narrow triumph at Southport, England, in 1933. Then the Americans took over, winning every series until the British rallied to win at Lindrick, in 1957. The competition became so one-sided that it came close to dying after World War II and managed to survive only because of the financial support of Robert Hudson, wealthy Portland, Oregon fruit dealer, and other patrons of the game.

In the 15 series played between 1927 and 1965, U.S. professionals won 13 and lost only 3. They were never beaten on American soil.

The format—two days of play consisting of four foursome and eight individual matches over 36 holes—remained unchanged until 1961 at Royal Lytham and St. Anne's where it was streamlined. The matches were cut from 36 to 18 holes and doubled in number. There were eight foursome matches—four in the morning and four in the afternoon—and 16 singles, divided the same way.

The change failed to alter the British luck. The Yanks won at St. Anne's-on-the-Sea, 14½ to 9½.

In 1963, at the East Lake Country Club in Atlanta, Georgia, renowned as the home club of the great Bob Jones, further experiments were made in an effort to tighten the competition and increase interest. The series was lengthened to three days and eight four-ball matches were added, making the program consist of eight two-ball, or Scotch foursome, contests; eight four-ball matches, with the best ball counting, and sixteen individual duels. With different lineups for the morning and afternoon, it became possible for a player to figure in as many as six points.

British fortunes were not improved by this change, either, and the powerful U.S. team led by Captain Arnold Palmer scored a resounding 23 to 9 victory, keeping intact the American record of never having lost on a U.S. course.

What was the reason for Britain's long string of failures? Had the pendulum of golf supremacy swung so decidedly to the new land across the sea? Was there a logical explanation for the repeated American victories, particularly on U.S. courses? These questions were debated on both sides of the Atlantic.

"It's the tough American tour that does it," said Bernard Hunt, one of England's top international players and leading money winner of the British circuit during the early 1960's. "Because of our climate, we can only play a part of the year. Because we are a small country, it is difficult for us to sustain spectator interest in more than a handful of tournaments. Americans follow the sun, play the year around for big purses, keep their games sharp, and become immune to pressure."

Peter Alliss, a second generation Ryder Cupper, took a different viewpoint. "We British are just as good as the Americans from tee to green, perhaps even slightly better," he said. "The Americans win on the putting greens. They are bolder putters. On putts of 4 to 10 feet, they bang the ball into the cup. We roll the ball into the hole."

Some observers blamed Britain's chronic failures in America on insistence of its players in use of the smaller British ball, six-hundredths of an inch less in diameter than the American ball. The argument was that, in the mild United States climate, there was no advantage to the smaller ball off the tee, where admittedly it bores better through gusty winds, while the larger American ball putted better and was more maneuverable around the greens.

Stating the American viewpoint, Palmer said he believed the U.S. pros won because they worked harder and were more dedicated. A British journalist commented: "It's become a mental block with our boys. They are beaten before they ever tee up the ball."

The U.S. superiority perhaps was not as pronounced as the final point totals might indicate. In the 1963 series at Atlanta, four of the matches lost by the British went to the final green, six to the seventeenth.

Membership on the Ryder Cup teams, carrying with it no monetary reward, became highly prized by players of both nations.

The 10-man U.S. team is selected by the Professional Golfers Association Executive Committee through an involved point system, but character and sportsmanship also are taken into consideration.

Ryder Cup point standings are figured on the basis of a predetermined formula in all official tournaments on the PGA tour, plus approved events such as the Masters, Western Open, Canadian Open, and U.S. Open.

In each tournament, except the PGA Championship which carries a higher value, points are awarded on the following basis: 70 for first, 42 for second, 28 for third, 21 for fourth, 18 for fifth, 14 for sixth, 11 for seventh, 10 for eighth, 8 for ninth and 6 for tenth—a total of 228 points in all. The PGA Championship offers 115 Ryder Cup points for the winner, with the others on the following scale: 70-45-35-30-25-20-15-10-10.

The British team is chosen on the basis of points scored in nine official PGA tournaments. The British PGA awards 100 points to the winner, 90 for second, 85 for third, 83 for fourth, and thereafter a drop of 2 points for each place down to fortieth, for which 11 points are given.

Unlike the PGA of America, which compiles Ryder Cup points over a two-year period, the PGA of Great Britain selects its team on the basis of performances for a one-year period just prior to the matches.

Ryder died in 1936 at the age of 77. His daughter, Mrs. Thomas Scarfe, took over his seed business. A prominent writer, lecturer, and philanthropist, she did not, however, continue her father's interest in golf.

RYDER CUP FACTS AND FIGURES

Most One-Sided Team Victory: United States 11, Britain 1, at Portland, Oregon, 1947.

Closest Matches: At Southport, England, 1933—Britain 6½ , United States 5½ , at Wentworth, England, 1953—United States 6½, Britain 5½.

Most times on Team: Dai Rees, Britain, 9 (1937, 1947, 1949, 1951, 1953, 1957, 1959, 1961, 1963). Second, Sam Snead, U.S., 7 (1937, 1947, 1949, 1951, 1953, 1955, 1959).

Most Matches Played: Dai Rees, Britain, 18 (won 7, lost 10, drew 1). Sam Snead, U.S., 13 (won 10, lost 2, drew 1). Gene Sarazen, U.S., 12 (won 7, lost 2, drew 3).

Most Matches Won: Sam Snead, U.S., 10.

Most Matches Lost: Dai Rees, Britain, 10.

Best Winning Percentage (Six Matches or More): Jimmy Demaret, U.S., won 6, lost none, drew none.

Most One-Sided Foursome Victory (36 Holes): 10 and 9, Walter Hagen and Denny Shute, U.S., over George Duncan and Arthur Havers, at Columbus, Ohio, in 1931; Lew Worsham and Ed Oliver, U.S., over Henry Cotton and Art Lees, at Portland, Oregon, in 1947.

Most One-Sided Individual Score (36 Holes): 10 and 8, George Duncan, Britain, over Walter Hagen, at Moortown, England, in 1929.

Chapter Thirty-one

The Walker Cup

At the end of World War I, people turned to sports on a broad scale in an effort to get their minds off the terrible tragedy they had just experienced. It was the dawn of the era known as the Golden Twenties. Outstanding personalities in various athletic fields gripped the imagination of the public. Golf followers were intrigued by the exploits of a young, baby-faced boy out of Atlanta named Bobby Jones.

The war had stimulated internationalism. Doughboys by the thousands had crossed the Atlantic to join in the big skirmish and had become acquainted with Europe. On the other hand, Europeans were eager to see the New World. The world had shrunk. It was only natural that people should start thinking in terms of worldwide competition in sports. In such an atmosphere the Walker Cup series was born in 1922.

This biennial contest between the best men amateur golfers of the United States and Great Britain, however, was not spontaneous. It took root—as an idea—in early experiments with matches between the United States and Canada. It gained substance with informal meetings in Britain. Finally, it became a reality.

In 1919, the Royal Canadian Golf Association invited the U.S. Golf Association to send an amateur team to Canada. The U.S.G.A. accepted. A 10-man team was formed with William C. Fownes, Jr., serving as captain. Other members were John Anderson, Eben Byers,

Charles (Chick) Evans, Jr., Bob Gardner, Bob Jones, Oswald Kirkby, Max Marston, Francis Ouimet, George Ormiston and Jerome Travers. The match was played at the Hamilton (Ontario) Golf Club on July 25, 1919, with five foursome matches in the morning and ten individual matches in the afternoon. The United States won, 12 to 3. The next year, a return match was played at the Engineers Country Club in Roslyn, New York, and the Americans repeated their victory, 10 to 4.

American amateurs clearly were superior to their northern neighbors. It was obvious that if an international competition should be inaugurated, it should be between the United States and Great Britain. American golf had grown to full manhood as the result of Francis Ouimet's astounding triumph over Britain's famous Harry Vardon and Ted Ray in the 1913 United States Open at Brookline, Massachusetts. Now it was ready to challenge its British ancestor on any and every front.

More and more Americans—professionals and amateurs, men and women—were crossing the ocean to seek the major British championships. In increasing numbers, the Britons were making assaults on the U.S. tournaments. In 1920, Bob Gardner gained the final round of the British Amateur at Muirfield, losing to Cyril Tolley in a rugged, 37-hole match. The same year, a large number of Britons, including Tolley, Roger Wethered, Lord Charles Hope, and Tommy Armour, played in the U.S. tournament at Roslyn, New York.

The British visitors were intrigued by the match between the United States and Canada and talked enthusiastically about entering such a series themselves. The seed of this idea already had been planted months before—among men in higher places.

The rules committee of the Royal and Ancient Club of St. Andrews, recognized as the ruling body of the game, had taken note of the astonishing growth of golf in America and had invited the executive committee of the United States Golf Association to participate in discussions dealing with modification of the playing code.

The U.S.G.A. was honored. Members of the executive committee set sail for Scotland in the spring of 1920 to talk rules changes, and, during off moments, to test the fabled seaside links where the sport was cradled. One of the most enthusiastic of the group was George Herbert Walker, then serving as president of the U.S.G.A. Walker had been a leading amateur in the St. Louis area before transferring his membership to the National Golf Links of America in Southampton, New York.

Walker returned to the United States thoroughly convinced that there was need for an international team competition among amateurs. He discussed it freely with fellow officials of the U.S.G.A. Then, on December 21, 1920, at a meeting of the executive committee in New York, he put his proposal on a formal basis. All golf-playing nations should be invited to compete, he said. He himself would donate a permanent cup to be known as the International Challenge Trophy.

The U.S.G.A. approved the idea. Early in 1921, an invitation went out to all countries to send an amateur team to the United States to compete for the new International Trophy, which already—much to the embarrassment of the donor—had been christened the Walker Cup. The Americans waited. Nobody came—not even the British.

It appeared that Walker's brainchild had died aborning. The Americans, however,

were not easily discouraged. Bill Fownes, who had organized the matches against Canada in 1919 and 1920, assembled another team and took it to Britain in the spring of 1921. It was a formidable group, headed by Francis Ouimet and the sensational American prodigy, Bob Jones, just turned 19. Others on the team were Chick Evans, Jesse Guilford, Paul Hunter, Wood Platt, and Fred Wright, Jr.

The match was played at Hoylake, scene of the 1921 British Amateur. The Americans gave an outstanding show in whipping the British, 9 and 3. The staid Royal and Ancient Club must have been duly impressed. At its regular meeting the following spring, it decided to accept—a year late—the U.S. Golf Association's bid for a challenge match.

The opening contest was set for Walker's home club, the National Links at Southampton on Long Island, but Walker had since been succeeded by Howard F. Whitney as president of the U.S.G.A. Whitney was in charge of hammering out the format with officials of the Royal and Ancient Club. Each country was to select eight players. The competition was to consist of four foursome matches and eight individual matches to be played over 36 holes during a two-day period.

The United States selected virtually the same lineup that had walloped the British the year before at Hoylake. Fownes was to serve as captain. Ouimet, Evans, Jones and Guilford were on the team along with Bob Gardner, Max Marston, Jess Sweetser and Rudolf Knepper. Bob Harris captained the British squad, which consisted of Cyril Tolley, Roger Wethered, Colin Aylmer, C.V.L. Hooman, W.B. Torrance, John Caven and Willis MacKenzie.

The Americans won three of the four foursome matches and captured five of the eight singles for a convincing 8-to-4 victory. One of the U.S. setbacks saw Sweetser lose an extra hole duel to Hooman, who won 1-up on the thirty-seventh. This became significant, because it turned out to be the only extra hole match on record in the series. Before the next meeting, the two countries decided not to

Members of the U. S. Walker Cup team get together for sailing to England from New York, April 26, 1947. They were, *left to right,* standing: Marvin Ward, Smiley Quick, Richard Chapman, Skee Riegel, A. F. Kramer, Jr., George Hamer, Jr., Willie Turnesa and Frank Stranahan; *left to right,* kneeling: Francis Ouimet, captain, Charles Littlefield, President of the U. S. Golf Association and Fred Bishop.

carry out to a conclusion matches which were even at the final hole, and in such cases, no points were to be awarded.

If the British hoped to get revenge in a return meeting on their home grounds, they were bitterly disappointed the next year when the Americans, accepting a British invitation, invaded St. Andrews to defend the cup. It was not so much the 6 and 5 American victory that inflicted a biting sting. It was the way the match was lost when it seemed securely in Britain's grasp.

The British won three of the four foursome matches on the first day, making it necessary for the United States to capture five of the eight singles if it was to retain the cup. In the individual contests, the host team jumped off to a quick advantage in the morning round and appeared headed for a certain triumph. At one stage the U.S. players, in their eight singles matches, were collectively down by 24 holes.

Then lightning struck, and the British golfers did not know what hit them. Francis Ouimet, down 2 holes with 3 to play, birdied the thirty-fourth and thirty-sixth holes to gain a half against Roger Wethered. George Rotan, 6 down after 14 holes, won 11 of the next 12 holes and crushed Willie Mackenzie, 5 and 4. Fred Wright, 2 down with 3 holes to play, swept the final 3 holes for a 1-up victory over Ernest Holderness. Max Marston, 1 down after the morning round, rallied for a 6 and 5 victory over Willie Hope. Finally, with the team score tied 5–5, the outcome hung on the battle between Dr. O.F. Willing of the American team and Britain's William Murray. Doctor Willing won the thirty-fourth and thirty-fifth holes for a dramatic 2 and 1 triumph that kept the Walker Cup in American hands.

The tenor of the series was set. The Americans won, 9 to 3, in 1924 at the Garden City Golf Club, but the British put up a good

225

scrap, carrying every match as far as the thirty-third hole. After 1924, it was decided that the matches should be held every two years instead of annually, but there was no blunting the sharp edge of American superiority.

The great Bob Jones, reaching the zenith of his game, paced the United States to successes in 1926, 1928, and 1930 before retiring in his Grand Slam year at the age of 28. During this period, the Atlanta Wonder scored the most one-sided triumphs of the international competition. In 1926, at St. Andrews, he crushed Cyril Tolley, 12 and 11. In 1928, at the Chicago Golf Club, he trounced Philip Perkins, 13 and 11, the biggest Walker Cup margin of all time. Two years later, Roger Wethered was the victim, 9 and 8.

The retirement of Jones failed to halt the United States' long winning streak. With players such as Jess Sweetser, Lawson Little, Johnny Goodman, John Fischer, and Charley Yates carrying the load, the Americans racked up the most smashing triumphs of the series during the next six years. They won, 8 to 1, at Brookline, Massachusetts, in 1932, with three matches halved; 9 to 2, at St. Andrews, in 1934, and in 1936 scored the first shutout with a 9–0 triumph at Pine Valley in Clementon, New Jersey.

United States amateurs won 9 straight meetings over a 14-year period—1922 through 1936—before their golfing cousins across the Atlantic were able to stem the tide. Even then, it was only a temporary hesitation.

The British beat an apparently smug and overconfident United States team at St. Andrews in 1938. The Americans had won the previous three meetings by humiliating margins. They fielded one of their strongest teams, headed by Charley Yates of Atlanta, who had just won the British Amateur at Troon. However, the British, captained by John Beck, gave a plucky, fighting performance and came off with a 7 and 4 victory.

Finally, they had won the Walker Cup. They were destined to keep it for nine years only because World War II intervened and play was suspended until 1947. When compe-

tition was resumed at St. Andrews, a new crop of American amateurs took over and re-asserted United States superiority. With players such as Willie Turnesa, Skee Riegel, Frank Stranahan, and Bud Ward, the United States fashioned an 8-to-4 victory that started a new winning skein.

In the ensuing years, the British never seriously threatened to win the cup again. The American assembly line kept a steady stream of talented amateurs flowing into combat. As soon as a leading amateur retired or turned professional, another just about as good was ready to step into his shoes. Charley Coe came up from Oklahoma City, Jim McHale from Philadelphia, Sam Urzetta from Rochester, New York. Princetonian Bill Campbell from Huntington, West Virginia, became a popular and effective member of the U.S. team, later its captain. Harvie Ward was a star in the early 1950's. Players such as Gene Littler, Ken Venturi, Tommy Aaron, and Jack Nicklaus flashed briefly on the Walker Cup scene and then turned to successful pro careers. The lure of professional gold failed, however, to attract Charley Coe, Bill Hyndman, Deane Beman, and the irrepressible Billy Joe Patton. They remained amateurs—and always ready for a Walker Cup call.

In 1963, the format was changed to include eight foursome matches and sixteen singles, all played over the 18-hole instead of the 36-hole route. At Turnberry, Scotland, that year the British put up a good fight, winning seven of the singles, losing six and halving three but the Americans prevailed by taking six of the eight foursomes.

Two years later, over the Five Farms course of the Baltimore Country Club, the British, led by 18-year-old Peter Townsend and 20-year-old Clive Clark, stepped off to an 8–3 lead on the opening day and split the morning foursomes on the second day for a 10–5 advantage.

The United States seemed definitely headed for defeat before rallying its forces in singles to gain an astounding 11–11 tie. At one stage the Americans were trailing in seven of the eight

Billy Joe Patton chips to the green at the fifth hole during the 1963 Walker Cup matches against England at Turnberry, Scotland. Patton and Richard Sikes beat Britain's Mike Bonallack and Stuart Murray in a match.

individual duels but the veteran Ed Tutwiler triggered a U.S. comeback that saw them win six, tie one and lose one of the final matches.

Clark had to sink a 34-foot birdie putt on the final hole in the final match to give the British a tie.

HIGH AND LOW SPOTS OF THE WALKER CUP

Most One-Sided Team Victory: 9–0, United States, 1936, at Clementon, New Jersey.

Biggest Singles Margin (36 Holes): 13 and 12, Bob Jones, U.S., over Philip Perkins, 1928, at Wheaton, Illinois.

Biggest Singles Margin (18 Holes): 7 and 5, Joe Carr, Britain, over Richard Sikes, 1963, at Turnberry, Scotland.

Biggest Foursomes Margin (36 Holes): 9 and 8, Billy Joe Patton and Charley Coe, U.S., over Mike Bonallack and Arthur Perowne, 1959, at Muirfield, Scotland.

Biggest Foursomes Margin (18 Holes): 5 and 3, Deane Beman and Charley Coe, U.S., over Mike Lunt and David Sheahan, 1963, at Turnberry, Scotland.

Most Walker Cup Appearances: 12, Francis Ouimet, U.S. Played 1922, 1923, 1924, 1926, 1928, 1932, 1934; captained team in 1936, 1938, 1947, 1949.

Most Walker Cup Matches: 16, Francis Ouimet, U.S. Foursomes, won 5, lost 3; singles, won 4, lost 3, halved 1.

Most Victories: 9, Francis Ouimet and Bob Jones.

Most Singles Victories: 5, Bob Jones.

The Curtis Cup:
The Women's International Series

The Curtis Cup, a biennial series between the leading women amateurs of the United States and Great Britain, never attained the broad scope envisioned by its donors, the Curtis sisters.

Harriot Curtis won the U.S. Women's Amateur Championship in 1906 and her sister, Margaret, who reputedly could hit the ball as far as most of the men of her day, succeeded her in 1907 and repeated in 1911 and 1912.

The Curtis sisters had a strong belief in the future of international golf, and as far back as the mid-1920's, they were trying to promote a worldwide competition involving women's teams from many nations. Both active in the affairs of the U.S. Golf Association, they offered to put up a permanent trophy for that purpose.

Meanwhile, the best American players were taking periodic voyages across the Atlantic to compete in British events and Britain's stars were returning the favor.

In 1924, the Women's Eastern Golf Association approached the British Ladies' Golf Union and the French Golf Union with a plan for a series of matches among the ladies of those three countries. Nothing came of it. Subsequent talks were held in 1927 and 1929, still with no results. It was decided that there was no means for financing such expensive expeditions.

Glenna Collett, the talented Rhode Island girl, took a group of American women abroad in 1930 to play a British team. It was an in-

formal match, without sanction or help from the U.S. Golf Association. But the event was such a resounding success that the inauguration of an official series became inevitable.

The idea was brought up again before the official ruling golf bodies of the United States and Britain in 1931. The British Ladies' Golf Union met in February and gave the plan its unqualified approval. Two months later, the USGA also agreed and voted to assume financial responsibility and administration of the matches.

The first matches were set for Wentworth, England, on May 21, 1932. They were to involve teams of the United States and Britain with the door left open for the admission of France when that country felt it was ready to compete. The offer of the Curtis sisters to donate a trophy was accepted and the Curtis Cup was born.

It was somewhat ironic that the trophy carried the following inscription: "To stimulate friendly rivalry between the women golfers of many lands." To the disappointment of the donors, the competition never expanded beyond the United States and Britain. Thirty-two years later, the Curtis sisters' dream was realized with the inauguration of the World Cup competition, open to women players of all lands, in Paris. The Curtis name was not on it.

The opening matches at Wentworth accented a point which already had become evident in the Ryder Cup and Walker Cup battles involving the men professionals and amateurs of the two countries—the pendulum of golf superiority had swung decisively away from the place of its birth to the New World.

The first Curtis Cup match was a one-day affair consisting of three foursomes and six singles. With one point given for each victory and one-half point for halved matches, the American ladies prevailed, 5½ to 3½. However, the British got some consolation from the fact that in the featured blue-ribbon singles duel, the brilliant British star, Joyce Wethered, defeated America's ace, Mrs. Edwin H. Vare, Jr., the former Glenna Collett, 6 and 4.

Standouts of the U.S. team were Virginia Van Wie and Mrs. L.D. Cheney, who figured in two points. Miss Van Wie teamed with Helen Hicks in firing a 68 for 17 holes in beating Enid Wilson and Mrs. J.B. Watson, 2 and 1, and then scored a 2 and 1 triumph over Wanda Morgan in singles. Mrs. Cheney and Maureen Orcutt won 1-up over Molly Gourlay and Doris Park in foursomes and then Mrs. Cheney crushed Elsie Corlett in singles, 4 and 3.

The United States repeated in 1934 when the series made its American debut at the Chevy Chase Country Club in Maryland, gained a tie in 1936 at Gleneagles, Scotland, and won again in 1938 at Manchester, Massachusetts, before there was a 10-year cessation because of World War II.

The American supremacy continued unchecked with resumption of the series in 1948 at Birkdale, England. The feature match sent Louise Suggs, the U.S. champion, against Philomena Garvey, one of the best women players produced on the British Isles in years. Two down with two holes to play, the intent Georgia girl won the last two holes to gain a dramatic tie.

In 1950, the matches were enlarged from 18 holes to 36 holes and the Americans used the occasion at the Country Club of Buffalo in Williamsville, New York, to score their most one-sided victory, 8½ to 1½. The only British triumph came in the foursomes in which

Frances Stephens and Elizabeth Price defeated Helen Sigel and Peggy Kirk, 1-up. Miss Stephens managed to halve her singles match with Mrs. Mark A. Porter.

Apparently stung by this indignity, the British women stormed back in 1952 at Muirfield in Scotland and racked up their victory in Curtis Cup competition. The margin was 5-4, with Elizabeth Price scoring the decisive point over Grace DeMoss of the American team, 3 and 2. Dorothy Kirby of Atlanta provided one of the thrills of the series with a magnificent comeback against Britain's Jean Donald. Five down with 11 holes to play, Miss Kirby rallied to tie the match on the thirty-fifth hole and win 1-up on the thirty-sixth when the British girl hit her approach shot into a bunker.

The backbones of the British ladies seemed to stiffen with the victory at Muirfield and for the next few years they proved far from a pushover for the Americans. The United States regained the trophy in 1954 at Ardmore, but lost it two years later to the British at Sandwich Bay, by another 5–4 margin, and in 1958, at the Brae Burn Country Club in West Newton, Massachusetts, could come off with no better than a tie.

Thus there was a four-year span before the Americans saw the trophy again. Led by Jo-Anne Gunderson, Anne Quast and Judy Eller, the U.S. women scored a 6½-to-2½ triumph at the Lindrick Golf Club in Nottinghamshire, England. Interest was intense among the Britons and a gallery of 12,000 showed up for the singles matches on the final day.

Virtually the same American team defended the cup in 1962 at the Broadmoor Golf Club in Colorado Springs and the match turned into a complete rout. The final score was 8–1, widest in the series, with the lone British point coming on an 8 and 7 victory by Mrs. Alastair Frearson over Judy Bell. The U.S. girls were magnificent. Mrs. Anne Quast Decker, the U.S. champion, shot a 74 in the morning and a 36 for the first 9 holes of the afternoon in routing Marley Spearman, 5 and

4. Phyllis Preuss fired a 75 in beating Jean Roberts, 1-up, and Clifford Ann Creed started with a 76 in winning 6 and 5 over Sally Bon-allack. It was one of the youngest British teams ever to play in the Curtis Cup, three of the girls being in their teens.

HIGH AND LOW SPOTS OF CURTIS CUP

Most One-Sided Team Victory: 8 and 1, United States, 1962, at Colorado Springs, Colorado.

Biggest Singles Margin (18 Holes): 7 and 5, Mrs. L.D. Cheney, U.S., over Pamela Barton, 1934, at Chevy Chase, Maryland; Mrs. Marjorie Ross Garon, Britain, over Mrs. O.S. Hill, 1936, at Gleneagles, Scotland.

Biggest Singles Margin (36 Holes): 9 and 8, Polly Riley, U.S., over Elizabeth Price, 1952, at Muirfield, Scotland; Margaret Smith, U.S., over Philomena Garvey, 1956, at Sandwich, England.

Biggest Foursome Margin (18 Holes): 5 and 4, Dorothy Kirby and Mrs. Julius Page, U.S., over Maureen Ruddle and Mrs. Val Reddan, 1948, at Birkdale, England.

Biggest Foursome Margin (36 Holes): 8 and 7, Jean Ashley and Mrs. Les Johnstone, U.S., over Mrs. Alastair Frearson and Ruth Porter, 1962, at Colorado Springs, Colorado.

Most Singles Victories: 4, Polly Riley, U.S.

Chapter Thirty-three

The Americas Cup

In the summer of 1951, just prior to the National Amateur Championship at the Saucon Valley Country Club in Bethlehem, Pennsylvania, leading amateurs of the United States and Canada played a friendly team match which proved to be very successful and popular. Officials of the U.S. Golf Association and the Royal Canadian Golf Association immediately began deliberations on making such a match a regular series.

By sheer coincidence at the same time this project was being discussed, the Western Golf Association came forward with a proposal for a similar series with Mexico. "Why not put the two plans together and form a hemispheric competition?" became a logical question.

Jerome P. Bowes, Jr., of Chicago, president of the Western Golf Association, presented the plan to the Royal Canadian Golf Association and the Asociacion Mexicana de Golf and offered to set up a permanent trophy to be called The Americas Golf Cup.

The idea met with an enthusiastic response. The series would be patterned after the Walker Cup competition. It would consist of three 36-hole three-ball sixsomes on the first day and six 36-hole three-ball matches on the second day. In each match, representatives of one country played simultaneously against the other two, one point to be awarded for each victory and each match to be played to its conclusion. The series would be staged every two years.

The first match was played on August 14–15, 1952, at the Seattle Golf Club in Seattle, Washington. The United States was expected to win easily. It fielded a powerful team headed by Harvie Ward, Frank Stranahan, and Charley Coe, but got something of a shock when the Canadians won the first three singles matches from both the United States and Mexico. Walter McElroy, Jerry Kesselring, and Nick Weslock crushed their Mexican opponents by one-sided scores and beat the U.S. aces, Ward, Stranahan, and Coe.

It was depth that finally brought the United States through the opening test, winning by a slender margin of two points. The United States scored 12 points, Canada 10, and Mexico 5.

The margin was even closer two years later when the event went to the London Hunt and Country Club at London, Ontario. The United States beat out Canada by a single point, 14 to 13, with Mexico failing to score. The decisive margin came in the foursomes in which the United States won two of the three matches. The six singles matches between the Americans and Canadians were so close that none was decided before the thirty-fifth hole. Three went the full thirty-six, one to the thirty-seven, and another to the thirty-eight. Don Cherry was forced the two extra holes for a victory over Nick Weslock for one of the vital U.S. points. America's Billy Joe Patton had to get birdies on 2 of the last 3 holes for his 2 and 1 victory over Walter McElroy.

It was not until the 1956 match at the Club Campestre de la Ciudad de Mexico that the Mexicans made a representative showing. Led by Harvie Ward, the United States made a runaway of the event, scoring 29½ points, but Mexico beat out Canada for second place, 13 to 11. The format was streamlined and matches were reduced to 18 holes. There were two separate 18-hole singles matches each day, thus doubling the number, with three-ball sixsomes played the first day and three-ball matches the second. Ward, the double National Amateur champion, figured in eight points for one of the outstanding individual performances of the series. He won all four of his singles matches and shared four more points in the foursomes.

The competition continued to rotate among the three participating nations, but there was no cracking the United States monopoly. The Americans won easily at the Olympic Club in San Francisco in 1958, but in 1960, at the Ottawa Hunt and Golf Club, had to rally to beat the Canadians by 1½ points.

In Monterrey, Mexico, in 1961, Jack Nicklaus headed the American team which scored 29 points, compared to 14 for Canada and 11 for Mexico. In 1963, it was the United States again at Des Moines, where the veteran Charlie Coe of Oklahoma City and Dick Sikes were the outstanding players in a 26½ to 19½ point triumph over Canada, with Mexico trailing with 8.

Chapter Thirty-four

The Canada Cup

One of the world's outstanding international golf competitions—the Canada Cup—was born of an idea and the accidental meeting of two men.

In the early 1950's, at one of the major American championships, a tall, well-dressed gentleman was stopped at the front gate. There was a mix-up on his credentials and he was having difficulty with the gatekeeper.

Nearby, Fred Corcoran, former tournament director of the Professional Golfers Association, noticed the trouble and strode over to the entrance.

"Why, Mr. Hopkins," Corcoran said, extending his hand to the harried visitor. "Are you having some trouble?"

With Corcoran's intercession, John Jay Hopkins, prominent industrialist and golf patron, was admitted to the grounds.

"Many thanks," Hopkins said to Corcoran. "Let's go somewhere where we can talk."

It was during this informal chat that Hopkins, president of General Dynamics Corporation, revealed to Corcoran a dream he had harbored for years—a truly worldwide golf tournament aimed at promoting good will among nations.

"I would like for you to run it for me," Hopkins said to Corcoran. "You're just the man."

Thus, the International Golf Association was born.

John Jay Hopkins, originator of the Canada Cup International matches, presents individual trophy to Ben Hogan at Wentworth, England, in 1956.

The first tournament was played on the Beaconsfield Golf Club course in Montreal, Canada, in 1953. Only seven nations responded: Canada, the United States, Argentina, Australia, Germany, Mexico, and a combined team of England and South Africa.

The United States sent its National Open champion, Julius Boros, and the reigning PGA king, Jim Turnesa. Americans, who had wrested domination of the game from the British, were, of course, heavily favored.

The first tournament was a 36-hole affair played by two-man teams. The best team score would win the Canada Cup, the best individual score the International Trophy.

If the Americans expected to win easily, they were in for a quick jolt. Antonio Cerda of Argentina turned in the best individual score, 140, and with his partner, long-hitting Roberto de Vicenzo, 147, captured the team prize with 287.

Canada, aided by Stan Leonard's runner-up 144, finished second. Australia was third and the English–South African combination of Harry Weetman and Bobby Locke was fourth. The Americans were keen disappointments, Boros shooting 150 and Turnesa 154 for fifth place at 304. Only Germany and Mexico fared worse.

The event attracted only mild interest, but the idea was firmly planted. Other countries immediately became interested.

The 1954 tournament was set for the Laval-sur-le-Lac Golf Club near Montreal. This time, 25 nations entered 2-man teams. The format was expanded to include 72 holes of medal play—1 round each day for 4 days.

Again emphasizing that golf had become an international sport, the Canada Cup was won by Australians Peter Thomson, 277, and Kel Nagle, 279, with a combined score of 556. Argentina's Cerda and De Vicenzo were second, followed by the U.S. team of Sam Snead and Jimmy Demaret. Canada's Stan Leonard won the individual International Trophy with 275.

Now the success of the venture was assured. Hopkins' dream of international good will

through golf was a reality. World interest in the project mushroomed. The tournament had no other way to go but forward.

"This is truly the Olympic Games of golf," said the enthused overseas competitors.

"The Canada Cup matches are the United Nations without double-talk," said America's Jimmy Demaret.

Corcoran immediately realized that if the Canada Cup were to achieve its true worldwide stature it was necessary to take the tournament out of the confines of Canada and put it on the road. It must be played on every continent.

This was a giant undertaking, but Hopkins was ready to go all-out in the fulfillment of his ideal. He solicited the support of other large business enterprises—Pan American Airways, American Express, and the Time-Life Corporation. The International Golf Association became a chartered nonprofit organization.

The prize money was token and incidental: $2,000 for the team championship, and $1,000 for the individual. However, all players had their traveling and living expenses paid and each man was given a $500 honorarium. For the fortunate participants, the tournament became the highlight of the season.

Each country was permitted to select its representatives. These normally were professionals, although there was no restriction against the use of amateurs. Britain was permitted to enter separate teams representing Scotland, England, Wales, and Ireland.

At first there was no formula for the selection of the U.S. team. The Open and PGA champions were picked for some of the early tournaments. Records were used as a gauge for tapping others. Finally, a system was devised whereby the host country, when the event was played outside the United States, would be permitted to choose the American players. These were picked from a list of six submitted by the Professional Golfers Association.

The Open and PGA champions—lame-armed Ed Furgol and husky Chick Harbert—were the American standard-bearers when the

234

Fred Corcoran, tournament director of the International Golf Association.

tournament moved into the United States for the first time in 1955, played at the Columbia Country Club in Washington, D.C. They finally restored U.S. golf prestige by winning the team trophy with a score of 560, 9 shots better than second-place Australia. The amazing Furgol, whose withered left arm was 8 inches shorter than his right, won the individual trophy in a playoff with Peter Thomson of Australia and Flory Van Donck of Belgium after tying at 279.

Then the tournament started reaching to the far corners of the globe. In 1956, it went to Wentworth in England, where Ben Hogan and Sam Snead successfully defended the title for the United States. The next year, Hopkins, the founder, died, but the tournament and his ideals carried on, first under Frank

235

United Press International

Arnold Palmer and Sam Snead admire Canada Cup which they won for the United States in the international matches at Buenos Aïres in 1962.

Pace, Jr., who took over as president of the General Dynamics Corporation, and later under a changing list of presidents of the International Golf Association.

The 1957 Canada Cup competition invaded the Orient for the first time, going to the Kasumigaseki Club on the outskirts of Tokyo. Mexico City got it in 1958, then Melbourne, Australia, and then Dublin, Ireland. The tournament returned to the Western Hemisphere in 1961, being played at the swank, new Dorado Beach Club in Puerto Rico, then on to Buenos Aires, Paris, Hawaii and Madrid.

Everywhere the tournament was played, there was a surge of golf interest, but no boom compared with that which followed the 1957 appearance in Tokyo. A bouncy little Japanese veteran named Torakichi (Pete)

Nakamura displayed phenomenal touch around the greens in setting the tournament individual scoring record of 274. He and his partner, Koichi Ono, also won the Canada Cup. The Japanese went wild. Almost immediately, golf became one of the most popular sports in the country. New courses mushroomed. Driving ranges sprouted. The sale of equipment multiplied.

No single nation, not even the United States, dominated the competition. Ireland won the team trophy, and a little-known Spaniard, Angel Miguel, captured the individual crown at Mexico City in 1958. Australians Peter Thomson and Kel Nagle delighted their fellow countrymen by winning at Melbourne in 1959, but Stan Leonard, the Canadian, topped the individual list. At Dublin, Sam Snead and Arnold Palmer combined for the team championship, but the leading individual was Belgian Flory Van Donck. Snead figured in U.S. victories in 1961 and 1962, but 1963 and 1964 were reserved for the mighty "Big Two" of American golf, Arnold Palmer and Jack Nicklaus.

The 1963 tournament was played over the Saint-Nom-la-Breteche course, about 12 miles from the heart of Paris. Until that time, golf had been regarded as a sport for the privileged classes in France. There were only 80 courses and some 15,000 players, one-third of them women.

Nevertheless, the French were intrigued by the appearance of the game's great and near-great and swarmed over the course by the thousands, interested mainly in those two American muscle men, Palmer and Nicklaus.

For the first time in the tournament's history, play had to be cut from the normal 72 to 63 holes because of a dense fog that enveloped the course.

Both Palmer and Nicklaus had to birdie the fifty-fourth hole to pull even with Spaniards Ramon Sota and Sebastian Miguel. However, on the final day, playing 9 holes instead of 18 because of the poor visibility, Nicklaus went on a birdie spree, starting 4-3-3-3-3-3. With 5 birdies in the first 6 holes, Nicklaus finished with a score of 237 for 63 holes and won the individual championship. Palmer, with 245, joined him in sharing the team title.

It was the sixth Canada Cup triumph in 11 years for the United States, which in the same period had won only four of the individual championships.

HIGH AND LOW SPOTS OF CANADA CUP

Individual 72-Hole Record: 272, Sam Snead, Puerto Rico, 1961.
Team Record: 557, Japan (Torakichi Nakamura 274, Koichi Ono 283), 1957; United States (Arnold Palmer 278, Sam Snead 279), Buenos Aires, 1962.
Largest Winning Margin, Individual: 7 strokes, Torakichi Nakamura, Japan, 1957.
Largest Winning Margin, Team: 14 strokes, United States, 1956.
Most Team Victories: United States, 6.
Most Individual Victories: Stan Leonard, Canada, 2.
Largest Individual Score: 366, Sjamsudin, Indonesia, 1959.
Largest Team Score: 726, Indonesia, 1959.

CANADA CUP RESULTS

1953, Beaconsfield Golf Club, Montreal, Canada

1. Argentina (Antonio Cerda 140, Roberto de Vicenzo 147)—287.
2. Canada (Stan Leonard 144, Bill Kerr 153)—297.
3. Australia (Ossie Pickworth 147, Peter Thomson 151)—298.
4. England–South Africa (Harry Weetman 149, Bobby Locke 150)—299.
5. United States (Julius Boros 150, Jim Turnesa 154)—304.
6. Germany (Georg Bessner 151, Hans Goernert 161)—312.
7. Mexico (Al Escalante 152, Juan Neri 169)—321.

Individual: 1. Cerda, 140; 2. Leonard, 144; 3. De Vicenzo, 147, and Pickworth, 147; 5. Weetman, 149.

1954, Laval-sur-le-Lac, Montreal, Canada

1. Australia (Peter Thomson 277, Kel Nagle 279)—556.
2. Argentina (Antonio Cerda 277, Roberto de Vicenzo 283)—560.
3. United States (Jimmy Demaret 278, Sam Snead 287)—565.
4. Canada (Stan Leonard 275, Jules Huot 295)—570.

5. Scotland (Thomas Haliburton 284, Eric Brown 287)—571.
6. France (Jean Garaialde 284, Francois Saubaber 289)—573.
7. England (Harry Weetman 284, Peter Alliss 290)—574.
8. Brazil (Mario Gonzalez 287, Ricardo Rossi 288)—575.
9. Belgium (Flory Van Donck 282, Arthur De Vulder 296)—578.
10. South Africa (Bobby Locke 284, Bert Thomas 294)—578.

Individual: 1. Leonard, 275; 2. Cerda and Thomson (tie), 277; 4. Jimmy Demaret, United States, 278; 5. Kel Nagle, Australia, 279.

1955, Columbia Country Club, Washington, D.C.

1. United States (Ed Furgol 279, Chick Harbert 281)—560.
2. Australia (Peter Thomson 279, Kel Nagle 290)—569.
3. Scotland (Eric Brown 285, John Panton 286)—571.
4. Argentina (Antonio Cerda 286, Roberto de Vicenzo 287)—573.
5. Belgium (Flory Van Donck 279, Arthur De Vulder 294)—573.
6. Germany (Friedel Schmaderer 287, Georg Bessner 288)—575.
7. England (Norman Sutton 287, Peter Alliss 288)—575.
8. Ireland (Harry Bradshaw 284, Fred Daly 296)—580.
9. Italy (Alfonso Angelini 288, Ugo Grappasonni 295)—583.
10. Canada (Stan Leonard 289, Pat Fletcher 295)—584.
11. Colombia (Raul Posse 289, Miguel Sala 295)—584.

Individual: 1. Ed Furgol, United States, 279, won in sudden death play-off with Peter Thomson, Australia, and Flory Van Donck, Belgium; 4. Chick Harbert, United States, 281; 5. Harry Bradshaw, Ireland, 284.

1956, Wentworth, England

1. United States (Ben Hogan 277, Sam Snead 290)—567.
2. South Africa (Bobby Locke 285, Gary Player 296)—581.
3. Canada (Stan Leonard 286, Al Balding 297)—583.
4. England (Ken Bousfield 291, Harry Weetman 295)—586.
5. Japan (M. Ishii 289, Y. Hayashi 297)—586.
6. Wales (Dai Rees 284, D. Smalldon 303)—587.
7. Scotland (Eric Brown 293, John Panton 296)—589.
8. Belgium (Flory Van Donck 283, Arthur De Vulder 312)—595.
9. Mexico (Roberto de Vincenzo 282, P. Clifford 316)—598.
10. Australia (Norm Von Nida 294, Peter Thomson 307)—601.
11. Ireland (Christy O'Connor 297, Harry Bradshaw 304)—601.
12. Spain (Angel Miguel 298, Sebastian Miguel 303)—601.

Individual: 1. Ben Hogan, United States, 277; 2. Roberto de Vicenzo, Mexico, 282; 3. Flory Van Donck, Belgium, 283; 4. Dai Rees, Wales, 284; 5. Bobby Locke, South Africa, 285.

1957, Kasumigaseki Golf Club, Tokyo, Japan

1. Japan (Torakichi Nakamura 274, Koichi Ono 283)—557.
2. United States (Sam Snead 281, Jimmy Demaret 285)—566.
3. South Africa (Gary Player 281, Harold Henning 288)—568.
4. Australia (Bruce Crampton 285, Peter Thomson 287)—572.
5. Wales (David Thomas 281, Dai Rees 292)—573.
6. Canada (Stan Leonard 283, Al Balding 293)—576.
7. England (Peter Alliss 288, Ken Bousfield 291)—579.
8. Brazil (Mario Gonzalez 290, Juan Querellos 291)—581.

238

9. Argentina (Antonio Cerda 288, Leopoldo Ruiz 298)—586.
10. Scotland (Eric Brown 292, John Panton 295)—587.

Individual: 1. Torakichi Nakamura, Japan, 274; 2. Gary Player, South Africa, Sam Snead, United States, and David Thomas, Wales, 281; 5. Stan Leonard, Canada, and Koichi Ono, Japan, 283.

1958, Mexico Golf Club, Mexico City

1. Ireland (Harry Bradshaw 286, Christy O'Connor 293)—579.
2. Spain (Angel Miguel 286, Sebastian Miguel 296)—582.
3. South Africa (Gary Player 291, Harold Henning 293)—584.
4. Wales (Eric Brown 289, John Panton 299)—588.
5. Australia (Frank Phillips 289, Kel Nagle 299)—588.
6. England (Peter Alliss 296, Bernard Hunt 297)—593.
7. Argentina (Leopoldo Ruiz 292, Fidel De Luca 302)—594.
8. Wales (David Thomas 294, Dai Rees 301)—595.
9. Venezuela (Manolo Bernardez 298, Teobaldo Perez 303)—601.
10. Colombia (Miguel Sala 288, Pablo Molina 315)—603.
11. Belgium (Flory Van Donck 287, Donald Swaelens 316)—603.

Individual: 1. Angel Miguel, Spain, 286, won in sudden death play-off with Harry Bradshaw, Ireland; 3. Flory Van Donck, Belgium, 287; 4. Miguel Sala, Colombia, 288; 5. Frank Phillips, Australia, and Eric Brown, Scotland, 289.

1959, Royal Melbourne Golf Club, Melbourne, Australia

1. Australia (Peter Thomson 275, Kel Nagle 288)—563.
2. United States (Sam Snead 281, Cary Middlecoff 292)—573.
3. Canada (Stan Leonard 275, Al Balding 299)—574.
4. South Africa (Gary Player 284, Harold Henning 296)—580.
5. England (Peter Alliss 293, Bernard Hunt 295)—588.
6. Wales (David Thomas 294, Dai Rees 296)—590.
7. Scotland (Eric Brown 292, John Panton 303)—595.
8. China (Chen Ching-po 292, Hsieh Yung-yo 305)—597.
9. Argentina (Leopoldo Ruiz 297, Fidel De Luca 304)—601.
10. Spain (Angel Miguel 30, Sebastian Miguel 301)—601.

Individual: 1. Stan Leonard, Canada, 275, defeated Peter Thomson, Australia, in sudden death play-off; 3. Sam Snead, United States, 281; 4. Gary Player, South Africa, 284; Kel Nagle, Australia, 288.

1960, Portmarnock Golf Club, Dublin, Ireland

1. United States (Sam Snead 281, Arnold Palmer 284)—565.
2. England (Harry Weetman 284, Bernard Hunt 289)—573.
3. Australia (Peter Thomson 286, Kel Nagle 288)—574.
4. Ireland (Christy O'Connor 286, Norman Drew 289)—575.
5. South Africa (Bobby Locke 289, Gary Player 289)—578.
6. Scotland (Eric Brown 286, John Panton 294)—580.
7. Belgium (Flory Van Donck 279, Arthur De Vulder 303)—582.
8. Wales (Dai Rees 289, David Thomas 295)—584.
9. Argentina (Fidel De Luca 290, Leopoldo Ruiz 297)—587.
10. Spain (Sebastian Miguel 292, Angel Miguel 295)—587.

Individual: 1. Flory Van Donck, Belgium, 279; Sam Snead, United States, 281; Arnold Palmer, United States, and Harry Weetman, England, 284; Peter Thomson, Australia; Christy O'Connor, Ireland, and Roberto de Vicenzo, Mexico, 286.

1961, Dorado Golf Club, Puerto Rico

1. United States (Sam Snead 272, Jimmy Demaret 288)—560.
2. Australia (Peter Thomson 280, Kel Nagle 292)—572.
3. Canada (Al Balding 283, Al Johnston 296)—579.
4. Ireland (Christy O'Connor 282, Norman Drew 300)—582.
5. Philippines (Ben Arda 286, Celestino Tugot 299)—585.
6. Wales (Davis Thomas 292, Dai Rees 295)—587.
7. Puerto Rico (Juan Rodriguez 290, Pete Cooper 299)—589.
8. South Africa (Ratief Waltman 293, Harold Henning 298)—591.
9. Argentina (Fidel De Luca 296, Leopoldo Ruiz 297)—593.
10. China (Hsieh Yung-yo 295, Chen Ching-po 299)—594.
11. Belgium (Flory Van Donck 297, Donald Swaelens 297)—594.

Individual: 1. Sam Snead, United States, 272; 2. Peter Thomson, Australia, 280; 3. Christy O'Connor, Ireland, 282; 4. Al Balding, Canada, 283; 5. Ben Arda, Philippines, 286.

1962, Jockey Club of San Isidro, Buenos Aires, Argentina

1. United States (Arnold Palmer 278, Sam Snead 279)—557.
2. Argentina (Roberto de Vicenzo 276, Fidel De Luca 283)—559.
3. Australia (Kel Nagle 283, Peter Thomson 286)—569.
4. England (Peter Alliss 278, Bernard Hunt 294)—572.
5. France (Jean Garaialde 287, Roger Cotton 298)—585.
6. Brazil (Mario Gonzalez 284, Jose Gonzalez 302)—586.
7. Uruguay (Juan Sereda 292, J. Esmori 294)—586.
8. Belgium (Donald Swaelens 291, Flory Van Donck 297)—588.
9. Wales (David Thomas 287, Dai Rees 301)—588.
10. China (Chen Ching-po 287, Lu Liang-hwan 302)—589.
11. Japan (Torakichi Nakamura 294, Tadashi Kitta 295)—589.

Individual: 1. Roberto de Vicenzo, Argentina, 276; 2. Peter Alliss, England, and Arnold Palmer, United States, 278; Sam Snead, United States, 279; Alfonso Angelini, Italy, 281.

Chapter Thirty-five

World Amateur Team Championship: The Eisenhower Trophy

It was clearly evident by the middle of the twentieth century that golf no longer was a British and an American monopoly. The international Canada Cup matches had spread the fairway gospel to the far reaches of the globe. Australia and New Zealand were turning out such top-flight players as Peter Thomson, Kel Nagle, and Bob Charles, all winners of the British Open. South Africa's Bobby Locke and Gary Player could match shots with the best. From Argentina came long-hitting Roberto de Vicenzo. Golf interest was rising in Japan and South America.

Such was the climate when Joseph C. Dey, executive director of the United States Golf Association, and other members of that ruling body decided in 1958 that there was need for an official world championship among amateurs. The Walker Cup, involving only Britain and the United States, did not completely fill the bill. The sport needed something on the order of the Davis Cup in tennis, open to any country with an interest in golf.

The idea was kicked around at the annual U.S.G.A. convention in New York in January. The plan was presented to the Royal and Ancient Golf Club of St. Andrews in March, receiving an enthusiastic reception. The two governing bodies decided to join hands in implementing the project. A planning conference was held in Washington, D.C., in May, attended by representatives of national amateur golf associations from 32 nations. The U.S. State Department threw its support behind the idea.

Out of the Washington conference came the blueprint for a world amateur team championship. Competition would be held every two years. It would be medal play over 72 holes, one round a day. Each country would be allowed four players but would count the total of the three best individual scores each day. Thus one score daily was discarded. The winner would be the team with the lowest over-all total for the four rounds.

With the format decided upon, the next question facing the amateur golf officials was: "What shall we call it?" There were suggestions that it be named the Bob Jones Trophy, honoring the man who had been such an inspirational figure in amateur golf. Finally, they found the name under their very noses: It should be the Eisenhower Trophy.

Dwight D. (Ike) Eisenhower at the time was President of the United States, the most sports-minded of all the nation's chief executives and a man with a deep devotion for the game of golf.

Eisenhower had played football and baseball at West Point, had once tackled the great Jim Thorpe of the Carlisle Indians. Later, he took a fling at pro football, played semipro baseball, and coached at a college in Texas. A career army man, he rose to the rank of five-star general and led the Allies to victory over Germany and Italy in World War II. In 1952, the American people elected him to the country's highest office.

The President found relaxation from his pressing duties by playing golf. He had a pitch-and-putt green built on the back lawn at the White House. When he needed a break, he sneaked over to the Burning Tree course and played a round with friends. His vacation retreat was the Augusta National Golf Club in Augusta, Georgia, site of the Masters, where he occupied a white cottage overlooking the tenth fairway. He was an avid golfer who occasionally shot in the 80's and blew a temper fuse when he missed a short putt. Pundits of the day jestingly predicted that Ike's pro, Ed Dudley, would be made a member of the Cabinet. The President's score was a classified secret.

If the Eisenhower Trophy was the ideal name for this new worldwide competition, then it was just as natural that the inaugural tournament should be played at St. Andrews, the cradle of the game. The first event was scheduled for October 8–11, 1958. It drew 115 players from 29 countries.

The United States fielded a formidable team composed of Charley Coe, William Hyndman III, Billy Joe Patton, and Dr. Frank Taylor. Bob Jones, confined to a wheelchair because of a crippling spine ailment, agreed to serve as captain, returning to the scene of his former triumphs.

Although the Americans were heavily favored, a surprise Australian team posted a score of 918 and appeared to be a certain winner until the United States came from nowhere to gain a tie. Hyndman, a veteran from Philadelphia, playing in the last group, made a birdie 3 on the seventeenth hole—the notorious "Road Hole" of St. Andrews' Old Course—and got a par 4 at the eighteenth for a 72. America also had 918.

Emphasizing the closeness of the competition, the combined British-Irish team was only one shot back at 919 and New Zealand was fourth with 921.

In the 18-hole play-off, the Australians defeated the United States, 222 to 224. The Australian playing captain, Robert Stevens, and Bruce Devlin clinched the trophy by knocking in birdie 3's on the final hole. It seemed rather fitting, in the spirit of the broadened scope of amateur golf, that the first Eisenhower Trophy should go to a nation of 10,000,000 people located at the bottom of the world.

The United States got a minor consolation in the fact that Hyndman shared individual honors with Devlin of Australia and Reid Jack of Great Britain. Each had 301 to tie for the lowest individual score.

The second tournament was staged at Merion Golf Club in Ardmore, Pennsylvania, just outside Philadelphia, September 28–October 1, 1960. There were 3 new teams, making a total of 32, and 126 players, 11 more than had competed at St. Andrews. However, before the week ended, it appeared that there was only one man on the course—big Jack Nicklaus of Columbus, Ohio.

Nicklaus shot consecutive rounds of 66-67-68-68 for a 72-hole score of 269 over one of the most testing championship courses in the world. The brilliance of the blond heavyweight's performance was accented by a comparison with Ben Hogan's score of 287 in winning the U.S. Open over the same course in 1950. Nicklaus' card beat that of Hogan by 18 strokes.

Led by Nicklaus, the United States team leaped into a big advantage in the first round and won going away with scores of 208-205-203-218 for 834, 42 strokes better than the runner-up Australian team, which registered 219-220-215-220 for 876. The combined British and Irish team was third with 881.

Although no official prize is awarded for individual scoring, Nicklaus was easily the leader. Deane Beman, holder of the National Amateur title at the time, had the second lowest score, 282, 13 shots off Nicklaus' pace. Devlin was third with 288, followed by the other two members of the American team, Hyndman and Robert Gardner, tied at 289.

Two years later, the world's leading amateurs journeyed to the Far East to contest for the trophy over the Fuji Golf Course in Kawana, Japan. The dates were October 10–13, 1962. Because of the distance, only 23 countries were represented.

The visitors found golf interest rocketing in Japan. This interest had been stimulated by the appearance of leading professionals for the Canada Cup matches in Tokyo in 1957 and turned into a national obsession by the surprise victory of two Japanese professionals, Torakichi Nakamura and Koichi Ono. Old courses were being stormed by new devotees. New courses were being built. Driving ranges and pitch-and-putt courses were everywhere.

The United States stepped off to the first round lead with a score of 212, thanks to a 69 by Richard Sikes, the public links champion, and a 70 by Beman. Three shots back after the opening day, Canada rallied in the rain and forged six shots in front of the Americans in the second round, 432 to 438. A second 69 by Sikes and a 70 by Beman helped the United States overtake Canada in the third round, 649 to 651, but the pressure was still intense.

On the final days, prospects looked dark for the Americans when Billy Joe Patton, the first player to finish, posted a fat 81. However, the other three members of the team played superbly. Beman fired a 4-under-par 66, best round of the tournament. Sikes posted a third 69. Labron Harris, Jr., the 1962 National Amateur Champion, added a 70.

When the adding machines stopped whirring, the United States was still on top, winner of the Eisenhower Trophy for the second time in a row, with a score of 854. Canada followed with 862 and the Britain-Ireland team was third with 874.

Gary Cowan of Canada had the best individual score, 68-71-72-69 for 280, 3 strokes lower than Sikes and 6 lower than Beman. Juan Antonio Estrada of Mexico, who, along with D.B.M. Shade of Britain, matched Beman's low round of 66, was fourth with 287.

The surprise of the tournament was the team from Nationalist China, which had finished twenty-sixth and twenty-first in the previous two events. The Chinese team finished sixth with a score of 892, one stroke ahead of the Australians, who had won the first competition in 1958.

Golf observers looked at this result with deep satisfaction. It was proof that golf was becoming a truly international game.

HIGH AND LOW POINTS

Lowest Over-All Team Score: 834, United States, Merion Golf Club, Ardmore, Pennsylvania, 1960.
Lowest Individual Score for 72 Holes: 269, Jack Nicklaus, United States, 1960.
Lowest Score for Single Round—66: Jack Nicklaus, United States, first round, 1960; Deane Beman, United States, fourth round, 1960; Juan Antonio Estrada, Mexico, fourth round, 1960.
Largest Team Score: 1104, Ceylon, 1960.
Largest Winning Margin: 42 strokes, United States over Australia, 1960.
Largest individual margin: 13 strokes, Jack Nicklaus, United States, over Deane Beman, United States, 1960.

EISENHOWER TROPHY RESULTS
1958, Old Course, St. Andrews, Scotland, October 8–11

	1st	2nd	3rd	4th	Total	Play-off
1. Australia	244	226	221	227	918	222
Douglas Bachli	81	77	78	79	315	77
Peter Toogood	84	76	71	79	310	75
Bruce Devlin	81	73	74	73	301	72
Robert Stevens	82	77	76	75	310	75

2. United States	233	232	225	228	918	224
Charley Coe	74	77	76	78	305	73
William Hyndman III	79	77	73	72	301	78
William J. Patton	80	78	76	79	313	75
Dr. Frank Taylor	81	79	76	78	314	76

3. Great Britain–Ireland, 919; 4. New Zealand, 921; 5. Argentina, 940; 6. Canada and South Africa (tie), 945; **8. France, 949; 9. Sweden, 957; 10. Italy, 963; 11. Belgium, 964; 12. Philippines, 970; 13. Spain, 974; 14. India and Switzerland** (tie), 981; **16. Bermuda, 985; 17. Germany and Kenya** (tie), 998; **19. Netherlands, 1005; 20. Japan, 1006; 21. Brazil, 1009; 22. Venezuela, 1015; 23. Finland, 1017; 24. Malaya, 1029; 25. Norway, 1040; 26. Republic of China and Portugal** (tie), 1049; **28. Austria, 1071; 29. Iceland, 1084.**

1960, Merion Golf Club, Ardmore, Pennsylvania, September 28–October 1

	1st	2nd	3rd	4th	Total
1. United States	208	205	213	218	834
Deane Beman	71	67	69	75	282
Robert Gardner	71	71	68	79	289
William Hyndman III	71	76	67	75	289
Jack Nicklaus	66	67	68	68	269

2. Australia, 876; 3. Great Britain–Ireland, 881; 4. South Africa, 893; 5. New Zealand, 895; 6. Canada, 906; **7. Mexico, 909; 8. Rhodesia–Nyasaland, 914; 9. Argentina, 917; 10. Sweden, 923; 11. Italy,** 935; **12. France, 937; 13. Germany, 940; 14. Philippines, 942; 15. Denmark, 952; 16. Japan, 954; 17. Belgium, 960; 18. Venezuela, 962; 19. Brazil, 972; 20. India, 975; 21. Republic of China and Switzerland** (tie), 977; **23. Norway, 979; 24. Peru, 999; 25. Bermuda, 1001; 26. Austria, 1005; 26. Netherlands, 1008; 27. Finland, 1023; 28. Portugal, 1035; 29. United Arab Republic, 1045; 30. Malaya, 1099; 31. Ceylon, 1104.**

1962, Fuji Golf Course, Kawana, Japan, October 10–13

	1st	2nd	3rd	4th	Total
1. United States	212	226	211	205	854
Deane Beman	70	80	70	66	286
Labron Harris, Jr.	73	77	72	70	292
William J. Patton	74	73	72	81	300
Richard Sikes	69	76	69	69	283

2. Canada, 862; 3. Great Britain–Ireland, 874; 4. New Zealand, 882; 5. Mexico, 887; 6. Republic of China, 892; 7. Australia, 893; 8. South Africa, 896; 9. Japan, 902; 10. Argentina, 905; 11. Italy, 912; 12. Germany, 926; 13. Philippines, 929; 14. India, 931; 15. Hong Kong, 942; 16. Sweden, 943; 17. Switzerland, 947; 18. Spain, 961; 19. Brazil, 964; 20. Bermuda, 980; 21. Peru, 985; 22. Malaya, 1036; **23. Pakistan, 1058.**

PART FOUR
by Robert Trent Jones

Chapter Thirty-six

Ten Great Courses

The early origins of golf, as it first developed along the linksland of Britain, were in marked contrast to the game and conditions of play as we know them today. The clubs were almost as crude as the limb that Sam Snead cut from a tree in his native Virginia hills to use when he took his first swing at a golf ball. The ball was made of feathers tightly compacted and hand-sewn in a leather case, and the greens and tees were merely hitting areas—natural plateaus of variable lengths. Some of the early rules held that "the teeing areas shall not be less than three club-lengths from the hole."

Try to imagine the condition of the putting green where the hitting area is only three club-lengths from the hole, and where the golfer, by puckering the sand with his fingers in order to form a little mound on which to place the ball through error, may take a good-sized divot.

The sheep and the rabbits were the cutting units, and the bunkers were formed by the swirling winds in the weak areas the grass could not cover. Because the pattern of play of many of the golfers had created an erosion problem through intensive use of the spot, power first began to show its ugly head in the period when the gutty ball superseded the feather ball.

Before 1848, when the gutty ball came into play, golf was not a game but a pastime, and it was only after this that the elements of the game began to form. Competition developed between players in various groups and it was only natural that local pride in its stellar players would bring about an Open championship. This was first played at Prestwick between 1860 and 1870. The first amateur championship of Great Britain was played at Hoylake in 1886. Some 19 years later, golf-course architecture was first recognized as belonging to the art of the game. Subsequently, the Haskell ball, the first rubber-cored ball, was developed. It was so superior to the gutty ball in distance and accuracy that, in a very crude form as compared to today's conditions, it laid the foundation for modern golf. It was quite natural that each of these revolutionary stages in ball and equipment made necessary, in its own trial-and-error fashion, changes in the architecture of the courses in the early play of the game over the linksland.

The player is the attacker and the architect is the defender. In a sense, it is a form of attack and counterattack, for the player, given modern tools and playing conditions, works to improve his game and skills to apply the pressure he hopes to achieve in order to bring the course to its knees. The architect calls on his ingenuity to create the defense that will frustrate, say, the long-driving Jack Nicklaus or the pin-point irons of Arnold Palmer without resorting to trickery.

Holes were considerably shortened when the gutty, with its additional length, came into fashion—perhaps to the extent of 20 percent. A comparable advantage arose when the

Haskell ball was developed. The improvement of the ball and the advent of the steel shaft, allowing for a swing pattern that increases distance and accuracy, have conspired to shorten the holes materially. As a result, there have been two, perhaps three, periods of reconstruction within this comparatively short period to bring the golf course back into competitive focus. This has been done by regrouping the hazards to defend against the attack based on the advantages the attacker has obtained from the equipment at his command.

Golf was started in America in a very primitive manner. John Reid, of Scottish descent, played what was probably the first game of golf in this country in a meadow behind his house in Yonkers, New York, in 1888. From that Sunday afternoon diversion, the first golf club in the United States developed, St. Andrews Golf Club, its name indicating the true reverence that the Old Course inspired even across the sea.

As we are indebted to the Scots and English for the game, we are similarly indebted to them for our principles of architecture. Early golf and its growth in the United States undoubtedly owed much to the interest, enthusiasm, initiative, and fine conception of design of Charles Blair Macdonald, our first amateur champion, who learned the game when he was being educated at St. Andrews, Scotland. Macdonald was responsible for the first course in Chicago, in 1893, but it was not until the National Links at Southampton, Long Island, New York, was built by Macdonald in 1907, that our golf began to come out of the "cow pasture" stage of golf-course architecture.

Macdonald became obsessed with the idea of building a truly classical golf course in America, incorporating in it the best features of the most famous holes of England and Scotland. In this way, he felt he could obtain an 18-hole golf course with each hole of outstanding quality. For although certain holes on each of the English and Scottish links were outstanding, these did not usually exceed two or three per course, with the remaining holes

falling into the fair category. In 1902, Macdonald went abroad to gather material. This consisted of playing on most of the courses, observing them, and discussing them with golfing friends. On the basis of these conversations, he decided that his plan was entirely feasible.

For four years he proceeded to gather ideas, and in 1904 he made a second trip to study foreign courses. This time, he made a detailed survey of the more famous holes, such as the "Alps," the "Redan," the "Eden," and the "Road Hole." He also drew 20 to 30 sketches of holes that embodied distinct features which in themselves seemed misplaced, but could be utilized in principle to harmonize with certain characteristics of undulating ground. Thus began the foundations of outstanding holes.

It was through the work of Macdonald and his disciples that golf began to spread throughout the United States. Many of the holes that Macdonald brought over were copied at other places. In addition, the emigration of English and Scottish professionals added to spreading the game in this country. Although many of the professionals laid out mediocre courses—"18 stakes on a Sunday afternoon"—some did some very fine work, such as the late Donald J. Ross, who became nationally famous in the United States as a designer of golf courses.

The influence of British architecture was also felt in the next era of our golf-course design, when the course at Pine Valley, in Clementon, New Jersey, was built by George Crump, a Philadelphia sportsman. With the advice and assistance of the English architect, H.S. Colt, Crump laid out what has now become one of the world's outstanding golf courses.

The courses in the 1920's developed into a pattern, based on punishing the golfer for the slightest error. This undoubtedly was due to an attempt to emulate Pine Valley, a strictly penal course, in modified form. As a result, our courses became overcluttered with traps, and our greens extremely small as target areas. The maintenance involved to keep such a course well groomed, as well as the dissatisfaction of the average golfer, led to the next revolution in golf-course architecture in the United States.

In the late 1920's, Dr. Alistair Mackenzie, the Scottish golf architect, came to America and began designing golf courses. The main principle of Mackenzie's technique was to revert from the penal to the strategic, and bring about the elimination of the overabundance of traps. In this same period, Stanley Thompson, a well-known Canadian golf-course architect and for many years my partner, was paralleling the Mackenzie idea at Jasper Park in the Canadian Rockies. It was at this time that Thompson and I became partners, because of our basic agreement on this philosophy of golf-course design.

It took the greatest name in American golf, Robert Tyre Jones, Jr., to give this new theory impetus. With Dr. Mackenzie, he created the Augusta National Golf Club Course. Jones had some theories of his own that modified some of Mackenzie's extremes and brought about a revolution in American golf-course architecture. It was Jones's belief that a really great course must be a source of pleasure to the greatest possible number of players and that it must require strategy as well as skill, or it could not continue to hold a player's interest. It must give the average golfer a fair chance and at the same time must require the utmost from the expert who tries to break par.

Jones's basic theory was influenced by his love for the Old Course at St. Andrews. I have had the opportunity of working with Robert Tyre Jones, Jr., in the remodeling of some of the holes at Augusta, and completely in the design of the Peachtree Golf Club in Atlanta, Georgia. We believe these courses exemplify the best principles of modern golf-course architecture.

Peachtree differs from Augusta somewhat, particularly in the basic principle of its green design. Each green has five or six definite pin positions, of which at least four are of such quality as to be ideal for tournament play. These positions represent the target area for the better golfer, whereas the whole green represents the target area for the average golfer. The greens are undulating in character, but not as severe nor as continuous in the tilt of the slopes nor in the crowns of the greens as they are at Augusta, the undulations at Peachtree being folds between the various pin positions. Peachtree's greens are larger, in keeping with this principle.

The greens at Peachtree and Augusta National are both of the plateau type for the most part, but the greens at Augusta fall from front to back, and the various pin areas at Peachtree fall in no general direction but take the nearest and obvious outlet to all sides of the green.

Another feature of Peachtree is the tremendous flexibility of the course, brought about by the extreme length of the tees. The course can vary from 5,700 yards to 7,400 yards in length, and yet, by the proper positioning of the pins, the holes are never tricky in character. By combining the two principles—the number of green positions and the number of the tee positions—it is possible to give an infinite variety to the course.

In reviewing the development of golf-course architecture in America and describing the changes brought about in the various eras, it must be taken into consideration that most of the American courses are inland in character. The golf-course architect no longer attempts to copy famous holes of British seaside courses in detail, as Macdonald did when he built the National Links of America. We now adapt those principles of good architecture that have developed, modifying the dunelike character of the seaside links to blend harmoniously with the existing contours, and to tie in with our maintenance equipment in the matter of upkeep.

The phrase "championship golf course" is so broadly used that one would expect a clean-cut knowledge of its meaning, but that is not the case. Times without number I am asked, "What is a championship golf course?" One must obviously assume that a championship golf course is one on which a championship can be played, but, as a definition, this is not enough. Championships have been played on both good and bad golf courses. One could assume that a course of extreme length would be classified as a championship golf course, but such also is not the case. Extreme length alone does not make a championship golf course. One could also expect that large greens would be a requirement in the making of a championship golf course, but, again, this is not necessarily the case. One would naturally expect that a profusion of trapping would also be a requirement in the making of a championship golf course, but this, too, is not necessarily the case. When one analyzes the characteristics of some of the well-known and accepted-as-great championship golf courses of the country, the above points are easily borne out.

Merion is not a long golf course in the modern sense, being only 6,700 yards in length. Augusta National, while having length, is not a profusely trapped golf course, having a total of only 23 traps on its full 18 holes. Big greens alone do not make a great golf course. Merion's greens are small, averaging only about 6,000 square feet, though some are smaller and some much larger, often being as large as 9,000 square feet. Pinehurst Number 2 has relatively small greens, as do the famed Pebble Beach and the Olympic clubs in San Francisco. Conversely, St. Andrews in Scotland, probably the most famous of all championship golf courses, has mammoth, acre-sized greens, primarily due to the fact that seven greens are in reality two greens, being played with two pin settings, thus becoming different holes from the opposite directions.

Scenic beauty does not necessarily make a championship golf course, although it does add to the enjoyment and pleasure of playing the course. Consider the contrast between Pebble Beach along the blue Pacific, Augusta National in one of nature's natural arboretum horticultural amphitheatres, or Pine-

hurst Number 2 in its pine-tree-framed sand dunes. All of these golf courses share one basic quality: character in the golf course. Character in the golf-course sense is similar to character in the human sense, in that character is attributed to those having strong individual points that make them stand out over others. While great golf courses should necessarily have beauty, they should, above all else, have great playing value.

Great shot value and playing value are inextricably linked. The tee shot must be hit straight as well as long within the scope of well laid-down limitations. The perfect shot on any given hole can be considered as in the "white" area. When the shot takes on a degree of error, it goes into the "gray" area. If the shot becomes exaggerated in its degree of error, the color becomes a deeper tone of gray until the badly missed shot goes into the "black" area. The values of a hole should be emphasized, so that the player can see at a glance what he must conquer to avoid penality. It can be traps, roughs, boundaries, water, trees, or just plain lack of position.

Rough will be very much a part of the penalty for misplaced shots in the Open championship, as it is traditional for the U.S. Golf Association Championship Committee to invoke rough as a form of penalty. The position of the trapping, the position of the ponds and creeks, the tilt or contour of the fairways, and the width as well as the narrowness of the fairways are all part of the formula making demands upon the player, rewarding accuracy and penalizing lack of it.

The green, of course, is the ultimate target. What is more enjoyable than to play a shot to a well-placed, beautifully designed green where the guarding traps, as well as the contours, are in harmony, and with a subtle pin position demanding from the golfer the greatest possible shot? The variety of green design is infinite. Elevated greens, terraced greens, tilted greens, mounded contours, flanked trapping on the sides, direct trapping in the front, creeks or water ponds to carry—these many varied green designs contribute to the joy of playing a golf course and to the miseries of failing to meet the persistent demands.

There is no single design for a championship golf course. Like the human beings who play them, they vary in character and style, yet they possess their own unique qualities setting them apart.

The great courses range from the Old Course at St. Andrews, craggy and cantankerous, just as Mother Nature molded her, to the Bellerive Country Club in St. Louis, representing the newest in modern techniques, receiving her first major test with the 1965 United States Open.

In between them, you have fabled Pine Valley in New Jersey, renowned as a nemesis for the great and near great; Pennsylvania's Merion, lacking the awesome length of some courses but testing and rich in tradition; Pinehurst, a 65-year-old legend in the sand-dune country of North Carolina; California's fabled Pebble Beach, with its rocks and rills and whistling winds; relatively new Dorado Beach in Puerto Rico, with its picture-postcard beauty; the Augusta National, majestic site of the Masters; Oakland Hills in Birmingham, Michigan, which Ben Hogan dubbed the "Monster"; and Firestone in Akron, Ohio, scene of the annual World Series of Golf and the course the pro golfers term the most difficult on the tour.

There are many other exacting and magnificent courses throughout the world but these are my personal "Top Ten."

Chapter Thirty-seven

Old Course at St. Andrews

There is something unique and special about St. Andrews, which is evident from the moment one gets one's first glimpse of it. Here is the majestic Royal and Ancient club house, the big expansive eighteenth green, the shops and clubs bordering the eighteenth fairway, the glimpse of the sea and the mountains, the green turf as it spreads like a carpet over its undulating, rolling, dunelike terrain, and the casualness of the villagers as they walk across fairways and through the paths between the dunes with their dogs and manifest the sheer joy of being there.

One gets a touch of nostalgia, as if one could see the golfers of yesteryear playing across these very same dunes, hear the hollow sound of the gutty ball, the crackling of a splintered shaft, or the munching of sheep keeping the grass closely cropped, the lawn-mowers of the day.

The course is very much alive today, particularly in the summer when the evenings are long, when golfers can be starting at 4 A.M. and playing until 11 P.M. The Old Course is, as it always has been, shaped like a long fisherman's hook, with its seven double greens to which golfers play on the way out and to which they return on the way back.

There is only one St. Andrews' Old Course, and nature built it. It would be outright folly for any architect to attempt a duplication, particularly an American architect on American soil. For while there are many who love it, there are many who dislike it intensely because they cannot understand the uphill and downhill lies, the blind bunkers, the blind green surfaces and the traps in the middle of the fairway that cannot be seen from the tee.

The Old Course at St. Andrews is starkly primitive. She is just as nature laid her out and fashioned her with winds and rains and receding seas down through the centuries. There is nothing false about her. No bull-dozer has ever touched her. Unlike American courses, which are built and molded to an architect's specifications and fitted with man-made hazards, St. Andrews has not a single artificial characteristic. She is nature's off-spring.

The area forming the most famous seaside links in the world started ages ago with a coastline of cliffs guarding the shores. It ran inland to where the River Eden makes its break for the sea, forming a perimeter now bounded by a belt of fertile farmland, an expanse of saltings, the Eden River and St. Andrews Bay.

As the sea withdrew from the higher ground, it left a series of sandy wastes with ridges and furrows broken by channels up and down which the tides flowed and ebbed. These channels dried out and formed dunes, ridges, and gullies of varying heights and widths. Threaded by small streams reaching for the sea, they became nesting places for the birds. The winds brought seeds from the inland and the bird-droppings provided rich fertilizer. Rich grasses sprouted. Heather, whins, and trees took root. Animals burrowed into the ground for protection against the wind and rain, forming natural bunkers. Thus a golf course was born.

By modern standards, old St. Andrews is not a pretty course, nor is it easy to play.

The first time Sam Snead, who won the British Open there in 1946, saw the course, it was through the glass window of a gully-jumper train up from London.

Looking out over the gray, craggy moors, Snead tapped the knee of a native passenger across the aisle and inquired, "What in the devil is that? It looks like an old, abandoned golf course."

"My God, sir," the Englishman replied, aghast. "That is the Royal and Ancient Club of St. Andrews, founded in 1754. And it is not now, nor ever will be, abandoned."

Sam choked back his embarrassment but turned to Lawson Little, his traveling companion, and said, "Down home, we plant cow beets on land like that."

Later, playing on the course, Snead wound up with a 160-foot putt on one of the massive double greens. His lag was 40 feet short. He was so angry he banged his putter against the toe of his shoe and bruised his big toe.

The Old Course was the despair of other masters of the game. The first time Bob Jones played there, he picked up in disgust midway in the third round. Defending his British Open crown there in 1933, Gene Sarazen hit a shot into the notorious Hell's Bunker on the fourteenth hole and took a triple bogey eight that cost him the title by a stroke. Walter Hagen won four British Opens but he never was able to conquer the hallowed old links by the sea.

Players of later generations also met their frustrations. Playing in the 100th Anniversary British Open in 1960, Arnold Palmer was derailed by the famous Road Hole—the seventeenth—where he went 5–5–5–4, while Australia's Kel Nagle played it 3–3–4–4 and beat out Palmer by a stroke.

Only recently, Dai Rees, one of Britain's most famous players, said that the Old Course should be remodeled to make it a modern golf course. I do not share this opinion, for I am one of its admirers and feel that the principles of many of its holes have been used over and over by better golf architects through the years to create what must be classed as superb golf holes. The first few rounds of golf played over the Old Course may be perplexing, the golfer may be puzzled in trying to understand the rhapsodies that have been expressed about the perfect strategic position of its traps, the subtle undulations of its huge double greens, the endless rolling character of its fairways rarely providing a level lie. But then he will thrill all the more when he hits a good shot and gets a just reward. Whenever he thinks out his round and plays the course according to his own game, he will be rewarded hole after hole and he will cherish the end result.

St. Andrews is particularly rough on the very bad shot, for it will probably carry one off into the whins or gorse and getting out of them can expend many a stroke.

The essence of strategic architecture is to encourage initiative and to reward the thinking golfer more than the unthinking golfer. In strategic architecture, well-executed shots are necessary but may often be secondary, for, if one has not thought through to the position one wants to be in at the end of the shot, one may find oneself with an impossible shot left to the green.

Of all the splendid holes at St. Andrews, the most renowned are the eleventh, or the Eden; the fourteenth, or the Long Hole; and the seventeenth, or Road Hole. The strategy of the eleventh, which measures 164 yards, is developed by its key hazard, the Strath bunker, a deep, heavy-lipped bulldog that patrols the access to the right-hand side of the green. The Strath sets up perfectly the function of Hill bunker to the left of the green and of the green itself, which slopes back-to-front at a very severe angle. When the wind is out in full force and blowing down the slope, it is next to impossible to keep a downhill putt from running off the green, no matter how gently you tap it. (I feel that at no other place but St. Andrews would such a slope be countenanced.)

The seventeenth, the famous Road Hole, is a par 5, as we would rate it here, which measures 467 yards. It is a very possible 4 and a very possible 7. To be in a position to reach the green in two, the golfer must take his courage in his hands on the tee and drive over Auchterlonie's drying sheds, which are situated in an out-of-bounds area that noses into the direct line between the tee and the choice side of the fairway. The long second shot must be played with true precision. A deep trap at the left of the green forces the player to hew to the right; there, running diagonally behind the green, is the road, and behind the road a stone wall.

They play as part of the course, and any guess at how often they have proved to be the difference between a match that was won and a match that was lost would be an almost astronomical figure. (Here again I feel that at no place but St. Andrews would such hazards be acceptable; on the Old Course, they are as natural as the gray stone of the houses which line the closing hole.)

As for the fourteenth, the Long Hole, the longest on the course, a brute of 527 yards, we have here the apotheosis of one cardinal tenet of golf architecture: A great hole always offers the golfer an alternate route to the green. The fourteenth, in fact, offers the golfer a choice of three alleys: left, center, and right. The intelligent golfer will wait until he arrives at the tee and take into account how the wind is blowing at that moment, and the other immediate conditions, before he chooses his route for that particular round. By any of the routes, he must tack his way skillfully to the green, avoiding the bunkers that lie in wait to change his peaceful sail into a hapless Odyssey.

Chapter Thirty-eight

Pine Valley

George Crump started to cut Pine Valley out of the thick pine forest of western New Jersey in 1912. The course was finished 10 years later. Crump gave to the golfing world an architectural masterpiece. It is a great tribute to Crump's magnificent talent that the holes remain the same as they did in 1912 when he first created them. Pine Valley has a spectacular grandeur different from that of any other course in the world. Its pine-tree-framed fairways accentuate the island design of the holes and the contrast between the green turf and the artistically patterned sand and sod has formed its sandy wastelands.

It is a terrifying course for the average golfer, who finds it difficult to get a straight 180 yards from the tee. It is not so difficult for the low handicap golfer, except on those few straight holes where he strays from his normal pattern and winds up in a clump of low growing junipers, for an inevitable double or triple bogey. Pine Valley is replete with classic golf holes great in the sense they would be magnificent holes even without its horrifying footprinted sandy wastes. Ten of the holes are great, five are outstanding, two are good, and one, the twelfth, is an ordinary hole that does not seem to belong to part of this great golf course.

What makes Pine Valley a course unlike any other in the world is the basic principle of its design, the island. From the tee, the fairway targets are islands of grass surrounded by sandy wastes and forests. The sandy wastes are terrifying—covered with low growing juniper, small, low-branched pines, undercut sod, pit holes, and troublesome bushes of varied descriptions. And the footprints in the sand are sure signs of misfortune. To the golfers of this world, Pine Valley's footprints are a record for all to observe. Since there is too much sand at Pine Valley for all of it to be raked, none of it is, and somewhere during the round, vast blasting from one of these footprints will become a back-breaking task. Most of the greens are island, too, and if they are not surrounded completely by sand they are surrounded by rough. These greens must be classed as among the best-molded, best-textured greens in the world.

One must really see Pine Valley to appreciate it, play it to know its joys and pitfalls, assault it to relish its combat, thrill with one's pars, laugh at one's calamities, and relish an experience in golf that one cannot obtain any other place in the world.

There are four holes at Pine Valley that I find particularly enjoyable to play: the second, third, thirteenth, and fifteenth. The second, a par 4, 350 yards long, demands a drive with a minimum carry of 175 yards to clear the badlands between tee and fairway. However, the golfer must be out about 220 yards in order to have the percentages with him when he plays the approach to the green. The green sits at the crown of a mesa-like ridge that climbs some 35 feet above the level of the fairway. It is understatement to say that there is no framework around the green to give it a receptive feeling. What the golfer is really faced with, as he looks up at the green from the fairway below, is the fearful incline of the ridge—yards and yards of heavy, raw sand on all sides. That, too, strikes me as understatement. The second is a Vesuvius in contour and it causes as many eruptions as any hole on the course.

To pick one short hole as better than another at Pine Valley is something like judging a beauty contest: It is all a matter of taste. If I were to continue with this analogy, I should label the third a "redhead." The tee on the third is elevated, the green is below you, about 175 yards away, and there is nothing around the green but sand—a veritable lake of sand. The front deck of the irregularly shaped green has a treacherous tilt, downhill from right to left. When the pin is positioned on this front deck, to find the green and hold it requires a shot played with the finesse of a Ryder Cupper. If you miss the green island . . . well, it is a good idea to count to 10 after fluffing your first "out"; it may save your counting to 10 when you are subsequently asked for your score.

The thirteenth, 439 yards long, presents one of the most challenging second shots you will ever encounter. After a good drive you will usually have a three-wood or four-wood left—rarely anything shorter than a three-iron under any conditions—and all you have to do is produce a shot that defeats the long, menac-

ing crescent of sand-land depressed below the level of the green, which curves with the dog-leg fairway for some 80 yards before the green. It is up to the player to judge mentally how much of this junior desert he believes he can carry. To reach the green, he must carry it all. The thirteenth is a nonpareil of "heroic" design. It requires great length, great control, and audacity. If your gamble fails, of course you are far worse off than the cautious golfer who has veered his ball away from the challenge, but the player has the privilege of deciding on the exact amount of his wager.

The fifteenth is a par 5 that has never been reached in two by any player; 584 yards long, its fairway becomes narrower and narrower as it climbs a long, gentle thicket-bordered slope to the small, tight green area. In other words, three excellent shots must be played—a rare requirement today in America where we are presently faced with a dearth of honest par 5's. Along with its golf-packed character, the fifteenth has immense beauty. I remember playing a round at Pine Valley not so long ago with Lowell Thomas, author and raconteur, who has traveled the world as widely as any man. On this fifteenth, after we had driven across the lake that separates the tee from the start of the fairway, Thomas turned and looked back across the water, then quietly gazed at the rest of the scene around us. "In all my travels," he said, "I do not think I've seen a more beautiful landscape. This is as thrilling as Versailles or Fontainebleau."

Chapter Thirty-nine

Merion Golf Club

The Merion Golf Club, which lies on the outskirts of Philadelphia, is somewhat like the city of San Francisco in that everybody loves it. The charm and dignity of its colonial club house, the parklike beauty of its great golf course, the magnificence of its trees, the quality of its rolling terrain are the ingredients, which, blended by some talented men, have produced one of the world's great golf meccas. Golfing drama as it has been presented over its lush green turf has been the pinnacle in America's golf history. It was here that Bob Jones won the fourth of his major championships in making the impregnable Grand Slam. It was here that Olin Dutra got up from a sick bed to seek his dramatic victory in the Open championship of 1934. It was here that Ben Hogan came back after his near fatal accident to win his third Open championship in an exciting play-off, and it was here that Jack Nicklaus in the World Amateur matches shot the lowest score in any major event with his four consecutive rounds.

Merion is an inland course, but it has the feeling of a seaside links. This is because the flowing lines of its beautifully formed greens have the rhythm of the dunes along the sea, and its artistically formed traps, oriented with sod and sand, have the appearance of serrated turf edged by the winds into the irregular eroded pattern that so pleases the eye. The demands of the superb individual holes at Merion are brought out by these famous white-faced traps, slashed in the faces of these green-sided mounds. The psychological factor is that the eye sends the message to the brain that in those white faces there lurks trouble. To see a pin nipped in close against the face of the sand is a challenge so brutally frank it makes the spine quiver. The problems are then obvious, and one must handle them with all the skill with which one is endowed.

From the very first hole, Merion confronts one with genuine golf. The first hole is just 360 yards long, relatively short for a championship course. There are two factors that make this hole amazingly effective, particularly for one built on flat terrain. First, it entices the player to drive as far as he can in order to get the most advantageous angle of entrance to the green, especially if the pin is on the right-hand side. Second, after a short drive or a pushed drive, the approach shot must carry over traps to get in close to the pin when it is set on the right. A hole that encourages the golfer to drive far increases the possibilities of a hook, and there is a trap at the 250-yard mark that will surely catch a long stray hook. If the tee shot is hit too hard to the right, there is a fairway trap with which to contend. Unless the tee markers are forward or the wind is behind, it is out of the range of even the long hitters, but players of professional caliber would do well to yield their power and play this tee shot discreetly, taking their chances on the accuracy of their second shots.

The second hole—which, for me, is one of the best par 5's in the country—is 555 yards long, bringing it within the range of the power-hitter's ability to reach in two. But with what consummate accuracy these two shots must be executed if they are to escape the threat of the out-of-bounds stakes that hug the narrow fairway from tee to green on the right. Yet if one does not hit his two most powerful shots and get as close as possible to the green, the third shot, especially when the pin is in the back left-hand corner of the diagonal green, is one of the meanest little pitches imaginable.

The third hole, 195 yards in length, has the elements of the Redan, but is not a copy. Both the tee and the green are plateaued with a valley between, and a deep trap on the diagonal protects the green at the right. Three traps flank the left-hand side of the green. The green is shaped like a pear, with the small end toward the front, and a pronounced terrace divides the upper and lower levels.

Hole after hole, Merion restates challenges of this order, requiring the golfer to place his tee-shot, but never insisting that he knock the cover off the ball, then throwing at him a succession of second shots to all kinds of green sites—a green that tilts forward at a sharp angle, a green that is best approached by a pitch-and-run played off an incline at the right of the apron, a green that is long and narrow but not too sternly trapped, a green that tilts backward to a central hollow and is further fortified by tough frontal trapping (which is eminently fair since the shot to the green is usually an eight-iron or a nine-iron), a green that is flanked with five traps in back and guarded in front by a lake, here a green that sits below you, there a green that sits above—a wonderful variety, each of them making the most of natural features of the terrain and geared to the golf sense of the individual hole. The eleventh hole is an excellent illustration. It is only 378 yards long, but even those golfers who have gone to pieces on it speak of it as one of the best holes of its length anywhere. It is the second shot that makes the eleventh. The green, small in area, lies just across a creek, which, after

bordering the fairway on the left, curves across the fairway before the green, then twists again and continues around the right-hand side of the green. If you hit this green with your second shot, you heave a sigh so deep that it is usually audible a mashie-shot away.

Among its other distinctions, Merion possesses one of the strongest finishes in golf, a stretch of five holes that sustains a proper pitch of solvable difficulty. The fourteenth, which starts this finish, is a 443-yard dog-leg to the left, flanked along that side by Golf House Road—out of bounds. There is a trap at the right at the 240-yard mark, and the urge to veer away from the road brings it frequently into play. While the green is on the same level as the fairway, the sharp lines of the greenside trapping make it seem a very tough target to hit and hold. The green surface is contoured with mild rolls that can be exasperating, since their actual negotiation is far more slippery than the eye first perceives.

The fifteenth is a dog-leg to the right. While the card gives the yardage of this hole as 395, during the championships the tee can be pushed back into the part of the sixteenth fairway, which serves as the alternate route on that hole. From this back tee, it takes a first-class shot to carry the traps at the angle of the dog-leg. There is not too much to be gained by this short-cut route except that, as usual, power is its own reward and sets up the chance to use a higher lofted club on the approach. The deep trap in front of the green, at the right, makes the approach most hazardous when the pin is positioned on the right-hand tongue of the green.

The sixteenth is perhaps Merion's most celebrated hole. This is the famous Quarry Hole, and the quarry has been used ingeniously. Following an accurately placed drive, the second shot—a strong four-iron up to a four-wood for the bigger players—must carry the quarry, as terrible a piece of wasteland as one would want to see. Trees have been allowed to grow wild and jungle-like at the base of the quarry, and sand has been flashed there.

259

Across the quarry, the green area has been placed astride a hilltop. The green itself, with its double terrace, is a perfect complement to the general ruggedness of this hole.

The seventeenth hole is a par 3, 220 yards long, and when the wind is slightly against you, even the professional stars will use woods. The green is situated well below the tee, framed by four traps that are handsomely shaped and oriented. The main strength of the green is in the boldness of its contours. The front deck lies about 4 feet below the upper deck, and the break between the two decks is severe.

The eighteenth hole, 458 yards long, is a grand finishing hole. The tee-shot is played over another arm of the quarry, and, from the back tee, it takes a reasonably good hit to carry the quarry and reach the fairway. Then it is either a long-iron or a controlled fairway wood home. The green takes conscientious reading.

Analyze Merion closely. It has something. It keeps the pressure on the tournament golfer all the way through to the home hole. It is harder on the average golfer than a course like the Augusta National, but its variety of fairway contours, the angles of its green surfaces, its contiguous "white faces," and the intelligence of its routing have made for a course that age has not withered nor custom staled.

Chapter Forty

Dorado

The world's renowned golf courses achieve their reputation because they have something extra. Pebble Beach has its spectacular seaside scenery. Banff, Jasper, and The Broadmoor in the Rockies have their spectacular mountain views; Augusta has its natural amphitheater. So, too, Dorado has something special.

Dorado lies on one of the most spectacular pieces of ocean beach in the Caribbean. It was cut out of a jungle of trees which now frame and define the fairways, making the course a natural arboretum. A natural lake and two artificially created lakes are interspersed throughout the play of the course.

Snead and his partner, the indestructible Jimmy Demaret, two oldsters, won the team title in the Canada Cup International Matches at Dorado in 1961, and Snead, playing as superb golf as he ever played in his life, won the individual event with a record breaking score of 274. Golf's most beautiful swinger was at his peak. Sam proved the age-old golfing adage that sweet swingers never die, neither do they fade away. Sam's shots were as straight as an arrow during the entire four rounds.

Many of the holes at Dorado are great. Individually, they are cunningly subtle, glamorously breath-taking, treacherously fatal, potentially devastating, charmingly horrifying, desperately demanding, grouchily mean, disastrously wet, blissfully tranquil. The third is a teaser (the "'cunningly subtle") where the shot is flanked by woods on the right and water on the left. The Sneads of the game, fearing the woods, will attempt a slight hook, but therein lies the subtlety, for the slightly controlled hook may become the uncontrolled pull. The ball then runs or plunges into the lake. Snead says it is unfair, too critical in the target area. On one round he went into the water, once he went into the woods, and twice he split the middle, but his four rounds were even par. Sam, I fear, will complain until he plays his last hole.

The fourth hole (glamorously breathtaking) has the tee on the lake. The golfer is shooting to the beautifully molded, well-trapped green, framed by the blue, white-capped, ocean—breathtaking indeed. The large green, cunningly contoured, demands gray matter as well as touch. Be happy for a par, and for being alive.

The fifth hole (treacherously fatal) is edged by the ocean at the tee. The golfer is driving to a dog-leg fairway, lake-flanked its full length on the left, tree-lined to the bend in the fairway on the right, and with a treacherous trap at the 250-yard mark. If you hug the shoreline with your tee shot, you will be in a position to carry the water with your second, a distance of some 230 yards, or fatally sacrifice a stroke to the lago. It is a birdie possibility with two good shots, and one can always hope to prove the magic formula "2 plus 1 makes 3," a blessed formula for egos; but with a hooked tee shot, and a hooked second, disaster lurks on the shoreline. Players have played themselves out of tournaments by taking high scores of 9, 10, and 11 here.

The ninth hole (potentially devastating) has a trap flank on the fairway at the 260-yard mark, and is tree-lined on both sides of its entire length. The green is tightly trapped on both sides from front to middle, and contoured with devious curves and terraces, making for treacherous putting. It is the master trap at the left, placed on the diagonal, that triggers a doubt (just before the forward press of the knee starts the flow of the swing)—fear then injects itself—and breaks the rhythm, sending the ball turning from right to left into its sandy waste. This master trap, with its narrow entrance, calls for a very demanding shot.

The eleventh (charmingly horrifying) is a picture hole with the tree-lined ponds running its full length on the left. The next grouping of grapefruit and palm trees flanks the right side of the fairway. Inside the tree line at the 260-yard mark there is a bold, avaricious-looking trap. The green, with its wide entrance, seems guileless as a child, but the crowned bold contour in the middle of the green and the subtle contours on the rest of the green make it a difficult task to get cozy with the pin. In addition, the lake on the left seems to sneak up to the very edge of the green to catch a slightly pulled pitch shot. Charming, indeed, if you get home in two.

The twelfth hole (desperately demanding) is as long as the Burma Road. It is tree-lined and trapped from the tee at the 260-yard mark; lake-flanked on the left to the 280-yard mark; over the Burma Road at the 200/350-yard mark; then downhill to the green at the 575-yard mark. The green is artistically molded, protected by a bold trap at the left, for a demanding pin position directly behind. The lake begins at the front right edge and wends its way the full right side and to the back of the green to catch a pushed or overplayed shot—demanding, demanding, demanding.

The thirteenth hole is grouchily mean, with a peninsula shaped green that extends slightly into the water on the left and back, the surface crown hiding the pin position in the back of the green, and with water the full 210 yards of its length. The hole is tree-lined at the right, and trapped at the right forefront of the green. With woods, water, and upside-down contours, mean is the word.

The seventeenth hole is disastrously wet in the Neptune sense. It is 190 yards long starting at the tee which is nestled in the trees. The lake runs its full length on the left-hand side, and it is trapped boldly and diagonally at the right forefront of the green, which is contoured with three distinct pin positions, divided by slightly crowned mounds. Woe unto the hooker as the ball plunges into this watery bottom—the water is deep, grave's end, and the ball is gone.

The eighteenth hole, blissfully tranquil, has wide and tree-lined fairways, ocean-flanked and windblown, a heavenly view in a paradise setting. The trap at the right edge of the rough at the 260-yard mark, tree-flanked its full length on both sides, and with a backdrop of trees, makes a beautiful finish for a felicitous experience.

Chapter Forty-one

Pinehurst

Pinehurst has passed its sixty-fifth year as America's number-one golfing Mecca. The legend of Pinehurst started with a wastelike sand-dune country in the North Carolina hills, which James Tufts found in the early 1890's. It is here that the late great architect Donald Ross created some of America's great courses. The tradition of these two great men has been carried on admirably by James Tufts' son Richard, who has added a fifth golf course at Pinehurst. Perhaps no one spot has sold the game more to the hinterlands than Pinehurst. For it was after playing at Pinehurst that many a guest would return home to his native heath, organize a club, and immediately write to Donald Ross.

As a result, Pinehurst has been a tremendous influence, which has been in keeping with the fine traditions of the game. The architecture of the courses at first was crude: Ross was mimicking the best he could find on the linksland of his native Scotland, and it was not until later in his career, with experience and with the aid of some talented associates, that he wisely used his accumulated knowledge and experience and constantly improved his own abilities as well as improving vastly the character of his golf courses at Pinehurst and elsewhere.

Ross created his greatest course, Number 2, at Pinehurst in the mid-thirties, when he completely revised a course that up until that time had had sand greens. When he finished, he stated that this was his masterpiece. There are some of us who may question this: I feel that the Seminole Links at Palm Beach was an equally masterful job. In March and April, Ross's five golf courses are a hubbub created by golf-happy people, both duffers and skilled alike. Pinehurst in the spring is delightful. You can smell the pine, see the beauty of the dogwood, hear the buzzing of the conversation that is nothing but golf (and in this sense it is somewhat like St. Andrews). This is golf, golf, golf!

Pinehurst's most famous course, Number 2, is routed over more or less level land, with only one pronounced change in the conformation of the terrain, a dip at the fifth hole. One of its most striking aspects is the isolation of the separate holes. Each becomes an individual unit, due to the fact that the pine trees planted early in the development now frame the holes completely. This framing accords the holes a third dimension, which adds immensely to their character and creates an aesthetic background that emphasizes the flowing lines of the architecture. The thick pine woods also offer a comforting protection when the cold winds sweep down from the north, as they are bound to do on occasion.

Americans, unlike the British, are not given to playing in the rain, but at Pinehurst they make what is perhaps their one exception. I dare say that more people play in the rain at Pinehurst than at any other golf course in America. In fact, if you can have a windbreaker and an umbrella, it is a rather pleasant thing to do, because the sand underfoot makes for relatively dry walking. In the rain, the pine trees seem to glisten, making each hole an individual jewel.

As to the character of the architecture of Pinehurst Number 2, the most striking feature is that the greens are extremely small, perhaps the smallest of any on our championship layouts. They are nicely formed, with their rhythmic sweeps carrying well out into the approach areas. This particular type of architecture makes the greens difficult to hit and at the same time makes for a chipping course that has no equal, since one is apt to be chipping more often here than at any other place I know. It is my feeling that Pinehurst is a more difficult test of golf for the nearly great golfer than it is for the truly great golfer, for here the big hitter carries all the fairway trapping, and his power, of couse, brings him within closer range of the green. With small greens as the targets, that edge in distance is important, because the nearer one gets to any target in any sport, the more often he is apt to hit it. It has been my feeling that a half-dozen cunningly placed pot traps at the 250-yard marks (measured from the backs of the tees) could make Pinehurst a truly formidable test for golfers of championship caliber.

Chapter Forty-two

Pebble Beach

Most people get their first view of Pebble Beach through a big picture window in the Lodge. The view is awe-inspiring, looking across the eighteenth green over Carmel Bay to the headlands of a craggy coastline beyond. From the same vantage point, the viewer looks upon the shoreline of the eighteenth hole from start to finish. Undoubtedly, this is a hole that must be classed as one of the world's great par 5's. Pebble Beach and Del Monte properties as a whole have a flavor which is truly indescribable; wooded hillsides and mountain areas, the view of the bay, the turbulence of the ocean, the clean crisp air, the blue sky and blue water.

Pebble Beach is unrivaled among our oceanside courses. It is routed along a craggy headland that drops abruptly into Carmel Bay and therefore must be called an oceanside course and not a linksland. Linksland indicates windswept sand dunes placed there by nature, resulting from the combined efforts of wind and sea. Pebble Beach is composed of two types of holes, those along the sea and those back from the sea. Those along the sea are superb, magnificent, outstanding, while those back from the sea can be classified as good. One or two of them must also be classified as ordinary. The least thrilling holes are probably the first, second, and third, and greatness begins with the fourth, which is not a long hole, but is toward the sea and is a very interesting drive and pitch.

The fifth is a short hole clustered in the trees. The length of its green and the tightness of its trapping and the overhanging branches of the trees make it a difficult little hole.

Then begins the start of five of the most spectacular holes in golf. The sixth hole is a 502-yard uphill hole to a plateaued green dangerously near an escarpment and flanked throughout, from the 200-yard mark, by the ocean and the cliffs. The seventh is one of the most spectacular holes of its length in the world—110 yards from an elevated tee down to the very edge of the ocean. It is a simple little eight- or nine-iron or possibly a wedge under ordinary conditions, but when the wind blows, as it does frequently in the wintertime, some of the better players in the country will use three-irons from this tee and still only barely reach the green. The eighth hole is spectacular both in its design and in its setting. The tee shot aims to a plateaued fairway with ample room for a good shot but none to spare for an extremely bad tee shot. The second shot demands a complete carry across the water and cliffs to a green site along the very edge of the ocean. What makes this hole particularly good is that the player having reached the target area from the tee can choose his length and in keeping with his ability can bite off as much as he chooses en route to the green. Number 10 has approximately the same setting and one looks on to the expansive beautiful white beach of Carmel Bay. These holes are 425 and 450 yards respectively, and they are terrifying for the golfer who is inclined to fade or push his shots. It requires two big shots to get to the green on both holes and both of them lie on the very edge of the cliff escarpment.

Number 11 starts the golfer back, since the shots are played away from the sea, but one will hardly be back far enough to lose the potency of the wind. Number 12 is a nicely designed little hole of 185 yards, with a master trap across the left-hand face of the green, trapped at the right-hand corner and nestled in a beautiful grove of trees. This is not an easy hole, and is particularly hard under wind conditions. Number 14 is an interesting par 5, 555 yards in length. The golfer hits to a target fairway area flanked with traps on the right and left. The second shot will undoubtedly stop just before the green, and the green itself is rather small in size and tightly trapped with deep traps across the face, both left and right. It is not the type of green to which one gets home in two very often, but it is quite possible that a Nicklaus or a Palmer with their best blows under favorable conditions can do so, but it would have to be an extremely accurate shot because of the tightness of the green surface. Number 15 is somewhat of an ordinary hole but Number 16 is a real gem. It is a slight dog-leg to the right where one plays into a grove of trees surrounded by a barranca. One must be accu-

rate or finish in the woods well below the green in the barranca and quite possibly be lucky if one is not stymied playing back to the pin.

Number 17 is a great par 3, 218 yards and normally dead into the wind. This is the hole where Arnold Palmer in the 1964 Crosby went down onto the beach and had to wait for the wave action to stop pushing his ball around before he could play back up onto the green surface. Now we come to the eighteenth, the great par 5 of the course and one of the great par 5's of golf. It is flanked its full length by Carmel Bay on the left. From the tee, one has definitely to carry in across an arm of the ocean if one wants to be in a close position. There is a tree in the middle of the fairway that can play havoc with a good tee shot because one might get dead up against it and not be able to play his second shot or one might be stymied in playing the second shot. If the shot is free, the second shot is not too difficult as one can protect himself by a slight fade. The shot onto the green becomes a testing one because the green is small and is trapped almost totally on all sides. Under pressure conditions, this hole can be nerveracking, and many a golfer has lost a tournament on this last hole because he could not keep the jitters from creeping into his swing.

Chapter Forty-three

Augusta National

The Augusta National started as a gleam in Bob Jones's eye and became the most celebrated golf course in America. As site of the Masters Tournament, it is the Mecca each spring of golf's nomads and of those who love the game. The Masters has become the symbol of the reawakening of the sport each year after a long winter's hibernation, and fans by the thousands swarm to the beautiful Georgia countryside for an extravaganza that has become a cross between a baseball World Series and a country fair.

The fate of a great golf course and of a great tournament was determined by one look. In 1931, Jones, having completed his immortal Grand Slam and gone into semi-retirement, began searching for a setting to lay out what he considered the perfect golf course. The moment he saw Berckmans' nursery property and its lovely ante-bellum mansion house on the outskirts of Augusta, Georgia, he knew he had found the perfect site. Here Jones decided to carve out a course that would incorporate the principles of some of the wonderful holes he had encountered during his illustrious career and to establish a tournament that would delight golfers. Not even Bob Jones could have visualized the impact that his course and his tournament ultimately would have on the golf world.

It is a setting that is the last word in skillfully nurtured natural beauty—a maze of color with forests of stately pines and flowering azaleas, dogwood, and redbud. Looking down from the club house, a bridal-white Colonial structure, one sees a natural amphitheater over which the course is laid out. It is possible to see the far end of the property. There a sharp escarpment rises, defining the course's border. This bank, covered with pines reaching high into the sky, presents a natural backdrop for a natural stage on which some of the greatest drama in American golf is enacted. This incline, from the club house dropping to its lowest point at Rae's Creek, is 120 feet long. Within this natural amphitheater some of the game's most classic holes have been developed.

The Augusta National is a meadowland course, with broad ribbons for fairways, tall pines, flashes of white sand and small lakes and streams providing hazards. Augusta has a clean, sprightly appearance, yet one of great beauty and majesty.

Bob Jones's theory was that a course should be not only a test of championship golf but also a pleasure to play. This concept he incorporated in Augusta National. The width of the fairways allows for latitude from the tees. Missed tee shots are not punished drastically, either by trapping or rough, making it a hitters' course. This is the reason that players such as Arnold Palmer, who won four Masters' crowns in the space of seven years, and Jack Nicklaus, who set a record of 271 in 1965, always play it well. They say you never have to call a man out of the crowd to present him the traditional champion's green coat—a champion golfer, a favorite, almost invariably wins.

In order to offset the freedom from the tee and the use of so few traps in the normal target areas and around the greens, the plateau principle of green design has been employed. On these plateaus, the sinuous rolls have defied the world's outstanding golfers. It is necessary to put the approach shots near the pin in order to reduce the chance of three-putting. This keeps golfers on constant edge, insidiously and continually tearing at their nerves.

While the outgoing nine has some interesting holes—particularly the third, the fourth, the fifth, and the seventh—it is not nearly as treacherous as the back nine, although the two sides play equal par: 36–36—72. The incoming nine constitutes perhaps the most nerve-racking test of championship golf in the United States. Many a golfer's dream has been shattered on that small stretch known as "Heartbreak Corner" the tenth through the thirteenth. Here championships have been won and lost.

The tenth is a stirring par 4, dropping into a beautiful valley with the green framed by pine trees. The eleventh has water flanking the left side of the green, always a challenge when the pin is tucked into the left corner. Whirlpool winds make the twelfth a tricky, frustrating par 3. The par 5 thirteenth, with its fronting creek, has snuffed out the ambitions of many a bold attacker.

The golfer's nerves get no rest after this ordeal. On the fifteenth, another par 5, the second shot must carry over a pond to the crowned green if one is to keep pace with the modern day sluggers. The short sixteenth has a two-level contoured green across its fairway of water. The two finishing holes are among the toughest in golf. No player can be sure of victory at Augusta until the last putt has dropped.

It was on the two closing holes that Palmer stole the championship from Ken Venturi in 1960, scoring birdies while Venturi was being measured for the green coat, and it was here also that Palmer, with victory in his grasp, lost the crown to Gary Player in 1961. Sam Snead blew a chance for the championship on the seventeenth in 1963.

The men who run the Masters are proud of their heritage. They feel it is their responsibility to see that the Augusta National be kept abreast of the times and never outdated. Changes are made constantly.

Two of the most marked changes have been made in the eleventh and sixteenth holes. I am proud that my contribution to developing these holes has contributed to the course's greatness. Once Number 11 was the easiest par 4 hole and Number 16 the easiest par 3 hole on the course. Now they are probably the toughest.

The eleventh originally was a 365-yard hole that called for a controlled fade on the drive and a simple pitch over some mounds to the green. To put more teeth in the hole, a new tee was built in the pine grove to the left of the tenth green, elevated so that there is a hollow between it and the crest of the target area. The hole was lengthened to 450 yards. Pines on the left stretch to a pond, which was created by damming a creek that flowed innocuously to the left of the green. The green was reshaped with a neck projecting to the left, surrounded by water on three sides. The hole becomes frightening when the pin is placed in this treacherous cape and most golfers elect to shoot for the fat part of the green rather than for the pin.

Since the hole was changed, both Hogan and Snead have blown the Masters at the harrowing eleventh. Going into the last round, each felt he had to gamble for a birdie there to win the championship. The result was that each hit his approach into the water and took penalty shots that wrecked his hopes.

Bob Jones compared the Augusta National to a fickle woman who must be petted and studied. "You cannot hammer her and push her around," the immortal Grand Slam king said, always talking about the course in personal terms. "Snap at her and she snaps right back. You cannot attack her. You must cajole her, treat her gently. You must sneak up on her if you expect to win."

Chapter Forty-four

Oakland Hills

The Oakland Hills golf course always will be remembered for a remark made by Ben Hogan at the presentation ceremonies after he had won his third National Open championship there in 1951. "I am happy," Hogan said dourly, "that I brought the monster to her knees."

Hogan was at the peak of his career at that time. He had survived a near fatal automobile accident and had astounded the golf world with his comeback victory in the 1950 Open at Merion. Now he was shooting for another Open, his goal to surpass the four Open crowns won by Willie Anderson and Bob Jones.

Along with others of the world's best golfers, the meticulous, almost flawless Hogan went out after Oakland Hills' rugged par 70, zealously guarded by sinister fairway traps planted, golfers said, at the normal target areas of the reasonably good hitters. The fairways were given hour-glass figures, the golfers complained, making it necessary to hit short rather than risk a run through the small alley way. "The fairways are so narrow," Dr. Cary Middlecoff said, "that the players and caddies have to walk single file, Indian fashion."

Walter Hagen, patriarch of professional golf, had another comment. "The course is playing the players instead of the players playing the course," he said, as the first three rounds were played without a single sub-par round.

Competitors in the 1951 Open experienced a psychological shock when they first encountered Oakland Hills. They had been playing over courses which, with few exceptions, had been laid out in the 1920's or earlier, and had been tailored for the equipment and playing conditions of that period. Such courses were all right for Hagen, Jones, Sarazen, and Armour, but hardly a test for the new breed, using steel-shafted clubs, balls that took off like rockets, and swing patterns that added greater length to every drive. They generated such power that their drives, whether straight or not, brought them so close to the green that only a little flip of the wedge or niblick was necessary to reach home. Par had lost its significance.

The 1951 Open, for the first time in years, put the players on a course that could take their heaviest blows and then hit back. It was a twentieth-century test for twentieth-century conditions. Players complained a while, then delighted in facing a real challenge. Before remodeling the course for the event for the U.S. Golf Association, I accumulated sufficient data to assess the values that related to the playing skills of the modern professional golfer. Then I related these values to the course.

Our first move was to fill in all the obsolete traps situated at the right and left sides of the fairways. These were 200 to 220 yards from the tee, no obstacle to the professional golfer of the 1950's. They had been put there in the 1920's to penalize the golfer who could not groove his tee shot. Against the modern professionals, they were useless hazards. The professionals—even the average hitters—found no difficulty in driving well past the hazards.

We replaced these traps with new ones, ranging from 230 yards to 260 yards from the tee. These changes were not unfair. They presented the top tournament player with the same sort of task—no harder and no easier—that the top players of that other generation experienced in the 1920's. He had to hit a straight tee shot or risk trouble. If he wanted to gamble on muscle, he might shoot over the traps. The choice was his.

We made other changes. We tightened the greens, protecting the tongue areas with additional trapping. On a few of the greens, we softened the contours that we thought might be too harsh or too tricky.

The cries that went up from the touring pros, accustomed to easy courses, split the heavens. Instead of the usual cluster of sub-par rounds, they struggled in with scores in the middle 70's and some even in the 80's. "Foul!" "Unfair!" they screamed. Instead of being able to approach with a wedge and putt for birdies on almost every hole, they found that a missed shot cost a stroke. This is the purpose of a truly championship course.

However, the field was thrown into confusion. There was no complaint against a particular hole or a particular group of holes. It was just that the golfers were not scoring as they had been accustomed to doing—and the experience was humiliating. The first reaction of the players was to be cagey. Instead of

trying to fly a tee shot over the fairway bunkers, they chose to play safe, use irons and three-woods off the tee, play short of the traps, and take a longer iron to the greens.

One of these was the razor-keen Hogan. His first round was a frustrating 76. He was disgusted with himself. Par escaped him again on the second round. On the third round Saturday morning, Hogan, his face a grim mask of determination, appeared to have the situation licked until he moved to the fourteenth. There he took a bogey and again failed to beat par.

At lunch, Hogan apparently took inventory. By playing safe, he had failed to beat par. So had everyone else. Perhaps the thing to do was attack. Clubbing down, off the tee, had only made for longer second shots and the increase in the chances for error.

So, during the last round, Hogan decided to attack. The change in tactics paid off. He used his driver off the tee on every par 4 and every par 5 hole. He played his approach for the pin instead of the fat part of the green. He finished with a 67—one of two sub-par rounds played in the entire tournament, the other being a last round 69 by Clayton Heafner. Hogan won the championship, and, after giving out his "monster" statement, called it the finest round of golf he had ever played.

To me, the most satisfying feature of the 1951 Open at Oakland Hills was that at the end of the tournament the best players were at the top. This is as it should be. The basic truth was accented: When a tournament is played on a championship course, such as Oakland Hills, you rarely get an outsider as the winner. The title goes to a great golfer.

Chapter Forty-five

Firestone

"Firestone," said Gary Player to me recently, "is the hardest golf course in the world for me to score well on consistently." The statement is not surprising because Firestone is a hard taskmaster. Hole by hole, shot by shot, the pressure is always on. One cannot let up for a moment, for a missed shot may take a heavy toll. It is indicative that in an analytical study of the last four major championship tournaments held on the Firestone course, the six most difficult holes, as computed from the scoring records, have never been the same over a four-year period. Eleven of the eighteen holes have fallen into the top six bracket of most difficult scoring holes.

We performed a major remodeling job on Firestone for the 1963 PGA championship. I was most amused by the remark made to me by Ted Kroll after he finished his first round at Firestone during the tournament: "What a transformation has been made on this golf course! We used to think that this course was a 'nothing' golf course, and now it has everyone tipping his hat."

The Firestone course flows over a gently rolling, naturally wooded Ohio countryside. Looking up the tree-lined verdant fairways from its elevated club house, one gets a sense of tranquility—that is, until one tees off on the first hole. Former Open champion Jack Fleck said, "Stepping on the first tee is like going to the movies and sitting through the previews of coming attractions, for this exacting starting hole gives you a peek of what is in store for you on the next 17 holes of this great golf course."

The third hole at Firestone, 450 yards, par 4, has been called a picture hole because of the beautiful tree-lined fairway and the pond that lies before the green, defending the hole. The hole is a dog-leg to the right, and the tee strategy calls for positioning the drive in the left center of the fairway. The placement of the tee shot is of utmost concern. Distance is a requisite, for if you lack distance you can have a treacherous second shot. The hole is downhill for about the first 270 yards. Hence the big tee shot requirement, for if you do not get to the level area of the fairway, you have a slightly downhill lie. With the large pond before the green to carry, your shot to the green must be flying high. A pushed tee shot will get you in the trees at the right and make an extremely difficult shot to the green. The green, lying just beyond the water, is a two-level and very large one. In playing the second shot, the difference between the front and back of the green can actually be two clubs. Jay Hebert, the winner of the 1960 PGA, called this "one of the most frightening golf holes in the country." From the records, and as expressed vehemently by that articulate Southern gentleman, Mr. Samuel Jackson Snead: "The fourth hole is just too much golf hole, too long and too hard." The tee lies back in trees and the drive must be projected through a tree-lined opening to a fairway that tilts perceptibly from right to left. There is a trap in the hillside slope at the 260-yard mark; to obtain a favorable position in the fairway, you must flirt dangerously with this well-located trap. The location of the trap and the tilt of the fairway necessitates a shot with a slight draw, and therein is the rub; for if the slight draw becomes a big hook, you will find yourself in the rough, and from there it is almost impossible to reach the green in two. Only after a perfect position in the fairway can you reasonably anticipate a par. The hole is slightly uphill to the green from the 250-yard mark. The green is well trapped, with its surface partially blind due to the difference in elevation. Par here is a thrill, and a birdie blissful exultation. Without question, number four is the toughest hole on the course.

The fifth hole at Firestone is the 230 yard, par 3 troublemaker. The entrance is guarded by two formidable Sahara-like traps, one on the left forefront and one along the right forefront and right side, and another on the back left-hand corner. The green is ample in size—in fact, large—making for a reasonable target. The surface is slightly undulating but not severe, and normally it takes a good three-wood to hit the green. Most players wisely will play for the center of the green, regardless of the pin position, and be completely happy with a par, for here, in the analytical studies, bogeys outrank birdies six to one.

"The sixth hole at Firestone follows five of the most difficult starting holes we encounter anywhere on the PGA tour," said Johnny Pott. The hole is 450 yards long with a slight dog-leg to the right. From the tee, one must thread the ball through the trees, at left and right, forming a funnel for the first 100 yards. The target area to the fairway is blind, and for that reason there are no fairway traps; the width of the fairway is more generous than on other holes. Like any hole of this length, power pays a premium. The long tee shot will leave a two- or three-iron to the green, but if the golfer is short off the tee, he is left with a three-wood from a down slope. The green itself is flanked both on the left and right

sides, with one trap on the left forefront nipping across the front left surface of the green, one at the back left-hand side and with more trapping along the full right-hand side of the green. There are two mounds on the green surface—a moderately large one on the left-hand side of the green, and a smaller one on the right-hand side. Pins placed directly behind either mound can make for some knee-knocker putts.

The ninth hole at Firestone is a beautiful tree-lined 465 yard, par 4. The roll is downhill all the way to the dip before the green. There are three traps in the target area—one at the left-hand side and two on the right-hand side, to catch the slightly strayed tee shot. The green is slightly small and elevated, with deep bunkers on both sides, and another shallow trap to the rear. This makes an extremely exacting green, for the second shot must be just right, both in length and accuracy. Don Fairfield shot one of the most brilliant rounds at Firestone in the third round of the American Classic when he shot the course record of 65. He said, after his round, "I believe I played the hole perfectly. My drive was down the middle of the fairway and my five-iron approach left me a 6-foot putt for a birdie, which I made. That was a mighty impressive birdie, for it gave me a record 31 for the front side. From there, I went on to a one under par 34 for the second nine, which made a record 65 for the round. That 65 was the greatest round of golf I've ever played in my life."

The tenth hole, 405 yards, par 4, is slightly dog-legged and tree-lined on the right. There are bunkers at the 250 yard mark, both left and right. "The big problem on 10," says Gene Littler, "are the bunkers. If you are fortunate enough to place the ball on the fairway between the bunkers, you are faced with a shot anywhere from a three- to a six-iron, depending on the condition of the wind, and the wind is usually against you." The green is elevated above the target area with a bold trap at the left. The green tilts from left to right. Through the back right-hand corner, there is a tongue area that makes the hole extremely difficult.

The sixteenth hole at Firestone has been called the "Monster," primarily because it wrecked Arnold Palmer's chance of winning the 1960 PGA championship, after he had won the Masters, the U.S. Open, and finished one shot back in the British Open and needed the PGA to make it three out of four in golf's current great Grand Slam. The sixteenth hole is a 625, par 5, from the very back of the tee. In recent years, it has been played from the forward position in the American Classic, making the hole somewhere around 575 yards in length. This makes a big difference in the play of the hole. Whereas the play to the 250-yard mark from the back of the tee reaches a target position in a level area with a trap at the right, when the hole is some 40 to 50 yards shorter, the ball lands on the downslope, running approximately 75 to 100 yards. This brings the green within range of the second shot, whereas, from the very back, this would be almost impossible except for a long-hitting Nicklaus, with a downwind helping. When Palmer lost the PGA, this hole proved to be his disaster. He pitched his tee shot in the trap to the right. He then hit his second shot into the trees in the right rough. The third shot was flubbed into a little creek on the same side of the fairway. A drop-out and a stroke to the green made him five, and then he three-putted. Gary Player says, "I've been around the world playing golf, and as far as I'm concerned, the sixteenth hole is one of the most challenging par 5's anywhere. I don't try to play it as anything but a par 5, and am very happy if I get a 4. From the shorter tee position, here is the way I generally play it: I drive off the tee and play slightly to the right and I play my second shot far to the left, avoiding the pond. This opens my third shot up, giving me the advantage of taking a shot to the green, and from here you don't have to play over water. The third shot must be high and have a lot of bite, for the green is slightly crowned and does not have too much depth. Any hole that causes you to think and play for position or otherwise extracts a penalty has got to be considered a great golf hole. The sixteenth does this."

The eighteenth hole at Firestone is tree-lined on both sides. The favorite position for this hole from the tee would be slightly to the right-hand side of the fairway. The hole doglegs slightly to the left, and the trees on the left-hand side can stymie the shot to the green. The green is large, trapped on the left and on the right, and the pin position can be nipped behind these provocative bunkers. The surface is slightly contoured, and makes for extremely treacherous putting if the ball is long as it sometimes may be on this big green. Arnold Palmer calls it one of the great par 4 finishing holes of golf.

Firestone is a great golf course and must be put in the blue-ribbon class as one of the country's outstanding tests.

Chapter Forty-six

Bellerive

It is not necessary that a course be old and hallowed, bloodied by decades of skirmishing with the titans of the game, to earn the distinction of being a true championship test. A case in point is the relatively new Bellerive Country Club in St. Louis, which made its bow in big-time golf as host of the 1965 United States Open.

Bellerive is a comparative youngster with its birth dating to 1959, when the club was relocated and a new course constructed, but she is big for her age and terribly precocious. She is the kind of course that talks up to punishing hitters such as Jack Nicklaus and Arnold Palmer, and teases precisionists such as Tony Lema and Ken Venturi.

This is the longest course ever to host the Open, measuring 7,191 yards—38 yards longer than the taxing Congressional course, which, in the intense Washington (D.C.) heat, left competitors gasping for air in 1964. Bellerive has six par 4 holes of 450 yards and over and two par 5's measuring 580 and 606 yards. The big hitters may get home on the first of these marathon holes—the eighth—but are unlikely to do so on the other, the seventeenth.

There are four good par 3's, with a meandering creek inviting vagrant shots on two of them. A creek also cuts diagonally across the 460-yard, par 4 twelfth, forcing a 220-yard tee shot to clear it. Gene Sarazen, a coiner of phrases, might call Bellerive "a real heavyweight—a Jack Dempsey among golf courses."

Rolling hills, creeks, and wooded slopes made Bellerive an ideal setting for a championship course. The greens are fairly large in size, undulating and varying from subtle to bold in character.

Bellerive is a course which demands both strength and accuracy.

One of the most trying holes is Number 4, a 470-yarder that is a modified par 5. I consider it one of the toughest of the par 4's. The trapping in the fairway should not be a troublesome factor, because it was originally placed for a par 5 hole, but the narrowing of the fairway at this point makes the rough become a hazard adequate to protect the strayed tee shot. The green is slightly elevated with three traps—one bold, large trap on the right and two small traps on the diagonal at the left side of the green. The green has a crowned center with pockets at the back and at the right-hand side. The green slopes from both sides to the front.

The fifth hole is not as long, measuring 466 yards, but it can be terrifying because of a pond at the 230-yard to 260-yard position. The fairway at this point tilts slightly toward the water.

The tenth is another par 5 converted to a par 4, made more difficult by a shallow green. The green is hard to hold because it was designed for a third shot pitch. There is an entrance to the right side of the hole, the left side being protected by a trap that cuts full across. A trap back of the green is ready to gulp shots that are overplayed. I consider the tenth the hardest hole on the course on which to score.

274

The par 4 twelfth, measuring 460 yards, puts a premium on the tee shot. Play is from an elevated tee, but the golfer must always be extremely accurate with his drive to avoid the trees that seem to crawl out into the middle of the fairway. If the target area is reached safely, the shot is to the green in the hillside, surrounded by trees and with flank trapping from the forward position back through two-thirds of the edge of the green. This makes for an extremely difficult second shot.

The fifteenth marks the beginning of one of the most difficult stretch runs in golf. On the 456-yard fifteenth, the tee shot must be well-placed in the center, since there are woods on the left and traps on the right. Because of the dip before the green, the left-hand trap in front is not visible unless one has a prodigious drive. The green sits on a plateau with a bank at its back, and a great second shot with precision is needed for good scoring.

The sixteenth is a gem of a short hole with an elevated green and a valley between it and the tee. While the green is approximately on the same level as the tee, the dip makes the green some 20 feet above the level of the approach area. The green is well trapped.

The seventeenth is a dog-leg to the right, with the tee nestling among the trees and the fairway tilting from left to right. The creek flanks the whole right-hand side of the fairway and trees are on the left. There is a nasty little pond in front.

The final hole presents a strong and dramatic finish. Played from a slightly elevated tee, the hole dog-legs to the left. The fairway is trapped heavily in the angle of the dog-leg some 260 yards from the tee. The second shot is played to a big green protected by cavernous traps.

The seventeenth is a longer par 5 than the eighth, but may be no easier to birdie. The eighth is strong enough to make the golfer earn every stroke he saves. Large trees engulf the target area from the tee. Even after a good drive, the second shot presents problems. The fairway is flanked by a creek along the full right-hand side. The trapping in the target area of the second shot must be carried in order to get into a safe position for the last pitch. The green is wide but not deep, with a trap directly in the front middle of the green. Another trap sits at the right forward position of the green. To reach this green in two is quite unlikely, even for long hitters such as Nicklaus, so the third shot has to be a pitching wedge.

For all its tender age, Bellerive has cultivated some mighty big muscles.

Chapter Forty-seven

Other Great Courses

Each of the famous courses included in this book is markedly different from each of the others. Each has its own distinctive personality, and, if each course did not, it would be safe to say it would not be outstanding. Since all the great golf courses cannot be included with diagrams in the limited space available in this book, it would appear to me to be remiss in not mentioning some of the great courses upon which major Open, PGA, or Amateur championships have been played. They should be included in the Hall of Fame of golf courses. There are also many courses that have local renown and undoubtedly would have national acceptance if major championships were played over them.

Outstanding courses are not similar to one another in character, and that is one of the pleasures of the game. For it would be boring indeed, if every golf course one played were an exact copy of every other golf course.

To me that is part of the charm of the game—imaginative use of any given piece of property will produce a course different from any other, the design having been adapted properly to the terrain makes the course outstanding. Individual characteristics of the holes of great courses leave indelible imprints on the golfer's memory after he has once played them—this is what puts these courses into a special category. These courses must include that ugly beauty, the Oakmont Country Club in Pittsburgh, Pennsylvania, which, with its pew traps and its treacherous greens,

must be considered as really great; Congressional, the scene of the 1964 Open championship, pieced together by combining the best of two 18's to make it an exciting championship course, with one of the greatest natural finishing holes—with a lake in front of the green enhancing the amphitheatre setting that held 30,000 people watching the final drama; Winged Foot at Mamaroneck, New York, where Bob Jones sank a curling 12-foot putt to tie Al Espinoza in 1929, going on to win the Open championship the next day in easy style, and where Billy Casper proved to be one of the current greats by his victory in 1959, 30 years later; the Olympic Club in San Francisco, where the unknown, Jack Fleck, caught Hogan with a birdie on the seventy-second hole and won the play-off to snatch from Ben what would have been his record fifth Open title; the Country Club of Brookline, with its dignified Back Bay setting and its undignified brutality enforcing a play-off at 293, the highest score in recent golfing history, in which the aging Boros beat the youthful Cupit and the great Arnold Palmer, 50 years after a youthful ex-caddy Francis Ouimet upset the great British stars Ted Ray and Harry Vardon to win the Open championship in 1913; Baltusrol, in Springfield, New Jersey, which received its fifth Open in 1967 and whose famous lower course, relatively level and majestically tree-lined, demands shots that are only worthy of a champion; Southern Hills in Tulsa, Oklahoma, a truly great golf course over a gently rolling terrain where, in 1958, Tommy Bolt, shooting brilliant golf, nipped Gary Player by a stroke for what could have been Gary's first major title; Oak Hill in Rochester, New York, that tree-lined beauty where Cary Middlecoff garnered his second Open championship, beating Julius Boros by a stroke; Medinah, in Chicago, Illinois, where Cary Middlecoff threaded the tree-lined fairways to win his first Open championship, beating Sam Snead by a stroke after he had three-putted the seventeenth green to let another Open slip from his grasp; Colonial Country Club in Forth Worth, Texas, one of the country's great championship tests, where Craig Wood, with a lame and braced back, won with a brilliant 284; Broadmoor at Colorado Springs, in a majestic mountain setting, where Jack Nicklaus won his first Amateur championship over a truly great golf course, starting a brilliant and still unended career; Canterbury in Cleveland, scene of the 1940 U.S. Open, won by Lawson Little after a play-off with Gene Sarazen shooting 70 to a 73, and scene of the 1946 U.S. Open Championship, in which Lloyd Mangrum won with a play-off requiring 36 holes to defeat Byron Nelson and Vic Ghezzi. Among the other courses that are sites for great championships, and others that certainly could be, are: Saucon Valley, Bethlehem, Pennsylvania; The Country Club of Cleveland, Cleveland, Ohio; The Cascades, Hot Springs, Virginia; The Dunes, Myrtle Beach, South Carolina; East Lake, Atlanta, Georgia; Golden Horseshoe, Williamsburg, Virginia; Royal Kaanapali, Maui, Hawaii; Cyprus Point, California; Los Angeles Country Club, Los Angeles, California; Shady Oaks Country Club, Fort Worth, Texas; Houston Country Club, Houston, Texas; Champions Course, Houston, Texas; The National Links,

Southampton, Long Island; Shinnecock Hills, Southampton, Long Island; North Hills, Long Island; Deepdale, Long Island; Meadowbrook, Long Island; Seminole, Palm Beach, Florida; Doral, Miami, Florida; Seaview, Atlantic City, New Jersey; Buffalo Country Club, Buffalo, New York; The Country Club of Detroit, Detroit, Michigan; Hazeltine National Golf Club, Minneapolis, Minnesota; Philadelphia Country Club, Philadelphia, Pennsylvania; Point O' Woods, Benton Harbor, Michigan; Kitansett at Marion, Massachusetts; Salem Country Club, Peabody, Massachusetts; Incline Village, Lake Tahoe, Nevada; Riviera Country Club, Pacific Palisades, California; Inverness, Toledo, Ohio; Banff, Canadian Rockies; Peachtree, Atlanta, Georgia; Boca Raton, Boca Raton, Florida; Country Club of Miami, Miami Bearch, Florida; Greenbriar, West Virginia; Shore Haven Golf Club, Connecticut; Duke University Golf Club, North Carolina; Air Academy, Colorado Springs, Colorado; Stanford Golf Club, Palo Alto, California; Pauma Valley, Escondito, California; Old Warson, St. Louis, Missouri; Milwaukee Country Club, Milwaukee, Wisconsin; Dallas Athletic Club, Dallas, Texas; Olympic Fields, Chicago, Illinois; Cherry Hill, Denver, Colorado; Birmingham Country Club, Birmingham, Alabama; Five Farms, Baltimore, Maryland; and Scioto, Columbus, Ohio.

Above and beyond their uniqueness, these courses possess a common fundamental characteristic. They are routed so that there is an interesting varied sequence of holes, the strategy of each individual hole being designed from the natural features of the terrain. They reward good shots and punish the poor shots of all classes of golfers in proportion to their accuracy or error. Courses that combine these qualities are assuredly in the great golf course category.

PART FIVE

Chapter Forty-eight

Ten Shots that Rocked the World

THE SHOT THAT AWAKENED AMERICAN GOLF

The ball traveled only 20 feet. It was just a putt, one of hundreds of such puts made at a critical time in an important golf championship. Yet this turned out to be one of the most important putts in the history of the game. It was responsible for the great awakening of golf in America.

"If I had not made that putt, I would never have tied Vardon and Ray for the championship," said Francis Ouimet. "Things certainly would have been different."

Ouimet was a scrawny caddy of 20 when he teed off in the 1913 U.S. Open Championship over the swank The (capital "T") Country Club of Brookline, Massachusetts. Golf was just gaining a foothold in the United States but it was a stuffy game confined largely to the rich. British players dominated the American tournaments.

The 1913 Open shifted from its usual June dates to September to permit the entrance of the famed British professionals Harry Vardon and Ted Ray, as well as other notables from overseas. No one doubted that the competition would be a duel between Vardon, the stylist, who had won five of his six British Open Crowns, and Ray, a massive figure towering over 6 feet and weighing more than 200 pounds, counting a flowing mustache.

Ray led the 36-hole qualifying with 148. Vardon was at 151. Ouimet, in cap and knickers and looking like a boy playing hooky from school, registered a creditable 152, but

drew scant attention. The championship was to be contested over two days—36 holes Thursday and 36 Friday.

High excitement swept the stodgy old club on Friday when the end of the morning round showed Vardon, Ray, and Ouimet tied after 54 holes at 225. Ouimet was a home-town boy, born in Wellesley Hills, but still an inexperienced amateur hardly expected to stand up to two of the world's foremost professionals.

It was a gray, rainy, miserable day as the tournament moved to its climax. Ray finished first with a 79, giving him 304. This hardly seemed adequate. Yet out on the course the others also were fading one by one—Wilfred Reid, MacDonald Smith, Johnny McDermott, Walter Hagen, Jim Barnes, and France's Louis Tellier.

Vardon, his putting touch shaken on the water-soaked greens, also had to settle for a 79, which left him tied with Ray. Then the roof fell on Ouimet, playing well back of the other two leaders. The young Boston caddy took a 43 on the outgoing nine and blew to a 5 on the short tenth. Spirits of the home-town gallery sagged. To tie for the lead, Francis had to play the last eight holes in 31—a seemingly hopeless task.

Only Ouimet did not despair. He parred the eleventh with four, took a bogey five at the twelfth, and now needed two birdies on the last six holes. He chipped in from the edge of the green on the thirteenth for a birdie, parred the fourteenth, fifteenth, and sixteenth. Now he needed another birdie with two tough finishing holes to go.

The seventeenth provided the life-saver. This was a 360-yard hole, dog-leg to the left. He hit a good drive and then for his approach chose a jigger, a club between the modern five- and six-iron. The ball sailed 20 feet past the pin.

It was a tough putt, a sliding, downhill assignment. The crowd framing the green was deadly silent. Ouimet looked over the line quickly and then took his stance. There was a blare of an automobile horn on a nearby road. The crowd fidgeted nervously. Ouimet did not move. He stroked the ball crisply. It rolled easily down the slope, hit the hole dead center, banged against the back of the cup, and dropped home. It was a birdie three. Pandemonium broke loose.

Ouimet, maintaining a tremendous calm, hit a good drive at the eighteenth, but left his second short. He chipped to within 5 feet, sank the putt for a 79 and a 3-way tie at 304.

The play-off the next day was anticlimactic. Ouimet got another three at the lucky seventeenth, relieving some of the pressure from Vardon, a stroke behind going to the hole. Vardon banged into a trap at seventeen and took a five. The Massachusetts caddy won easily with a 72 to Vardon's 77 and Ray's 78.

News of the sensational victory was carried on page one of many of the nation's newspapers. Golf received a stimulus in the United States, and Ouimet acknowledged later: "That one putt did it."

THE EAGLE THAT WON THE OPEN FOR BYRON NELSON

Byron Nelson was one of the all-time masters of golf. It would have been a tragedy indeed if he, as in the case of Sam Snead, had been denied the one title every player wants— the United States Open.

It was unfortunate that Lord Byron reached his peak during the years of World War II, when play in the National Championship was suspended. It was during this span that he set scoring records that lasted for decades and won 11 straight PGA tour tournaments, an achievement that never has been challenged, and probably never will be.

Nelson did get his name on the U.S. Open trophy, however. The year was 1939 and the site was the Spring Mill course of the Philadelphia Country Club.

It took the unforgettable blowup by Sam Snead—an eight on the final hole when a six would have tied—to set up a three-way play-off among Nelson, Craig Wood, and Denny Shute, and it took a single fantastic shot to win it.

That was an eagle deuce on the fourth hole of the second round of a 36-hole play-off.

When Snead took his horrendous tour of the traps on the final hole of the 1939 Open, Nelson, Wood, and Shute were left tied for first with 72-hole scores of 284.

Nelson had to sink a wicked 10-foot birdie putt on the final hole to tie Wood at 68 through the first 18 extra holes. Shute, his putting sour, was eliminated when he shot a 76.

A second 18-hole play-off followed between Nelson and Wood. Nelson dropped a birdie putt at the third hole and took a one-stroke lead. Then the pair moved to the fourth, followed by a tremendous gallery of several thousand.

The fourth at Spring Mill is a difficult 460-yarder, well-trapped and playing par 4. Nelson said later that he felt certain that this hole could well prove the turning point of the match. Both players were determined to reach the green in two and go for birdies.

Both drives were good, in the fairway, and reasonably long. Wood used a wood club and got his second onto the green about 25 feet from the cup. Nelson deliberated more than usual. He could not decide whether to use a brassie or a one-iron.

"My irons always had been pretty good and I figured that I would have a better chance of both reaching the green and controlling the shot if I used a one-iron," Byron recalled later. "I knew I couldn't make a mistake."

Nelson said he concentrated on this particular shot as much as he had ever concentrated in his life. The gallery, lining the fairway and framing the green, was deathly quiet as Nelson took his stance.

"I knew it was good when I hit it," Lord Byron said. "My swing was just right, the impact was perfect. I know I had never hit a better iron."

Nelson watched the ball fly toward the green but he lost sight of it as it fell to earth. He heard a loud roar.

"I knew then it was close," he said. "I didn't know until I walked to the green that it had rolled into the hole for an eagle two. Craig Wood had played four holes in par and was three down. I was determined to protect that lead."

Nelson did. He shot a 70, Wood a 73, and Byron had his first only National Open with what he called "the greatest shot of my life."

THE NICKLAUS THAT AWED EUROPE

Most of the historic shots of the great champions were made in major tournaments before swarming galleries. They were usually climactic shots. They decided titles and launched careers.

Only a handful of hardy spectators—200 at the most, one of them a former King of England—saw Jack Nicklaus unleash one of the greatest and most important shots of his career. Although few saw it, reports of it spread like a runaway brush-fire, and to Europeans, at least, the Golden Bear became golf's miracle worker.

The date was Monday, October 28, 1963. The place was the Saint-Nom-la-Breteche Golf Course, 12 miles from the heart of Paris. The occasion was the windup of the eleventh International Golf Championship and Canada Cup matches, played in Europe for the first time.

Nicklaus and Arnold Palmer were playing for the United States against picked teams from 32 other nations, and they found it far from a breeze. The two Americans had to sink birdies on the fifty-fourth hole to gain a tie with two amazing Spaniards, Sebastian Miguel and Ramon Sota, at the three-quarter mark, with one round to play. Nicklaus was even with South Africa's Gary Player in the individual competition.

Then an eerie, souplike fog blanketed the area, limiting visibility to less than 100 yards. The final round on Sunday, October 27, had to be postponed, and on Monday, when the fog persisted, it was decided to play in the semidarkness, limiting the final round to nine holes.

When the two American players reached the sixth tee, they learned that the Spaniards, playing beautifully, had gone ahead by one stroke. The Spaniards were playing in front of the United States team.

American hopes dropped quickly when both Palmer and Nicklaus—firing blind into the dense fog—hit bad approach shots on the sixth, a 430-yard, par 4, uphill hole. Arnold Palmer's shot landed in a bunker at the left of the green, 85 feet from the flag. Jack Nicklaus found himself in the right trap, 70 feet away.

Bogeys appeared the fate of each, and with them little chance of overtaking the Spaniards in the three holes remaining.

Palmer blasted first. The ball landed 15 feet beyond the pin, seemed momentarily to stop, and then spun back 10 feet toward the cup as if yanked by an unseen yo-yo.

The gallery gasped. The rumble of disbelief was still echoing around the hillsides when Nicklaus took his stance in the other trap. His head was barely visible from the other side of the green. Three times he walked to the top of the bunker to look at the location of the hole. Then he buried his feet in the sand, paused, and swung.

The ball came out in a beautiful arch, took one bounce, and plunked into the cup.

"Incredible," said one spectator.

"Magnifique," yelled another.

"Magic—sheer magic," repeated others.

The Duke of Windsor, watching from in front of the green, became so excited he fell off his shooting stick.

It was a birdie three for Nicklaus—his fifth three in a row and his fifth birdie in the first six holes.

Nicklaus went on to play the 9 holes in 32, 4 under par. He won the individual International Trophy with a 63-hole score of 237, 5 shots ahead of Spain's Miguel and South Africa's Player. The Americans won the team trophy with a three-stroke margin over Spain.

Nicklaus never rated the sensational trap shot in Paris as the most significant of his career, personally finding it hard to choose between an eight-iron shot that gave him a 1-up victory over Charlie Coe in the 1959 National Amateur or the bold 4-foot putt he sank on the seventeenth hole of his play-off with Arnold Palmer for the 1962 National Open title—but he could never convince the Europeans.

They never stopped talking about the young Golden Bear and his five straight three's, climaxed by the unbelievable trap shot, in the Canada Cup at Paris in 1963.

THE SHOT THAT SEALED
BEN HOGAN'S COMEBACK

Tension crackled like a berserk electric charge at the Merion Golf Club, outside Philadelphia, on that hazy Saturday afternoon in June, 1950.

The fiftieth United States Open Championship was drawing to its climax and in the thick of the drama was the dour, determined Texas Hawk, Ben Hogan.

This was not just another Open for the 37-year-old iron-master from Fort Worth. It was his first National Championship since the near-fatal automobile accident on a Texas highway 18 months before that had left him a battered, broken heap.

Could Hogan come back? This was what all of the golf world was asking. No one wondered

about that more than perhaps Hogan himself. Now he was face-to-face with the answer.

Merion was one of the nation's historic courses, the site where Bob Jones completed his Grand Slam by winning the National Amateur in 1930. It was also an exacting layout, one that challenged the best in men and surrendered to none.

The test was particularly grueling for Hogan. His legs, shattered in the automobile accident, had not fully healed. There were circulation problems, and each night, after his play, he was forced to return to his hotel room and put his legs in traction to restore the flow of blood.

On the course, he walked with slow, stiff-legged deliberation. Spectators looked at him and winced, but the expression on the face of the Hawk never changed. His jaw was grim, his lips tight, and his eyes sparkled with fire under his familiar white cap.

The last day of the Open, 36 holes under severest pressure, has been known to break the back and spirit of strong and healthy men. It was no wonder that the fans were watching Hogan's every labored step with deep concern.

At the club house, the big scoreboard showed George Fazio and Lloyd Mangrum in with a score of 287. On the course, challengers were dropping like leaves on an autumn day— all except Hogan. He was plodding along close to par, still within reach of the title.

Hogan faltered with bogeys at the fifteenth and seventeenth; then he came up the eighteenth, a difficult finishing hole, needing a par 4 to tie. He knew what his assignment was.

It takes a big drive and a fine iron shot to get home on this 458-yard finishing hole at Merion, and indications were that the gallant little man from Texas finally was weakening. Mustering his strength, Hogan hit a good drive—long and straight to the middle of the fairway.

He chose to play a two-iron to the green. He studied the shot a long time before he finally took a last puff on his cigarette and assumed his stance. Thousands lined the fair-

This is a remarkable rear camera view of the two-iron shot to the final green which Ben Hogan made in the 1950 U. S. Open at Merion. The shot enabled Hogan to tie for the title and then win the play-off.

way and packed around the green, but they were muted by the tension of the occasion.

Hogan swung into the shot. The ball sailed low and straight toward the green, but a bit to the left. Finally, the crowd let out a tremendous roar. Hogan rolled his putt 3 feet past the hole, and then sank coming back. He had his four and his tie for the title.

The 18-hole play-off was anticlimactic. No one doubted that destiny now could deny the game bantam his prize. Hogan fired a 69, beating out Mangrum by 4 shots and Fazio by 6.

The thousands who witnessed Hogan's two-iron shot to the final green acclaimed it the greatest shot under pressure that the fabulous Hawk ever played.

Hogan, a perfectionist to the end, disagreed. "It wasn't a good shot at all," he said later. "I wanted to be 25 feet closer to the hole."

ARNOLD PALMER'S 1960 MASTERS FINISH

Arnold Palmer made many a dramatic and climactic golf shot. Drama was the trademark of the rugged, colorful professional from Latrobe, Pennsylvania, in his sweep to a record bag of Masters championships as well as victories in the U.S. and British Opens. It was as if Palmer purposely saved the big shot for the big occasion. It was this faculty which endeared him to millions.

As for Palmer himself, there is no doubt about the shot he considers the most important one of his career. It was the six-iron shot to the final green which won him the 1960 Masters.

It was a thunderclap finish.

Palmer was on the tee at the par-5 fifteenth when news reached him that Ken Venturi had fired a final round 70 for 283. With four of the toughest finishing holes in golf ahead of him, Palmer needed two birdies to win.

Venturi was stashed away in Cliff Roberts' inner sanctum, trying on the green champion's jacket for size, answering questions from a picked handful of newsmen and awaiting presentation ceremonies when Palmer started his charge.

Palmer missed his birdie at the fifteenth and also parred the 190-yard, par-3 sixteenth.

"You've got it," a newsman said to Venturi. "Nobody's going to play those last two holes in two under par."

Venturi smiled wanly. He was afraid to hope.

Palmer now faced the seventeenth and eighteenth holes. He had stood in the same position the year before, with victory in his grasp, only to blow it by overhitting his approach on the seventeenth and missing a 4-foot putt on the eighteenth to finish bogey-bogey.

On the 400-yard, par-4 seventeenth, Palmer determined this time to keep the ball short. After a good drive, he pitched and the ball bit. He was 35 feet away. Bill Casper, Palmer's playing companion, putted out, and then Palmer, hunched over the ball with his legs forming an "X," stroked the putt. It rolled into the hole. A birdie three. Now Arnie needed only a par on the final hole to tie.

He boomed his drive 300 yards down the middle of the fairway. The crowd—total attendance for the day was put at 35,000—lined the fairway and swarmed around the green. Venturi, pale and nervous, watched on television.

Around 120 yards short of the green, Palmer yanked out a six-iron. He took a last puff on a cigarette and dropped it on the ground. He tugged at a glove on his left hand and took a jerk at his trousers—familiar gestures when he starts to move.

The crowd began murmuring and the noise was like an ocean swell. "Quiet, please. Everyone please be quiet," bellowed Ralph Hutchinson, the lavishly-dressed professional announcing at the eighteenth green.

"I knew what I had to do to win," Palmer said later. "I've got to admit the tension was terrific."

He swung crisply and the ball sailed for the green. There was a tremendous roar when it hit near the cup and rolled 6 feet away. Palmer still had a putt left, and the specter of the miss the year before came up to haunt him. He played for a break and the ball went squarely into the hole. A second birdie—and the championship.

"I don't think any single shot gave me a greater thrill, or was more important to me," Palmer said afterward.

THE PUTT THAT TRIGGERED
BOB JONES'S GRAND SLAM

It was just a 12-foot putt, hardly worth comparing with a double eagle, a hole-in-one, or a blast into the cup from out of a sand trap. Yet Grantland Rice, the famed syndicated sportswriter, and O.B. Keeler, Bob Jones's Boswell, both called it their greatest thrill in a quarter of a century of following the game—and neither saw it.

The putt took on added significance because of the circumstances under which it was made and the history it apparently unfurled.

Bob Jones sank the putt June 29, 1929, on the seventy-second and final hole of the United States Open Golf Championship. The site was the West Course of the Winged Foot Golf Club at Mamaroneck, New York.

The putt gave Jones a tie and ultimately the championship. He had won two of them before and he was destined to win a fourth, in his Grand Slam year of 1930. Nevertheless, Jones himself said he never made a more important shot.

These were the circumstances:

It was the final round of the tournament and as Jones left the twelfth green he appeared a certain winner. He had a six-stroke lead over his nearest challenger, Al Espinosa, with only six holes to play. Nobody made up that kind of a deficit on the great Jones.

Suddenly the tournament experienced a sharp turn of fortunes.

Espinosa, with a fat eight at the twelfth, shrugged his shoulders and conceded he had blown his chance. Loose and relaxed, he proceeded to play the last six holes in 22 strokes for a closing 75—a total score of 294.

Jones, playing behind the veteran professional, relaxed. He bogied the thirteenth, took a disastrous seven at the fifteenth, and 3-putted the sixteenth from 20 feet. Now he had dissipated his 6-stroke lead and needed to finish 4–4 for a tie.

Excitement was electric. Spectators swarmed onto the course. Sportswriters tore up their leads of a Jones victory and rushed to the closing holes to catch the drama. Among these were Grantland Rice and O.B. Keeler.

Jones got his four at the seventeenth. On the eighteenth, he hit a good drive up the middle but his pitch caught the rim of a deep bunker and rolled down the embankment, stopping in the tall grass just short of the sand.

Jones chopped the ball out of the heavy grass. The ball rolled onto the green but stopped at 12 feet from the flag. It was a tough putt over curving terrain. He would have to play a break of at least a foot to get it into the hole.

"I couldn't look," Keeler said later. "I was afraid if I watched he would miss the putt." Rice said he also turned his head away and waited for the crowd reaction.

They heard a sharp click. Then they waited for what seemed like endless minutes. There was a gasp, then a loud roar. Jones had made it. He had tied Espinosa for the title.

Viewers said later the ball had rolled slowly over the ice-slick green, hesitated, seemed to stop, then dropped home. It was one of Bob's famous "dying ball" putts.

If he had missed, Jones would have shot an 80, his first in the Open Championship. He would have blown a six-stroke lead and the title. Many speculated that such a collapse might have wrecked his brilliant career.

Instead, Jones went out the next day and shot rounds of 72 and 69 to crush Espinosa in the play-off by the margin of 23 strokes.

"I will always believe," Rice wrote later, "that the remainder of Bobby's career hung on that putt and that from this stemmed the Grand Slam of 1930."

WALTER HAGEN'S MIRACULOUS
SHOTS THAT FAILED

For many years, when old-timers gathered around the locker rooms in Britain to discuss momentous golf shots, precedence was given to a Walter Hagen shot that failed to come off. Golf-minded Britons regarded it as more dramatic than most of the successful shots that clinched championships and changed golfing history.

It was a shot that could have hit home, but did not. Nevertheless, it served to accentuate the brashness and showmanship of this swashbuckling American professional who excited world galleries for two decades.

The occasion was the 1926 British Open Championship at the Royal Lytham and St. Anne's course. Bob Jones had finished the 72 holes in 291 for the lead. It looked secure as Hagen came to the par 4 final hole needing an eagle 2 to tie—secure, that is, to everyone except the cocky Hagen.

"It had been done before, I thought it could be done again," the Haig explained later.

Hagen's drive on the eighteenth was straight down the middle and long enough. It left him a 150-yard approach to the green.

Hagen strode a few yards toward the green to survey the assignment. Jones and the British star, J.H. Taylor, watched tensely from the club house balcony.

Jones acknowledged later that he felt fidgety and uneasy. "I didn't know what this fellow might do," Bobby said.

Hagen walked back to his ball and then turned to the official scorer, standing nearby.

"Would you please go up and hold the flag?" Hagen requested.

The scorer looked at the Haig incredulously and blinked. He thought he must have misunderstood.

"What's that again, sir?" he said.

"I'd appreciate it if you would go up and hold the flag," Hagen repeated.

Hagen said it loud enough this time for many in the gallery of 10,000 packed around the green and along the fairway to hear. A buzz went through the crowd. "Does this man really expect to sink that shot?" "Who does he think he is?"

There was some method in Hagen's seemingly mad request. By concentrating the attention of the gallery on the official holding the flag 150 yards away, he eased his own tension.

Hagen said later he could concentrate on his shot. If he should miss, the gallery would consider the official—not Hagen—a goat for holding the stick at such a distance.

The Haig set himself over the ball. There was not a move or a sound when he swung crisply through the ball.

The shot was better than Hagen dared hope under the circumstances. It flew straight at the pin, landed on the edge of the green, and rolled toward the hole. The crowd gasped.

The ball, rolling at a fast pace, skipped over the hole and dropped into a shallow scooped-out sand trap at the back of the green. The applause was deafening.

Had the flag stick been left in the hole, the ball probably would have struck it and plunked into the hole for a tying deuce. It seemed immaterial that Hagen took a bogey five and finished third at 295.

"I turned my back on you, Walter," Jones told Hagen later. "A guy with that much confidence would be fool lucky enough to make it."

BILLY JOE PATTON'S MOMENT OF GLORY

The distinctive feature of the Masters Golf Tournament is that it never has been won by an amateur, but the big April spectacle in Augusta, Georgia, got a fright in 1954. That was the year of Billy Joe Patton's spectacular charge and his unforgettable hole-in-one.

Billy Joe Patton shows his usual exuberance during the 1954 Masters. This was the year Billy Joe made his hole-in-one and came within a stroke of being the first amateur ever to take the title.

Billy Joe was a scrambling, exciting lumber executive from Morganton, North Carolina, who left an indelible print on golf in the mid-1950's, when Ben Hogan was at his peak. A leading amateur, Patton attracted large galleries because of his flair for driving the ball a country mile, battling his way miraculously out of trouble, and all the while carrying on a running dialogue with his worshipful following.

His greatest moment of glory came in the 1954 Masters, the year after Hogan had made his triple slam of winning the Masters, U.S., and British Opens.

Billy Joe started by winning the driving contest, the day before the tournament opening, with a prodigious drive of 338 yards on his first of three drives. Told he was entitled to two more drives, he said, "No thanks, I might miss the next one altogether."

The bespectacled, crew-cut North Carolinian, slamming and joking his way out of traps and rough, tied old E.J. (Dutch) Harrison for the opening round lead with a 70, 2 strokes better than defending champion Hogan and 4 better than Sam Snead.

The crowd flocked behind the uninhibited amateur the next day and, playing in a stiff wind, he delighted the flock with a 74 which gave him the undisputed lead at 144. Hogan had 145, Snead 147.

Newsmen had a holiday. "Hold on, boys," Billy Joe cautioned. "I may shoot an 80 tomorrow." He did not go quite that high but he did scramble to a 75 under easier playing conditions, and with 219 he fell 5 shots back of a rallying Hogan.

On the final round, the bulk of the gallery deserted Patton and flocked to the two old pros, Hogan and Snead. It stacked up as a strictly Hogan-Snead show.

Hogan was putting out on the third green when a loud roar rumbled through the trees. "It's Billy Joe," somebody yelled and there was a stampede toward the area of the ovation—the sixth hole.

There Patton had just sunk a hole-in-one to move back into contention.

The sixth at Augusta is the "Juniper Hole," 190 yards, par 3, a steep slope from tee to green. The pin was placed dangerously close to the edge of the green, and only a gambler would go for it.

Nobody ever denied Billy Joe was a gambler. He chose a five-iron, changed his stance a couple of times, and hit. The ball cleared the front edge of the green, rolled toward the cup, and finally lodged against the pin. The pin was carefully removed, and the ball dropped—a hole-in-one.

Fired by new confidence, Billy Joe took a hitch in his belt and started moving. He birdied the eighth and ninth, passed Snead, and caught Hogan. Disdaining caution, he hit out boldly on every shot and fired at the pin on every green. On the par 5 thirteenth, he went for the green and dumped his approach into the water, winding up with a double bogey seven. It was costly. Snead and Hogan tied for first at 289, Patton one stroke back at 290. Snead won the play-off.

Billy Joe never regretted it. "I didn't come to play safe," he said.

LEW WORSHAM'S $62,000 EAGLE

No single golf shot, except possibly Gene Sarazen's double eagle in the 1935 Masters, has created as much attention as Lew Worsham's $62,000 eagle in the 1953 World's Championship at Tam o' Shanter in Chicago.

The circumstances could not have been more dramatic. The tournament was the world's richest at the time. It was being shown on national television, before the eyes of millions. The shot, last of the day, produced a movie-thriller climax.

The date was Sunday, August 9, 1953, the final day of Industrialist George May's All-America and World Championship tournaments, which lured leading golfers in quest of the fabulous prize money.

Chandler Harper, playing in the next to last threesome, thrilled the viewers by lacing his second shot in the 370-yard, par 4 finishing hole to within 1½ feet of the pin and sinking for a birdie three.

This gave Harper a 72-hole score of 279 and apparently the first prize of $25,000 cash plus a series of $1,000 exhibitions. Only one group remained on the course.

The big TV cameras zeroed in on the smiling Harper and he was being congratulated as the winner when the final threesome lumbered down the eighteenth fairway. In the

Diagram of Lew Worsham's wedge shot on the final hole of the World Tournament at Tam o'Shanter in 1953. The shot enabled him to win the $25,000 first prize.

threesome were Doug Ford, Dave Douglas, and Lew Worsham, playing in semiprivacy.

Few knew it, but Worsham needed only to duplicate Harper's birdie to tie for first place and necessitate a play-off. His drive was down the middle, nestling in a good lie in the little valley between the elevated green and elevated tee. He was 104 yards—by measurement—from home. The green was guarded on the left and right by trees. A small river ran in front of it.

While officials and well-wishers were swarming around the happy Harper at the eighteenth green, Worsham, the 1947 Na-

tional Open champion from Oakmont, Pennsylvania, swung easily through the ball. The ball soared to the green, hit about 25 feet short of the pin, rolled over a small ridge and into the cup.

Pandemonium followed. The eagle deuce gave Worsham a 31 for the back 9 and a score of 278, winning by one stroke.

First prize was $25,000 and an option to play exhibitions at $1,000 each for George May. Worsham played 37 of these, making his total prize money $62,000.

The shot and its attendant victory was tasteful to the Oakmont pro for another rea-

291

Here's the record of Lew Worsham's fantastic shot that won the Tam o'Shanter World Golf Championship in 1953. At the *left,* Worsham swings for his approach. The ball bounced on the green and rolled into the cup.

son. The year before, in the same tournament, Worsham had a four-stroke lead with nine holes to play but drove out of bounds on the fourteenth and fifteenth holes to blow his chances.

Observers estimated at first that the eagle was made with a wedge from 140 yards. Later, from movie film, Worsham had the distance measured and it was put exactly at 104 yards.

"I knew it wasn't 140 yards; I couldn't hit a wedge that far," Worsham said. "The club I used was a double service wedge. It was a combination of sand and pitching wedge."

George May later abandoned sponsorship of the Tam o'Shanter tournament because of constant conflicts with the Professional Golfers Association and some of the players, but not before erecting a small monument to one of the greatest—and most profitable—golf shots ever played.

GENE SARAZEN'S DOUBLE EAGLE

In the early days of the Masters Tournament, when only a handful of sportswriters covered the event instead of the hundreds who came later, the press quarters were set up on the second floor porch of the Augusta

National Club's white club house, overlooking the eighteenth green.

There, men such as Alan Gould of The Associated Press, Henry McLemore of the United Press, Bill Richardson of *The New York Times,* Grantland Rice, and O.B. Keeler pecked out stories that were read around the world.

Such was the setting on a crisp April day in 1935 with the second Masters going into its final-round climax.

Handsome Craig Wood had just holed a birdie three on the seventy-second hole for a score of 282. Green-coated officials and spectators rushed up to congratulate him. He appeared the certain winner. A few players were still on the course, none apparently with a chance for the title.

This was not an age of quick communication. No telephone wires stretched to the outlying holes. There were no walkie-talkies. Reporters depended on runners, usually unemployed Negro caddies, to get their details.

Alan Gould of the AP was preparing his night lead based on a Craig Wood victory when one of his runners came up puffing with a report from the course.

"Mistuh Sarazen had a two at fifteen," the runner said.

"A two!" blustered Gould. "Go back out there and get the score right."

No. 15 was a 485-yard, par 5 hole. Nobody made it in two.

Moments later, the runner returned, still breathless. "Yes, suh, Mister Gould, it really was a two."

Sarazen was just moving to the fifteenth when he squinted at the club house in the distance and saw the commotion raised by Wood's finish. Word drifted back on Wood's score.

"What do I need to win?" the bouncy Gene asked his Negro caddy, Stovepipe.

"Let me see," the caddy figured. "You need four three's." Par in was 5-3-4-4.

Walter Hagen, playing with Sarazen, hit his second short of the pond guarding the green. Sarazen, always a go-for-broke competitor, knew this would not be enough. To insure a birdie four on the hole, he had to clear the water.

His drive was about 250 yards but the lie was close. He and his caddy deliberated over whether to use a three-wood or four-wood and finally decided it would take a four to give the ball its needed loft.

Gene took out a lucky ring and rubbed it on Stovepipe's close-cropped head. Both laughed. The tension eased.

"I rode into the shot with every ounce of strength and timing I could muster," Sarazen said later. "The split-second I hit the ball, I knew it would carry the pond."

The ball flew like a rifle shot, not more than 30 feet in the air. The ball dropped on the green and rolled into the cup. The small crowd framing the green let out a thunderous roar. This brought hundreds streaming from the club house.

The shot had carried 235 yards. It was a rare double eagle two.

Now the gallery had swelled to 5,000. Sarazen got his three on the short sixteenth, missing a 10-foot putt for a birdie, then parred the seventeenth. Now Gene needed a birdie three on the final hole to win, a par to tie.

As tension mounted, the determined little battler hit a good drive and then cut a four-wood through the crosswind to the green, 30 feet from the cup.

Gene babied the putt to within 3 feet and then sank for 282 and a tie. The crowd went wild. With the momentum generated by his surging finish, Sarazen beat Wood by 5 strokes in the 36-hole play-off the next day.

And Alan Gould apologized to his runner.

Chapter Forty-nine

The Ever-Changing Principles of Play

The basic principle of golf, tracing back to the hardy Scots of the 1700's, is to play the course as you find it and not to touch the ball until you lift it from the hole. Down through the years, this rigid code however, has been unable to endure the tampering of the rules architects. The rules of the game are constantly undergoing change, with no solid platform of agreement among the two powerful governing bodies, the Royal and Ancient Club of St. Andrews and the United States Golf Association, and those who dominate the competitive phase of the sport, the professionals.

Despite strong efforts in the middle of the twentieth century to arrive at a uniform world playing code, full agreement failed. The result was that the British played by one set of rules with a different size ball, the Americans by another, the pros by still a third, and the rest of the world took its choice.

The prohibition against touching the ball in the course of play vanished. The stymie rule became a casualty. Originally, in match play, golfers were compelled to leave the balls as they lay on the green even when one obstructed the path toward the hole of another. The stymie was abolished as unfair and as not in keeping with the principles of the game. Then came the right to lift a ball and clean it on the green.

The privilege of lifting and cleaning a ball on the green was a source of bitter dispute among America's golf fathers in the 1920's and almost brought a rupture between the U.S. Golf Association and the powerful Western Association. The right to lift and clean became law. In the 1960's, the ritual was observed and abused to such an extent that the game became draggy and a bore. Frequently, it took 5 and 6 hours for a foursome to complete an 18-hole round. Cries went up to revert to the no-cleaning rule, but no immediate action was taken.

This was not in the spirit of the original 13 rules, called the "Articles and Laws in Playing the Golf," adopted by the Royal and Ancient Club of St. Andrews in 1754.

These are the rules, in their original language:

"1. You must tee your ball within a club-length of the hole.

"2. Your tee must be upon the ground.

"3. You are not to change the ball which you stroke off the tee.

"4. You are not to remove Stones, Bones of any Break-club for the sake of playing your ball, except upon the fair green, and that only within a club-length of your ball.

"5. If your ball come among water, or any watery filth, you are at liberty to take your ball, and throw it behind the hazard, six yards at least; you may play it with any club and allow your adversary a stroke for so getting out your ball.

"6. If your balls be found anywhere touching one another, you are to lift the first ball 'til you play the last.

"7. At holing, you are to play your ball

honestly for the hole, and not to play upon your adversary's ball, not lying in your way to the hole.

"8. If you should lose your ball by its being taken up, or in any other way, you are to go back to the spot where you struck last, and drop another ball, and allow your adversary a stroke for the misfortune.

"9. No man, at holing his ball, is to be allowed to mark to the hole with his club or anything else.

"10. If a ball be stop'd by any person, horse, dog or anything else, the ball so stopped must be played where it lies.

"11. If you draw your club in order to strike, and proceed so far in the stroke as to bring down your club—if then your club shall break in any way it is to be accounted a stroke.

"12. He whose ball lyes farthest from the hole is to play first.

"13. Neither trench, ditch nor dyke made for the preservation of the links, nor the scholars' holes, nor the soldiers' lines, shall be counted a hazard, but the ball is to be taken out, teed and played with any iron club."

The first rules used by Americans were half as many and more concise in their wording. This proved to be one of the chief areas of disagreement between the British and Americans down through the years. The British tended to expand the rules, the Americans to retract and employ the simplest language possible.

The first rules in the United States were published November 7, 1893—five years after the St. Andrews Club was founded in Yonkers, New York. The rules applied to play for the John Reid Championship Medal Tournament.

They were:

"1. Competitors shall note each other's scores, checking same at each hole.

"2. If a ball be lost, the player shall return as nearly as possible to the spot where the ball was struck, tee another ball and lose a stroke.

"3. All balls shall be holed out, and when play is nearest the hole shall have the option

of holing out first. Throughout the green, a competitor can have the other competitor's ball lifted, if he finds that it interferes with his stroke.

"4. A ball under penalty of two (2) strokes may be lifted out of a difficulty of any description and teed behind the same.

"5. Competitors may not discontinue play because of bad weather.

"6. The penalty for a breach of any rule shall be disqualification.

"7. The ordinary rules of golf, so far as they are not at variance with these special rules, shall apply to this match."

With two different, but not drastically contrasting, codes, the British and Americans continued to go their individual ways. Representatives of the Royal and Ancient and the U.S.G.A. conferred in 1921 and 1922 on adopting a uniform set of standards but the meetings never got farther than the talking stage.

The two groups came close to getting together in 1946, but the British, with Bernard Darwin serving as chairman of the rules committee, declined to adhere to some key points. A basic difference of opinion lay in the penalty for unplayable lies and out of bounds. The British decreed loss of distance only. The United States imposed a sterner fine—loss of distance and one stroke.

With these exceptions, the two bodies sought to play under a similar code in 1947 and 1948. After the two years, the plan was declared unworkable. Each side went back to its own standards, varying more in the wording than in the intent. The Americans liked a streamlined version, simply written, with several rules incorporated into perhaps one. The British wanted to be more wordy and specific.

In 1951, word drifted across the Atlantic that the very austere Royal and Ancient Club again was ready to talk about a single worldwide code. The United States sent over a rules delegation which held three meetings—the first at the Royal Automobile Club of London; the second at the House of Lords as guests of Lord Brabazon of Tara; and the third in the old gray edifice of the Royal and Ancient Club at St. Andrews.

The result was finally a uniform code, to become effective January 1, 1952. The U.S.G.A. and the Royal and Ancient would play under one set of rules. The only difference was in the size of the ball, a difference never resolved. The British ball, while the same weight, was 1/64th of an inch smaller in diameter than the American ball. It was deemed better to bore through the winds on the blustery seaside links. The Americans preferred the bigger ball, regarded as more maneuverable and easier to putt. Neither was willing to concede this 1/64th of an inch.

While the two big amateur governing bodies were playing one set of rules, the touring professionals in America were using another. These rules were more liberal in many respects, stiffer in others. They were not as punitive in the case of unplayable balls. They were more punitive in the case of a ball striking an unattended flagstick from the area around the green—two strokes in medal play and loss of hole in match instead of no penalty at all, as under the U.S.G.A. and R&A regulations.

The uniform code lasted eight years. In 1960, the United States adopted a two-year experiment reducing penalties for lost balls, unplayable lies, and out of bounds. The British did not change. After two years, the U.S.G.A. found the experimental changes not entirely to its liking and reverted to its former regulations.

The honeymoon between the U.S.G.A. and the R&A ended in 1963. Rules experts of the two bodies went into conference at Turnberry, Scotland, in May, and when they emerged they were as far apart as they had ever been. They decided to disagree. The net result was that the U.S.G.A. moved closer to the American professionals and farther away from its British cousins.

The principal differences in the new rules, effective for the United States January 1, 1964, concerned the flagstick, unplayable lies, and provisional balls. The U.S.G.A. imposed the penalties for hitting the stick from the putting green or within 20 yards of the hole. The British stuck to no penalties. On the unplayable lie, the penalty was reduced from two strokes to one stroke for a drop.

Further, under the U.S.G.A. code, a provisional ball could be played only for one lost or out of bounds. No provisional ball was allowed for a ball unplayable or in a water hazard. The British continued to allow a provisional ball for one lost, out of bounds or unplayable.

Thus uniformity took another blow—perhaps a lethal one.

Chapter Fifty

The U.S. Golf Association:
Zealous Guardian of the "Spirit of the Game"

To the millions of men, women, and children who play golf in the United States—the figure was placed at 8,000,000 in 1965—the United States Golf Association is a benevolent but stern parent. It makes the rules. It regulates handicaps. It keeps a sharp eye on equipment. It conducts tournaments. It is a zealous guardian of amateurism and protector of the spirit of the game.

It was a threat to the spirit of the game that resulted in the formation of the U.S.G.A. in 1894. With the rapid growth of golf in America, the establishment of a ruling body was certainly inevitable, but it was speeded by a ridiculous controversy and a sore-losing Irishman named Charles Blair Macdonald.

Charlie Macdonald, from a wealthy Chicago family, was sent to Scotland for schooling when he was a youngster in the 1870's. He attended St. Leonard's in St. Andrews and it was natural that he should fall under the influence of the Old Course by the sea. He was able to get the best equipment from the shop of Old Tom Morris. He became an avid golfer, and a very good one. He was able to play with Young Tom Morris, one of the greats of the era.

Golf was just beginning to take root in the United States when Macdonald returned home. Because of his experience at the birthplace of the game, he became an almost legendary figure among those who were just learning to hack their way over the primi-

tive courses emerging in the Midwest and East.

In the summer of 1894, members of the Newport Golf Club decided to stage a championship tournament over a new nine they had built at Rocky Farm. Invitations were sent to all the leading players of the day, who were merely a handful. Macdonald was naturally the heavy favorite.

It was a 36-hole stroke play tournament, four times around the course. Macdonald lived up to his advance billing by shooting a first day 89 for a four-stroke lead. On the second day, he had one of his shots roll against a stone wall bordering the course and he had to take a two-stroke penalty. He skied to 100 and the tournament went to a local member, W.G. Lawrence, with 88.

Macdonald was furious. He contended that the stone fence was not a legitimate hazard and that the penalty was unfair. Furthermore, he insisted, a championship should be determined by match, not medal, play.

The St. Andrews Club in New York agreed to stage a match play event in October to settle the issue once and for all. Again invitations went out. Again there was a good response, 27 players from 8 clubs, one of them the tempestuous Macdonald.

Macdonald swept through his early matches but lost an extra-hole final to Laurence Stoddard. The blustery Chicagoan and his Midwest supporters took the defeat hard. Macdonald said he had been ill the night before and this was not really a true test. Also, he said, a championship cannot be determined in an invitation event by one club. It must have the approval of all clubs.

The bantering between pro-Macdonald and anti-Macdonald forces caused concern among some of the golf leaders, principally Henry O. Tallmadge of St. Andrews, Lawrence Curtis of The Country Club in Brookline, Massachusetts, and Theodore A. Havermeyer of Newport, who decided that the game needed a guiding spirit.

Tallmadge was designated to write letters to five principal clubs—the Chicago Golf Club, The Country Club, Shinnecock Hills, Newport, and St. Andrews—urging each to send two delegates to a meeting in New York for the purpose of setting up an organization.

The meeting was held December 22, 1894, at the Calumet Club, at Fifth Avenue and 29th Street. Besides the three sponsors—Tallmadge, Curtis, and Havermeyer—those present included Charlie Macdonald and Arthur Ryerson of Chicago, General Thomas Barber and Samuel Parris of Shinnecock Hills, Samuel Sears of Brookline, and John Reid of St. Andrews.

A fight developed immediately over who should be president. Tallmadge wanted Reid, the recognized father of American golf. Curtis nominated Havermeyer. The latter was a mustachioed millionaire known as the "Sugar King." Curtis argued that Havermeyer's influential position in the business world would give the organization added prestige.

The argument sold a majority of the delegates. Havermeyer became the first president of the U.S.G.A. Curtis was named the first vice-president, Tallmadge secretary, and Parrish treasurer. They formed the first executive committee of the association.

Another dispute arose over the name. The first name given was the Amateur Golf Association of the United States. This was changed at the second meeting to American Golf Association, with the idea it might include Canada. Finally, the U.S. Golf Association became the official title.

On February 8, 1895, Macdonald and Reid submitted a list of by-laws and a constitution. Regular meetings were held at the home of the president, Havermeyer, on the southwest corner of Madison Avenue at 37th Street, across from the house of J. Pierpont Morgan. From the very beginning, however, things failed to run smoothly.

Members of the executive committee bickered constantly. One of the big arguments revolved around the definition of the term "amateur." Another developed over foreign players. Reid and Macdonald were sticklers for rules and met opposition from some of the more liberal-minded members. Macdonald, who had learned the game in Scotland, resented any attempt to Americanize the game. Golf as played in Scotland was a religion to him. At one meeting, only three committee members showed up.

The Tuxedo and Essex County Clubs resented the fact they had not been invited to join the U.S.G.A. Curtis took the blame for the omission, Tallmadge apologized formally, and the two were admitted. When Meadow Brook on Long Island made a similar complaint, open bids were sent to all clubs. The Philadelphia Country Club, Richmond County and Lakewood in Washington, D.C., were given allied memberships in March, 1895.

In 1901, the U.S.G.A. came face-to-face with one of its first problems involving amateurism. The Casper Whitney magazine, *Outing*, published an article declaring that Walter Travis and Arthur Lockwood should be ruled professionals because they accepted free golf and board privileges at resort hotels in the South. W. B. Thomas, then U.S.G.A. president, was asked to take action. He refused, but the fuss continued.

Travis figured in another controversy after winning the British Amateur Championship in 1904. The Royal and Ancient Club of St. Andrews banned the Schenectady putter, a unique blade with the shaft placed in the middle, with which Travis had beaten the cream of British golf. The R&A asked the

U.S.G.A. to follow suit. The U.S.G.A. declined at first, then later barred center-shafted and other freak clubs as a "menace to the art of club-making." This stand was reversed years later and center-shafted putters were made legal.

The U.S.G.A. brought down an avalanche of criticism on its head in 1916 when it declared Francis Ouimet a nonamateur. Ouimet, the one-time caddy who defeated Britain's Harry Vardon and Ted Ray for the National Open Championship in 1913, had become an American sports hero. He was credited with taking golf out of its restrictive society corset and making it a game for the people. In the eyes of most people, he could do no wrong.

The golf fathers refused to let their ethics be swayed by popular opinion. Ouimet had opened a sporting-goods store in Boston. Under strict interpretation of the amateur code, the U.S.G.A. said, he was making his livelihood from the game. While this did not make him a professional, it rendered him a nonamateur.

The nation's newspapers took up the cudgels in Ouimet's behalf. He had been employed by a sporting-goods store before his historic Open victory at Brookline, they insisted, and thus he was not capitalizing on his success.

The dispute brought a rupture in the ranks of the U.S.G.A. The Western Golf Association refused to honor the U.S.G.A.'s ruling and permitted Ouimet to play in Western events. A bitter rivalry ensued between the U.S.G.A. and the Western Association which was to continue long after the former Boston caddy was given back his amateur standing following World War I.

The feud between the two organizations carried into the 1920's, and it appeared for a while that the power of the U.S.G.A. might be doomed. George O. Pfeil of Memphis, Tennessee, president of the Western Association, recognized the danger of this and moved to conciliate the differences. He succeeded. Later he was nominated for the presidency of the U.S.G.A.

The U.S.G.A. proceeded to grow in strength and prestige.

From a total of 50 courses in 1895, the game spread to 1,040 courses by 1900 and 7,112 in 1965. As the sport mushroomed and produced great personalities, the U.S.G.A. steadfastly stuck to its guns as the guardian of the spirit of the game.

No person was so big that he or she could escape the strict playing code of the watchful and firm parent.

Babe Didrikson Zaharias, heroine of the 1932 Olympic Games, was disbarred from amateur golf because she endorsed an automobile in an advertisement. She applied for reinstatement, got it, won the Women's National Amateur in 1946, the British Ladies Championship in 1947, and then turned professional.

John Dawson, one of the game's great swingers, was similarly disbarred for commercial activities but was reinstated in the 1940's. He was runner-up to Skee Riegel in the National Amateur at Del Monte, California, in 1947.

Harvie Ward won the U.S. Amateur in 1955 and 1956 and was acclaimed the world's leading amateur when he ran afoul of the U.S.G.A. The golf fathers found him indiscreet in the matter of accepting expenses for tournaments and imposed a two-year probation on him, which later was reduced to one year. The handsome graduate of the University of North Carolina never recovered from the crack-down and quickly dropped out of the big-time golf picture. Expense irregularities also provoked suspension of a large part of a college golf team—North Texas State—in the 1940's. The players returned to good standing, and many of them, including Billy Maxwell, winner of the 1951 National Amateur, went on to great success in the game.

The first executive director of the U.S.G.A. was Thomas J. McMahon, who began his duties in 1922. He is credited with adopting a regular system of holding tournaments. He set up the first public scoreboard—a 4-footer called "gigantic" in that day—and hired an accountant to keep it. He also first started charging spectators for admission. Originally, the tournaments were free, but the crowds were wild and unruly. It was decided that by charging $1 or $2 it might be possible to dissuade the curious from attending and attract true fans.

McMahon was succeeded by Joseph C. Dey, a Philadelphia sportswriter, on December 10, 1934, and under Dey's astute guidance the U.S.G.A. became one of the most suaccessful of all sports organizations. It built up a strong reputation for integrity. It gained the respect and confidence of amateurs and professionals alike. And it never stopped looking after the "little men in golf."

By 1965, the game had attracted 8,000,000 regular players—that is, those playing 15 rounds or more a year—with another 1,000,000 who played the game less frequently. It was estimated that 126,000,000 rounds of golf were played a year, over 703,700 acres, at an expense of $1,855,000,000.

These statistics proved, the U.S.G.A. said, that golf's need for a national authority was greater than ever.

Chapter Fifty-one

The Professional Golfers Association

The touring tournament professional, whose name is splashed across newspaper headlines and is known in almost every household, makes up only a small fraction of the Professional Golfers Association of America. For every golfer who plays the game as a means of livelihood, there are 15 professionals serving the nation's golf clubs and other key positions in the game.

The PGA, by its own definition, is a voluntary, incorporated, nonprofit membership association of golf professionals banded together in mutual interests. Formed by a handful of pioneers in 1916, it had grown to 5,200 members by 1964, serving 7,477 golf clubs and 7,250,000 golfers.

It lists the following as its objectives:

1. To elevate the standards of the profession.

2. To promote interest in the game.

3. To protect the mutual interests of members.

4. To promote tournaments.

The PGA says its major aim is to stimulate growth of golf. Through a broad public-relations program, educational films and literature, it has sought to bring the game to the masses and erase the idea, prevalent as late as the 1930's, that golf is a sport for the wealthy.

The organization also has moved to raise the stature and standard of the professional. When the PGA was formed in 1916, there were only a handful of golf teachers. They were obscure, poorly paid, and regarded as second-class citizens by the swank country clubs which placed the tag of "gentlemen" only on the amateurs.

The PGA's two big showcases are the PGA Championship, which started with the organization's birth, and the tournament tour, which in 1964 offered 40 sponsored competitions for a total prize-money offering of $2,400,000.

The PGA also sponsors the Seniors' Teacher Trophy Championship, National Golf Club Championship, the National Golf Club Match Play Championship, the Quarter Century Club Championship, the Senior-Junior Best-Ball Championship, and National Golf Day.

National Golf Day was originated in 1952 for both promotional and benevolent purposes. Golfers throughout the country—men, women, and children—pay a fee to match their own handicap scores over their home courses with the scores of the U.S. Open and PGA champions, playing at a selected site. Medals are awarded to those who "Beat the Champion."

Through the first 12 years 1,092,500 people paid $1,122,871 to participate. The money went to the National Golf Fund, Inc., for charitable and other worthwhile projects. These included caddy scholarship programs, golf for the crippled and blind, and educational and relief projects.

For more than 20 years, the PGA also has sponsored a Hole-in-One Club, keeping a permanent record of those golfers who hit a once-in-a-lifetime shot. The record enrolled for a single season was 6,675 in 1961.

Prior to 1916, there was no national organization of golf professionals. Some regional associations flourished, but as a general rule the pros were a disorganized, unnoticed, unappreciated lot. A regional association was formed in Chicago in 1907 and a New England association in 1914.

On January 17, 1916, a number of professionals were invited to a luncheon given by Rodman Wanamaker, son of the Philadelphia department store magnate, John Wanamaker, at the Taplow Club in New York.

Wanamaker suggested to the pros that they form a national organization. As an incentive, he said he would put up $2,580 as prize money for a tournament to be conducted along the lines of Great Britain's News of the World Match Play Championship. Several prominent amateurs, including Francis Ouimet, John G. Anderson, A.H. Tillinghast, Joseph Appel, W.W. Harris, Jason Rogers, and P.C. Pulver, attended the meeting and enthusiastically endorsed Wanamaker's idea.

The pros were sold. An organizing committee was selected with James Hepburn as chairman, Herbert W. Strong as secretary, and James Maiden, Robert White, Gilbert Nicholls, Jack Mackie, and Jack Hobens as other members. At a subsequent meeting on January 24, 1916, the group decided that a constitution should be drafted.

The constitution committee consisted of Rogers, Hobens, Mackie, Strong, and G.C. Ennever. Appointed on February 7, 1916, the committee needed only two weeks to draft the constitution, which was approved at a meeting in New York on February 24, 1916. A total of 82 charter members, including 78 in Class A, were elected April 10, 1916. An additional 145 members, 139 in Class B, three in Class C, and three in Class D, were added June 5, 1916.

The Association's first annual meeting was held June 26–28 at the Radisson Hotel in Minneapolis. Thirty-nine members attended.

Robert White was elected the first president, George Fotheringham and James Maiden vice-presidents, and Herbert Strong secretary-treasurer. A 24-man executive committee was chosen, with 9 members from the Metropolitan New York section, 6 from the Middle States, 3 from New England, 3 from the Southeast, 1 from the Central section, 1 from the Northwest, and 1 from the Pacific Southwest.

At a meeting at Garden City, New York, on July 14, 1916, the executive committee accepted Wanamaker's offer to donate $2,580 in prize money, a trophy and various medals for the first United States professional championship tournament. A trophy and a gold medal were to go to the winner, a silver medal to the runner-up, a bronze medal for each of the semifinalists, and medals also for the low scorers in the seven qualifying sections. The PGA decided to call the tournament the Championship of the Professional Golfers Association of America.

Thirty-one PGA members competed in the first tournament at the Siwanoy Country Club in Bronxville, New York, October 10–16, 1916. The winner was Long Jim Barnes, who beat Jock Hutchison, Sr., 1-up in the final match. First prize was $500.

Interest in the game mushroomed. The PGA flourished. By the beginning of World War II, in 1941, membership in the PGA had grown to 2,041. There was a natural decline during the war, but the PGA prepared itself for the postwar boom by hiring a full-time executive secretary and counsel in 1943. Membership rolls jumped to 2,300 in 1947, 4,000 in 1957 and a high of 5,200 in 1964.

The PGA resisted efforts to establish strong one-man—or czar—control as in professional baseball and football. It chose instead to operate on an assembly plan with functions delegated to committees and management vested in an executive committee made up of the president, secretary, treasurer and 11 vice-presidents.

The vice-presidents represent the PGA's districts, including from three to five sections.

The eleventh is the chairman of the tournament bureau and representative of the tournament players.

When the tour grew to such enormous proportions, there were moves among some of the tournament players to break away from the parent organization. The effort failed. Most of the touring pros, while demanding a greater voice in the conduct of the tour, preferred remaining with the PGA. The PGA tournaments are run under agreements with local sponsors. The sponsors put up the prize money and the PGA provides all scheduling and technical tournament services, including direction under a six-man field staff.

Most of the operational work of the PGA at the national level is handled by the staff of the PGA National Headquarters. These offices were located in Dunedin, Florida, until 1964, when they were transferred to the PGA National Golf Club at Palm Beach Gardens, Florida. This became the winter rendezvous for PGA members, gathering there for clinics, seminars, and a diversified winter tournament program.

To be eligible to apply for membership in the PGA, an applicant must be 21 years of age and must have served at least 5 years in one of the following categories:

1. A head professional at a recognized golf club or course.

2. An assistant to a head professional at a recognized club or course.

3. An approved tournament player, under an agreement with the PGA, playing in a minimum of 25 tournaments a year.

4. Any combination of these various phases.

Members fall into various classifications, ranging from A to J.

The principal classification is Class A. These are the members who govern and control the association. They include those regularly engaged as professionals at recognized clubs and courses, those who own or lease such facilities, and those who qualify in other ways. They alone have the right to vote, hold office, attend executive meetings, and endorse applications for membership.

The other classifications are:

Class Junior A: Assistants employed by professionals at recognized clubs as club-makers, teaching assistants, shop assistants, and playing assistants.

Class B: Professionals who have left the profession but who remain actively engaged in other capacities of golf which are not such to make them eligible for Class A.

Class F: Members who are temporarily unemployed and unable to meet the obligations of regular membership as Class A or B.

Class E: Honorary members.

Class G: Life members.

Class J: Inactive members.

A professional can be elected to PGA membership only in Class A, Class Junior A and, in certain instances, Class B. Approved tournament players are not considered PGA members. They are learning the business by playing the PGA tour.

One of the knottiest problems to confront the PGA in the modern era has been television. With the growth of sports interest on the home screens, golf became a natural and a lucrative commodity. A series of filmed weekend shows became popular on the networks, but even more desirable was live television of the weekly tournaments. This was the point of dissension.

The sponsors insisted that, since they were the ones putting up the prize money and taking the big financial risk, they should receive the TV receipts. The players argued that it was show business. They, the pros, were the actors on the stage. They deserved the major portion of the television money. A long and bitter war—and even a stalemate—appeared inevitable until a solution was reached in Chicago on August 5, 1964.

Warren Cantrell, president of the PGA, and James L. Hyde, Jr., president of the International Golf Sponsors Association, announced jointly an accord giving part of the proceeds to the sponsor and part to the players, with the latter adding their share to the tournament purse.

The breakdown varied. The agreement affected only about half the 40 tournaments. The others either had no television commitments or operated independently of the PGA. The independents included such giants as the Masters and the U.S. Open, which insisted on maintaining control of the TV purse strings—and went unchallenged.

Chapter Fifty-two

The Ladies' Professional Golfers Association

In the 1940's, the name of Babe Didrikson Zaharias was one of the most magnetic in golf. In popularity, in newspaper and radio exposure, the talented Texas athlete refused to be overshadowed by the men stars of the day— Ben Hogan, Byron Nelson, and Sam Snead. The public wanted to see and read about her. Fans came out in droves to watch her in her few tournament appearances.

Unlike the men, with their prospering professional tour, the Babe had no regular stage on which to show her wares. It was not until Mrs. Zaharias placed management of her affairs in the hands of the enterprising promoter, Fred Corcoran, that the situation was rectified.

Corcoran got a prominent manufacturer of women's clothing, Albert Handmacher, interested in backing women's golf for commercial reasons. A cross-country women's tournament was organized under the name of the Weathervane, a label carried in Handmacher's smart women's suits.

With Mrs. Zaharias as the leading attraction, the ladies modeled Handmacher's suits and played golf, starting on the West Coast and working their way east. There were cash prizes at each stop. At the end of the swing, a women's team was chosen to play a picked team in Britain. There always were poses in the trim suits. The girls fidgeted but bore it.

This was the origination of what was to become the ladies' tour. With only a handful of professional players, the loosely-knit Women's PGA was formed. The group even managed to launch a National Women's Open Tournament in 1946. Corcoran, busy with the PGA and other interests, volunteered his services as a counselor but he was in no position to take over full responsibility of the organization. Furthermore, the women did not have enough money to retain him.

The ladies struggled along as best they could until September, 1950, when a meeting was called in Wichita, Kansas, for the purpose of establishing a body to govern women's professional golf.

Out of this meeting came the Ladies' Professional Golf Association. Patty Berg, regarded as the dean of women's golf, was named the first president. There were 11 charter members: Babe Zaharias, Patty Berg, Alice Bauer, Marlene Bauer, Louise Suggs, Sally Sessions, Betty Jameson, Bettye Danoff, Shirley Spork, Helen Dettweiler, and Marilynn Smith.

At first, tournaments were few and prizes small. It was hardly worth the effort, but the women stuck it out. Gradually, the tournaments increased. By 1964, there were 34 official tournaments on the tour with prize money totaling around $325,000. In 1963, Mickey Wright won $31,269.50, in contrast to the $3,400 earned by Mrs. Zaharias in 1948.

The LPGA membership also ballooned. By 1964, the organization had 125 members, half of them playing professionals and the other half teaching professionals.

The women patterned their administration along the lines of their big brother, the PGA. Management of their national affairs was vested in an Executive Committee, consisting of a president, vice-president, secretary, treasurer, and member-at-large. Committees were formed to work in such areas as tournament operations, clinics, statistics, television, membership, and sponsor information.

In 1962, the LPGA hired Leonard Wirtz as full-time Ladies' PGA Tournament Director, with headquarters in Cincinnati. A year later, Nan Berry Ryan, formerly of the PGA Magazine and Public Relations staff, was taken on as Public Relations Director. She operated out of Kirkwood, Missouri.

The LPGA set its aims as: (1) help popularize golf among women and young people; (2) promote assistant and head professional jobs for its members.

In keeping with the latter idea, the LPGA launched a series of National Golf Schools, to be held annually. The first was staged in 1960 in Ann Arbor, Michigan, with an attendance of 65. The school covered all phases of teaching and golf technique. A second school was held in Ann Arbor the next year. Subsequently, the project moved to other golfing areas.

The LPGA established a Ladies' Golf Hall of Fame in 1950. A committee of six men was formed to select the first players to be inducted and to be enshrined at the Augusta Country Club in Augusta, Georgia. Seven immortals of American golf were selected the first year. They were Joyce Wethered Amory, Margaret Curtis, Alexa Stirling Fraser, Beatrix Hoyt, Dorothy Campbell Hurd, Virginia Van Wie, and Glenna Collett Vare.

Four professionals were named in 1951—Babe Zaharias, Betty Jameson, Patty Berg, and Louise Suggs; Betsy Rawls was added in 1960 and Mickey Wright in 1964.

In 1952, Betty Jameson donated a trophy to be awarded yearly to the player with the lowest-scoring average in official LPGA tournaments. She requested that the award be named for the great American player, Glenna Collett Vare. To qualify for the trophy, it was necessary that a player compete in 80 percent of the tournaments.

LEADING MONEY WINNERS OF THE LPGA

Year	Player	Amount
1948	Babe Zaharias	$ 3,400.00
1949	Babe Zaharias	4,650.00
1950	Babe Zaharias	14,800.00
1951	Babe Zaharias	15,087.00
1952	Betsy Rawls	14,505.00
1953	Louise Suggs	19,816.25
1954	Patty Berg	16,011.00
1955	Patty Berg	16,492.34
1956	Marlene Bauer Hagge	20,235.50
1957	Patty Berg	16,272.00
1958	Beverly Hanson	12,639.55
1959	Betsy Rawls	26,774.39
1960	Louise Suggs	16,892.12
1961	Mickey Wright	22,236.21
1962	Mickey Wright	21,641.99
1963	Mickey Wright	31,269.50
1964	Mickey Wright	29,800.00

LPGA VARE TROPHY WINNERS

Year	Player	Rounds	Average
1953	Patty Berg	65	75.00
1954	Babe Zaharias	66	75.48
1955	Patty Berg	72	74.47
1956	Patty Berg	77	74.57
1957	Louise Suggs	49	74.64
1958	Beverly Hanson	84	74.92
1959	Betsy Rawls	95	74.03
1960	Mickey Wright	75	73.25
1961	Mickey Wright	87	73.55
1962	Mickey Wright	101	73.67
1963	Mickey Wright	95	72.81
1964	Mickey Wright	75	72.46

Chapter Fifty-three

The Tour: From Hamburgers to Cadillacs

The professional golf tour, a thriving $3,-000,000-a-year enterprise in the mid-1960's, started out on a shoestring, a layer cake, and a few long-distance telephone calls. It went from hamburgers and $2-a-night stands to limousines and luxury for the tournament pros—a handful of struggling artisans in the 1920's, a breed of capitalists 40 years later.

History is cloudy on exactly how and when the tour started. Most golfers of the period traced it to informal tournaments staged in the Miami (Florida) area before and shortly after World War I. Walter Hagen's exhibition tours gave it impetus. A telephone campaign by Estelle Armour, wife of Tommy Armour, and Jo Espinosa, wife of Al Espinosa, set up a primitive network of early sponsors.

Long Jim Barnes recalled that in the early days before 1920, he and such players as Jock Hutchison, Tommy McNamara, Alex Smith, and Walter Hagen frequently got together for friendly competitions in Florida.

"There was just one prize," Barnes said. "Often it was just a big layer cake put up by one of the hotels."

Later, Tommy Armour, Al Espinosa, Bobby Cruickshank and their wives got together and decided to try to promote some tournaments.

Mrs. Espinosa telephoned a group of friends in El Paso, Texas. Yes, the friends decided, if Armour, Espinosa and Cruickshank could guarantee their appearance, money could be raised for an open tournament.

The tournament was staged on cotton-seed hull greens. Pros and amateurs of the area competed against the big-name pros. The gallery was negligible. The prize money amounted to little more than $1,000. This was in 1927.

The next year the tournament was canceled. This time, Mrs. Armour got on the telephone. She had an influential friend in Chicago. However, he was in Hot Springs, Arkansas, taking health baths. Standing in a bath with only a towel around him, the influential Chicagoan agreed to hold a tournament in Chicago.

So it went in the early days. A scattered tournament here and there, no organization, purses so small the entire effort hardly seemed worthwhile. Most of the tournaments were held in the winter at resort areas. The summer circuit did not start until 1930.

The pioneer of the winter circuit was the Texas Open, played on the Brackenridge public course at San Antonio in 1922. Jack O'Brien, a newspaperman, was the spark behind the project. He got a group of wealthy Texans to put up $5,000 prize money, regarded as a fabulous figure for that day.

Scattered tournaments began popping up elsewhere. There was one at Sacramento, with prize money of $2,500, and another at San Diego, 600 miles south. In 1927, the Los Angeles Open was inaugurated with a total purse of $10,000. This figure was regarded as earth-shaking.

307

Horton Smith recalled that when he turned professional in 1926, the only playing pros, besides himself, were Hagen and Joe Kirkwood, the transplanted Australian who later became famous as a trick-shot artist.

"Leo Diegel joined us later as the private professional for millionaire Edward B. McLean," Smith said. "Then later, Wild Bill Mehlhorn. I recall, we played in the LaGorce Open in 1929. I won and got a check for $1,000. I mailed the check home to my father to show him that golf could be a profitable business."

The summer circuit was started in 1930. The St. Paul Junior Chamber of Commerce raised $10,000 for a tournament to follow the National Open. Still, tournament golf remained a struggling venture.

More successful than those scattered 72-hole events were the exhibitions featuring the stars of the period. The great Hagen, with newsman Bob Harlow as his personal manager, made capital with his reputation and flair for showmanship.

Harlow, who at one time served as director of the tour, worked with Hagen for 12 years. He served as advance man, made contacts with the newspapers and radio stations, wrote a golf column and then helped promote the tournaments.

He kept Hagen moving. The Haig said he played in every city with a population over 25,000 in the United States. The flamboyant professional from Rochester, New York, made a habit of latching onto the best player of the day, usually the U.S. Open champion, and playing exhibitions with him across the country.

When Horton Smith emerged in 1929 as the "Joplin Ghost," the hottest golf commodity since Bob Jones, Hagen signed him for 100 exhibitions. They paid their own expenses. Hagen received 40 percent, Smith 40 percent, and Harlow 20 percent of the guarantee. It became a terrific grind.

"We played as many as 5 or 6 exhibitions a week," Smith said. "Once we had 11 straight matches around Michigan, Indiana and Ohio prior to the National Open. Another time, we played 33 consecutive days across Illinois, Missouri, Oklahoma, Texas, Kansas, Nebraska, Colorado, Utah, and Idaho."

Hagen, a great showman and a natural-born gambler, insisted on a side bet of $1 on each stroke. At the end of 100 exhibitions, Smith had to pay $22. "Walter really hated to lose a buck," Horton recalled. "He worked as hard for a six as he did for a birdie two."

The first actual tournament bureau organizer was Hal Sharkey, sports editor of *The Newark Evening News* (New Jersey). Sharkey worked without pay—a labor of love. He would go to California for the Rose Bowl football game, and, while there, line up tournaments for the golfers. He did the same in Florida while covering the baseball camps.

Sharkey started putting a tour schedule together in 1927 and 1928. Appreciative of his efforts, the golfers decided to cut him in on the purse. Usually, this was 10 percent of the winner's prize.

In 1930, Sharkey turned over $5,500 to the Professional Golfers Association and suggested that a tournament manager be hired. The PGA obtained Francis J. Powers, a Chicago sportswriter. Powers later was succeeded by Harlow, who is credited with popularizing the tour because he had golf, gypsy, and showmanship in his blood.

Harlow was the first to put out a PGA player record book. He produced a tournament sponsors' guide and developed press releases and bulletins for both the players and press. He still maintained his private interests, a connection with Walter Hagen, and a column which he marketed to newspapers.

The Professional Golfers Association, foreseeing the tournament boom, decided that it needed a full-time tour director. In January, 1936, in the locker room at Pinehurst, North Carolina, scene of the North and South Tournament, George Jacobus, PGA president, offered the post to Fred Corcoran. Corcoran accepted.

Corcoran was a husky Irishman from Boston, who, like Harlow, had a deep-seated love for golf and a knack for promoting it. He had a trip-hammer mind. He had a flair for promotional gimmicks. He had the respect of both golfers and newsmen. Under his guidance over a 12-year period, the game made unbelievable strides.

When Corcoran took over there were 10 tour tournaments, with prize money ranging from $3,000 to $10,000. They were the Los Angeles Open, $10,000; Oakland, $5,000; Sacramento, $3,000; San Francisco, $5,000; Bing Crosby, $3,000; Houston, $3,000; Miami, $5,000; St. Petersburg, $5,000; St. Augustine, $3,000, and the Masters at Augusta, $5,000.

Their total prize money amounted to $52,-000. In 1964, eight golfers alone made more money. Jack Nicklaus topped the individual money list with $113,284.50.

"I took the job on a salary of $75 a week and $5 a day expenses," Corcoran later said. "I had to do everything. I was the advance man, going into the town early to set up publicity. I helped with the program, drew up pairings, supervised the setting of the pins and showed up at the first tee to get the tournament properly under way."

Corcoran remained tournament director until 1948, when he resigned to assume new responsibilities of personal management. He guided the business affairs of such notables as Sam Snead and Babe Didrikson Zaharias in golf and Ted Williams and Stan Musial in baseball. He remained with the PGA in an advisory capacity.

When he gave up the reins, Corcoran left the tour in a healthy condition. Purses had skyrocketed. There were more than 30 tournaments on the year-round schedule with prize money totaling $750,000.

Corcoran was instrumental in getting George S. May, wealthy Chicago business consultant, interested in the game. In 1941, May launched the All-America Tournament at Tam O'Shanter and became the father of the $100,000 purse. He later expanded the event into a two-week affair involving both amateurs and professionals, women and men. To the All-America he added the World's Championship, with a top prize of $50,000 which could be stretched to $100,000 through exhibitions.

With the departure of Corcoran, the tour lost the strong, dominant figure. The PGA had a steady parade of managers—George Schneider, a former player; Howard Capps; Ray O'Brien; and Harvie Raynor.

In 1955, the PGA hired Ed Carter, a high-powered promoter who had been successful in advertising, printing, and public-relations work. He set to work embellishing the giant which Corcoran had created. The job took on various splinters. Carter confined himself largely to dealing with sponsors—that is, selling the product. An information office was opened, with a New Englander named Jim Gaquin in charge. The actual job of running the tournament at the scene was turned over to another man—Harvie Raynor at first, then Joe Black.

Despite the constant changes, the tour mushroomed. Golf soared toward a peak of popularity. More people were playing. More wanted to watch the stars. Television was bringing its big magic eye to the fairways.

Whereas in the 1920's and 1930's there was only a handful of tournament players, and mothers were advised to discourage their sons from taking up the game as a profession, the lists grew into the hundreds. Golfers prospered.

The climb to affluence was reflected in the money winning tables. In 1934, Paul Runyan led the official individual earnings with $6,767. Johnny Revolta was No. 1 the following year with $9,543. Ben Hogan led in 1940 with $10,656. In 1964, there were 40 players who won $19,350 and more. Twenty-one were in the $25,000-plus bracket. Two thousand different players competed on the tour. More than 100 of these were regulars.

"It's amazing how the tour has changed," Fred Corcoran reflected when he examined the new picture. "In the old days, they made the circuit by train or in beat-up old cars. They took rooms at $2 a night with a bath down the hall. They went down to the corner to eat hamburgers. Now every pro golfer has 11 pairs of white shoes (in the case of some it was 100). He drives a Cadillac. He dresses like Walter Hagen and Jimmy Demaret. He goes first class."

As the tour moved through the 1960's, it was almost impossible to tell the "haves" from the "have nots." Young men starting on the tour often managed to get financial backing from friends back home. Even if unable to break into the money column, they ate, lived, and dressed well. Manufacturing companies were generous in supplying the athletes, always in the public eye, with shirts, slacks, shoes, and equipment. The barnstorming pros became a breed—young precisionists, natty, business-like, often accompanied by their own business managers or lawyers.

None capitalized on his ability more than Arnold Palmer, the son of a Latrobe, Pennsylvania, professional, and a player whose faculty for miraculous comebacks made him the darling of the galleries in the late 1950's and early 1960's.

At his peak, Palmer needed five lawyers to handle his myriad business ventures. He was actor, writer, teacher, and business tycoon as well as tournament golfer. It was said that every one of America's 7,000,000 golfers fell in some way under the Palmer influence. They wore Arnold Palmer hats, Arnold Palmer shoes, and Arnold Palmer gloves. They played with Arnold Palmer clubs and balls and rode in Arnold Palmer carts. They got lessons from him in books, newspapers, and on television.

Palmer owned his own equipment manufacturing business, said to be worth more than $1,000,000. He was the largest stockholder in a nationwide chain of putting courses. He was associated with two full-length golf clubs and owned part of a third. He produced hand carts, driving nets, practice balls and cut three long-playing record albums on instruction. He owned a printing company, an insurance agency, and an investment firm.

Additionally, he was part owner, producer, and commentator of his own television show. He appeared in the movies. He charged $5,000 for an exhibition and $2,000 for taking a bow on a television show. During his best years, he reportedly paid tax on an income exceeding $750,000.

While he was the No. 1 financial genius of the game, he was not alone in reaping big rewards. Players such as Jack Nicklaus, Gary Player, Julius Boros, Tony Lema, Ken Venturi, and Bill Casper also turned their tournament golf success into great wealth.

Mark McCormick, a Cleveland attorney who served as manager for Palmer, Nicklaus and Player, said that a victory in any of the major championships—the U.S. Open, Masters or PGA—could be parlayed into $1,000,000.

And Long Jim Barnes had to settle for a cake.

Chapter Fifty-four

The Golf Boom: Where Do We Go From Here?

Seventy-seven years after drawing its first breath in a primitive cow pasture in Yonkers, New York, on a crisp, windy February 22 in 1888, golf in America found itself to be more than a robust, growing institution. It was a veritable monster, so big, so rich, and developing at such a rapid rate that even its most devoted well-wishers were inclined to stop and ask: How long can this boom last? Where do we go from here?

Statistics released by the National Golf Foundation revealed this amazing growth by the end of 1964:

Number of golfers	8,000,000
Number of golf courses, regulation	7,112
Par-3 courses	781
New courses opened for play in 1964	292
New par-3 courses	90
Additions to existing courses	88
Estimated capital invested in golf facilities	$1,855,000,000
Acres devoted to golf facilities	751,200
Golf driving ranges	4,500

The astounding advance of the game was not limited to the United States. Great Britain, where the game was spawned, was experiencing a new awakening of interest. Japan was stricken with the "bug," devotees and courses multiplying at a staggering rate. An Asian pro tour was inaugurated that jumped from Manila to Hong Kong to Tokyo and Taiwan. France, Belgium, Spain, Italy, and other European countries which had been cool to the sport for years began clearing away unused pastures for courses.

The greatest strides, however, continued to be made in the United States.

Prize lists of $100,000 became routine on the $3,000,000 professional tour and $200,000 the target of any ambitious promoter who wanted to hold the world's richest tournament. Crowds were so large at the major events—the Masters, Open, and the PGA—that methods of handling them became a growing headache for the directors. The size of the turnouts at the Masters in Augusta, Georgia, never officially announced but estimated at $40,000 on a single day, caused sponsors to consider a restriction of the ticket sale—an unheard-of phenomenon in golf.

An example of the exploding golf boom was the 1965 Professional Golfers Association Championship at Ligonier, a remote steel center in the mountains of western Pennsylvania. The tournament manager, Ed Carter, termed it the first $1,000,000-tournament in the sport. The breakdown included $400,000 in admissions, $300,000 in advertising in the program, $182,000 for television rights, and $118,000 in concessions.

Television contributed materially to the bonanza. In the 1960's, it was almost impossible to flick on a TV dial on the weekend without catching a couple of professional golfers striding down the fairway. The majority of these were taped shows, matching the game's leading players in challenge or elimi-

Wide World

Masters crowds thirty years apart show the amazing growth of the game.

Above, only a handful watch Gene Sarazen putt out on the final green in his play-off with Craig Wood for the 1935 championship—the year Sarazen made his double eagle to tie. *At the right,* this is only part of the swarming thousands who packed around the green and the fairways to watch Jack Nicklaus hit his finishing shots in his 1965 Masters triumph.

nation contests, with ultimate prizes running into the hundreds of thousands of dollars. One program in color pitted leading players of many nations on exciting courses throughout the world. It was not rare for a star such as Arnold Palmer or Jack Nicklaus to compete

with himself for viewers on rival channels. Palmer became producer, commentator and star performer of his own show.

Such affluence spawned a new breed of golf professional—a young business tycoon with a personal manager, a secretary and a host of outside interests. Some of the standout players—Palmer, Nicklaus, Gary Player, and Tony Lema, particularly—became so involved in money-making enterprises that they began to find less and less time for their golf. As a result, their games suffered.

Most of Arnie's business problems were turned over to a friend, Mark McCormack of Cleveland, one of five lawyers handling Palmer's affairs. Palmer also employed two full-time secretaries.

The business manager became an integral part of professional golf, and one of the most successful was McCormack. Besides Palmer, McCormack also handled Jack Nicklaus and Gary Player, the other two members of the so-called "Big Three," as well as two of the most prosperous of the overseas invaders, Bob

Charles of New Zealand and Bruce Devlin of Australia.

McCormack's chief competition came from Fred Corcoran, who, besides making a name for himself as a tournament director, extended his fame by becoming personal manager for such sports celebrities as Sam Snead and Babe Didrikson Zaharias in golf, Stan Musial and Ted Williams in baseball. When Snead began fading, Corcoran started building a new stable headed by Tony Lema, winner of the British Open in 1964, and Ken Venturi, the American Open champion the same year.

As golf moved through the 1960's its greatest concern lay—paradoxically—in its almost berserk growing popularity. Galleries became a tremendous problem. The game was threatened with loss of interest through overexposure on television.

Crowds for the major tournaments became so large that drastic measures had to be taken for gallery control.

The Masters, with foresight, headed off the problem for a while by erecting natural mounds and amphitheaters which gave the spectators unobstructed views on many of the holes. It became a habit for golf followers to plant themselves at certain vantage points—with picnic lunches—and never move all day.

The size of the Masters galleries grew from a handful when the tournament was begun in 1934 to 10,000 a day, then 20,000 and finally 40,000 and 50,000. Officials declined to release attendance figures but in 1965 it became necessary to stop the sale of tickets for the third and final rounds on Saturday and Sunday—a sport precedent.

Another precedent was set when a group of college students were caught counterfeiting both tickets to the tournament and parking stickers, both a scarce and valuable commodity. They had a well-organized ring which printed the fake credentials at the University of Georgia.

It became almost impossible to flick on a television dial on the week-end without catching a glimpse of one of the current fairway heroes doing his chores. Even those closest to the sport feared that the screened shows—like the Westerns and hillbilly comedies—might suddenly lose their glamor. "People can take only so much," one tournament sponsor said. "Palmer is as exciting to them now as Hopalong Cassidy used to be—but remember they got tired of Hopalong."

Not many of the professionals on the tour went hungry. Nicklaus led the money winning list in 1964 with $113,284.50, with Palmer just behind him at $113,203.37. Thirty-six players collected $20,000 or better in official money. Most of them doubled it in unofficial earnings—money made in unsanctioned tournaments, exhibitions, and TV appearances.

Even those golfers unable to break even on the tour did not become destitute. Most of the youngsters attempting to crash the tour were backed by sponsors, usually home-town syndicates which put up enough money to allow their boy to live and travel in style and which shared in his winnings if he made good. Sporting goods and clothing manufacturers flooded the locker rooms with free equipment and apparel. A player striving to make ends meet was able to wear just as fleecy a sweater and just as swanky a pair of gilded shoes as Palmer or Nicklaus. A few dozen new golf balls were always stocked away on the top shelf of the locker.

Appendix

The 1966 Masters had Arnold Palmer's name written all over it. It was an even year, and hadn't Arnie won every even year since 1958? In addition, the 36-year-old people's choice had dumped details of his myriad, multi-million-dollar business enterprises into the lap of his attorney and manager, Mark McCormack, and shutoff the telephone. He was lean and hard and concentrating again on golf.

This was the Palmer of old. He was smoking again, easing his tensions with quick puffs on a cigarette—he was determined. After a sixteen-month slump, during which he won only one tournament, he had come out fighting on the Winter Tour. He won the Los Angeles Open, he finished second in the Bing Crosby Tournament and he lost a play-off to Doug Sanders in the Bob Hope Desert Classic. It was only natural that bookmakers should establish him a 4–1 favorite and Arnie's Army should come out in full numbers to see their hero make good his comeback by winning his fifth Masters title.

Palmer's cause was aided by other factors. His keenest rival, Jack Nicklaus, had played only one tournament on the Pacific Coast before taking off for South Africa on a golfing, hunting and fishing safari with the other member of the Big Three, Gary Player. Now the Golden Bear was back, but performances at Miami and Orlando on the Florida circuit showed that he was not at his sharpest. Player put in a casual appearance on the tour three weeks before the Masters and began struggling to put all the pieces together. Another formi-

dable threat, Bill Casper, had spent much of the winter in the Far East, climaxing his campaign with exhibitions for U.S. troops in Viet Nam.

Who, then, was there to challenge the master of the Masters? There was the Dixie dandy, Doug Sanders. Hotter than a dollar pistol, he had won three tournaments and missed a fourth only through an oversight—failure to sign his scorecard while leading by four strokes at Pensacola. But Sanders had a short, punchy swing, cultivated during his caddie days, and observers said he lacked the power to tame the massive Augusta National course. Gay Brewer, Jr., the pug-nosed fighter from Dallas, was playing marvelously and no one questioned his muscle off the tee, but, did he have the poise to stay with the favored Big Three, which had won seven of the last eight Masters and the last six in a row? The judgment was negative.

The Augusta National course, in the words of Bob Jones, has a personality which changes with the whims of nature. She can be gentle as a kitten—as she was in 1965 when Nicklaus set the winning record of 271 by nine strokes—or, she can be as cantankerous as a jilted woman. When the 1966 tournament opened on Thursday, April 7, winds with gusts up to 40 miles an hour whistled through the stately pines. The fairways had been watered to slow the run of big drives and the greens were as hard and slick as a marble top table.

Augusta was showing her fingernails. This became obvious as the bulk of the field of 103 of the world's best golfers attacked and met a fusillade of bogeys. Palmer, playing well up to that point, fell victim to "Devil's Elbow"—the treacherous corner which includes the 11th, 12th and 13th holes. He bogeyed the 11th and took a double bogey at the short No. 12, which he termed the "toughest par three in all golf," and finished with a 74. Player, his putting touch cold, also had a 74. Ben Hogan, an unsettling shadow out of the past, scored a 53.

The wind had intensified by the time Nicklaus teed off late in the day and there was another apparent distraction for the blond bombardier from Columbus, Ohio. On the previous day, at midnight, he had received news that four friends—one of them a former schoolboy pal with whom he golfed and fished—had died in a plane accident en route to Augusta to watch him play. Perhaps the news had sent him into a state of unconscious shock. At any rate, Jack paid no attention to the swirling winds, the glass-top greens and other subtle treacheries of the Augusta National. He hooked his drive on the first hole but recovered magnificently and sank a 25-foot putt for a birdie 3. He birdied the fourth and ninth, escaped a bogey at the Devil's Elbow, added his fourth birdie with a fine four-iron shot at the par five 13th and finished with a four-under-par 68. He led the tournament by three shots. Bill Casper, Don January, Mike Souchak and the veteran amateur, Charles Coe, were closest at 71—the only ones in the field able to crack Augusta's 72 par.

"Another Nicklaus runaway," spectators mumbled when the men came back Friday for the second round against the rugged layout. Again it was cold and windy; the Augusta National looked as menacing as ever. It was the kind of day that should have put more daylight between Nicklaus and the rest of the field, but who can account for the vagaries of this game?

Perhaps it was a delayed reaction to his personal tragedy. Maybe it was just a case of a cold, recalcitrant putter. At any rate, Nicklaus, the man who had cowed the course 24 hours earlier by not taking a single bogey,

now found the broad, undulating greens a complete mystery. He three-putted five greens and missed seven putts of five feet and less, three of them no more than 18 inches. When he totaled his score, he had a fat 76.

This opened the door and the first to barge through it were Paul Harney, a prematurely-graying home professional from Sutton, Massachusetts, and Peter Butler, a strapping British Ryder Cup player from Birmingham, England, tied for the lead at 143. Palmer snapped back with a 70 that sent his Army into orbit and found himself tied with Nicklaus, Sanders, Don January and Bob Rosburg, one stroke back at 144. Hogan was at 145 and Player, who hit what he called "my greatest shot ever" in digging a ball out of a mud bank at the 12th and dropping it into the hole for a birdie deuce, was out of contention at 151. Now instead of a rout, the Masters had a horse race. Twenty golfers were bunched within four shots of the top.

On the third day, the bulk of the gallery, estimated at between 40,000 and 50,000, fought and strained for a peek at the blue ribbon pairing of Palmer and Hogan, the two kings of different eras. Hogan, his jaws like a vice under his familiar white cap, looked like the master of the 1950's as he rifled shots from tee to green but putting nerves still troubled him. He three-putted three of the outgoing holes and turned in 38, two over par. Palmer also had putting troubles and made the bend in 37.

At the 10th, Hogan came alive again, chipping in from 35 feet. Then he sank a 30-foot putt for a birdie at the 11th and he was back in the fight. The bantam Texan faltered on the finishing holes but finished with a par 72 and a rousing salute from Arnie's Army. Palmer shot 73. Asked about the cheering, Hogan said, "I think the cheers were about even."

Meanwhile, Tommy Jacobs, a handsome, 10-year veteran of the tour best remembered for his record-tying 64 in the second round of the U.S. Open at Washington, D.C., in 1964, was making his presence felt in another area.

Jacobs ran in an eagle at the long 13th and registered a third round 70 which placed him in a tie with Nicklaus at 216. Big Jack continued to miss putts that he normally made.

The 36-hole leaders, Harney and Butler, had faded badly. Now Palmer and Hogan were tied at 218, only two shots out of the lead, and level with them was the husky, long-hitting Brewer, hardly noticed although he had won four tour tournaments since the fall of 1965. Sanders remained a threat at 219. Between this group and the leaders was another player drawing virtually no attention, raw-boned Don January at 217.

Brewer, paired with Palmer, turned a deaf ear to the chants and screams of Arnie's Army and proceeded to shoot into the temporary last round lead with a 33, three under par, on the front nine. Palmer stuck close with a 34. Hogan, January and Sanders faded. Sweeping down the torturous back nine, Brewer was in front—refusing to be shaken by the growing pressure—and Nicklaus and Jacobs both had a chance.

Then the tournament reached its climax on a note of high drama. Of the leaders, Brewer and Palmer were the first to reach the 72nd green, a tough, uphill par four. Brewer was one under par and Palmer two over. Brewer's approach rolled to the back of the green, 60 feet from the pin. He had to get down in two if he hoped for a clear-cut victory. He putted. The ball swerved and stopped seven feet past the cup. He stroked the putt for his par well but the ball hung on the left lip of the cup. He had to settle for a 72 and a score of 288, even par. Dejected, he plopped himself on the side of the green, head in his arms, to await developments.

Out on the course, tension was mounting. Jacobs had birdied the 15th and now needed only par the rest of the way to tie. Nicklaus also got his bird at the par-five 15th and now also was level with Brewer in relation to par. The gallery—and a national television audience—steeled itself for the exciting finish.

At the final hole, Jacobs, needing a par four to tie, hit his drive off the toe of his club and sent the ball into the rough at the bottom of the hill. Then he produced a magnificent four-wood shot that bounded on the green and spun back to within ten feet of the cup. He missed his bird but got a par for a tie.

Nicklaus, playing just behind at the 400-yard 17th, sent a nine-iron shot to within three feet of the cup. A birdie here and a par on the final hole would clinch the title. But Jack's putting miseries attacked him again. He missed. He slammed a booming drive on the last hole and laced his approach 40 feet past the pin. He needed two putts to get down. The Masters had its second three-way tie in history. In 1962, Palmer had won a similar play-off over Gary Player and Dow Finster-wald. This time, Palmer and Sanders were tied at 290, two srokes back.

The 18-hole play-off on Monday was anti-climactic. Only about 12,000 fans showed up for the spectacle, and most of these were season ticket holders. The day was warm and sunny, conditions ideal.

"I've had three chances to win this tournament and blown them," Nicklaus said. "I hope I don't blow it again. It seems that nobody wanted to win this one."

Everybody was now convinced that Nicklaus would take it—everybody, that is, except the mild-mannered Jacobs. Tommy ran home a 25-foot putt on the first hole and stepped off to a quick lead. Nicklaus caught him with a birdie at the second hole and Brewer, bogeying, began losing ground that he could never regain. It seemed that Brewer was suffering from the after-effects of his three-putt nightmare on the 72nd hole the day before.

Jacobs played Nicklaus shot for shot on the outgoing nine but as the threesome turned into the back side it became obvious that this time Big Jack's strength and talent were not to be denied. At the 11th, Nicklaus sank a 25-foot putt for a birdie and moved ahead for the first time. He increased this advantage to two when Jacobs bogeyed the 12th. It was at this 155-yard teaser, with a small target, water in front and a steep bank in back, that all hope died for Brewer. He hit his tee shot into the water and took a double bogey five.

Jacobs went boldly for his birdie on the par five 15th and made it but Nicklaus knocked in a 15-foot, downhill putt to remain two strokes in front. Refusing to give ground, Big Jack played on in with a two-under-par 70. Jacobs shot 72 and Brewer, despite a pair of comeback birdies, finished with 78.

Nicklaus thus wrote another record into the tournament of the green coats. In 1963, at the age of 23, he had become the youngest man ever to win the Masters. Two years later, in 1965, he set the 72-hole record with 271, seventeen under par. Now he had become the first ever to put Masters titles back-to-back.

Jack attributed the play-off victory to a last-minute change in putting technique.

"I watched the replay of Sunday's matches on television," he explained. "I noticed that my eyes were not directly on the line of flight of the putt. I went out and practiced putting until dark Sunday. It made all the difference in the world."

Nicklaus' caddie for the last six years, Willie, got a check for $3,000.

"I saw this boy in 1959 when he was an amateur and I knew he would be the greatest golfer in the world," Willie said. "He is. He'll be winning the Masters for the next ten or fifteen years and we got a deal to stick together. You might say, I got a pretty good annuity here."

Index

A. G. Spalding Co., 15
A. 1 ball, 15
Aaron, Tommy, 226
Adair, Perry, 74
Adair, Rhona, 181
Age of Steel, 84
Agrippa Ball, 15
Agrippa Mold, 15
Air Academy Golf Club, 277
All-American Open, 91, 290, 309
All-America Women's Tournament, 154
Allegheny Country Club, 154
Alliss, Percy, 72
Alliss, Peter, 221
Alps, 249
Alves, Grange, 214
Amateur Golf Association of the U.S., 298
Amateur Public Links Championship, creation of, 201–203
American Amateur: see U.S. Amateur
American Ascendancy, Era of, 177
American Classic, 272–273
American Express, 234
American Golf Association, 298
America's Golf Cup, 138; development of, 231–232
American Open, 215
Amory, Joyce Wethered: see Wethered, Joyce
Anderson, James, 176, 223
Anderson, John G., 302
Anderson, Willie, 44–47, 88, 102, 167–169, 269
Apawanis Club, 44, 46, 68, 169
Appel, Joseph, 302
Apple Tree Gang, the, 34–35, 189
Ardmore Open, 154
Ardsley Club, 205
Argentina, 234, 241
Armour, Estelle, 307
Armour, Tommy, 60, 74, 81, 87,

95, 148, 177, 197–199, 219, 223, 269, 307
Armstrong, Arthur, 202
Arnie's Army, 122–123, 125, 133, 139, 141, 159, 162
Aronimink Golf Club, 156
Asociacion Meixicana De Golf, 231
Associated Press, the, Athlete of the Year of, 91; women athletes of the Year of, 155
Astor, John Jacob, 35
Atlanta Athletic Club, 75
Atlantic City Country Club, 48, 169, 210
Auchterlonie, Laurie, 169
Auchterlonies, 14, 21
Augusta National Golf Club, 64, 101, 119, 123, 132, 141; formation of, 183–186, 214, 242, 250–252, 260–261; description of, 267–268, 290, 292–293, 306
Augusta National Invitation (later the Masters), 186
Aulbach, George, 201
Australia, 16, 178, 234–235, 241
Australian Open, 157, 182
Avery, Nathaniel (Iron Man), 130
Aylmer, Colin, 224

B. F. Goodrich Co., 15
Badminton Book, 176
Baker, Ann, 208
Ball, John, 176, 179
Balloon Ball, 16
Baltimore Country Club, 226
Baltusrol Club, 44, 46, 78, 88, 95, 105, 116, 118, 169, 203, 212, 276
Banff Country Club, 261, 277
Barber, General Thomas, 298
Barber, Jerry, 17, 199
Barnes, Jim, 51–52, 56, 68, 76, 177; 1st PGA champion, 196–198; 219, 281, 302, 307, 310

Barnum, John, 215
Barrett, Beatrice, 206
Barron, Herman, 215
Barton, Pamela, 206
Bath, 150
Bauer, Alice, 152, 211, 305
Bauer, Marlene, 152, 211, 217, 305
Baxter, Rex, 217
Bayer, George, 163
Beack, John, 226
Beaconsfield Golf Club, 234
Beard, Frank, 158
Beardsley Park, 68
Belgium, 311
Bell, Judy, 229
Belle Meade Country Club, 215
Bellerive Country Club, 156, 158–159, 252; description of, 274–275
Belmont, Oliver, 35
Belmont Springs Country Club, 206
Belt, the, 30, 40
Bemen, Deane, 181, 193, 226, 242–243
Berckmans, Baron Prosper Jules Alphonse, 184–185, 267
Berg, Patty, career of, 151–152, 206, 210, 305–306
Berthellyn Cup, 150
Bethpage State Park, 202
Beverly Country Club, 206
Big Double, of Mickey Wright, 154
Big Three (Hogan, Nelson, Snead), 88
Big Three (Palmer, Player, Nicklaus), 141, 158, 313
Bing Crosby Tournament, 161, 309
Bird, May, 205
Birmingham Country Club, 199, 277
Biscelli, Fred, 68
Bishop, Ted, 203

Black, Joe, 209
Blackwell, Ted, 48, 180
Blakely, Willie, 216
Boca Raton Country Club, 277
Boit, Florence, 35
Bolstad, Lester, 202
Bolt, Tommy, 119, 156, 277
Bonallack, Sally, 230
Boros, Julius, 108, 118, 133, 139, 234, 276–277, 310
Bounding Billies, 15
Bourne, Alfred, 184, 214
Bowles, Jerome P. Jr., 231
Boyd, Tom, 197
Brady, Mike, 50, 60, 169
Brae Burn, 60, 62, 79, 229
Braid, Jamie, 40, 176
Breckenridge Park, 117, 307
Brentwood Country Club, 147–148
British Amateur, 48–49, 74, 76, 78, 80, 86–87, 119, 171; development of, 179–181, 191, 193, 223–224, 226, 298
British Ladies' Championship, 148–149; development of, 181–182, 206–207, 210, 299
British Ladies' Golf Union, 228
British Open, 17, 21–22; 1st champion of, 30; 38, 40, 42–43, 57, 59–60, 62–63; won by Sarazen, 66–67; Hagen's 1st try at, 70; 72, 74, 76, 78–80, 95–96, 102, 108–109, 124, 133, 139, 156–158, 161–162, 167–168, 171; development of, 174–179; 182–183, 215, 219, 241, 254, 273, 281, 286, 298, 290, 314
British PGA, 221
Broadmoor Golf Club, 137, 229, 261, 277
Brooklawn Club, 70
Brookline: see The Country Club
Brooks, Arlene, 217
Brown, Mrs. Charles, 204–205
Brown, David, 46, 169
Brown, Eric, 109
Brownlow, W. G., 180
Bruning, Barbara, 217
Buffalo Country Club, 170, 229, 277
Buick Open, 161
Burke, Billy, 100, 187
Burke, Jack Jr., 119, 121, 159
Burkemo, Walter, 199
Burma Road, 262
Burning Tree, 242
Byers, Eben, 48, 223
Byrd, Sam, 93

Caddy, evolution of, 7
Calamity Jane (Jones' Putter), 186

Calcutta Pool, earliest form of, 4
Calumet Club, 298
Campbell, Alex, 54
Campbell, Bill, 194, 226
Campbell, Dorothy, 206, 306
Campbell, Frank, 203
Canada, 10, 16, 32, 223–224, 231–232, 234, 243
Canada Cup, 17, 134, 140, 156, 158; development of, 233–234; 236–237, 241, 243, 261, 283–284
Canadian Open, 105, 150, 197, 221
Canroe Brook Country Club, 206
Canterbury, 73, 87, 277
Cantrell, Warren, 303
Capps, Howard, 309
Carlsmith, Merrill, 216
Carnoustie, 103, 108–109, 150, 176, 178, 181
Carr, Joe, 181
Carter, Ed, 309, 311
Cascades Inn, 99
Cascades, the, 277
Casper, Billy, 109, 118–119, 159, 199, 276, 286, 310
Cassidy, Hopalong, 314
Cavemen, theoretical origin of golf, 3
Caven, John, 224
Centennial Anniversary British Open, 125
Cerda, Antonio, 234
Challenge Golf, 127
Champion Belt, the, of Prestwick, 174–175
Champions Course, 277
Championship Cup, 177
Chapman, Richard, 181
Charles I, 8
Charles II, 8
Charles, Bob, 133, 139, 179, 241, 313–314
Cheney, Mrs. L. D., 229
Cherry, Don, 231
Cherry Hills, 88, 109, 124, 137, 277
Chevy Chase Country Club, 229
Chi Chi's Bandidos, 159
Chicago Club, 35–37, 44, 167, 169, 189, 226, 298
Choate, Allison, 216
Chole, early Belgian golf, 4–5
Choulla (see Chole)
Christy, Andy, 62
Ciuci, Al, 68
Civil War, the, 32, 50, 184
Clark, Captain Charles, 214
Clark, Clive, 226–227
Clark, Jimmy, 203
Clark, Tom, 215
Cleveland Country Club, 86, 277
Cleveland Open, 161

Club Campestre, 232
Coe, Charles, 137, 193–194, 226, 231–232, 242, 284
Coleman, Fay, 82
Collett, Glenna, 150–151, 181, 206, 208, 216, 228–229, 306
Colonial Country Club, 105, 277
Colt, H. S., 249
Columbia Country Club, 76, 235
Columbus Country Club, 162
Commonwealth countries, 16–17
Company of Gentlemen Golfers: see Edinburgh Golfers
Compston, Archie, 220
Congressional Country Club, 159, 274, 276
Conley, Peggy, 208
Conrad, Joe, 181
Cooper, Lighthorse Harry, 74, 81, 87, 95, 134
Corcoran, Fred, 82, 84, 100, 114, 211, 233–234, 305, 308–310, 314
Corlett, Elsie, 229
Cornelius, Kathy, 211
Cossar, Simon, 19
Cotton, Henry, 17, 178
Cowan, Gary, 243
Cox, Robert, 205
Crampton, Bruce, 139
Crawford, McGregor and Canby Co., 23
Creed, Clifford Ann, 230
Crews, Mrs. John: see Orcutt, Maureen
Cricket Influence, the, 18
Crocker, Fay, 212
Crosby, Bing, 100, 266
Cruickshank, Bobby, 72, 77, 307
Crump, George, 249, 256
Cryder, Duncan, 35, 190
Cupit, Jackie, 276
Curtis Cup, 27, 144, 205, 216; development of, 228–230; inscription on, 228
Curtis, Harriot, 205–206, 228
Curtis, Laurence, 35, 298
Curtis, Margaret, 205–206, 228, 306
Cypress Point, 148, 277

Dallas Athletic Club, 277
Daniels, Skip, 72
Danoff, Bettye Mims, 211, 305
Darwin, Bernard, 40, 295
Davies, Richard, 181
Davis Cup, 241
Dawson, Johnny, 216, 299
Deal, 176–177
Decker, Mrs. Anne Quast: see Quast, Anne
Decker, Mrs. Jay D., 208
Deepdale Country Club, 277
de Maglione, Margarita, 154

Demaret, Jimmy, 88, 90, 103, 130, 164, 188, 199, 234, 261, 310
DeMoss, Grace, 229
Dempsey, Jack, 74, 146, 274
Denver Open, 164
Detroit Country Club, 277
Dettweiler, Helen, 305
DeVicenzo, Roberto, 109, 129, 234, 241
Devlin, Bruce, 242, 314
Dey, Joseph C., 156, 211, 241, 299
Dickinson, Gardner, 117
Dickson, Andrew, 9, 18
Diegel, Leo, 60, 63, 74, 80, 95, 198–199, 220, 308
DiMaggio, Joe, struckout by Babe Zaharias, 147
Dimples, nicks on ball, 14
Donald, Jean, 149, 181, 229
Dorado Beach, 164, 236, 252, 261; description of, 261–262
Doral Country Club, 277
Doubleday, Abner, 32
Douglas, Dave, 291
Douglas, Findlay, 48, 191
Douglas, Robert, 174
Dowling, Jack, 196
Druid Hills, 211
Dudley, Ed., 164, 185, 187, 242
Duke of Windsor, 55, 62, 284
Duke University Golf Club, 277
Duncan, George, 59, 219–220
Dunes, the, 277
Dunn, Jamie, 11, 30
Dunn, Willie, 11, 30, 35, 167, 190
Durham, James, 11
Dutra, Olin, 73, 147, 258

East Lake Course, 38, 43, 74–75, 220, 277
East Potomac Park, 201–202
Eastern Open, 150
Eclipse Putty Ball, 15
Eden, 249, 254
Edgar, J. Douglas, 197
Edinburgh Golfers, Honourable Company of, 10, 27, 40, 176
Edinburgh, Town Council of, Sunday Law of, 9; 10
Edward VIII: see Duke of Windsor
Eisenhower, Dwight D., 241–242
Eisenhower Trophy, 132; creation of, 241–243, 258
Eller, Judy, 217, 229
Engineers Country Club, 197, 223
England, 3, 6–11, 41, 47, 78, 191, 228–229, 234, 249, 311
England, King of, 55, 283
English Invasion, Era of, 176
Ennever Golf Club, 302
Epsie, J. Clark, 215

Espinosa, Al, 79, 220, 276, 287, 307
Espinosa, Jo, 307
Essex Country Club, 44, 167, 205–206, 298
Estrada, Juan Antonio, 243
Euclid Club, 191
Eureka Ball, 14
Evans, Chick, 49, 54, 62, 68, 79, 170, 191, 193–194, 196, 223–224
Evanston Golf Club, 216

Fairfield, Don, 272
Farrell, Johnny, 54, 57, 70, 79, 220
Farwell, John B., estate of, 35
Faulkner, Max, 178
Fazio, George, 66, 108, 284–285
Feather Balls, 12–15, 20, 28, 144, 247
Ferguson, Bob, 21, 176
Ferrera, Charley, 202
Ferrier, Jim, 197, 199
Finsterwald, Dow, 119, 199
Firestone Country Club, 139, 199, 252; description of, 271–273
Fisher, John, 226
Fishwick, Diana, 181
Five Farms Country Club, 277
Fleck, Jack, 109, 112, 118, 271, 276
Flood, Val, 215
Florida Country Club, 216
Flossmoor Country Club, 78
Forbes, Duncan, 10
Ford, Doug, 119, 291
Forest Hills Country Club, 154
Forest Park, 202
Forgan, Robert, 21–22
Forgotten Middles, the, 118
Forrester, Jack, 197
Fotheringham, George, 302
Foulis, Dave, 15
Foulis, James, 167
Fownes, William C. Jr., 223–224
Fox, Valerie, 102, 105, 109
France, 3, 181, 228, 237, 311
Fraser, Alexa Stirling: see Stirling, Alexa
Frearson, Mrs. Alastair, 229
French Amateur, won by Ouimet, 54
French, Emmett, 187, 197
French Golf Union, 228
French Lick Spring Golf Course, 198
French Open, 58, 150, 182
Fresh Meadows, 72,
Fruitlands (Augusta National), 184
Fuji Golf Course, 242
Furgol, Ed., 116, 118, 234–235

Gaguin, Jim, 309
Garden City Club, 48–49, 191, 225

Gardner, Bob, 75–76, 137, 223–224 242
Garvey, Philomena, 181, 229
Gavin, Mrs. W. A., 150
General Dynamics, 233, 236
General Electric, 23
Germany, 234, 241
Ghezzi, Vic, 277
Ginger Beer Hole, 29
Girl With a Golf Club, portrait of, 144
Glen Cove Club, 48
Glen Garden Country Club, 105
Glen View Club, 46
Glenna Collett Vare Trophy, 152, 155, 306
Goff, Captain of, 10
Gold Dust Twins, 91
Golden Bear (Jack Nicklaus), 132–133, 141, 283–284
Golden Horseshoe, 277
Golden, Jimmy, 187
Golden, John, 197, 220
Goggin, Willie, 198
Golf, Articles and Laws in playing, 294
Golf Hall of Fame, of the LPGA, 155, 306
Golf House: see U.S.G.A. Museum
Golf Inn, 41
Goodman, Johnny, 79, 84, 100, 171, 226
Gordon, George, 214
Gordon, Jacqueline, 149, 181
Gosford, 7
Gould, Alan, 293
Gourlay Ball, 14
Gourlay Family, 14, 19
Gourlay, Molly, 229
Graham, Archibald, 49
Grainger, Isaac, 97
Grand Slam, 74, 80, 82, 84, 86, 103, 123, 125, 177–178, 181, 184, 191, 226, 258, 267, 273, 284, 287–288
Great Triumvirate, Era of the, 176
Greenbriar Hotel and Country Club, 99–100, 117, 206, 277
Green Monster (Augusta), 143
Greig, William, 175
Griscom, Frances, 205
Grout, Jack, 136
Guilford, Jesse, 16, 224
Guldahl, Ralph, 64, 86, 88–89, 97
Gullane, 149, 181
Gunderson, JoAnne, 208, 217, 229
Gunn, Watts, 78, 191
Gutta Percha Balls, 14–15, 20–22, 28, 33–34, 42, 247
Gutties: see Gutta Percha Balls

Haas, Freddie, 91
Hagen, Era of, 197

Hagen, Walter, 51–52; career of, 56–63; 64, 70, 74, 78, 82, 87, 95, 104, 108, 116, 134, 158, 160, 170, 177, 187, 196–199, 202, 219–220, 254, 269, 281, 288, 293, 307–308, 310
Haig, the: see Hagen, Walter
Hale American Open, 105
Hamilton Golf Club, 223
Handmacher, Albert, 305
Hanson, Beverly, 152, 211
Harbert, Chick, 119, 199, 234
Harding, Warren G., 202
Harding, Warren G., Team Trophy of, 203
Harlow, Bob, 57–58, 308
Harmon, Claude, 103
Harper, Chandler, 199, 290
Harriman, H. M., 191
Harris, Bob, 224
Harris, Labron Jr., 243
Harris, W. W., 302
Harrison, E. J. (Dutch), 215, 290
Haskell Ball, 247–249
Haskell, Coburn, 15
Havemeyer, Theodore A., 35, 37, 298
Havers, Arthur, 177
Hazeltine Country Club, 277
Heafner, Clayton, 270
Heartbreak Corner, 268
Hebert, Jay, 117, 119, 199, 271
Hebert, Lionel, 119
Hecker, Genevieve, 205
Held, Edmund R., 201
Hell's Bunker, 254
Hell's Corner, 141
Henley Ball, 15
Hepburn, James, 302
Herd, Alexander, 42
Herd, Fred, 44, 168
Herd, Sandy, 20
Herron, Davison, 76
Hershey Country Club, 90
Hezlet, May, 181
Hicks, Helen, 210, 229
Higgins, Bill, 216
Higgins, Warren, 216
Hill, C. Alec, 17
Hilton, Harold, 40, 48–49, 180, 191
Hines, Jimmy, 187
Hobens, Jack, 302
Hoblitzel, Fred, 82
Hogan, Ben, 17; explaining Vardon, 43, 44; a 1900 edition of, 46; 64; 66–67, 87–90, 93–94, 96, 98; career of, 102–114; 116, 118–119, 121, 125, 130, 132, 135–136, 142, 157, 159, 162, 169, 178; record in Masters of, 188; 199, 211, 235, 242, 252, 258, 268–270, 276, 284–286, 289–290, 305, 309

Hogan, Valerie: see Fox, Valerie
Holbrook, Harry, 34
Holderness, Ernest, 225
Hole-in-one Club, 301–302
Holland, 3; golf ball tariffs from, 6; 12–14
Holscher, Bud, 117
Holston Hills, 93
Homans, Gene, 82, 191
Homestead Hotel, 99
Honourable Company: see St. Andrews' Golfers
Hooman, C. V. L., 224
Hope, Lord Charles, 223
Hope, Willie, 225
Hopkins, John Jay, 233–235
House of David, Babe Zaharias team member of, 146
House of Lords, 295
Houston Country Club, 277
Houston Open, 117, 309
Hoylake, 80, 176, 181, 224, 247
Hoyt, Beatrix, 151, 205, 306
Hudson, Robert, 220
Hunnewell, Arthur, 35
Hunt, Bernard, 220
Hunter, Paul, 224
Hunter, Willie, 76
Huntington Valley Club, 150
Hurd, Dorothy: see, Campbell, Dorothy
Hutchinson, Horace G., 9, 20–21, 179–180
Hutchinson, Jock, winning British Open, 23; 70, 77, 177, 196–198, 214–215, 302, 307
Hutchinson, Ralph, 286
Hyde, James L. Jr., 303
Hyndman, Bill, 194, 226, 242

Incline Village, 277
Industrial Revolution, 22
Intercollegiate Championship, 49
Interlachen, 80–81, 151, 206
International Canada Cup Trophy, 140, 284
International Challenge Trophy, 224
International Golf Association, development of, 233–234; 236
International Golf Sponsors Association, 303
International Trophy: see Canada Cup
Inverness Country Club, 95, 118, 277
Inverness Invitational for Women, 154
Inwood Country Club, 77, 170, 197
Ireland, 31, 181, 234, 236

Issler, Martin M., 215
Italy, 241, 311

Jack, Reid, 242
Jack's Pack, 162
Jacobs, George, 308
Jacobs, Tommy, 159–160, 217
Jacques, Herbert, 16
James I, introduced golf to England, 8–9; 27
James II, 6
James II (Duke of York), 8–9, 18
James IV, 4–5, 12
James V, playing at Gosford, 7
James VI, 12, 18
Jameson, Betty, 207, 210, 305–306
Jamieson, Andrew, 78
January, Don, 199
Japan, 241–243, 311
Jasper Park, 250, 261
Jeu de Mail: see Pell Mell
John Reid Championship Medal Tournament, 295
Johnstone, Mrs. Ann Casey, 208
Jolly, Jack, 214
Jones, Robert P., 74
Jones, Robert Tyre, forerunner of, 30; 38, 40, 44, 46, 54, 56–58, 60, 62, 64, 66–67, 70, 72; career of, 74–84; 86–87, 94–95, 102, 104, 108, 116, 119, 121, 132, 134–135, 137–138, 143, 146, 169–171, 176–177, 180–181; develops Augusta, 183–186; 191, 206, 214, 220, 223–224, 226, 242, 250, 254, 258, 267–269, 276, 284, 287–288, 308
Juniper Hole, 290

Kasumigaseki Club, 236
Kauffmann, Karl F., 202
Keeler, O. B., 77, 83, 287, 293
Kerrigan, Tom, 196
Kesselring, Jerry, 231
Kidd, Willie, 214
King, Rufus, 193
Kinnan, Alexander P. W., 34
Kirby, Dorothy, 148, 154, 229
Kirk, Peggy, 148, 229
Kirkby, Oswald, 223
Kirkwood, Joe, 219, 308
Kitansett Country Club, 277
Knepper, Rudolf, 224
Knollwood Country Club, 191
Kolf (Dutch golf), 4
Knight, A. W., 48
Knoxville Open, 93
Kroll, Ted, 271

Ladies' Golf Hall of Fame: see Golf Hall of Fame
Ladies' Golf Union, 181
Ladies' PGA, 151–152, 154, 210–211; development of, 305–306

Ladies' PGA Championship, 155
Ladies' PGA, Executive Committee of, 306
Ladies' Professional tour, 144; development of, 305
LaGorce Open, 308
La Jolla Country Club, 153
Lakewood Country Club, 298
Lamb, Henry, 20
Landale, Bailie William, 174
Larchmont Country Club, 68
Lard, Allan, 23
Latrobe Country Club, 129
Laurel Valley Country Club, 130
Laval-sur-leLac Golf Club, 234
Lawrence, W. G., 36, 189–190, 297
Leed, Herbert, 189
Leitch, 150, 181
Leith Links, 9–10, 27, 174
Lema, Champagne Tony, 117–118, 158; career of, 160–162; 163, 179, 274, 310, 313–314
Lema's Legion, 162
Leonard, Stan, 234, 236
Lesser, Pat, 217
Lewis, Charles, 137
Lily Pad Shot, of B. Jones, 81
Lind, Dean, 216
Lindrick Golf Club, 229
Little, Lawson, 23, 66, 73, 84, 86, 100, 171, 181, 191, 193, 226, 254, 277
Littler, Gene, 84, 116–117, 138–139, 226, 272
Llanerch Country Club, 199
Lloyd, Joe, 44, 167
Locke, Bobby, 60, 178, 199, 234, 241
Lockhart, Robert, 33–34
Lockwood, Arthur, 298
London Hunt and Country Club, 231
Long Hole, 254–255
Lord Brabazon, 295
Los Angeles Country Club, 277
Los Angeles Open, 100, 107, 126, 138, 307, 309
Low, Carrie, 34, 144
Low, George, 114
Lowery, Eddie, 52, 118, 121
Lucky International, 164

McAuliffe, Ray, 202
McCormack, Mark, 310, 313–314
McDermott, Johnny, 46, 50, 56, 88, 95, 169–170, 281
McElroy, Walter, 231
McEwen, Douglas, 19, 21
McEwen, Peter, 19, 21
McHale, Jim, 226
McIntyre, Barbara, 181–182, 217
McLean, Edward B., 308

McLemore, Henry, 293
McLeod, Fred, 197, 215
McMahon, Thomas J., 299–300
McNamara, Tommy, 50, 307
McSpaden, Harold (Jug), 88, 91
MacClain, E. M., 23
MacDonald, Charles Blair, 35–37, 189–190, 249, 297–298
MacFarlane, Willie, 54, 78, 197
Macfie, Allan Fullarton, 179
MacKay, Pauline, 205
MacKenzie, Alister, 185, 250
MacKenzie, Willis, 224–225
Mackey, Lee, 108
Mackie, Jack, 302
Maiden, James, 75, 302
Maiden, Stewart, 38, 75, 78
Malone, Mary, 78
Manero, Tony, 88, 95, 97
Mangrum, Lloyd, 88, 90, 108, 142, 277, 284–285
Mann, Willie, 38
Manufacturers' Golf and Country Club, 216
Marr, Dave, 131, 159
Marston, Max, 78, 223–225
Martin, Fred, 99
Mary, Queen of Scots, 7, 144
Massachusetts State Amateur, 54
Master, The, 64; speed record at, 66; 67, 84, 87–90, 100, 102, 104–105, 108–110, 119, 121, 123–124, 126, 130, 132–134, 139, 141, 156–159, 164, 178–179; development of, 183–188; 199, 214, 221, 242, 252, 267–268, 273, 286, 288, 290, 292, 304, 309–311, 314
Maxwell, Billy, 117, 299
May, George, 290–292, 309
Mayer, Dick, 118
Mayne, William, 14, 18
Mead, Edward S., 35, 190
Meadow Brook Club, 204–205, 277, 298
Medinah Country Club, 97, 277
Mehlhorn, Bill, 70, 198, 219–220, 308
Melfort Ball, 14
Melvill, James, 8, 14
Memphis Country Club, 215
Meridian Hills Country Club, 208
Merion Cricket Club, 75, 78, 82, 104, 107, 132, 137, 191, 242, 251–252; description of, 258–260; 269, 284
Metz, Dick, 88
Mexico, 138, 231–232, 234
Miami Country Club, 203, 277
Miami Open, 309
Middlecoff, Cary, 64, 66, 84, 98, 109, 118–119, 269, 277
Middlesboro Club, 34

Midlothian Country Club, 62, 168, 206
Miguel, Angel, 236
Miguel, Sebastian, 237, 283–284
Milwaukee Country Club, 277
Minikahda Country Club, 79
Minneapolis Golf Club, 199
Mitchell, David, 202
Monster, the (Oakland Hills), 252
Monster, the, at Firestone, 273
Montrose, Marquis of, 9
Moore, Archie, 104
Moraine Country Club, 91
Morey, Dale, 194
Morgan, J. Pierpont, 298
Morgan, Wanda, 229
Morris County Country Club, 205
Morris Era, 175
Morris, Old Tom, 11, 14, 21, 27–30, 33, 175, 297
Morris, Young Tom, 21–22, 30, 35, 40, 175–176, 297
Mount Pleasant Park Golf Course, 202
Muirfield, 10, 40, 42, 78, 137, 176, 180, 223
Murphy, Bob, 194
Murray, Father Francis, 159
Murray, William, 225
Musial, Stan, 309, 314
Musselburgh Links, 10, 27, 29–31, 42, 150, 176
Myopia Hunt Club, 46, 168–169

Nagle, Kel, 125, 156, 158, 178, 234, 236, 241, 254
Nakamura, Torakichi (Pete), 236, 243
National AAU and Olympic Tryouts, entered by Babe Zaharias, 144
National Amateur: see U.S. Amateur
National Golf Club Championship, 301
National Golf Club Match Play Championship, 301
National Golf Day, 301
National Golf Foundation, 311
National Golf Fund, Inc., 301
National Golf Links of America, 224, 249–250, 277
National Open: see U.S. Open
National Women's Amateur: see U.S. Women's Amateur
National Women's Open: see U.S. Women's Open
Nationalist China, 243
Nelson, Byron, 87–94, 97, 105, 132, 134, 182, 188, 199, 277, 282–283, 305
New Orleans Open, 70

Newport Club, 35–37, 167, 189–190, 204, 297–298
Newport Tournament, 189–190
News of the World Championship, 196, 302
New York Metropolitan Amateur Championship, 48
New Zealand, 16, 241–242
Nichols, Bobby, 159; career of, 162–163; 200
Nichols, Gil, 46, 302
Nichols, Joe, 202
Nicklaus, Jack, 64, 66, 84, 94, 101–102, 121, 123, 125–126, 130; career of, 132–143; 156, 158–164, 171, 179, 182; Masters record, 188; 193, 199–200, 217, 232, 237, 242, 247, 258, 266–267, 273–275, 277, 283–284, 309–310, 312–314
Nicklaus, L. Charles, 136
North and South Open, 89, 105, 308
North and South Women's Open, 150, 152
North Berwick Course, 30
North Hills Country Club, 277
North Shore Country Club, 84
Number 2 (of Pinehurst), 251, 263–264

Oak Hill, 277
Oakland Course, 48
Oakland Hills, 78, 88, 96–97, 103, 108, 117, 138, 252; description of, 269–270
Oakland Open, 100, 105, 309
Oakmont, 76, 78–79, 87, 95, 98, 108, 133, 139, 197, 276
O'Brien, Jack, 307
O'Brien, Ray, 309
Ocobo Ball, 15
Oconomowoc Club, 46
Odell, General Jacob, 189–190
Ogden Country Club, 155
Ogden, Phil, 202
Ohio Open, 137
O. K. Ball, 15
Oklahoma City Open, 130, 161
Old Tom Morris Ball, 14
Old Warson Country Club, 277
Oliver, Ed (Porky), 106
Olympia Fields, 79, 98, 199, 277
Olympic Club, 109, 193, 232, 251, 276
Olympics, entered in by Babe Zaharias, 146–147; 207, 210, 299
Ono, Koichi, 236, 243
Open Championship Cup, 167, 171
Orange County Open, 161
Orcutt, Maureen, 148, 206, 216, 229

Ormiston, George, 223
Ottawa Park, 201
Ottawa Hunt and Golf Club, 232
Ouimet Caddy Scholarship, 55
Ouimet, Francis, 38, 43; winning 1913 U.S. Open, 51–53; career of, 54–55; 56, 68, 74, 76, 82, 84, 170, 191, 193, 201, 223–225, 276, 281–282, 299, 302
Outing, a Casper Whitney magazine, 288

Pace, Frank Jr., 235–236
Paganica, Roman golf, 3
Page, Mrs. Estelle Lawson, 148
Page, Mrs. Julius A. Jr., 152
Palmer, Arnold, 17; qualities associated with, 30; 59–60, 62, 84, 94, 100, 110, 117–119, 121; career of, 122–131; 132–135, 137–141, 143, 156–164, 171–172, 178–179, 182, 188, 199, 220–221, 236–237, 247, 254, 266–268, 273–274, 276, 283–284, 286–287, 310, 312–314
Palmer Method, 164
Palmer, Milfred (Deac), 127
Palmer, Winnie: see Walzer, Winnie
Palm Springs Golf Classic, 159
Pan American Airways, 234
Park, Doris, 229
Park, Willie Jr., 21
Park, Willie Sr., 22, 27, 29; 1st British Open champ., 30; 174–176
Park's Special Ball, 15
Parks, Sam Jr., 87
Parris, Samuel, 298
Paterson, Reverend Dr. Robert, 14
Patersone, John, 9
Paterson's Patent, 14
Patton, Billie Joe, 121, 226, 231, 242–243, 288–290
Pauma Valley Country Club, 277
Peachtree Golf Club, 250, 277
Pearson, Isette, 150, 181
Pebble Beach, 79, 132, 138, 251–252, 261; description of, 265–266
Pelham Golf Club, 197
Pell Mell, early French golf, 5
Perfect Foot Roll, of Sam Snead, 101
Perkins, Phil, 72, 79, 226
Pfeil, George, 299
Philadelphia Country Club, 217, 277; Spring Mill course of, 282; 298
Philadelphia Phillies, 62
Philp, Hugh, 19, 21
Picard, Henry, 187
Pinehurst Country Club, 105, 251–252; description of, 263–264; 308

Pine Valley, 226, 249, 252; description of, 256–257
Pittsfield Club, 46, 168
Platt, J. Wood, 215, 224
Player, Gary, 17, 67, 126, 130, 138, 141, 143; career of, 156–158; 178, 182, 197, 199, 241, 268, 271, 273, 277, 283–284, 310, 313
Point O' Woods, 277
Port St. Lucie Country Club, 215
Porter, Mrs. Mark A., 229
Pott, Johnny, 272
Potter, Thomas Owen, 179
Powers, Francis J., 308
Pressler, Mrs. Leona, 151
Prestwick, 21–22, 27–31, 42–43, 86–87, 174–176, 179, 247
Prestwick Era, 175–176
Preuss, Phyllis, 230
Price, Elizabeth, 229
Professional Golfers Association (PGA), 38, 84, 100, 114; 72-hole record of, 117; creation of, 196; 214, 219, 233, 234, 272, 282, 292; development of, 301–304, 306, 308–309
PGA Championship, 17, 57, 60, 63, 66–67, 70, 72, 87, 90–91, 96, 106, 125, 130, 133–134, 139, 156, 159, 162, 179; development of, 196–200; 214, 221, 234, 271, 273, 301–302, 310–311
PGA, Executive Committee of, 221
PGA National Club, 215, 303
PGA National Headquarters, 303
PGA Seniors, 67; development of, 214–215
Pronation, 112–113
Pulver, P. C., 302
Pung, Mrs. Jacqueline, 207, 212
Putnam, Kingman, 34

Quarry Hole, 259
Quarter Century Club Championship, 301
Quast, Anne, 208, 217, 229
Quick, Smiley, 203

Ragan, Dave, 117–118, 139
Rancho Santa Fe Open, 100
Rattray, John, 10
Ravenscroft, Gladys, 206
Rawlins, Horace, 167
Rawls, Betsy, 152, 155, 211–212, 306
Ray, Ted, 38, 43, 50; losing 1913 U.S. Open to F. Ouimet, 51–53; 56, 64, 68, 74, 76, 95, 170, 201, 223, 276, 281–282, 299
Raynor, Harvey, 309
Redan, 249, 259
Red Cross Open, 91

Rees, Dai, 109, 254
Reid, John, 32–35, 37, 144, 189, 249, 298
Reid, Mrs. John, 34, 144
Reid, Wilfred, 50–51, 281
Revolta, Johnny, 86, 91, 309
Revolutionary War, the, 32
Rice, Grantland, 147, 287–288, 293
Richardson, Bill, 293
Richmond County Country Club, 298
Riegel, Skee, 226, 299
Riley, Polly, 154, 210
Riviera Country Club (Hogan's Alley), 106–107, 277
Road Hole of St. Andrews, 242, 249, 254–255
Robbins, Thomas C., 216
Robert Forgan Ball, 14
Roberts, Clifford, 183–186, 188, 286
Roberts, Jean, 230
Robertson, Allan, 11, 14, 22, 28–30
Robertson, Davie, 14
Robinson, Sugar Ray, 104
Rochester Country Club, 56, 62, 208, 211
Rodgers, Phil, 139, 217
Rodriguez, Juan (Chi Chi), 159; career of, 163–164
Rogers, Jason, 302
Rolland, Douglas, 179
Rolling Hills Country Club, 211
Romack, Barbara, 154, 208, 217
Roman Legionnaires; played earliest form of golf, 3
Rosburg, Bob, 117, 128, 199
Roslyn Country Club; scene of 1920 U.S. Amateur, 54; 76
Ross, Donald J., 249, 263
Rotan, George, 225
Royal and Ancient: see St. Andrews, Royal and Ancient Club
Royal Automobile Club, 295
Royal Blackheath; first English course, 8–9; 27, 30
Royal Canadian Golf Association, 223, 231
Royal Kaanapali, 140, 277
Royal Liverpool Club, 31, 179
Royal Lytham; scene of 1926 British Open, 60; 176–177, 181, 219–220, 288
Royal Montreal Club, 33
Royal North Devon, 31
Royal St. George's Club, 31, 48, 176
Royal Warrant; as clubmaker, 18
Rubber Golf Balls, 15, 20, 22
Rucker, Betty Jean, 148
Rudolph, Mason, 216–217
Runyan, Paul (Little Poison), 86, 186–187, 198, 215, 309

Russia, 22
Ruth, Babe, 74, 146
Ryan, Nan Berry, 306
Ryder Cup; forerunner of, 8; 17, 57, 67, 87; creation of, 219–222, 228
Ryder, Samuel A., 219, 221
Ryerson, Arthur, 298

Sacramento Open, 309
St. Andrew's; birthplace of golf, 7; 27–31, 33, 40, 42, 62, 76, 78–80, 95, 125, 161–162, 174, 176–179, 181, 190, 225–226, 242, 250–255, 263
St. Andrews Golfers, Society of, 10, 19; Royal and Ancient title granted, 28; 174
St. Andrews, Ladies Golf Club of, 144, 150
St. Andrews, Museum of Royal and Ancient Club of, 186
St. Andrews, Old Course of, 27–29, 249–252; description of, 253–255; 297
St. Andrews, Royal and Ancient Club, 8; rules of, 10; 12–13; size of ball dispute, 16–17; 18, 20–22; on shape and number of clubs, 23–24, 27, 35, 40, 48, 50; Ouimet elected captain of, 54–55; 144, 167, 224, 241, 254, 294–296, 298
St. Anne's-on-the-Sea, 42, 60, 78, 86, 133, 139, 176–177, 179, 181, 219–220, 288
St. Augustine Open, 309
St. Louis Country Club, 97, 150
Saint-nom-la-Breteche, 140, 283
St. Paul Junior Chamber of Commerce, 308
St. Petersburg Open, 309
Salem Country Club, 152, 277
Salisbury Course, 160, 198
San Antonio Open, 89
Sande, Earl, 74
Sands, Charles E., 37, 190
Sands, W. H., 205
Sandwich, 40, 42–43, 62; scene of 1933 British Open, 66; 72, 177, 179
San Francisco Open, 309
Saraceni, Federico, 67–68
Sarazen, Gene, 17; using new club to win British and American Opens, 24; 57; career of, 64–73; 74, 77, 84, 87, 108, 116, 130, 134–135; on tour with Babe Zaharias, 147; 153, 157, 160, 170, 177, 182–183, 188, 197–199, 202, 215, 219–220, 254, 269, 274, 277, 290, 292–293
Sargent, George, 215

Sargent, Miss N. C., 205
Saucon Valley Country Club, 231, 277
Savannah Golf Club; archives of, 32
Sayers, Ben, 21
Scarfe, Mrs. Thomas, 221
Schenectady Putter; used by W. Travis, 48; 298
Schneider, George, 309
Scioto Country Club, 78, 136, 220, 277
Scotland; cradle of the game, 3–5; royal deterents in, 6; 10, 22, 29, 33–34, 178, 181, 189, 224, 229, 234, 249, 263, 297–298
Scott, Lady Margaret, 150, 181
Scottish Rifle Volunteer Corps; member of Wimbledon, 31
Sears, Evelyn, 206
Sears, Samuel, 298
Seattle Golf Club, 231
Seaview, Country Club, 277
Seminole Links, 263, 277
Senior-Junior Best Ball Championship, 301
Seniors' Teacher Trophy Championship, 301
Serrick, Bill, 202
Sessions, Sally, 210, 305
Shady Oaks Country Club, 277
Sharkey, Hal, 308
Shawnee Country Club, 198, 206
Sherman, Clara Callender, 148, 207
Shinnecock Hills; first incorporated course, 35; 167, 189–190, 204, 277, 298
Shore Haven Country Club, 277
Shotts, John C., 34
Shute, Denny, 86–87, 89, 97, 177, 186, 282
Sigel, Helen, 148, 229
Sikes, Richard, 202–203, 232, 243
Silver Club; origin of, 174
Simpson, Archie, 180
Simpson, George, 169
Siwanoy Country Club, 196, 302
Skokie Country Club; scene of 1922 U.S. Open, 66; 70, 170
Smith, Alex, 44, 46–47, 49, 95, 150, 168, 191, 307
Smith, A. W., 167
Smith, Horton (Joplin Ghost), 23, 81, 87, 90; first Augusta champion, 186–188; 220, 308
Smith, Macdonald, 23, 46, 51–52, 56, 66, 72, 74, 80–81, 95, 186, 281
Smith, Margaret (Wiffi), 181
Smith, Marilyn, 211, 305
Smith, Willie, 44, 168
Snead, Sam, 17, 64, 88–90; career of, 93–101; 104–105, 107–108,

329

110, 117, 121, 132, 134, 136, 139, 164, 178, 188, 198–199, 215, 234–237, 247, 254, 261, 268, 271, 277, 282, 290, 305, 309, 314
Somerville, Ross, 82
Soncrant, Milton, 202
Sota, Ramon, 237, 283
Souchak, Mike, 116; PGA record of, 117; 125
South Africa, 178, 234, 241
South African Open, 157
Southern California Open, 148
Southern Hills Country Club, 148, 156, 194, 207, 276
Spain, 284, 311
Spalding Wizard, 15
Sparling, George, 70
Spearman, Marley, 229
Spokane Athletic Round Table, 210
Spork, Shirley, 305
Spring Mill Course of Philadelphia Country Club, 282
Spring Mill Country Club, 89, 97
Stafford, Louis, 203
Standish Cup, 201
Standish, James D. Jr., 201
Stanford Golf Club, 277
Starmount Forest Country Club, 210
Stephens, Frances, 229
Stevens, Robert, 242
Stewart, Marlene, 181, 208, 212
Stirling, Alexa, 75, 150–151, 206, 306
Stoddard, Laurence, 36, 189–190, 297
Stone, Beth, 217
Stovepipe, 293
Stranahan, Frank, 109, 119, 181, 226, 231
Streit, Marlene: see Stewart, Marlene
Strong, Herbert W., 302
Studinger, George, 215
Suggs, Louise, 148, 152–153, 181, 211, 229, 305–306
Sunningdale, 78
Super Ball; outlawing of, 17
Sweeny, Robert, 128, 181
Sweetser, Jess, 77–78, 82, 180, 224, 226
Szwedko, Andy, 202

Tallmadge, Henry O., 34, 37, 298
Tam o'Shanter, 152, 154, 290, 292, 309
Taylor, Dr. Frank, 242
Taylor, J. H., 40, 42–43, 168, 176, 288
Taylor, William, 15

Teacher, William and Sons, Ltd., 215
Tellier, Louis, 50, 56, 281
Texas Open, 117, 307
The Country Club, Brookline, Massachusetts, 35, 38; awakens golf in U.S., 50; scene of 1913 U.S. Open, 50–53; 54, 56, 62, 74, 77, 84, 86, 133, 139, 170, 201, 223, 226, 276, 281, 298
Thomas, Lowell, 257
Thomas, W. B., 298
Thompson, Stanley, 250
Thomson, Jimmy, 87
Thomson, Peter, 17, 158, 178, 234–236, 240
Thorp, J. G., 191
Thorpe, Jim, 241
Thunderbird Classic, 110, 139, 161
Tilden, Bill, 74
Tillinghast, A. H., 302
Time-Life Corporation, 234
Titleholders Tournament, 152
Titusville Country Club, 70
Toledo Country Club, 76
Tolley, Cyril, 223–224, 226
Torrance, W. B., 224
Torza, Felice, 199
Tournament of Champions, 117, 130
Townsend, Peter, 226
Trailer Kids, 116, 118
Travers, Jerome D., 44, 46, 49, 54, 170, 191, 223
Travis, Walter J., 15; using new club to win British Amateur, 23; 44, 47–49, 179–180, 191, 298
Troon Golf Club; the big room, 18; 70, 176, 179, 226
Tufts, James, 263
Tufts, Richard S., 55, 263
Turnberry; conference at, 296
Turner, Gilbert, 34
Turnesa, Jim, 234
Turnesa, Joe, 198, 219–220
Turnesa, Mike, 91
Turnesa, Willie, 181, 193, 226
Turnure, Mrs. Arthur, 205
Tutwiler, Ed, 194, 227
Tuxedo Country Club, 298

Union Hardware Company, 23
United States, 11, 16, 22, 32; first course, 33; 35, 37–38, 41, 43, 47, 108, 138, 144, 156, 177, 179, 181, 189, 191, 196–197, 201, 219, 221, 223–226, 228–229, 232, 234, 236–237, 241–243, 249–250, 268, 281–283, 295–297, 311
United States Amateur; first championship, 37; 47; won by J. Travers, 49; 74, 76–79, 82, 86,

116, 119, 123, 128, 132, 137–138, 167, 171, 179–181; development of, 189–194; 196, 202–204, 231, 242, 284, 299
United States Golf Association (U.S.G.A.); size of ball dispute, 16–17; 18; on the shape and number of clubs, 23–24; 27; creation of, 36–37; 55, 90, 97, 121, 148, 156, 179, 185; creation of, 190; 193–194, 201–203, 205, 211, 214–216, 223–224, 228, 231, 241, 251, 269, 294–297; development of, 297–300
United States Golf Association, Executive Committee of, 201–202, 211, 216, 224
United States Golf Association Girls' Junior Championship, 217
United States Golf Association Junior Amateur Championship, 214; development of, 216–217
United States Golf Association, Museum of, 3, 12, 32, 205
United States Golf Association, Public and Municipal Golf Course Committee of, 201
United States Golf Association, Public Links Committee of, 203
United States Golf Association Senior Amateur Championship, 214; development of, 215–216
United States Golf Association Senior Women's Amateur Championship, 214; development of, 216
United States Golf Association Women's Amateur, 148, 150, 152, 154; development of, 204–208; 210, 216–217, 228, 299
United States Open, 17; first championship, 37; 38–39, 43–44, 46, 48, 50–54; won by F. Ouimet in 1913, 55–56; 57, 62; won by Gene Sarazen in 1922, 66; 68, 70, 72–80, 84, 87–89, 94–98, 101–110, 112, 116–118, 124–125, 132–134, 138–139, 156–159, 161; development of, 167–172; 176, 178–179, 183, 186, 196–197, 199, 201–202, 215–216, 221, 223, 234, 242, 251–252, 269–270, 273–274, 277, 281–284, 286–287, 290–291, 299, 301, 304, 308, 310–311, 314
United States Women's Open, 152, 154; development of, 210–213, 305
University of Georgia, 314
University of North Carolina, 299

Upham, John P., 34, 144
Urzetta, Sam, 119, 226

Valley Country Club, 154
Vanderbilt, Cornelius, 35
Vanderbilt, W. K., 35, 190
Van Donck, Flory, 235, 237
Van Wie, Virginia, 151, 206, 229, 306
Vardon Grip, 20, 38, 70
Vardon, Harry, 20, 38, 40–43, 46, 50; losing 1913 U.S. Open to F. Ouimet, 51–53; 56, 64, 68, 74, 95, 102, 168–170, 176, 201, 223, 276, 281–282, 299
Vardon, Tom, 41–42
Vardon Trophy, 38, 159
Vare, Edward H. Jr., 151, 206
Vare, Glenna Collett: see Collett, Glenna
Vare Trophy: see Glenna Collett Vare Trophy
Venturi, Ken, 52, 118, 121, 123; career of, 159–160; 216, 226, 268, 274, 286, 310, 314
Vines, Ellsworth, 206
Virginia, Country Club of, 137
Vishnu, Statue of, 14
Von Elm, George, 78, 191

Wales, 31, 234
Wales, Prince of, 8
Walker Cup; forerunner of, 8; 17, 27, 54, 76, 78, 80, 82, 87, 128, 137, 179–180, 193; development of, 223–227; 228, 231, 234, 241
Walker, Cyril, 57, 78, 196–197
Walker, George Herbert, 224
Wall, Art Jr., 119
Wallace, Fielding, 185
Wallace, James, 87
Walsh, Richard J., 201–202
Walzer, Winnie, 128–129
Wanakah Country Club, 217
Wanamaker, John, 302
Wanamaker, Rodman, 196, 199, 302
Wanamaker Trophy, 197

Ward, Harvey, 52, 119–121, 181, 193, 226, 231, 232
Ward, Marvin (Bud), 193, 226
Washington Park, 168
Watch Hill Club, 44
Watrous, Al, 78, 198, 215, 219–220
Watson, Mrs. J. B., 229
Way Bert, 215
Weathervane, 305
Wee Burn Club, 206
Weetman, Harry, 234
Wellshire Golf Course, 203
Weslock, Nick, 231
Westchester Country Club, 110
Western Golf Association, 231, 294, 299
Western Open, 89, 164, 215, 221
Western Women's Open, 148, 152
West Virginia Open, 99
Westward Ho! 179; first English seaside course, 31
Wethered, Joyce, 150, 181, 229, 306
Wethered, Roger, 80, 150, 177, 181, 223–225
Whigham, H. J., 191
Whitcombe, Charles, 220
White Brand Ball, 14
White Melfort Ball, 14
White, Robert, 302
Whitney, Casper, 298
Whitney, Howard F., 224
Wigham, Sybil, 150
William IV, 28
Williams, Eddie, 215
Williams, Henry, 199
Williams, Ted, 309, 314
Willing, Dr. O. F., 225
Wills, Helen, 74
Wilson, Enid, 229
Wilson, James, 19, 21
Wilson, Virginia, 150
Wimbledon Club, 31, 150, 181
Winged Foot Country Club, 79, 109, 119, 276, 287
Winthrop, R. D., 205
Wirtz, Leonard, 306

Women's Eastern Golf Association, 228
Women's National Doubles, 206
Women's Open, 152, 154
Women's PGA: see Ladies' PGA
Wood, Craig, 66, 86, 89–90, 97, 105, 186–188, 277, 282–283, 293
Worcester Country Club, 78, 219
Work, Bertram G., 15
World Amateur: see Eisenhower Trophy
World Amateur Team Championship, 132, 137
World Cup, 228
World Seniors' Championship, 215
World Series of Baseball, 188, 267
World Series of Golf, 133–134, 139, 156, 158, 252
World War I, 40, 95, 150–151, 170, 176, 181, 197, 206, 223, 299
World War II, 64, 88, 116, 119, 148, 202, 207, 216, 220, 226, 229, 241, 282
World's Championship, 290, 309
World's Championship (for women), 152, 154
Worsham, Bud, 128
Worsham, Lew, 97, 290–292
Wright, Frederick Jr., 215, 224–225
Wright, Mickey, 152; career of, 153–155; 212, 217, 305–306
Wright, William, 203
Wysong, Dudley Jr., 138

Yates, Charlie, 181, 226
Yonkers; first course in United State, 33–35; 249
Yonkers, St. Andrews Club of, 34, 36, 144, 189, 249, 295, 297–298

Zaharias, George, 148–149, 152
Zaharias, Mildred Didrikson (Babe); career of, 144–149; 150–155, 181, 207, 210–212, 299, 305–306, 309, 314

J. C. Dollman's
"The Sabbath Breakers"
1896

Courtesy of Golf Digest Magazine